QUALITATIVE
RESEARCH
PRACTICE

QUALITATIVE RESEARCH PRACTICE

A Guide for
Social Science Students
and Researchers

Edited by

JANE RITCHIE AND JANE LEWIS

Los Angeles | London | New Delhi
Singapore | Washington DC

SAGE Publications Ltd
1 Oliver's Yard
55 City Road
London EC1Y 1SP

SAGE Publications Inc.
2455 Teller Road
Thousand Oaks, California 91320

SAGE Publications India Pvt Ltd
B 1/I 1 Mohan Cooperative Industrial Area
Mathura Road
New Delhi 110 044

SAGE Publications Asia-Pacific Pte Ltd
3 Church Street
#10-04 Samsung Hub
Singapore 049483

British Library Cataloguing in Publication data

A catalogue record for this book is available
from the British Library

ISBN 0 7619 7109 2
ISBN 0 7619 7110 6 (pbk)

Library of Congress Control Number 2002109391

Typeset by C&M Digitals (P) Ltd., Chennai, India
Printed and bound by CPI Group (UK) Ltd, Croydon, CR0 4YY

Contents

Notes on Contributors

The **National Centre for Social Research** is Britain's largest independent social research organisation. It was established in 1969 and is registered as an educational charity, with a staff of almost 200. The National Centre carries out statistical and qualitative research across all the major social policy areas, specialising in the application and development of rigorous research methods. Its work is commissioned, primarily by central government departments but also by other public bodies, or initiated by the Centre itself and funded by research councils and foundations. Researchers at the National Centre often work in collaboration with other research teams, or with academics and others with specific substantive expertise. The Centre has housed a number of ESRC Research Centres and other joint centres over the years.

The **Qualitative Research Unit** was established within the National Centre in 1985. It specialises in the design, conduct and interpretation of research studies using in-depth interviews and focus groups. The Unit now has a staff of 19 people. The Qualitative Research Unit and the Centre more generally has a longstanding interest in the development of research methods and standards. The Qualitative Research Unit runs a programme of short courses in in-depth interview and focus group research methods, and provides tailored research teaching for university departments and units and other research groups.

All the contributors to this book are current or past members of the Unit who have published extensively on qualitative research studies. They have a wealth of experience of carrying out qualitative research studies in varied fields of social research and policy, and all have been involved in the Unit's teaching on research methods.

Editors

JANE RITCHIE is a psychologist and has worked exclusively in social policy research throughout her career. She founded the Qualitative Research Unit at the National Centre for Social Research in 1985 and was the Unit's Director until 1998. She was one of the originators of Framework – a qualitative analysis method now widely used in the UK.

JANE LEWIS is Director of the Qualitative Research Unit at the National Centre. She has a background in law and began her social research career using qualitative and survey research methods in a management consultancy context. She moved to the National Centre in 1994 to specialise in qualitative research and its application to social policy, and succeeded Jane Ritchie as Director of the Qualitative Research Unit in 1998.

Contributors

Sue Arthur's academic background is in history and law. She began her professional research career working for the Equal Opportunities Commission where she undertook and commissioned research on gender equality issues. She also worked at the Policy Studies Institute carrying out qualitative and quantitative research. She moved to the National Centre's Qualitative Research Unit in 1998, where she is a Research Director.

Gillian Elam has spent her career in social research, initially managing and commissioning research at the then Department of Social Security and subsequently specialising in qualitative research as a Senior Researcher at the National Centre. She is now a freelance qualitative research consultant and teaches qualitative research methods at Birkbeck College.

Helen Finch, a former National Centre Research Director, holds degrees in social science and in fine art. She worked at the National Centre for 20 years where, as a founding member of the Qualitative Research Unit, she was involved in setting up and developing courses in focus groups. She now works as a group analytic psychotherapist.

Jill Keegan has been a leader in the arena field of qualitative fieldwork methods for the last 35 years and played a central role in the creation and development of the National Centre's Qualitative Research Unit. She has been involved in projects covering a wide spectrum, from almost every aspect of social policy research to generating scripts for verbatim theatre. She now works as an independent researcher and is currently involved in a filmed documentary project exploring different interview techniques.

Robin Legard received his initial training in qualitative research at the National Centre more than 20 years ago. After a 12 year period as a freelance researcher, he returned to the National Centre as a Senior Researcher in 1994. He has special responsibility for fieldwork skills within the Qualitative Research Unit. He has a degree in Modern Languages and worked as both a teacher and an actor before embarking on a research career.

James Nazroo is a Reader in Sociology and head of the Health and Social Surveys Research Group of the Department of Epidemiology at University College London. He also holds a honorary position in the Department of Psychiatry and Behavioural Sciences at UCL, where he teaches research methods on the MSc in Sociology, Health and Healthcare. He was a Senior Researcher at the National Centre for several years where he worked on both qualitative and statistical studies.

William O'Connor is Deputy Director in the Qualitative Research Unit at the National Centre. His academic background is in sociology and social policy. He joined the National Centre in 1994, working initially in statistical research before moving to the Qualitative Research Unit. With Kandy Woodfield, he is developing a computerised method of Framework, the analytical method originated by the Qualitative Research Unit.

Dawn Snape began her professional research career in 1991 as a Project Researcher in the Qualitative Research Unit of the National Centre. She subsequently left the National Centre to lecture in research methods at the Universities of Bristol and Plymouth, as well as continuing to carry out research. In 1997 Dawn re-joined the National Centre where she is currently a Research Director with an interest in both qualitative and quantitative research methods.

Liz Spencer is a sociologist with 30 years' experience of qualitative research in both academic and applied policy contexts. While a Research Director in the Qualitative Research Unit from 1985 to 1993 she collaborated in the conception and development of Framework with Jane Ritchie. She is now a partner in New Perspectives, an independent research consultancy, and teaches qualitative research methods at the University of Essex.

Kit Ward has worked as a specialist qualitative research interviewer for a major part of her career, following a period as a health professional. She has led the advancement of qualitative fieldwork methods both within the National Centre and through her teaching in the wider research community. Kit Ward now works as an independent researcher with a range of social research organisations and consultants.

Clarissa White, a Senior Associate Director at BMRB Qualitative, spent 11 years working in the Qualitative Research Unit. During this time she developed the application of focus group methods for public consultation purposes, including in deliberative polls, citizens' juries and consultative panels. Before joining the National Centre she had a career in television as a researcher on current affairs programmes.

Kandy Woodfield is a Deputy Director of the Qualitative Research Unit at the National Centre. She co-ordinates the qualitative research training provided by the Qualitative Research Unit and is involved in developing a computerised version of Framework, the analytical method used there. Prior to joining the National Centre in 1997 she was involved in academic research and teaching focusing on socio-legal issues, political science and research methods.

Editors' Acknowledgements

We owe a sincere debt of gratitude to the many people who have helped to create this book. Foremost among them are the principal contributors to individual chapters for the enthusiasm and thought they brought to the task. They had to write their chapters alongside busy research lives and it is a tribute to their commitment that they achieved this so ably.

Among the authors, we are particularly grateful to Liz Spencer, who also carried out an initial review of the literature. This informed all the chapters and we are grateful for the theoretical guidance and wise counsel she gave us throughout. She has been an unstintingly generous and stimulating colleague to all of us.

We would like to thank Sue Johnson, the librarian at the National Centre, for her tireless help with locating literature. We owe warm thanks to Lydia Cole and Elisabeth Valdani for their skilful work on the manuscript, and for the calmness with which they dealt with final changes.

Also within the National Centre, we thank our other colleagues, particularly those now and formerly members of the Qualitative Research Unit. They have helped to hone the skills and approaches of the National Centre's practice of qualitative research. But a significant impetus for this book also came from the people who have attended our short courses in qualitative research methods over the years. Their questions and reflections have influenced our approaches, and the way we think about what we do.

We are also grateful for the support of the organisations which have funded our studies. We have been lucky enough to work with many highly skilled and insightful researchers outside the National Centre and have learnt enormously from their collaboration. But none of this would have been possible, of course, without the people who participated in our studies over the years. They have perhaps taught us most of all.

We acknowledge with gratitude the support of our editorial team at Sage, particularly Michael Carmichael and Zoe Elliott. We would also wish to thank the two thoughtful (although anonymous) readers of an earlier draft for the very helpful comments and suggestions they made.

Jane Ritchie
Jane Lewis

Preface

This book is about qualitative research and how to do it. It documents the practice of qualitative research, both for those who are embarking on studies for the first time and for those who want to gain further understanding of its methodological principles. It is intended for those working in applied policy fields as well as those concerned with the development of social theory more generally.

The book has been written by a team of practising researchers from the current and past staff of the Qualitative Research Unit at the National Centre for Social Research. The National Centre is an independent social research institute which is dedicated to research for the development and evaluation of public policy. The Qualitative Research Unit specialises in the conduct of in-depth research, primarily involving individual interviews and focus groups, for explanatory, evaluative or strategic purposes. The authors who have contributed to the book have drawn on experience of designing, conducting, analysing and reporting on qualitative studies as a central part of their everyday work.

The methods described have been developed over several decades. They have been refined and enhanced in response to an ever widening repertoire of applications. There is particular emphasis on data generated through in-depth interviews and focus groups, two data collection methods widely used in more applied qualitative inquiry. This focus means that less attention is given to the study of naturally occurring data, such as observation, documentary analysis, discourse and conversation analysis, although the origins and uses of these methods are discussed. There are also a number of excellent texts on the use and conduct of such methods and key references to these are given throughout the chapters. It should also be noted that many of the principles described in relation to working with interviews and focus groups have relevance for the full repertoire of qualitative methods.

There are many forms of qualitative research, each shaped by different epistemological origins, philosophies about the nature of scientific inquiry and its outcomes and varying prescriptions for methodological rigour. A brief overview of these is given in Chapter 1 by way of a context to the subsequent chapters. This review also helps to locate our particular approach to qualitative research which is based on three central tenets. First, qualitative research needs to be conducted in a rigorous way, with an explicit methodological base to inform its design and execution. Second, we believe that there is a 'reality' to be captured in terms of the social constructs, beliefs and behaviours that operate, albeit a diverse and multifaceted one. We also recognise the fluidity of this reality but see it as sufficiently stable to inform the development of contemporary social policy and theory. Third, and related, we hold the view that small-scale qualitative studies can be used to draw wider inference about the 'social world', provided that there is appropriate adherence to the boundaries of qualitative research.

But, as qualitative research specialists, our primary wish is to honour the many alternatives offered to us in different approaches to qualitative research. Qualitative research scholars have provided a rich array of 'styles' and 'schools' from which to learn and it is part of the intellectual challenge to draw on these as needed. As Seale has argued in discussing the 'quality' of qualitative research

> ... pragmatic social researchers can use philosophical and political debates as resources for achieving certain mental attitudes, rather than a set of underlying principles from which all else must flow, creating unnecessary obstacles to flexible and creative inquiry ... One can, then, understand such debates as conversations stimulating methodological awareness among researchers, rather than laying foundations for truth. (1999: 26)

We hope this book will display not only the principles that lie behind our own 'school' of qualitative research but also some of the differing perspectives that can lead to alternative decisions in designing and conducting research studies.

The book provides a guided tour of the qualitative research process, beginning with a discussion of the different forms, roles and uses of qualitative research, moving through design, sampling, data collection and analysis. We end with two chapters on how – and why – evidence from qualitative research can be used to deepen understanding of society and its individual communities, and some requirements for its reporting.

At the end of each chapter, a summary is given of the key points that have been covered. This is followed by a description of key terms used that may not be familiar to all readers. Also at the end of each chapter is a short list of texts we would recommend for further reading. These are volumes that either we have found particularly enlightening on the subject matter of the chapter or which provide a useful overview of different perspectives or approaches. In choosing these, we have tried to avoid too much repetition of the same texts for different chapters. Where they do repeat, they tend to be authors who have written definitively about the whole qualitative research process or are particular favourites of ours because of their insightful commentary.

We should perhaps end by saying that we see qualitative research as a blend of empirical investigation and creative discovery – or, as noted by other authors, as a mix of science and art. But it is this delicate fusion that can leave unease about the safety of its use or worries about its methods of conduct. We hope this book will show that, properly executed, qualitative research is a skilled craft that brings unique understanding of people's lives and the social phenomena that form them.

1

The Foundations of Qualitative Research

Dawn Snape and Liz Spencer

We begin with a brief history of qualitative research, its traditions and philosophical underpinnings. This is not intended as a comprehensive and detailed account, but rather as edited highlights of an evolutionary process. There are several reasons why it is helpful to understand something of the background of qualitative research before going on to discuss the specifics of how to do it.

First, it is important to recognise that there is no single, accepted way of doing qualitative research. Indeed, how researchers carry it out depends upon a range of factors including: their beliefs about the nature of the social world and what can be known about it (ontology), the nature of knowledge and how it can be acquired (epistemology), the purpose(s) and goals of the research, the characteristics of the research participants, the audience for the research, the funders of the research, and the position and environment of the researchers themselves. This chapter considers how differences in the mix of these factors have led to distinctive approaches to qualitative research.

Second, it has been argued that it is important to be aware of the philosophical debates and the methodological developments arising from them in order to secure the quality of the research produced (and therefore the degree to which its findings are accepted, and by whom). Although this view is widely held by researchers from a range of different backgrounds, there is some divergence over how quality can and should be ensured in qualitative research. Some writers argue that different methodological approaches are underpinned by particular philosophical assumptions and that researchers should maintain consistency between the philosophical starting point and the methods they adopt. Indeed, maintaining consistency is seen as one way of producing more 'valid' findings (Morse et al., 2001). By contrast, others believe that the methods associated with a range of philosophical positions each have something to offer. Thus, they argue that better quality work is produced if the full range of research tools and quality assurances available are considered (Seale, 1999). Despite these different perspectives, there is general agreement that an understanding of this background will encourage and contribute to better research practice.

Finally, as noted in the Preface, the practices and approach to qualitative research discussed in this book have developed and evolved within a particular research environment and culture. As the preceding discussion indicates, it is important to appreciate that there is no one right and accepted way of doing qualitative research and the methods we use reflect a particular mix of philosophy, research objectives, participants, funders and audiences relevant to applied policy research. It is therefore important that readers understand where and how we situate our approach within the broader field of qualitative research in order to assess the value and appropriateness of the research practices we describe for their own purposes. We have attempted to provide a clear indication of this at the end of the chapter.

Defining qualitative research

Most texts on qualitative research begin with some attempt to define what is meant by this term, either theoretically or practically, or both. We will follow in this time honoured tradition because it is important to understand the diversity inherent in this term and also because it is impossible to discuss qualitative research practice without defining what is meant by it. However, providing a precise definition of qualitative research is no mean feat. This reflects the fact that the term is used as an overarching category, covering a wide range of approaches and methods found within different research disciplines.

Despite this diversity and the sometimes conflicting nature of underlying assumptions about its inherent qualities, a number of writers have attempted to capture the essence of qualitative research by offering working definitions or by identifying a set of key characteristics. In the second edition of their *Handbook of Qualitative Research*, Denzin and Lincoln offer the following definition:

> Qualitative research is a situated activity that locates the observer in the world. It consists of a set of interpretive, material practices that makes the world visible. These practices … turn the world into a series of representations including fieldnotes, interviews, conversations, photographs, recordings and memos to

the self. At this level, qualitative research involves an interpretive, naturalistic approach to the world. This means that qualitative researchers study things in their natural settings, attempting to make sense of, or to interpret, phenomena in terms of the meanings people bring to them. (2000: 3)

Some of the key defining qualities highlighted by Denzin and Lincoln are supported in other definitions. In particular, there is fairly wide consensus that qualitative research is a naturalistic, interpretative approach concerned with understanding the meanings which people attach to phenomena (actions, decisions, beliefs, values etc.) within their social worlds:

> The way in which people being studied understand and interpret their social reality is one of the central motifs of qualitative research. (Bryman, 1988: 8)

Some researchers have also focused on key aspects of methodology as defining characteristics of qualitative research (see for example Bryman, 1988; Denzin and Lincoln, 2000; Hammersley and Atkinson, 1995; Holloway and Wheeler, 1996; Mason, 2002; Miles and Huberman, 1994; Patton, 2002). These key aspects include: the overall research perspective and the importance of the participants' frames of reference; the flexible nature of research design; the volume and richness of qualitative data; the distinctive approaches to analysis and interpretation; and the kind of outputs that derive from qualitative research. Certain data collection methods have also been identified with qualitative research such as: observational methods, in-depth interviewing, group discussions, narratives, and the analysis of documentary evidence. However, it is important to note that practitioners of qualitative research vary considerably in the extent to which they rely on particular methods of data collection. Box 1.1 provides an overview of the methodological stances most commonly associated with qualitative research.

Finally, some writers define qualitative research in terms of what it is *not*. For example, Strauss and Corbin (1998) delineate qualitative research as any research not primarily based on counting or quantifying empirical material:

> By the term 'qualitative research' we mean any type of research that produces findings not arrived at by statistical procedures or other means of quantification. (Strauss and Corbin, 1998: 11)

In order to avoid becoming overly focused on the variations that make simple definitions of qualitative research difficult to attain, it is perhaps helpful to highlight key elements which are commonly agreed to give qualitative research its distinctive character. These include:

- aims which are directed at providing an in-depth and interpreted understanding of the social world of research participants by learning about their social and material circumstances, their experiences, perspectives and histories

BOX 1.1 METHODOLOGICAL STANCES ASSOCIATED WITH QUALITATIVE RESEARCH

Perspective of the researcher and the researched

- Taking the 'emic' perspective, i.e. the perspective of the people being studied by penetrating their frames of meaning
- Viewing social life in terms of processes rather than in static terms
- Providing a holistic perspective within explained contexts
- Sustaining empathic neutrality whereby the researcher uses personal insight while taking a non-judgemental stance

Nature of research design

- Adopting a flexible research strategy
- Conducting naturalistic inquiry in real-world rather than experimental or manipulated settings (though methods vary in the extent to which they capture naturally occuring or generated data – see Chapter 2)

Nature of data generation

- Using methods of data generation which are flexible and sensitive to the social context in which the data are produced
- Using methods which usually involve close contact between the researcher and the people being studied, where the researcher is the primary instrument

Nature of the research methods used

- Main qualitative methods include: observation, in-depth individual interviews, focus groups, biographical methods such as life histories and narratives, and analysis of documents and texts

Nature of analysis/interpretation

- Based on methods of analysis and explanation building which reflect the complexity, detail and context of the data
- Identifying emergent categories and theories from the data rather than imposing a priori categories and ideas
- Respecting the uniqueness of each case as well as conducting cross-case analysis
- Developing explanations at the level of meaning rather than cause

Nature of outputs

- Producing detailed descriptions and 'rounded understandings' which are based on, or offer an interpretation of, the perspectives of the participants in the social setting
- Mapping meanings, processes and contexts
- Answering 'what is', 'how' and 'why' questions
- Consideration of the influence of the researcher's perspectives

- samples that are small in scale and purposively selected on the basis of salient criteria
- data collection methods which usually involve close contact between the researcher and the research participants, which are interactive and developmental and allow for emergent issues to be explored
- data which are very detailed, information rich and extensive
- analysis which is open to emergent concepts and ideas and which may produce detailed description and classification, identify patterns of association, or develop typologies and explanations
- outputs which tend to focus on the interpretation of social meaning through mapping and 're-presenting' the social world of research participants.

As discussed in Chapter 2, qualitative methods are used to address research questions that require explanation or understanding of social phenomena and their contexts. They are particularly well suited to exploring issues that hold some complexity and to studying processes that occur over time.

We offer this simplified overview as a working definition of qualitative research to provide some parameters for the research practices described in the rest of this text. That notwithstanding, we recognise that the search for an all-inclusive definition of qualitative research goes on and will probably continue to do so given the array of approaches and beliefs it encompasses.

The historical development of qualitative research

The history of qualitative research should be recounted and appreciated within the wider context of the evolution of social research more generally. Against this wider backdrop, it is possible to see how approaches most closely associated with qualitative research were developed to overcome some of the perceived limitations of the prevailing methods used to study human behaviour. This account is provided here not to disparage or dismiss quantitative enquiry but to show how qualitative and quantitative traditions have developed in contrasting ways and the thinking that has underpinned them. Indeed, we would suggest that despite their different origins and assumptions, both qualitative and quantitative research methods have unique and valuable contributions to make to social research practice, a point we revisit later in the chapter.

The development of empiricism and positivism

We begin our history with the philosopher, René Descartes, who in 1637 wrote his *Discourse on Methodology* in which he focused on the importance of objectivity and evidence in the search for truth. A key idea in his writing was that researchers should attempt to distance themselves from any influences that might corrupt their analytical capacity. Another important idea in social research was proposed by seventeenth-century writers such as Isaac Newton and Francis Bacon who asserted that knowledge about the world can be acquired through direct observation (induction) rather than deduced from abstract propositions. Similarly, David Hume (1711–76) who is associated with the founding of the empirical research tradition suggested that all knowledge about the world originates in our experiences and is derived through the senses. Evidence based on direct observation and collected in an objective and unbiased way are key tenets of empirical research.

Following in their footsteps, Auguste Comte (1798–1857) asserted that the social world can be studied in terms of invariant laws just like the natural world. This belief is the basis of a school of thought (or paradigm) known as 'positivism' which was a major influence in social research throughout the twentieth century. Although positivism has been interpreted in many different ways by social researchers, beliefs and practices associated with positivism usually include the following (Bryman, 1988):

- the methods of the natural sciences are appropriate for the study of social phenomenon
- only those phenomena which are observable can be counted as knowledge
- knowledge is developed inductively through the accumulation of verified facts
- hypotheses are derived deductively from scientific theories to be tested empirically (the scientific method)
- observations are the final arbiter in theoretical disputes
- facts and values are distinct, thus making it possible to conduct objective enquiry.

The development of interpretivism

Against this backdrop, the early development of ideas now associated particularly with qualitative research can be linked to the writing of Immanuel Kant who in 1781 published his *Critique of Pure Reason*. Kant argued that there are ways of knowing about the world other than direct observation and that people use these all the time. He proposed that:

- perception relates not only to the senses but to human interpretations of what our senses tell us
- our knowledge of the world is based on 'understanding' which arises from thinking about what happens to us, not just simply from having had particular experiences

- knowing and knowledge transcend basic empirical enquiry
- distinctions exist between 'scientific reason' (based strictly on causal determinism) and 'practical reason' (based on moral freedom and decision-making which involve less certainty).

Qualitative research has generally (though not exclusively) been associated with this set of beliefs. Those practising qualitative research have tended to place emphasis and value on the human, interpretative aspects of knowing about the social world and the significance of the investigator's own interpretations and understanding of the phenomenon being studied.

Another key contributor to the development of interpretivist thought and the qualitative research tradition was Wilhelm Dilthey. His writing (during the 1860s–70s) emphasised the importance of 'understanding' (or 'verstehen' in his native German) and of studying people's 'lived experiences' which occur within a particular historical and social context. He also argued that self-determination and human creativity play very important roles in guiding our actions. He therefore proposed that social research should explore 'lived experiences' in order to reveal the connections between the social, cultural and historical aspects of people's lives and to see the context in which particular actions take place.

Max Weber (1864–1920) was very influenced by Dilthey's ideas and particularly his views on the importance of 'understanding' (or verstehen). However, rather than taking a strictly interpretivist stance, Weber tried to build a bridge between interpretivist and positivist approaches. He believed that an analysis of material conditions (as would be undertaken by those using a positivist approach) was important, but was not sufficient to a full understanding of people's lives. Instead, he emphasised that the researcher must understand the meaning of social actions within the context of the material conditions in which people live. He proposed two types of understanding: direct observational understanding, and explanatory or motivational understanding. He argued that there is a key difference in the purpose of understanding between the natural and social sciences. In the natural sciences, the purpose is to produce law-like propositions whereas in the social sciences, the aim is to understand subjectively meaningful experiences.

The school of thought that stresses the importance of interpretation as well as observation in understanding the social world is known as 'interpretivism'. This has been seen as integral to the qualitative tradition. The interrelatedness of different aspects of people's lives is a very important focus of qualitative research and psychological, social, historical and cultural factors are all recognised as playing an important part in shaping people's understanding of their world. Qualitative research practice has reflected this in the use of methods which attempt to provide a holistic understanding of research participants' views and actions in the context of their lives overall.

The development of qualitative research methods and challenges to the scientific method

From the late nineteenth century and throughout the twentieth century qualitative research methods developed and became more widely adopted. They evolved as researchers became more sophisticated and aware of the research process, but also as they responded to challenges from other methodologies and paradigms, particularly positivism and postmodern critiques.

Within sociology and anthropology, early qualitative research often took the form of ethnographic work which flourished in both America and Britain. Early examples of ethnographers include Malinowski, Radcliffe Brown, Margaret Mead, Gregory Bateson and Franz Boas, all of whom studied 'native' populations abroad, and Robert Park and the work of the Chicago school where the focus was on the life and culture of local groups in the city about whom little was known. Later, in the middle of the twentieth century, many community studies were carried out including those by Young and Willmott and by Frankenburg in the UK, for example. Sociology also saw the development of ethnomethodolgy (Garfinkel, 1967; Silverman, 1972) – the study of how, in practice, people construct social order and make sense of their social world and symbolic interactionism (Blumer, 1969; Mead, 1934; Thomas, 1931) – the study of symbolic meanings and interpretations attached to social actions and environments. Within historical studies there has been a strong tradition in the use of oral history (Plummer, 2001; Thompson, 2000) – the use of people's 'life stories' in understanding experiences and social constructions.

Throughout this period, however, survey research methods also became more widespread and quantitative researchers were increasingly influenced by positivism, modelling their approach on the methods of the natural sciences. Positivism became the dominant paradigm within social research and qualitative research was often criticised as 'soft' and 'unscientific'. In response to these criticisms, some qualitative researchers (for example Bogdan and Taylor, 1975; Cicourel, 1964; Glaser and Strauss, 1967) attempted to formalise their methods, stressing the importance of rigour in data collection and analysis. Denzin and Lincoln (1994) refer to this period as the 'modernist' phase.

By the 1970s, however, positivism itself and the legitimacy of social research based on the 'scientific method' began to be debated. Particular concerns arose in relation to:

- whether it is possible to 'control' variables in experimental research involving human 'subjects' to achieve unambiguous results
- whether the elimination of contextual variables in controlled experimental conditions is an appropriate way to study human behaviour
- whether it is appropriate to disregard the meaning and purpose of behaviour in controlled experimental studies

- whether overarching theories of the world and aggregated data have any relevance and applicability to the lives of individuals
- whether emphasis on hypothesis testing neglects the importance of discovery through alternative understandings.

These challenges encouraged the use of qualitative research as a means of overcoming some of the perceived limitations associated with the scientific method. In practice, this meant that qualitative methods began to be seen as a more valid and valuable approach to research. Qualitative research began to be adopted (in a somewhat patchy way) across a range of disciplines, including those which have traditionally relied upon the use of controlled experiments to study human behaviour (such as social psychology, clinical research).

In addition to criticisms of positivism, new approaches also challenged some of the basic assumptions of qualitative research. One such challenge has come from postmodern critiques, such as poststructuralism and deconstruction, which not only question the notion of objectivity but also maintain that the concepts of meaning and reality are problematic. It is argued that there are no fixed or overarching meanings because meanings are a product of time and place. The researcher cannot produce a definitive account or explanation, and any attempt to do so is a form of tyranny because it suppresses diversity. Denzin and Lincoln (1994) claimed that this resulted in a crisis for social researchers: the researcher cannot capture the social world of another, or give an authoritative account of his or her findings, because there are no fixed meanings to be captured.

Another challenge came from critical theory in the form of Neo Marxism and, subsequently, feminism, and race research which maintain that material conditions, social, political, gender, and cultural factors have a major influence on people's lives. Within these approaches, research findings are analysed primarily according to the concepts of race, class or gender, rather than the analysis being open to concepts which emerge from the data. The value of the findings is judged in terms of their political and emancipatory effects, rather than simply the extent to which they portray and explain the social world of participants.

One of the responses to these challenges was a call for greater equality between the researcher and research participants, a perspective particularly emphasised in feminist research. Feminist researchers argued that there was a power imbalance in the way that research was structured and conducted (Bowles and Klein, 1983; Oakley, 1981; Roberts, 1981) and this led to questioning and some refinement of both the researcher's and the participants' roles. Similarly, in other arenas, social research was increasingly being viewed as a collaborative process and researchers were developing ways to involve the study population in setting the research agenda (Reason, 1994; Whyte, 1991; Reason and Rowan, 1981). At the same time, the use of 'action research' – whereby research findings feed directly back into the environments from which they are generated – was widening, inspired by similar demands for more participatory and emancipatory research processes.

Meanwhile, the importance of 'situating' the perspective of the researcher was being emphasised. This was to encourage a more reflexive approach to research findings rather than the traditional approach in which the researcher takes an authoritative, 'neutral' stance. Alongside this, others have attempted to find ways of letting research participants tell their own story directly, rather than writing about their lives as an outsider. To some extent, this was a basic tenet of the tradition of oral history even though the researcher often interpreted the life stories given to develop their historical perspective. But by the turn of the twentieth century there had been a major growth in the use of narrative and biographical methods (Chamberlayne et al., 2000; Roberts, 2002). This was partly to provide greater understanding of phenomena in the context of people's own accounts of their personal development and histories but also because of the previously described challenges to ways of involving study participants in generating research evidence.

Within psychology, the other primary social science concerned with the understanding of human phenomena, the growth of qualitative methods has taken place much later than in sociology. Some of the earliest uses of qualitative methods, developed around the middle of the twentieth century, occurred in the fields of personal construct theory – the study of psychological constructs that people use to define and attach meaning to their thinking and behaviour (see for example Bannister and Mair, 1968; Harré and Secorde, 1972; Kelly, 1955). Other longstanding strands of enquiry took place in ethogenics which is concerned with the roles and rules through which people choose to act or not act (Harré and Secorde, 1972; Marsh et al., 1978); and protocol analysis which explores the 'thinking' processes that are manifest when people are engaged in cognitive tasks (see Gilhooly and Green, 1996). But it was not until the late 1980s that qualitative methods were being more systematically used in psychological research. Even then there was still deep resistance to qualitative research as a method of investigation (see Richardson, 1996) despite increasing calls for more interpretative and participatory approaches (Reason and Rowan, 1981). Psychology, as a discipline, was still deeply locked into emulating scientific enquiry with a heavy emphasis on the experimental method.

As a consequence, it was only within the last decade of the twentieth century that qualitative methods were more widely accepted within British psychological research practice (Nicholson, 1991; Richardson, 1996). Since then, there has been what has been termed an 'explosion' of interest in qualitative research and rapid growth in its applications within psychological enquiry (Bannister et al., 1994; Henwood and Nicholson, 1995; Robson, 2002; Smith et al., 1995). Qualitative methods are being used in a number of fields of psychology although with particular interest in the fields of cognitive and social psychology. Increasingly ethnomethodological approaches, discourse analysis and grounded theory are being used as methodological approaches in psychological investigation (Richardson, 1996). Qualitative methods are also being used in more applied fields like clinical and educational psychology.

In the context of discussing the psychological uses of qualitative research, it is important to acknowledge the role played by market research in developing qualitative methods for applied purposes. As Walker (1985) describes, there is extensive use of qualitative methods in the market research industry and many of the techniques developed there have been transferred to other social science settings. The use of projective techniques for understanding the imagery surrounding phenomena is one example, the ever increasing applications of focus groups another.

As qualitative research has evolved over the course of the twentieth century, responding to different challenges, a number of 'schools' or approaches have emerged as outlined above. In order to give a sense of the diversity of approaches now used within the field of qualitative research, Box 1.2 summarises the central aims and disciplinary origins of a range of these different traditions.

Key philosophical and methodological issues in qualitative research

Ontology

As this brief history of qualitative research demonstrates, deciding how to study the social world has always raised a number of key philosophical debates. Some of these issues relate to 'ontology' and are concerned with beliefs about what there is to know about the world. Within social research, key ontological questions concern: whether or not social reality exists independently of human conceptions and interpretations; whether there is a common, shared, social reality or just multiple context-specific realities; and whether or not social behaviour is governed by 'laws' that can be seen as immutable or generalisable.

As has been indicated, one of the key ontological debates surrounds whether there is a captive social reality and how it should be constructed. In broad terms, there are three distinct positions, realism, materialism and idealism. *Realism* claims that there is an external reality which exists independently of people's beliefs or understanding about it. In other words there is a distinction between the way the world is and the meaning and interpretation of that world held by individuals. *Materialism* also claims that there is a real world but that only material features, such as economic relations, or physical features of that world hold reality. Values, beliefs or experiences are 'epiphenomena' – that is features that arise from, but do not shape, the material world. *Idealism*, on the other hand, asserts that reality is only knowable through the human mind and through socially constructed meanings.

BOX 1.2 TRADITIONS OF QUALITATIVE RESEARCH

Research tradition	Disciplinary origins	Aims
Ethnography	Anthropology/ sociology	Understanding the social world of people being studied through immersion in their community to produce detailed description of people, their culture and beliefs.
Phenomenology/ ethnomethodology	Philosophy/ sociology	Understanding the 'constructs' people use in everyday life to make sense of their world. Uncovering meanings contained within conversation or text
Leading to Conversation analysis	Sociology/ linguistics	Analysing the way different conversations are structured and the meanings they contain
Discourse analysis	Sociology	Examining the way knowledge is produced within different discourses and the performances, linguistic styles and rhetorical devices used in particular accounts
Protocol analysis	Psychology	Examining and drawing inference about the cognitive processes that underlie the performance of tasks
Symbolic interactionism	Sociology/social psychology	Exploring behaviour and social roles to understand how people interpret and react to their environment
Leading to Grounded theory	Sociology	Developing 'emergent' theories of social action through the identification of analytical categories and the relationships between them
Ethogenics	Social psychology	Exploring the underlying structure of behavioural acts by investigating the meaning people attach to them
Constructivism	Sociology	Displaying 'multiple constructed realities' through the shared investigation (by researchers and participants) of meanings and explanations
Critical theory	Sociology	Identifying ways in which material conditions (economic, political, gender, ethnic) influence beliefs, behaviour and experiences

These three positions have been continually debated but also modified so that they are understood in less extreme terms. For example, Bhasker (1978) argues for 'critical realism', Hammersley (1992) for 'subtle realism' in which social phenomena are believed to exist independently of people's representations of them but are only accessible through those representations. Meanwhile, there are also differing positions within idealism. Some idealists maintain that it is possible for meanings and representations to be shared or collective, while those holding a relativist position argue that there is no single reality, only a series of social constructions (see Hughes and Sharrock, 1997 for a fuller discussion of these two positions). Materialism is the most difficult position to sustain within qualitative research because qualitative research focuses directly on meaning and interpretation. Nevertheless, critical theorists might be considered to be neo-materialists in that they believe that social structures based on class, race or gender are experienced as having an external, immutable reality.

An underlying ontological issue has concerned whether the social and natural worlds exist in similar ways or whether the social world is very different because it is open to subjective interpretation. Some early commentators believed that the social world was similar to the physical world and was governed by universal, causal laws. Most contemporary qualitative researchers maintain that the social world is regulated by normative expectations and shared understandings and hence the laws that govern it are not immutable.

Epistemology

'Epistemology' is concerned with ways of knowing and learning about the social world and focuses on questions such as: how can we know about reality and what is the basis of our knowledge? There are three main issues around which there is debate in social research.

The first concerns the relationship between the researcher and the researched. In the natural science model, phenomena are seen as independent of and unaffected by the behaviour of the researcher, consequently the researcher can be objective in his or her approach and the investigation can be viewed as value free. While some qualitative researchers subscribe to this model, others believe that, in the social world, people are affected by the process of being studied and that the relationship between the researcher and social phenomena is interactive. In this case, the researcher cannot be objective and cannot produce an objective or 'privileged' account. Findings are either mediated through the researcher ('value-mediated'), or they can be negotiated and agreed between the researcher and research participants. Between these two positions, some researchers propose 'empathic neutrality', a position that recognises that research cannot be value free but which advocates that researchers should make their assumptions transparent. The influence of these assumptions on the ways data are collected and analysed is one strand of the 'reflexivity' called for on the part of researchers. The second relates to the impact of the research process on the participants and the evidence produced (see Chapter 10).

A second point at issue surrounds theories about 'truth'. This links back to views about similarities or differences between the natural and social worlds. In the natural sciences, the dominant theory of truth is one of correspondence – that is, there is a match between observations or readings of the natural world and an independent reality. An alternative view, known as the intersubjective or coherence theory of truth, and proposed as more appropriate for the study of the social world, suggests that this 'independent' reality can only be gauged in a consensual rather than an absolute way. If several reports confirm a statement then it can be considered true as a representation of a socially constructed reality. Finally, there are those who argue for a pragmatic theory or truth, which rests on the premise that an interpretation is true if it leads to, or provides assistance to take, actions that produce the desired or predicted results.

A final area of debate concerns the way in which knowledge is acquired. The main options are through induction by looking for patterns and association derived from observations of the world; or through deduction whereby propositions or hypotheses are reached theoretically, through a logically derived process. In other words inductive processes involve using evidence as the genesis of a conclusion; deductive processes use evidence in support of a conclusion. Although qualitative research is often seen as an inductive approach, it is not a singularly defining characteristic of qualitative research. Inductive reasoning is used in other forms of enquiry and the processes of sampling and generalisation from qualitative research involve both induction and deduction.

When comparing quantitative and qualitative methodologies, it is common for these to be equated with different positions on the merits of scientific enquiry. The former is seen to investigate the social world in ways which emulate the 'scientific method' as used in the natural sciences, with an emphasis on hypothesis testing, causal explanations, generalisation and prediction. By contrast, qualitative methods are seen to reject the natural science model and to concentrate on understanding, rich description and emergent concepts and theories. Again, however, this distinction is not clear cut: some qualitative approaches have sought to emulate natural science models, and not all quantitative studies are based on hypothesis testing but can produce purely descriptive and inductive statistics.

An underlying difficulty in all these debates surrounds the conception of 'scientific' investigation and what it constitutes. There is much debate about what 'science' is and what that means for both methods of research enquiry and the 'empirical' nature of the evidence they produce (Chalmers, 1982). Indeed, some suggest that there is a 'story book' image of scientific enquiry (Reason and Rowan, 1981), a scientific 'fairy tale' (Mitroff, 1974), in which depictions of the way scientific investigation is carried out bear no resemblance to the reality of what innovative scientists actually do. There is also questioning of the natural sciences – physics and mathematics in particular – as the originating disciplines for defining what counts as 'scientific' (Hughes and Sharrock, 1997; Sloman, 1976). It has been suggested that had the definition of 'scientific' method been based on other natural sciences, such as geology or botany, in which historical perspectives and classification are integral to rigorous investigation, then it might have been differently conceived. Perhaps most crucially, there are now serious challenges to the view that the natural world is as stable and law-like as has been supposed (Gleick, 1987; Lewin, 1993; Williams, 2000). All of these issues raise important questions about the status of 'scientific method' around which so much epistemological debate in the social sciences has taken place.

It is important to recognise that there are no definitive answers to these many philosophical questions. They simply relate to different views of the social world and different beliefs about how, in practice, it can and should be studied. The purpose here is to highlight the different stances that social researchers may take on these issues and to show how different beliefs give rise to different research practices. These are summarised in Box 1.3. It is left to the reader to decide where he or she stands on these larger questions and to consider the implications of this for his or her own research practice.

Pragmatism and the 'toolkit' approach to social research

The diverse ontological and epistemological perspectives within the qualitative tradition, and the adoption of positivist ideals among some qualitative researchers, indicate that qualitative and quantitative methods should not necessarily be seen as opposed approaches to research. On a practical level, some researchers have begun to emphasise the importance of appreciating that qualitative and quantitative research methods can and should be seen as part of the social researcher's 'toolkit'. They are encouraging greater acceptance of pragmatism in choosing the appropriate method for addressing specific research questions, rather than focusing too much on the underlying philosophical debates (Seale, 1999).

According to this view, qualitative and quantitative research should not be seen as competing and contradictory, but should instead be viewed as complementary strategies appropriate to different types of research questions or issues. In the latter part of the twentieth century, there was much discussion and development of 'multi-method, transdisciplinary' research which employs a range of different methods and draws on expertise from a range of alternate disciplines, as appropriate to the research questions. In an attempt to overcome the previously entrenched epistemological positions of positivism and interpretivism, some have begun to examine more closely not only the philosophical, but also the practical realities of each.

BOX 1.3   KEY ONTOLOGICAL AND EPISTEMOLOGICAL STANCES

ONTOLOGICAL STANCES

The nature of the world and what we can know about it

Realism

- an external reality exists independent of our beliefs or understanding
- a clear distinction exists between beliefs about the world and the way the world is

Materialism (a variant of realism)

- an external reality exists independent of our beliefs or understanding
- only the material or physical world is considered 'real'
- mental phenomena (e.g. beliefs) arise from the material world

Subtle realism/critical realism (a variant of realism, influenced by idealism)

- an external reality exists independent of our beliefs and understanding
- reality is only knowable through the human mind and socially constructed meanings

Idealism

- no external reality exists independent of our beliefs and understanding
- reality is only knowable through the human mind and socially constructed meanings

Subtle idealism (a variant acknowledging collective understandings)

- reality is only knowable through socially constructed meanings
- meanings are shared and there is a collective or objective mind

Relativism (a variant of idealism)

- reality is only knowable through socially constructed meanings
- there is no single shared social reality, only a series of alternative social constructions

EPISTEMOLOGICAL STANCES
How it is possible to know about the world

Positivism

- the world is independent of and unaffected by the researcher
- facts and values are distinct, thus making it possible to conduct objective, value free inquiry
- observations are the final arbiter in theoretical disputes
- the methods of the natural sciences (e.g. hypothesis testing, causal explanations and modelling) are appropriate for the study of social phenomena because human behaviour is governed by law-like regularities

(Continued)

BOX 1.3 *(Continued)*

Interpretivism

- the researcher and the social world impact on each other
- facts and values are not distinct and findings are inevitably influenced by the researcher's perspective and values, thus making it impossible to conduct objective, value free research, although the researcher can declare and be transparent about his or her assumptions
- the methods of the natural sciences are not appropriate because the social world is not governed by law-like regularities but is mediated through meaning and human agency; consequently the social researcher is concerned to explore and understand the social world using both the participant's and the researcher's understanding

Those in favour of transdisciplinary, multi-method research strategies have suggested that purism about the epistemological origins of a particular approach may undermine our ability to choose and implement the most appropriate research design for answering the research questions posed. Indeed, some feel that philosophical positions have been allowed to undermine pragmatic considerations and that a more helpful balance might be struck between philosophy and pragmatism (Bryman, 1988; Silverman, 1993). This has led to the suggestion that different research methods should be viewed as part of a research toolkit, including both qualitative and quantitative techniques. The tools thus available to the researcher can be used as appropriate in different research contexts and to address different research questions.

While the need to move towards more transdisciplinary and multi-method research is increasingly being proposed, the ways in which this is envisaged vary. Some have suggested that it is possible and appropriate to mix methods associated with different paradigms within the same study. Others, however, have argued that multi-method research designs should only extend to the use of different methods from within the same paradigm. The latter would appear to limit the potential for combining qualitative and quantitative methods within the same study. Indeed, there is some debate about whether mixing methods across paradigms may lead to a lack of analytical clarity because each method relies on different assumptions in data collection and produces different types of data which may be difficult to reconcile. Ultimately, most authors on this subject have deferred to readers to draw their own conclusions about the value of these different arguments and to choose for themselves whether they will espouse pragmatism or adhere more strictly to particular epistemological stances. For those choosing the former, a range of strategies for combining qualitative and quantitative methods have been suggested (see Chapter 2).

Although some have attempted to focus more on the tools available to researchers than the philosophical assumptions underlying different research methods, others remain sceptical about this approach. Within disciplines based on natural 'science' particularly (for example, clinical research or psychological research), debate continues as to whether and how it is appropriate to use qualitative research methods which start from a different set of assumptions about the nature of reality and ways of knowing than those traditionally espoused in these fields (Stange, p. 351 in Crabtree and Miller, 1999). A key dilemma concerns whether it is feasible to maintain a positivist stance to research undertaken using quantitative methods while also accepting the more interpretivist or constructivist stances which tend to underpin some qualitative methods. It is said that combining both approaches in a single study poses particular difficulties unless the researcher neglects the epistemological bases of the different methods and adopts a largely pragmatic stance focusing on research methods as techniques divorced from their philosophical foundations (Richardson, 1996). This remains an area of ongoing controversy that has yet to be adequately resolved even among proponents of multi-method, transdisciplinary approaches to research.

The 'approach' within this book

Earlier in the chapter we indicated the importance of situating the approach described in the subsequent chapters, which has been developed in the domain of applied social policy, within broader methodological debate. In this section, we therefore indicate the main parameters within which researchers working in this tradition operate, and the beliefs which underlie their work. It is important to stress, however, that different research environments will vary in how they can be placed and individual researchers will differ in where they would situate themselves. For us all, beliefs and practices evolve.

First, it is perhaps useful to stress two key aspects of the context in which the use of qualitative methods within social policy has developed. A primary factor is that research is commissioned and funded by public bodies (government departments being by far the largest spenders) which intend to use that research in the design and development of policy and practice. As funders, they have certain requirements of the research they commission. Influential, too, is the fact that the dominant research paradigm within this context was, and to some extent remains, quantitative. Those funding and commissioning qualitative research also make extensive use of quantitative data. Many of the organisations and institutes which practice qualitative research within the applied policy context have strong traditions of conducting quantitative research, and many individual research practitioners are skilled in both methods.

These features mean that particular emphasis is placed in applied policy research on producing qualitative evidence that has been rigorously collected and analysed, is valid, able to support wider inference, as neutral and unbiased as possible and clearly defensible in terms of how interpretations have been reached. It also means that emphasis is placed on research findings which are accessible and which can be translated into policy planning and implementation.

What is important to note here is that adherence to these principles and our approach to implementing them means that we do not fit neatly into any one recognised 'school' of qualitative research and instead, we borrow from many different traditions within the social research field generally. This eclecticism can be a significant strength. However, in the existing literature, practising researchers appear reluctant to acknowledge and delineate the boundaries of their beliefs and practices where these do not mesh with existing recognised traditions of qualitative research. As a result, certain practices are generally acknowledged or aspired to, but the beliefs underlying these practices are rarely explicitly discussed or debated.

This gives rise to what has been informally termed 'generic qualitative research' (Morse, 1998); that is research which appears to have been carried out without reference to other qualitative research traditions and where the beliefs of researchers and their relationship to their research practice is never explicitly discussed. According to some researchers, not having the opportunity to assess the degree of consistency between the researchers' beliefs and the research practices used makes it impossible to evaluate the quality of research.

The following sections therefore map the key parameters within which we carry out qualitative research for applied social policy purposes. As far as can be judged, these same parameters would apply to many other individuals and institutions that carry out qualitative research within the same field.

Ontological position (or what it is possible to know about the world)

In terms of ontological position, or what we believe it is possible to know about the world, we adhere most closely to what Hammersley (1992) describes as 'subtle realism'. That is, we accept that the social world does exist independently of individual subjective understanding, but that it is only accessible to us via the respondents' interpretations (which may then be further interpreted by the researcher). We emphasise the critical importance of respondents' own interpretations of the relevant research issues and accept that their different vantage points will yield different types of understanding. But we do not feel that diverse perspectives negate the existence of an external reality which can be 'captured'. Rather, we believe that that external reality is itself diverse and multifaceted. The diversity of perspectives thus adds richness to our understanding of the various ways in which that reality has been experienced, and our underlying aim is to apprehend and convey as full a picture as possible of the nature of that multifaceted reality.

Epistemological position (or how it is possible to find out about the world)

Our epistemological stance reflects the fact that the historical context is largely one of quantitative research. Our approach therefore draws on aspects of the scientific method, particularly in its most recent conceptions, but has been adapted to suit the nature of qualitative data and the goals of qualitative research. To an extent a parallel adaptation has to occur in quantitative research since specific features of the scientific method are not necessarily reflected in, nor appropriate for, statistical social enquiry. Thus, we can pinpoint a number of features traditionally associated with empirical research that influence the conduct of applied social policy research.

A key feature is a striving to be as objective and neutral as possible in the collection, interpretation and presentation of qualitative data. Researchers generally take particular care in data collection to minimise the extent to which the researcher influences the views of research participants during the course of interviews or focus groups. Although individual researchers have different perspectives on this issue, researchers generally do *not* divulge personal information about themselves during data collection and are trained to use open, non-leading questioning techniques. We also recognise that while researchers can 'strive' for neutrality and objectivity, we can never attain this aspiration fully (nor indeed, do we believe that this is possible in other types of social research). This relates back to our ontological stance of subtle realism where we acknowledge that personal interpretations are important both in terms of study participants' perspectives of reality, and in terms of researchers' understanding and portrayal of study participants' views.

Reflexivity is important in striving for objectivity and neutrality. We try to reflect upon ways in which bias might creep into our qualitative research practice, and acknowledge that our own backgrounds and beliefs can be relevant here. However, while policy customers welcome guidance about the reliance they can place on particular research findings, they generally make no requirement to know the values and beliefs of the researchers they fund. It is therefore important that researchers provide as much information as possible, in terms of both technical details of conduct and potential bias, so that others can scrutinise the 'objectivity' of the investigation.

Other tenets of the scientific method that we strive to achieve relate to reliability and validity. We accept that differences in the nature of quantitative and qualitative data mean that these terms should not be applied in a standard way to both types of research. Nevertheless, we believe that both are important features of qualitative research, and attainable aspirations. They are also essential elements when considering ways in which wider inference from a study can be drawn. This is discussed in detail in Chapter 10.

In addition to aspects of our epistemological stance relating to the scientific method, the approach embraces aspects of interpretivism and pragmatism. Our acceptance of interpretivism is reflected in practices which emphasise the importance of understanding people's perspectives in the context of the conditions and circumstances of their lives. We therefore seek to obtain thick description and as much detailed information as possible about people's lives (from their own perspectives and, to a more limited extent, our own observations either of the circumstances in which they live or their engagement with the research issues). We also see the researcher's interpretations as important provided that these can be clearly delineated from those of the participants. In evolving our interpretations, we adhere as closely as possible to their accounts, but acknowledge that deeper insights can be obtained by synthesising, interlocking and comparing the accounts of a number of respondents. We also utilise other forms of inferential and theoretical thinking to place our interpretations in a broader context. The process of interpretation is discussed in Chapter 9.

Acknowledgement is also made of the importance of accessibility of research findings to research funders and commissioners, and to those whose policies and practices it is intended to inform. This means that our interpretation is grounded in the accounts of individual respondents, but employs language, conceptualisation and categorisation that is not their own. Where our interpretations move beyond the explicit data provided by individual respondents, we place great importance on ensuring that the building blocks used by researchers in arriving at their interpretations are clearly visible to the reader. This means that in our reporting, we take care to show how more abstract interpretations offered by the research relate specifically to the data provided by study participants.

Lastly, we align ourselves with other pragmatists because we believe in the value of choosing the most appropriate research method or methods to address specific research questions. We are more interested in ensuring a suitable 'fit' between the research methods used and the research questions posed than we are in the degree of philosophical coherence of the epistemological positions typically associated with different research methods. We believe that quality and rigour in research practice have more to do with choosing the right research tools for the job than with limiting ourselves to combining only those research methods which are viewed as philosophically consistent.

This means that we are happy to combine qualitative and quantitative methods in the same study where this is viewed as necessary and helpful in answering the research questions posed. We acknowledge that qualitative and quantitative data do not calibrate exactly, but see this as a manifestation of the different ways in which each method contributes to an understanding of the research question. Inconsistency and contradiction need to be acknowledged and explanations for them sought, but we do not believe this undermines the value of either. But, more crucially, we see the quest for replication in evidence produced by different research methods as a false trail. Instead our search is for complementary extension – that is using different forms of evidence to build greater understanding and insight of the social world than is possible from one approach alone.

KEY POINTS

- Qualitative research covers a broad range of approaches which are linked to different beliefs about what there is to know about the social world and how to find out about it. Although definitions vary, the aims of qualitative research are generally directed at providing an in-depth and interpreted understanding of the social world, by learning about people's social and material circumstances, their experiences, perspectives and histories.
- The history of qualitative research must be understood in the context of wider developments in research methods generally and social research methods in particular. The development of qualitative research was strongly influenced by ideas about the importance of understanding human behaviours in their social and material contexts; and by the need to understand the meanings that people attach to their own experiences. 'Interpretivism', which is integral to the qualitative research tradition, is seen to overcome some of the perceived limitations associated with 'positivism', the tradition most commonly associated with statistical social enquiry.
- Qualitative research has seen many developments over the course of the twentieth century and a number of different 'schools' have emerged. Those that have been most formative include ethnography, phenomenology and ethnomethodology, symbolic interactionism and grounded theory, constructivism and critical theory. There has also been a widening of interest in the use of qualitative methods in disciplines that previously relied on quantitative research and experimental methods and in more applied fields. This is part of a broader recognition that researchers may need to adopt a more pragmatic stance in their research and draw on different resources available to them (both qualitative and quantitative) to address research questions.

KEY TERMS

Ontology is concerned with the nature of the social world and what can be known about it. A key ontological debate concerns whether there is a captive social reality and how it should be constructed on which there are three distinct positions. **Realism** claims that there is an external reality which exists independently of people's beliefs or understanding about it; **materialism** holds that there is a real world but that only material features of that world hold reality; and **idealism** asserts that reality is only knowable through the human mind and socially constructed meanings. Qualitative researchers vary in their ontological stances but there is a common understanding that the social world is governed by normative expectations and shared understandings and hence the laws that govern it are not immutable.

Epistemology is concerned with the nature of knowledge and how it can be acquired. The main epistemological stances are **positivism** which holds that methods of the natural sciences are appropriate for social enquiry because human behaviour is governed by law-like regularities; and that it is possible to carry out independent, objective and value free social research. The opposing view, known as **interpretivism**, claims that natural science methods are not appropriate for social investigation because the social world is not governed by regularities that hold law-like properties. Hence, a social researcher has to explore and understand the social world through the participants' and their own perspectives; and explanations can only be offered at the level of meaning rather than cause. Qualitative research is largely associated with interpretivism.

There is also epistemological debate about the relative merits of **induction** and **deduction**. Induction looks for patterns and associations derived from observations of the world; deduction generates propositions and hypotheses theoretically through a logically derived process. Although qualitative research is often viewed as a predominantly inductive paradigm, both deduction and induction are involved at different stages of the qualitative research process.

Further reading

Bryman, A. (1988) *Quantity and Quality in Social Research*, London: Unwin Hyman

Denzin, N.K. and Lincoln, Y.S. (2000) *Handbook of Qualitative Research*, 2nd edition, Thousand Oaks, CA: Sage. In particular 'Introduction: The discipline and practice of qualitative research' and Y.S. Lincoln and E.G. Guba's 'Paradigmatic controversies, contradictions and emerging confluences'

Hammersley, M. (1992) *What's Wrong with Ethnography?*, London: Routledge

Hughes, J. and Sharrock, W. (1997) *The Philosophy of Social Research*, London: Longman

Seale, C. (1999) *The Quality of Qualitative Research*, Oxford: Blackwell

2

The Applications of Qualitative Methods to Social Research

Jane Ritchie

The previous chapter has described the different traditions of qualitative research and the particular 'school' of research that forms the backcloth to this book. It also described the main defining features of qualitative research and, in this second chapter, we consider what these features bring to social enquiry.

We begin the chapter with an overview of the different functions of qualitative research in addressing the types of research questions that arise in social research. There is then some discussion of the roles of different qualitative research methods in investigating and portraying social phenomena. The final section describes ways in which qualitative research can be used in harness with statistical enquiry.

Theoretical and applied research

When describing the uses and roles of different research methods, a distinction is sometimes made between theoretical, pure or basic research, and applied research. Theoretical research is concerned with the aim of testing, generating or enhancing thinking within a particular discipline. 'Basic researchers work to generate new theories or test existing theories' (Patton, 2002: 215). Applied research is concerned with using the knowledge acquired through research to contribute directly to the understanding or resolution of a contemporary issue. As such, its objectives are usually set or shaped by specific information requirements or by the need to gain insight into an existing problem.

In the social sciences generally, and in social research in particular, there is some debate about whether it is useful or even valid to distinguish between applied and theoretical research. The arguments that underpin that debate centre around the necessary and inherent interaction between social theory and social research (Hakim, 2000; May, 2001; Rossi and Lyall, 1978; Silverman, 2000b). Consequently, it is suggested that all research is based on certain theoretical assumptions, even if these are implicit, unacknowledged or ill formed. Similarly, it is argued that all forms of social research can contribute to 'theory' by providing greater understanding of, and knowledge about, the social world. Either way, there is a view that social research is at its most useful when theoretical insights and social investigation are mutually enhancing such that the collection of evidence 'is informed by theory and interpreted in the light of it' (Bulmer, 1982: 152). Indeed, as Silverman has said of social theory more generally, 'Without theory, research is impossibly narrow. Without research, theory is mere armchair contemplation' (2000b: 86).

Although, the boundaries between applied and theoretical research are somewhat blurred in social enquiry, the term 'applied social research' is often used to denote studies that have the objectives of developing, monitoring or evaluating policy and its related practice (Hakim, 2000; Patton, 2002; Walker, 1985). The policy or programme under review may be relevant to national, regional, local or institutional concerns and may take place in any one of numerous policy fields spanning education, employment, social security, housing, environment, health, social care, poverty, race relations, criminal justice and so on. The objectives of the research may be wide reaching in terms of understanding underlying social problems or receiving cultures or they may be highly focused on specific services, interventions or legislation. As such, the remit of social policy research, like the policy process itself, is multifaceted and extensive. It also requires an understanding of social theory to provide context to, and more fully interpret, the evidence generated.

The growth in applied qualitative research

Until the latter part of the twentieth century the use of qualitative methods was much more evident in research that was concerned with developing social theory than in more applied settings. As Chapter 1 described, qualitative research has a longstanding history of contributing to an understanding of social structures, behaviours and cultures. But the wide scale use of qualitative methods to aid directly in the development and appraisal of social policy occurred much later. This was certainly so in the UK but also occurred in other countries, like the US, which had equally strong traditions of using qualitative methods (Filstead, 1979). It has been argued that one of the main reasons for this was that policy-makers saw 'information' or 'evidence' as synonymous with numbers (Bulmer, 1982; Weiss, 1977). Even in the 1960s and 1970s, when there was significant growth in the conduct of policy related research, the main methods used were statistically based, often involving sample surveys. As it was then observed, the demand for 'hard facts' about social conditions established a normative statistical methodology for social policy research (Payne et al., 1981).

But as in other fields, there were increasing calls for much greater utilisation of qualitative methods in order to understand more fully the nature of the problems that social policies had to address, and to appraise those policies once implemented (Rich, 1977; Weiss, 1977). In other words, it was seen as having a crucial role in providing the 'enlightenment' or 'knowledge for understanding' that was needed for social policy concerns (Janowitz, 1971; Scott and Shore, 1979). And while there has been considerable growth in the use of qualitative research in social policy over the last few decades, its potential is still felt to be underutilised (Rist, 2000).

One of the more recent debates that has drawn particular attention to this surrounds the interest in 'evidence based' policy and practice (Davies et al., 2000; Morse et al., 2001). The term was first used in medical research ('evidence based medicine') to define 'the conscientious, explicit and judicious use of current best evidence in making decisions about the care of individual patients' (Sackett et al., 1996: 71) but has now been adopted more widely in other policy fields. In discussions about evidence based policy or practice, it soon came to light that evidence from qualitative research was being given much lower status than that derived from 'scientific' or statistical enquiry (Madjar and Walton, 2001). While this has been widely challenged, it reflects the persistent view that only 'facts' constitute evidence and that these are best derived from research involving numbers. As we will go on to show, this very limited view of 'evidence' will leave many questions essential to social policy misconceived or inadequately understood.

The functions of qualitative research

To consider the particular role of qualitative methods in providing the kinds of information and understanding needed in social research, it is useful to consider some of the broader functions of social investigation. These have been defined in various ways, depending on the purpose of the classification. In more theoretical research, for example, distinctions are often made between the functions of theory building, hypotheses testing and content illumination. Alternatively, in applied research, the policy-making cycle is sometimes used to define the different types of research needed during the key stages of policy-making – that is formulation, implementation and appraisal.

From these and other such divisions, it is possible to identify a broad, although comprehensive, classification as follows:

- Contextual – describing the form or nature of what exists
- Explanatory – examining the reasons for, or associations between, what exists
- Evaluative – appraising the effectiveness of what exists
- Generative – aiding the development of theories, strategies or actions.

Different forms of research can contribute to each of these functions in quite distinct ways and this is discussed later in this chapter. Here we are concerned with the kinds of evidence that qualitative research can provide within each of these broad categories.

Contextual research is concerned with identifying *what* exists in the social world and the way it manifests itself. A major feature of qualitative methods is their facility to describe and display phenomena as experienced by the study population, in fine-tuned detail and in the study participants' own terms. It therefore offers the opportunity to 'unpack' issues, to see what they are about or what lies inside, and to explore how they are understood by those connected with them. Such evidence can be used to:

- Map the range of elements, dimensions, classes or positions within a social phenomenon, for example

  - how do parents define 'good behaviour' in their children; how do their children define it?
  - what perceptions of politics do young people hold?
  - what dimensions are contained within the concept of a 'standard of living' or 'a good standard of living'?

- Display the nature or features of a phenomenon, such as

  - how does racism manifest itself?
  - how is social isolation experienced?
  - what does 'community participation' involve?

- Describe the meaning that people attach to an experience, event, circumstance or other phenomenon

  - what does it mean to be a grandparent?
  - how does it feel to have a criminal record?
  - what is the significance of a marriage ceremony to those involved?

- Identify and define typologies

  - what characterises different groups amongst people who experience social exclusion?
  - what are the different models for organising 'self help' groups?
  - what defines different approaches to vocational counselling for young unemployed people?

These functions of qualitative research have been called descriptive or exploratory by other authors (Marshall and Rossman, 1999; Robson, 2002) and indeed both are key features of contextual research. The essential purpose is to explore and describe participants' understanding and interpretations of social phenomena in a way that captures their inherent nature.

Explanatory research is concerned with *why* phenomena occur and the forces and influences that drive their occurrence. Because of its facility to examine subjects in depth, qualitative research provides a unique tool for studying what lies behind, or underpins, a decision, attitude, behaviour or other phenomena. It also allows associations that occur in people's thinking or acting – and the meaning these have for people – to be identified. These in turn may indicate some explanatory – even causal – link. This makes it possible to identify:

- the factors or influences that underlie a particular attitude, belief or perception, for example

  - what are the underlying factors leading to racism?
  - what influences people's views about environmental protection?
  - what shapes people's beliefs about poetry?

- the motivations that lead to decisions, actions or non-actions

  - why do people gamble?
  - why do people 'decide' not to have children – or how does 'voluntary' childlessness occur?
  - what leads people to become involved in volunteer activities?

- the origins or formation of events, experiences or occurrences

  - why does homelessness occur?
  - how do different systems for managing and controlling household income and expenditure evolve?
  - what are the barriers that inhibit the use of preventive health services?

- the contexts in which phenomena occur

  - in what circumstances does housing eviction take place?
  - what conditions give rise to the longevity of marital partnerships?
  - in what environments does traffic blight occur?

The role of qualitative methods in seeking and providing explanation is widely recognised within a range of different epistemological approaches (Giddens, 1984; Layder, 1993; Lofland and Lofland, 1995; Miles and Huberman, 1994). There is, however, debate about whether 'causes' of social phenomena can be truly detected, with some arguing that cause and effect in social enquiry can only be speculative (for full discussion see Chapter 8). Even assuming that is so, qualitative methods still have a crucial role in identifying the important influences and in generating explanatory hypotheses.

Evaluative research is concerned with issues surrounding how well does it work, a question that is central to much policy related investigation. In order to carry out evaluation, information is needed about both processes and outcomes and qualitative research contributes to both. Because of its flexible methods of investigation, qualitative methods are particularly adept at looking at the dynamics of *how* things operate. They can also contribute to an understanding of outcomes by identifying the different types of effects or consequences that can arise from a policy and the different ways in which they are achieved or occur. Such information can be used to:

- identify the factors that contribute to successful or unsuccessful delivery of a programme, service or intervention, for example

  - what factors contribute to the successful resettlement of people who are homeless?
  - what institutional factors lead young people to become excluded from school?
  - what makes an employment programme 'interesting' or 'boring' for participants?

- identify the effects of taking part in a programme or initiative on participants and how they occur, such as

  - what impact does a welfare to work programme have on the employment activity of its participants?
  - how do environmental conservation schemes change behaviour?
  - what are the psychological consequences of youth detention schemes?

- examine the nature of the requirements of different groups within the target population

  - what are the needs of different ethnic groups in responding to health promotion programmes?
  - how do different groups of older people respond to home security initiatives?
  - what are the requirements of different constituencies of people taking part in adult literacy schemes?

- explore a range of organisational aspects surrounding the delivery of a programme, service or intervention

  - what are the requirements of personal advisers for the effective delivery of debt counselling services?
  - how can funding most effectively be used in community development schemes?
  - what organisational structures are needed to support social work interventions for adoption?

- explore the contexts in which interventions are received and their impact on effectiveness

    - how do the personal circumstances of lone parents affect their participation in employment related programmes?
    - how does the nature of relationship breakdown affect receipt of family mediation services?
    - how do different personal or domestic circumstances affect secure parole arrangements?

The list of evaluative questions that qualitative methods can help to address is almost endless and much has been said about the role of qualitative methods in the evaluation of policy initiative and programmes. Patton (1988, 1997, 2002), in particular, has identified an extensive array of different types of evaluative functions for qualitative research. These include 'goal free' (that is looking at actual, rather than intended, effects); 'responsive' (to diverse stakeholder perspectives); 'connoisseurship' (which uses the evaluators' perceptions and expertise to draw conclusions); and 'utilisation-focused' (which derives from the intended use and users of the evaluation) (Patton, 2002).

One of the most widely used distinctions in evaluative research is between formative and summative modes of enquiry, a concept originally introduced by Scriven (1967) with much subsequent development (Herman et al., 1987; Patton, 2002; Rossi and Freeman, 1993). In brief, formative evaluations are designed to provide information that will help to change or improve a programme or policy, either as it is being introduced or where there are existing problems with its implementation. Summative evaluation is concerned with the impact of an intervention or policy in terms of effectiveness and the different outcomes that have resulted. There is a commonplace conception that qualitative methods can only contribute to formative research, a view that is very open to challenge. Rist (2000), for example, details a number of ways in which qualitative methods can address questions that arise when the impacts and outcomes of a policy or programme are being assessed.

Generative research is concerned with producing new ideas either as a contribution to the development of social theory or to the refinement or stimulus of policy solutions. Because qualitative research seeks to capture emergent concepts and is not overly predetermined in coverage, the potential for original or creative thoughts or suggestions is high. It also allows ideas to be generated through, and then placed in, the 'real' contexts from which they arise. It therefore has the potential to:

- develop new conceptions or understandings of social phenomena

    - the nature of 'social exclusion'
    - social models of disability
    - changing conceptions of 'family' and family relationships

- develop hypotheses about the nature of the social world and how it operates

  - the role of religious conflict in newly developing racial tensions
  - the nature of parenting in the twenty first century
  - the nature of the social structures that lead to 'workless' households

- generate new solutions to persistent social problems

  - innovative schemes to provide effective support for frail older people living alone
  - ways of intercepting cycles of disadvantage
  - identifying the nature of interventions to stop bullying at school

- identify strategies to overcome newly defined phenomena or problems

  - reduce overreaction to the threat of biological warfare
  - ways of restoring declining rural economies
  - mechanisms to encourage greater preservation of scarce environmental resources

- determine actions that are needed to make programmes, policies or services more effective

  - changes that are needed to help reduce hospital waiting lists
  - ways of encouraging car owners to make greater use of public transport
  - mechanisms for the early detection of child abuse

As was noted earlier, the role of qualitative methods in contributing to social theory has a well honoured heritage. Its applications in generating ideas and solutions for developing and reviewing policy and practice are as yet under exploited (Rist, 2000; Weiss, 1988). This is likely to alter with the enhanced understanding of qualitative methods that has taken place over the latter part of the twentieth century, with the increase in public consultation and with changing review mechanisms for integrating policy and practice through demonstration projects.

   The following chapters of this book will describe in detail the art of conducting qualitative research such that the functions described above are fulfilled to an optimum level. But it is important to emphasise again here that it is because of the exploratory, interactive and interpretivist nature of qualitative enquiry that it can make the kinds of contributions it does. Indeed all the defining features described in Chapter 1 allow qualitative research to provide evidence of a unique kind such that knowledge and understanding of social phenomena, and the contexts in which they arise, is extended.

Qualitative research as an independent research strategy

In the last section of this chapter we describe the various circumstances in which a combination of qualitative and quantitative methods might be used in the conduct of social research. But, as will be evident from the preceding discussion, there are many occasions when a qualitative approach will be the *only* approach needed to address a research question. A number of authors have identified the kind of circumstances in which this might be so (Denzin and Lincoln, 1998; Marshall and Rossman, 1999; Patton, 2002; Walker, 1985). There is general agreement that the factors that determine whether qualitative methods should be the principal or sole method used are centrally related to the objectives of the research. That is, it is the nature of the information or evidence required that will lead to a choice of a qualitative approach. So for example, if the major purpose of the research is concerned with understanding context or process, or is consultative or strategic in its aim, then qualitative evidence alone may be needed. But there are other factors, primarily related to the subject matter under investigation, that will necessitate a single research approach which is qualitative in form. These arise when the phenomena being studied hold certain features.

- *Ill defined/not well understood*   Qualitative research is sometimes used as a prelude to statistical enquiry when the subject matter needs to be more clearly understood or defined before they can be measured. There are perhaps more circumstances where qualitative research is needed to provide greater understanding of the nature of an issue or problem, but where measurement of its extent is not of interest. This can arise with newly developing social phenomena, such as the need for successful resettlement of refugees in disadvantaged urban areas; where previous knowledge or understanding has not fully explained occurrences or circumstances that are known to be widespread (for example, teenage use of drugs); or where refinements to understanding are needed (for example, the strengthening of citizenship). The open and generative nature of qualitative methods allow the exploration of such issues without advance prescription of their construction or meaning as a basis for further thinking about policy or theory development.

- *Deeply rooted*   There are subject areas in which the phenomena that need to be studied will be deeply set within the participants' personal knowledge or understanding of themselves. These may be related to the origins of long-standing values or beliefs (for example, beliefs about personal autonomy); to the formative influences on particular attitudes or behaviours (for example, gender roles); or to responses to events that have been very distressing, joyous or emotional (for example, feelings about becoming a parent for the first time). The nature of such phenomena makes it likely that participants will need very delicate and responsive questioning – and time – to explore the issues for themselves. They will also need continuing help in moving below initial or stylised responses to reach inner knowledge that has either been suppressed, or has remained largely unconscious.

- *Complex*   Similar issues arise in the study of complex subject matter where there is a need to understand phenomena which are innately intricate or conceptually difficult to relate. The complexity may lie in the nature of the subject itself – for example, technical matters like fiscal policy or philosophical questions like the nature of spirituality. Alternatively, it may be that the intricacy relates to the level of unpacking that is needed to formulate a position, view or belief. This can often be the case, for example, where cognitive processes, such as judgements or decisions are the focus of the study (for example the ways judgements are formed in criminal proceedings). Again, participants will need time to reflect both on the issue itself and on their own thinking and will require facilitative questioning to help them in the process.

- *Specialist*   A related point concerns the collection of information from individuals or groups that have a singular or highly specialised role in society. Examples would be public figures, leading professionals or 'experts' or senior representatives of organisations. If their views are being sought from the vantage of their particular positions, then the nature of the information is likely to require exploratory and responsive questioning. This is partly because the nature of the subject coverage is likely to be complex and/or involve aspects of system process but also because their perspectives are likely to be fairly idiosyncratic.

- *Delicate or intangible*   Certain subjects in social research are difficult to capture because they are so fragile in their manifestation. Again this might be because of the nature of the phenomenon itself which is either ethereal or unseeable (for example the 'culture' of a community); or it might relate to the elusive nature of feelings or thoughts that an event or circumstance provokes (for example, empathetic response to other people's grief). Here, carefully framed and responsive questioning or observation is needed to help participants uncover and relay the delicacy of their perceptions and responses.

- *Sensitive*   As will be discussed in Chapter 6, it is hard to predict the subject matters that might prove distressing or emotive to individual participants. Virtually any subject matter could turn out to raise sensitivities, depending on the circumstances or experiences of the person concerned. But there are also subjects which, by their very nature, are likely to generate emotional and often painful responses. Some obvious examples would include relationship breakdown, physical or sexual abuse, bereavement or life threatening illness. While predetermined questioning of such subjects is possible – indeed has often been carried out – there are practical and ethical limits to what it can achieve. Certainly any in-depth investigation of such matters will require finely tuned questions that are responsive to the particular circumstances of the individual; and sensitive facilitation to help people to describe feelings or emotions that may be very distressing or have previously gone unexpressed.

The features described above are some of the main determinants of using qualitative research as an independent mode of research enquiry. In all cases they are the kinds of subject matter that are difficult to address in structured surveys. As has been repeatedly stressed, the crucial questions in the choice of research methods surround the nature of the information that the research needs to provide.

In this context, it is perhaps important to warn against the other factors that can inappropriately influence the choice of qualitative research as the method to be used. Sometimes restricted budgets or time scales lead to a choice of small-scale qualitative methodology when this is not suited to the type of information required. In other circumstances, the particular orientation of a researcher or a funding body will influence the use of qualitative methods rather than the research questions that need to be addressed. It is therefore important that both research funders and researchers themselves ensure that there is good fit between the specification for the enquiry and the methods used to yield the information required.

The functions of different qualitative methods

It has already been stressed that the use of qualitative methods will be heavily influenced by the aims of the research and the specific questions that need to be answered. A further, although related issue, concerns the type of qualitative approach to be used to address the issues concerned. Just as qualitative and quantitative research offer different 'calibrations' of the social world, so too do different approaches and methods for collecting qualitative data. In this section we consider briefly the range of options available and the kinds of evidence they yield. Choosing which to use is considered further in Chapter 3 which deals with qualitative research design.

Approaches to collecting qualitative data can be divided into two very broad groups – those that focus on naturally occurring data and those that generate data through the interventions of the research.

Naturally occurring data

Many of the methods used in qualitative research were developed to allow investigation of phenomena in their natural settings. They provide data which is an 'enactment' of social behaviour in its own social setting, rather than a 'recounting' of it generated specifically for the research study. They are of particular value where behaviours and interactions (whether acted, spoken or written) need to be understood in 'real world' contexts. This would be relevant, for example, in studies concerned with an understanding of a particular culture or community and the implicit, as well as explicit, tenets and 'rules' that govern it. Alternatively, naturally occurring data may be needed when the researched behaviour involves elements that are subconscious or instinctive, is complex or delicate in its manifestation, or where there are concerns about the likely veracity of participants' representations of what has occurred.

There are a number of different approaches that have been developed to study phenomena in naturally occurring settings. These include

- *Participant observation* in which the researcher joins the constituent study population or its organisational or community setting to record actions, interactions or events that occur. This not only allows phenomena to be studied as they arise, but also offers the researcher the opportunity to gain additional insights through experiencing the phenomena for themselves. This method is integral to anthropological and ethnographic research because it provides 'direct experiential and observational access to the insiders' world of meaning' (Jorgenson, 1989: 15).

- *Observation* offers the opportunity to record and analyse behaviour and interactions as they occur, although not as a member of the study population. This allows events, actions and experiences and so on, to be 'seen' through the eyes of the researcher, often without any construction on the part of those involved. It is a particularly useful approach when a study is concerned with investigating a 'process' involving several players, where an understanding of non-verbal communications are likely to be important or where the behavioural consequences of events form a focal point of study.

- *Documentary analysis* involves the study of existing documents, either to understand their substantive content or to illuminate deeper meanings which may be revealed by their style and coverage. These may be public documents like media reports, government papers or publicity materials; procedural documents like minutes of meetings, formal letters or financial accounts; or personal documents like diaries, letters or photographs. Documentary analysis is particularly useful where the history of events or experiences has relevance, in studies where written communications may be central to the enquiry (for example organisational research, studies of public awareness or information) and where 'private' as well as 'public' accounts are needed. Documentary sources may also be needed when situations or events cannot be investigated by direct observation or questioning (Hammersley and Atkinson, 1995).

- *Discourse analysis* examines the construction of texts and verbal accounts to explore 'systems of social meaning' (Tonkiss, 2000). It examines ways in which 'versions of the world, of society, events and inner psychological worlds are produced in discourse' (Potter, 1997: 146) with an interest in both their cognitive conception and their interpretation for social action. The analysis may be based on a variety of different sources containing discourse including written documents, speeches, media reports, interviews and conversation. As such, discourse analysis draws in features of both documentary analysis and conversation analysis (see below) although always with a focus on what the content and structure of the discourse conveys.

- *Conversation analysis* involves a detailed examination of 'talk in interaction' to determine how conversation is constructed and enacted. The aim is to investigate social intercourse, as it occurs in natural settings, in 'an attempt to describe people's methods for producing orderly social interaction' (Silverman, 2001: 167). It is based on the assumption that conversation is a basic social system through which social order is both achieved and displayed and thus its study offers insights into how order is gained, sustained or overruled. Partly for this reason, conversation analysis is concerned with the structural and sequential organisation of conversation as well as its substantive content.

Generated data

Generated methods involve 'reconstruction' (Bryman, 2001) and require re-processing and re-telling of attitudes, beliefs, behaviour or other pheno-mena. The experience, thought, event, behaviour or whatever, is mentally re-processed and verbally recounted by study participants. Generated data give insight into people's own perspectives on and interpretation of their beliefs and behaviours – and, most crucially, an understanding of the mean-ing that they attach to them. These methods are needed in a variety of research settings, partly because they provide the only means of under-standing certain psychological phenomena, such as motivations, beliefs, decision processes, but also because they allow participants' reflections on, and understanding of, social phenomena to be gained.

Again there are different ways in which data can be generated.

- *Biographical methods* which use life stories, narratives and recounted biographies to understand the phenomena under study. In certain respects these are the most 'naturalistic' of the generated methods in that they allow participants a high degree of freedom to shape and order the reconstructions in their own way. The term encompasses study of a range of different types of material, both written and spoken, including life and oral histories, biographical and autobiographical accounts and 'docu-ments of life' (Plummer, 2001). Biographical methods are of particular value in determining how 'life experience can be understood' within 'contemporary cultural and structural settings' and 'has the important merit of aiding the task of understanding major social shifts, by includ-ing how new experiences are interpreted by individuals within families, small groups and institutions' (Roberts, 2002: 5)

- *Individual interviews* are probably the most widely used method in quali-tative research. They take different forms but a key feature is their ability to provide an undiluted focus on the individual. They provide an oppor-tunity for detailed investigation of people's personal perspectives, for in-depth understanding of the personal context within which the research phenomena are located, and for very detailed subject coverage. They are also particularly well suited to research that requires an understanding of deeply rooted or delicate phenomena or responses to complex systems, processes or experiences because of the depth of focus and the opportunity they offer for clarification and detailed understanding.

- *Paired (or triad) interviews* are in-depth interviews but carried out with two (sometimes three) people at the same time. They provide an opportunity for individual depth of focus but also allow participants to reflect on, and draw comparisons with, what they hear from others. This can be of particular value when investigating subjects in which dialogue with others may play an important part, or where two people form a naturally occurring unit (for example, partners, colleagues, friends etc.). They can also be useful when the subject matter is complex or unfamiliar to participants and there is benefit in interactive or joint reflection.

- *Focus groups[1] or group discussions* involve several – usually somewhere between four and ten – respondents brought together to discuss the research topic as a group. They are used where the group process will itself illuminate the research issue. They are sometimes described as a more naturalistic research setting than in-depth interviews but as the setting will generally have been engineered solely for the purposes of the study, the degree of naturalism should not be exaggerated. But they do provide a social context for research, and thus an opportunity to explore how people think and talk about a topic, how their ideas are shaped, generated or moderated through conversation with others. Because group discussions allow participants to hear from others, they provide an opportunity for reflection and refinement which can deepen respondents' insights into their own circumstances, attitudes or behaviour. They also provide an opportunity for direct and explicit discussion of difference as it emerges in the group. They are ideal for creative thinking and are a better setting for using stimulation materials or projective techniques (see Chapter 7), which can seem contrived in a one-to-one situation.

Mixing qualitative approaches

The concept of a 'mixed method' approach to research is often discussed in the context of combining qualitative and quantitative methods (see Chapter 1). But the same principles apply to using more than one qualitative method to carry out an investigation since each brings a particular kind of insight to a study. For example, interviews are often used in combination with observation

---

1 The terminology of focus groups has changed somewhat over the last few decades. Earlier terms used were 'group interviews' or, in the UK at least, 'group discussions'. As Fontana and Frey (2000) note, the term 'focus groups' was coined by Merton, Fiske and Kendall (1956). That term has always been used consistently in market research, and is now increasingly used in broader social research settings. We use the terms 'focus group' and 'group discussions' interchangeably throughout this book. The former is probably now the most widely recognised term. But the latter conveys better the idea of a group which may be more or less focused or structured depending on the requirements of the study, and in which data is generated and shaped through discussion.

methods so that there can be understanding of how events or behaviours naturally arise as well as reconstructed perspectives on their occurrence. Similarly individual interviews and focus groups are often used in the same study. For example, focus groups might be used as an initial stage to raise and begin to explore relevant issues which will then be taken forward through in-depth interviews; or might be used after in-depth interviews to discuss the issues at a more strategic level. A design combining say individual interviews and some later conversation analysis might be used for similar reasons. As with all decisions about the choice of methods, the objectives of the study and the nature of the data required to meet them will be central to the use of two or more qualitative approaches. It will also be affected by the epistemological orientation of the researcher and their views on the integrity of different methods for investigating the central phenomena under study.

Combining qualitative and quantitative methods

There is much debate in social research about whether qualitative and quantitative approaches should, or even can, be combined. Some writers argue that the approaches are so different in their philosophical and methodological origins that they cannot be effectively blended. Others, while recognising the very different ontological and epistemological bases of the two paradigms, suggest that there can be value in bringing the two types of data together. But even within the latter context it is often emphasised that the purpose of bringing different approaches together is to yield different types of intelligence about the study subject rather than simply to fuse the outputs from qualitative and quantitative enquiry:

> With multiple methods the researcher has to confront the tensions between different theoretical perspectives while at the same time considering the relationship between the data sets produced by the different methods. (Brannen, 1992a: 33)

We are of the view that there can be benefit in harnessing qualitative and statistical enquiry provided that the two methods, and the data they generate, can be clearly delineated. Certainly, within social policy research, the potential for combining the two approaches is considerable (DePoy and Gitlin, 1998). Many of the questions that need to be addressed require measurement of some kind but also greater understanding of the nature or origins of an issue. Each of the two research approaches provides a distinctive kind of evidence and used together they can offer a powerful resource to inform and illuminate policy or practice. To illustrate, Box 2.1 provides an example of how qualitative and quantitative methods would contribute quite differently to a study about the nature of homelessness and the types of interventions

BOX 2.1 STUDY OF HOMELESSNESS: CONTRIBUTIONS OF QUALITATIVE AND QUANTITATIVE METHODS TO DIFFERENT RESEARCH FUNCTIONS

Functions of research	Qualitative methods to explore/understand	Quantitative methods to determine
Contextual	The nature of different forms of homelessness The experience/meaning of being homeless	The extent to which different forms of homelessness exists The characteristics of homeless people
Explanatory	The events leading to homelessness/ circumstances in which it occurs Why homelessness continues	Factors statistically associated with homelessness Characteristics/ circumstances that correlate with different lengths of homelessness
Evaluative	Appraisal of any interventions experienced Formative factors in bringing periods of homelessness to an end	Extent to which different forms of homelessness services are used Extent to which interventions achieve required outcomes
Generative	Suggestions/strategies for supporting homeless people/ helping people to avoid homelessness	Prediction of future levels of homelessness Levels of requirement for different forms of provision/intervention

required. As can be seen, qualitative research would be addressing questions surrounding the nature of homelessness, how or why it arises, and appraising ways in which different forms of preventive or rehabilitative intervention can be made most effective. Meanwhile quantitative research would be concerned with the measurement of levels of homelessness, their distribution among the population, the extent to which homelessness services are used and future levels of provision required. In other words, both the aims and the outputs are of a quite different nature and it is this that can make their combined use so powerful.

Several authors have provided useful frames of reference for optimising the strengths of the two approaches in combination (see for example Brannen, 1992b; Bryman, 1988, 2001; Hammersley, 1996; Morgan, 1998). Each of these suggests possible sequential relationships that may exist between the conduct of qualitative and quantitative studies and this is a framework we will use here for elaboration. Very simply, qualitative research may precede statistical enquiry, may accompany statistical investigation or may be used in some form of follow up study. Each of these linkages is considered below.

Preceding statistical enquiry

A traditional role for qualitative research has been to help in devising areas of questioning for statistical study. This is particularly valuable in studies where the subject matter under investigation is new or underdeveloped and where qualitative methods can help to define terminology, concepts or subjects for investigation. Similarly, preliminary qualitative research can be of value when the subject matter is complex and where some identification of the underlying constructs is needed before relevant questions can be structured. This is particularly useful in cases where a battery of items is to be compiled to measure attitudes or behaviours. The qualitative work can not only identify the appropriate dimensions to include but also generate the 'real life' language in which they should be framed.

Another developmental use is to generate hypotheses for statistical testing. Because of its facility for in-depth investigation, qualitative research can point to possible connections between phenomena that might be difficult to detect through other means. Preliminary research can therefore help to identify the relevant variables for inclusion and indicate what kinds of association between them might be sought.

Defining the dimensions of sample segmentation can be another output of preliminary qualitative research. As is discussed in Chapter 8, the identification of typologies amongst the study population is a prevalent output of qualitative analysis. Developmental research can help to designate the different groups or locations that exist among the study population and identify their defining characteristics. If these can then be captured in predefined questioning, statistical enquiry can measure the size of the sample segments and show how they distribute in relation to other variables.

It is important to note that qualitative work undertaken for design purposes does not need to be discarded once its developmental role is fulfilled. It is often the case that the material collected in preliminary work can be used subsequently to illuminate statistical findings or to provide illustrative accounts or case studies, even if a full analysis is not conducted of its content. Alternatively, if the preliminary study is appropriately designed as a self-standing study, then the findings from the qualitative work might be separately reported.

Alongside statistical enquiry

Qualitative and quantitative methods can be used in tandem to study the same or different phenomena. They might also be used with the same participants or with different participants depending on the purpose of the enquiry.

It is often the case that there is a need to examine both the number and nature of the same phenomenon. Sometimes it is possible to isolate the different dimensions and then provide some measurement of them, as was described in the preceding section. Other times the phenomenon is too complex or delicate to be captured fully in statistical enquiry and qualitative research is needed alongside to provide the detail or understanding that is required.

There are also occasions where qualitative and quantitative research are brought together in the study of the same phenomenon but then divide in terms of what is explored. This occurs when the starting point is the same measurement or indicator but for which different types of information are required. An example might be levels of overspend in different areas of service provision. Both qualitative and quantitative research would have common ground in identifying areas in which overspend is greatest in each spending authority. Quantitative research might then be used to provide a profile of expenditure in different areas over a number of years or to compare the characteristics of the high spending areas with lower spending authorities. Qualitative research meanwhile might explore the processes through which expenditure is controlled or the factors that have led to changes in patterns of overspend.

There are many opportunities to use qualitative and quantitative methods in combination to study different phenomena in the same field of enquiry. Box 2.2 shows a short list of examples where the data from the two approaches might be complementary in a similar area of investigation. The items listed in the qualitative column are ones which hold some dynamic element (for example interactions, systems, processes) or ones that need in-depth information. In contrast, the quantitative column contains items which can be most easily categorised and hence be counted.

It is often important to know something of the contexts in which phenomena occur or the consequences to which they may lead. Sometimes it is possible to do this through quantitative measurement alone (for example the incidence of different types of illness/disability in different occupational groups; the effects of different illnesses/disabilities on employment activities). But there are often occasions where the context or consequences need to be understood at a deeper level and for which qualitative investigation will be needed. The cultural requirements of certain ethnic minority groups for effective health service delivery might be one such example.

As has already been noted, qualitative research is able to explore influences that are too complex or delicate to be captured through structured methods. It can therefore fruitfully be combined with statistical enquiry to investigate underlying factors that may be causing a phenomenon to occur. For example, in virtually any enquiry of barriers to service use there will be a role for qualitative methods. Although quantitative research will be able to

**BOX 2.2   COMPLEMENTARY USES OF QUALITATIVE AND
QUANTITATIVE DATA IN STUDYING LINKED PHENOMENA**

Area of investigation	Qualitative investigation	Quantitative measurement
GP consultations	Nature and content of interactions between GPs and patients	Length and frequency of consultations
Environmental conservation	Resistances against conservation practices	Levels of participation in different conservation schemes
Child sexual abuse	Circumstances in which child sexual abuse had arisen	Characteristics of people reporting child sexual abuse
Friendship	How friendships are gained and sustained	Size and characteristics of friendship networks
Gender roles in household financial systems	Origins of female/male roles in household financial systems/how they evolved	Distribution of financial systems across different households

identify the barriers at a global level – that is, awareness, access, cost, convenience, applicability and so on – it will be less able to explain the origins of these barriers or how they deter people from service use.

The need to use qualitative and quantitative methods is particularly evident in evaluative studies. Indeed, it could be argued that it is not possible to carry out comprehensive evaluation without the use of both methodologies. At a simple level, this is because some measurement of outcome is usually needed (requiring quantitative methods) accompanied by some investigation of process (requiring qualitative methods).

As a follow-up to statistical enquiry

Possibly one of the most underutilised ways of using qualitative and quantitative research together is to follow statistical research enquiry with a qualitative study, yet this is a particularly powerful way of combining the two approaches. There are many instances where statistical enquiries present findings that need further explanation or where more detail or depth about a phenomenon is needed.

Follow-up can also be useful to explore issues among particular subgroups of interest. This may be because the size of the subgroup is small and of insufficient scale for any detailed statistical analysis. But it can also usefully occur when the statistical study has shown that the group in question may have an important perspective on the subject matter of enquiry or where it is clear that there are unexplored areas to investigate. For example, in a survey carried out among people who were registered as disabled for employment purposes, it was found that an unexpectedly high proportion of those in the more severely disabled category were working in open, as opposed to sheltered, employment. This led to a qualitative follow-up study to explore how open employment had been gained, sustained and retained among people with more severe disabilities (Thomas, 1992).

There is also a case to be made for using the two approaches in some kind of interactive sequence to extend learning or knowledge about an issue. For example, qualitative research might be used as a follow-up to a survey to provide greater understanding of the factors underlying a problem. It might then be that indicators of those factors, already existing in the survey data set, could be used for subsequent modelling or statistical testing. In any such uses, the important requirement is to recognise the linkages between the two sources of information and to maximise their association.

When using qualitative and quantitative research in harness, it is important to recognise that each offers a different way of knowing about the world. Although they may well be addressing the same research issue, they will provide a different 'reading' or form of calibration on that issue. As a consequence, it should not be expected that the evidence generated from the two approaches will replicate each other. Instead the purpose of interlocking qualitative and quantitative data is to achieve an extended understanding that neither method alone can offer. It is then up to the researcher to explain why the data and their 'meaning' are different. But authors have commented that this is often avoided. Instead, the findings of one method or approach become dominant and 'conflicts between the data (and the sources of their reconciliation) may be somewhat hidden from view' (Bryman, 1988: 155).

TRIANGULATION

In this context, the issues surrounding triangulation hold some relevance, a term first used in connection with the validity of 'measurements' derived from structured quantitative data (Campbell and Fiske, 1959). Triangulation involves the use of different methods and sources to check the integrity of, or extend, inferences drawn from the data. It has been widely adopted and developed as a concept by qualitative researchers as a means of investigating the 'convergence' of both the data and the conclusions derived from them (Denzin, 1994). It is also often cited as one of the central ways of 'validating' qualitative research evidence (see Chapter 10).

In this latter context, there has been a longstanding debate about the extent to which triangulation offers qualitative researchers a means of verifying their findings. There are many strands to these discussions (see for example Denzin, 1989, 1997; Fielding and Fielding, 1986; Flick, 1992; Hammersley and Atkinson, 1995; Seale, 1999; Silverman, 1993) but two key points are recurrent in the challenges to its validating functions. First, there is criticism from an ontological perspective that there is no single reality or conception of the social world to ascertain and that attempting to do so through the use of multiple sources of information is futile. Second, it is argued on epistemological grounds, that all methods have a specificity in terms of the type of data they yield and thus they are unlikely to generate perfectly concordant evidence. As a result of these concerns, several authors now argue that the value of triangulation lies in extending understanding – 'or adding breadth or depth to our analysis' (Fielding and Fielding, 1986) – through the use of multiple perspectives or different types of 'readings'. In other words, the 'security' that triangulation provides is through giving a fuller picture of phenomena, not necessarily a more certain one.

This chapter has explored some of the many uses of qualitative research, primarily as an independent method of investigation but also in combination with statistical enquiry. Although its applications are virtually limitless, there is still some resistance to employing a qualitative approach, particularly in certain domains where an addiction to numbers is still prominent. Nevertheless, there has been a seismic shift in attitudes to qualitative methods, partly as a result of greater appreciation of what they can do but also because of a need for greater and more refined understanding of social issues. There is nothing to suggest that the ever widening use of qualitative research will abate for many generations to come.

KEY POINTS

- Until the latter part of the twentieth century the use of qualitative methods was much more evident in research that was concerned with developing social theory than in more applied settings. This was particularly so in social policy research where there had been some resistance to treating qualitative research findings as 'evidence'. While there has been considerable growth in the use of qualitative research within this sector, its potential is still felt to be underutilised
- A broad classification of the functions of research is described, based on the nature of the information or understanding it brings. This is categorised as: contextual research which describes the form or nature of what exists; explanatory, examining the reasons for, or associations between, what exists; evaluative, appraising the effectiveness of what exists; and generative – aiding the development of theories, strategies or actions. Qualitative research, like statistical enquiry, has a specific role to play in each of these functions.
- There are circumstances in which qualitative research may be the sole or principal method needed to address a research question. These are centrally related to the nature of the research information or evidence required. There are also factors related to the subject

matter under investigation, specifically where it is ill defined or not well understood; deeply rooted; complex; specialist; delicate, intangible or sensitive.

- Approaches to collecting qualitative data can be very broadly divided into two groups – those that focus on naturally occurring data (for example, observation, documentary analysis, discourse analysis); and those that generate data through the interventions of the research (for example, narrative accounts, interviews, focus groups). Each approach – and the methods within it – yields data of specific kinds and will be suited to different kinds of research objectives.

- The potential for combining qualitative and quantitative research is considerable. Several authors have provided useful frames of reference for optimising the strengths of the two approaches in harness. Each of these suggests possible sequential relationships that may exist between the conduct of qualitative and quantitative. Qualitative research may precede statistical enquiry, may accompany statistical investigation or may be used in some form of follow up study. Each mode of linkage offers a number of different roles for qualitative research. But, when using qualitative and quantitative research in harness, it is important to recognise that each offers a different way of knowing about the world and it should not be expected that the evidence generated from the two approaches will replicate each other.

KEY TERMS

Theoretical research is concerned with the aim of testing, generating or enhancing theoretical or academic thinking within a particular discipline. **Applied** research is concerned with using the knowledge acquired through research to contribute directly to the understanding of a contemporary issue. Applied social research is often equated with **social policy research**, which has the objectives of developing, monitoring or evaluating policy and its related practice.

Formative evaluations are designed to provide information that will help to change or improve a programme or policy, either as it is being introduced or where there are existing problems with its implementation. **Summative evaluation** is concerned with the impact of an intervention or policy in terms of effectiveness and the different outcomes that have resulted. Qualitative methods can contribute to both.

Naturally occurring data, such as observation and analysis of documents, conversation and discourse provide an 'enactment' of social phenomena in their original settings. **Generated data** such as those provided by in-depth interviews and focus groups yield a 'recounting' of phenomena, originated specifically for the research study.

Triangulation involves the use of different methods and sources to check the integrity of, or extend, inferences drawn from the data. There is much debate about whether the value of triangulation is to **validate** qualitative evidence or lies in extending understanding through the use of multiple perspectives or different types of 'readings', often termed as **multiple method** research.

Further reading

Brannen, J. (ed.) (1992b) *Mixing Methods: Qualitative and Quantitative Research*, Aldershot: Gower
May, T. (2001) *Social Research Issues, Methods and Process*, 3rd edition, Buckingham: Open University Press
Patton, M.Q. (2002) *Qualitative Research and Evaluation Methods*, 3rd edition, Thousand Oaks, CA: Sage
Rist, R.C. (2000) 'Influencing the policy process with qualitative research' in N.K. Denzin and Y.S. Lincoln (eds) *Handbook of Qualitative Research*, 2nd edition, Thousand Oaks, CA: Sage
Silverman, D. (2000b) *Doing Qualitative Research: A Practical Handbook*, London: Sage
Walker, R. (ed.) (1985) *Applied Qualitative Research*, Aldershot: Gower

3

Design Issues

Jane Lewis

A good qualitative research study design is one which has a clearly defined purpose, in which there is a coherence between the research questions and the methods or approaches proposed, and which generates data which is valid and reliable (see Chapter 10 for a full discussion of these concepts). It is also one which is realistic, conceived with due regard both for practical constraints of time and money and for the reality of the research context and setting. As Bechhofer and Paterson write, '[r]esearch design is always a matter of informed compromise' (2000: 71).

A number of writers also emphasise the need for flexibility in research design. Maxwell (1996) identifies the key components which should influence research design but stresses that the relationships between them are elastic and non-linear, and that the overall design will need to be modified in interaction with the research setting. Social research will always involve an element of the unknown if it is not simply to duplicate what is already established (Pole and Lampard, 2002), and a key strength of qualitative research in particular is that it can explore unanticipated issues as they emerge. Design in qualitative research is not therefore a discrete stage which is concluded early in the life of a study: it is a continuing process which calls for constant review of decisions and approaches. But this can never be a replacement for rigorous planning.

This chapter explores five key aspects of research design: the development of research questions; decisions about research settings and populations and how a study needs to be built around them; the time frame for data collection; the choice of data collection methods; and the negotiation of research relationships (including the issues of access and ethics). It concludes by summarising the key decisions that need to be made about the conduct of each stage of the study, particularly with a view to determining the resources and time required, and flags the chapters of this book which deal in more detail with each stage.

Defining the research questions

Research questions need to meet a number of requirements (Bryman, 2001; Holloway and Wheeler, 1996; Marshall and Rossman, 1999; Morse, 1994; Pole and Lampard, 2002). They need to be:

- clear, intelligible and unambiguous
- focused, but not too narrow
- capable of being researched through data collection: not too abstract, or questions which require the application of philosophy rather than of data
- relevant and useful, whether to policy, practice or the development of social theory
- informed by and connected to existing research or theory, but with the potential to make an original contribution or to fill a gap
- feasible, given the resources available
- of at least some interest to the researcher.

Where studies are generated by researchers themselves, the process usually involves an initial idea or topic (which may be more or less clearly defined). The researcher will have personal theories or hunches, which are then developed through systematic review of existing theory and research (Marshall and Rossman, 1999). As this process unfolds, the idea begins to be framed as more specific questions. The researcher becomes clearer about the intellectual puzzle (Mason, 2002), about what exactly it is they want to describe and explain, and about the more detailed questions they will need to address. Commissioned research involves a rather different process, beginning with a specification of the study by the funder, detailing the objectives and questions to be addressed in levels of detail which vary considerably between commissioners. The researcher needs to consider whether the research questions are sufficiently clear, of value and interest, and how they relate to existing research. In either case, they are then developed into specific proposals for design and method, and (in the case of generated research) an application for funding.

There is much discussion within the wider literature about the role of existing theory and research in shaping research questions in qualitative research studies. Qualitative research does not usually use the deductive model of a priori development of hypotheses to be tested through data collection. But an understanding of how the study can be informed by and build on existing knowledge or ideas, and a tentative theory or conceptual framework (Maxwell, 1996; Miles and Huberman, 1994) are important aids to design. At the same time, a fixed theoretical position is unhelpful. Qualitative researchers have hunches and working ideas, but they need to remain open to emergent concepts and themes (Layder, 1993), and it is not helpful to go into data collection burdened with preconceived theories and ideas (Hammersley and Atkinson, 1995).

A balance thus needs to be struck. Silverman (2000b: 63–7) for example warns against three unhelpful approaches: 'simplistic inductivism' in which researchers immerse themselves in the research setting, hoping that constructs and ideas will emerge through in-depth exposure; 'kitchen sinkers' whose minds are cluttered by unordered and unstructured ideas, and 'grand theorists' who need to be reminded of the role of new data in their study. But it is important to have a good sense of the substantive issues that the research topic involves, and to be clear about how they build on, and might add to, what has been generated by previous research. As Janesick has written, qualitative researchers have 'open but not empty minds' (2000: 384).

Although these early ideas inform the initial design and data collection, the relationship between design, data and theory is a multi-directional one. Bryman describes the researcher 'oscillating between testing emergent theories and collecting data' (2001: 269), a process described by Becker (1970) as 'sequential analysis'. Berg (2000) and Maxwell (1996) also stress the interactive, iterative and non-linear linkages between theory and data. Early decisions about design need to be reviewed as the study proceeds and new ideas emerge. This should not be seen to undermine the importance of a clear focus on the research objectives and of good quality design and planning: there are limits to how far design and data collection can be changed without the study losing coherence. However, it is important to keep the design under review as the study proceeds, and to allow theory and data collection to inform each other.

Building design around research settings and populations

Selecting research settings and populations involves identifying those which, by virtue of their relationship with the research questions, are able to provide the most relevant, comprehensive and rich information. This decision will flow from what the research questions are, but will be informed by existing literature or understanding of the research context. These issues are discussed in detail in Chapter 4. Here, however, we focus on two broader issues which relate to the way in which design needs to be built around the research settings and populations selected: the role of comparisons in qualitative research, and the role of case studies.

Building comparison into qualitative research designs

Some writers argue that comparison is an important feature of research design. It is seen as something that should inform the selection of research locales and populations, that aids theory building, and that enhances the solidity of research findings (Bechhofer and Paterson, 2000; Bryman, 2001; Pole and Lampard, 2002). There is also discussion of the importance of control – a particular feature of comparison in which two groups are constructed to differ in respect of one key variable, so that the effect of that variable can be understood. Control is particularly relevant in evaluative studies where the design may involve comparison between an 'action' or 'treatment' group which received or used the intervention being evaluated and a control group which did not, so that the effect of the intervention can be investigated. But control also has a more general application in helping to aid understanding of the relationship between the controlled variable and other aspects of the research phenomenon.

Bechhofer and Paterson argue that comparison and control lie at the heart of good research design, whether qualitative or quantitative:

> Designing a piece of empirical research requires the researcher to decide on the best ways of collecting data in research locales which will permit meaningful and insightful comparisons. At the same time, the research design must achieve the control which gives some degree of certainty that the explanations offered are indeed superior to competing explanations … [T]he need to achieve control applies as much to the most natural and participatory fieldwork situations as to experimental ones. (2000: 2)

There is some disquiet in the literature about the application of comparison in qualitative research. For example, Bryman (2001) argues that it is harder to retain contextual insight in comparative studies. Stake argues that focusing on comparison detracts from the intensity of single case description and thus can lead to less precision: 'Uniqueness and complexities will be glossed over … Differences are fundamentally more inaccurate than simple measurements' (2000: 444).

Although comparison does need to be handled carefully if the individual meaning of data is to be retained, it can be a highly effective aspect of qualitative research design and analysis. But the nature of comparison in qualitative research is very different from in quantitative research. The value of qualitative research is in understanding rather than measuring difference. Qualitative research can contribute by:

- identifying the absence or presence of particular phenomena in the accounts of different groups
- exploring how the manifestations of phenomena vary between groups
- exploring how the reasons for, or explanations of, phenomena, or their different impacts and consequences, vary between groups

- exploring the interaction between phenomena in different settings
- exploring more broadly differences in the contexts in which phenomena arise or the research issue is experienced.

Comparisons may be drawn between groups around which the sample design was structured, or may be between groups which emerge inductively from the analytical process.

It may also involve control groups. Control groups are more strongly associated with quantitative designs and with measurement of the effect of the intervention. But they can have a role to play in qualitative research, provided that they contribute to the specific objectives of the study and are used in ways that are consistent with the nature of comparison in qualitative research. For example, in a study of experiences of lone parenting, a control sample of couple parents would be of value if the objective was to isolate the particular strains and pleasures of lone parenting. This would identify which experiences are also a feature of couple parenting, and how their manifestations differ between the two groups. A study of a service being piloted in particular areas might, if an objective was to understand the nature of its impact, be enhanced by including a control group of people where the pilot is not on offer, who are otherwise akin to the sample of service users. This would provide detailed understanding of what happens in the absence of the service, and will focus understanding of what the service therefore adds.

However, a control group may be less illuminating if the purpose is to understand how the service contributes to the impacts experienced by the intervention group. The most valuable data here is likely to come from in-depth research (possibly longitudinal – see below) with the intervention group, exploring their perceptions of impacts and of how the service contributes to them. Although control groups can be a useful feature of qualitative research design, they need to be used with a clear purpose.

Qualitative samples structured around comparison can easily become over large. Each comparison group sample needs to be large enough to reflect the diversity of its parent population (see Chapter 4), since intensive analysis will involve looking at differences within as well as between the comparison group samples. They also require a slightly more structured approach to data collection, so that similar issues can be explored across the sample (see Chapter 5).

Building case studies and structural linkage into qualitative research design

The term 'case study' is strongly associated with qualitative research although it is used in a variety of ways. Indeed, it sometimes appears to be used as a synonym for qualitative research.

The particular features associated with case studies are variously seen as:

- the fact that only one case is selected, although it is also accepted that several may be (Bryman, 2001; Stake, 2000)
- the fact that the study is detailed and intensive (Bryman, 2001; Platt, 1988)
- the fact that the phenomenon is studied in context (Cresswell, 1998; Holloway and Wheeler, 1996; Robson, 2002; Yin, 1993, 1994)
- the use of multiple data collection methods (Creswell, 1998; Hakim, 2000; Holloway and Wheeler, 1996; Robson, 2002; Yin, 1993, 1994).

Although these descriptions are very helpful, it remains a little difficult to see exactly what it is that makes a case study distinctive. In essence, we see the primary defining features of a case study as being multiplicity of perspectives which are rooted in a specific context (or in a number of specific contexts if the study involves more than one case). Those multiple perspectives may come from multiple data collection methods, but they may also derive from multiple accounts – collected using a single method from people with different perspectives on what is being observed.

In these circumstances, the sample design is structured around context(s) rather than around a series of individual participants. The focus might be for example a process (such as the legal resolution of relationship breakdown, with the case involving husband, wife, their legal representatives, their children), or an organisational context (such as a school, with the case involving governors, principals, teachers, students and parents). Less complex designs might involve only two people in each case, such as a couple, or a professional and their client.

The integration of different perspectives on the context or interaction means that case study designs can build up very detailed in-depth understanding. They are used where no single perspective can provide a full account or explanation of the research issue, and where understanding needs to be holistic, comprehensive and contextualised.

Case studies raise a number of questions at the design stage. Early understanding of the study contexts is important for decisions about the criteria on which cases will be selected for study, and about the composition of each case – which are the key participants to be involved, how this varies between different cases or sites. There may be differences in the precise populations involved in each setting, and a decision needs to be made about how much consistency there should be between cases. The number of cases and the number of participants in each needs to be considered carefully. Mapping the full range and diversity of case types and incorporating all the key players in each may result in very large overall samples. Some compromise between breadth and depth of case coverage may be required. Finally, thought will also need to be given to how to organise analysis in a way that allows the contributions of different members of each case to be compared. In practice, case study analysis can become very complex, with comparisons made between different actors within a single case, between cases, and between groups of participants across cases.

Selecting the time frame for research

Study design also involves decisions about the time frame for research – particularly the period of or point in time to which the research will relate, and the number of episodes of data collection required.

The timing of research

Determining the appropriate timing of research in relation to the process or event which is its subject involves considering what perspectives on that process or event are implied by the study objectives. For example, a study exploring how people make decisions about retirement, the factors influencing their decision and the nature of retirement planning would imply fieldwork close to the actual event of retiring. If the study were instead to focus on the impact of retirement and the adequacy of retirement planning, this would imply fieldwork some time after the event. In investigations of new initiatives, services or policies, the appropriate timing will depend on whether the focus of the study is, for example, monitoring the implementation of the policy, exploring delivery, or questions about overall impact and effectiveness.

Determining the appropriate timing for research thus requires real clarity about the research objectives and priorities. But often studies have competing objectives which require collection of data about both earlier and later experiences. This raises the question of whether a single data collection period is sufficient.

The number of research episodes and the role of longitudinal research

SINGLE RESEARCH EPISODES
Many research studies involve only one episode of fieldwork. This would be appropriate, for example, if the focus of the study is on the current manifestation of the research subject, if what is being studied is expected to be relatively stable.

Even if there is a dynamic or changing quality to what is being studied, a single episode of fieldwork may be sufficient. Because qualitative research involves probing and clarification, fairly detailed retrospective accounts can be collected. The dynamic process can also be reflected in the sample design. For example, in a study of people's experience of cancer treatment (Farrell and Lewis, 2000), it was recognised that the stages of development of cancer have important implications for people's experiences of it. The sample was therefore designed to ensure that people at different stages in the development of cancer were included. The sample design meant that, for different participants, different stages could be explored as current phenomena. Retrospective questioning meant that earlier stages could also be explored.

Retrospective questioning can be supported by using instruments such as specially designed calendars or diaries. However, there are limits to what is feasible. There is a danger of deterioration in the quality of data collected through problems with recall, distortion and post-event rationalisation (see Dex, 1995, for a full discussion). If the process of change is an important aspect of what is being researched, and especially if the processes involved are complex or the timespan substantial, a single episode of data collection will not be enough.

LONGITUDINAL QUALITATIVE RESEARCH STUDIES

Longitudinal studies – involving more than one episode of data collection – are long established in quantitative research and in ethnographic research traditions, but have become prominent only relatively recently in other forms of qualitative research. In both qualitative and quantitative studies, longitudinal research takes two broad forms: panel studies in which the same people are interviewed more than once, and repeat cross-sectional studies in which subsequent samples of new participants are interviewed. (This latter model is sometimes described as a cohort study, although that term is also used specifically to describe studies which involve repeated research among the same generational group within a wider population – such as a particular age band, or those born within the same week.)

Panel studies are used to explore micro-level change, where the focus of change is the individual. This may be because the research itself is an intervention which is expected to prompt change. For example, if the subject is likely to be intangible or unfamiliar to people, reconvening (typically) focus groups or (less typically) in-depth interviews after a short interval captures people's thoughts as they develop over a period of reflection following the first research intervention. More often, though, the purpose of panel studies is to capture a process that evolves over a longer period, or to look at impacts, consequences and outcomes that are more than short term. These would be critical issues if the phenomenon being studied is intended to prompt change – for example, a mediation service designed to encourage co-parenting after relationship breakdown, or a service designed to help people to move into and towards work.

The role of qualitative research here is not to measure change – this is the job of surveys which incorporate a panel design. Instead it is to describe the different types of changes that take place or the different outcomes that result, to account for them by showing how they arise, and to explain how and why there are differences between sample members. Qualitative research explores the broader context within which change takes place, and so can capture the full set of factors that participants perceive as contributing to change or outcome.

Cross-sectional studies are used to explore macro-level change, where the focus of change is not the individual but the wider context within which they are situated. Cross-sectional designs would be used for example in a study exploring changing societal influences on attitudes (what shapes views about gender roles, for example). Comparisons are drawn between the two samples, and the role of qualitative research would be to identify new factors or experiences, to explore how they have arisen and to explain their consequences.

Some studies require a combination of panel and cross-sectional design. For example, the qualitative research element of an evaluation of a welfare to work service aimed at disabled people (Loumidis et al., 2001) involved three waves of fieldwork with participants. The first explored the experiences of an early cohort of participants. The second wave involved a new sample of participants who had entered the programme more recently (the cross-sectional element). The third involved reinterviewing a sample of those interviewed at waves one and two (the panel element) but also included a further cross-sectional new sample of recent users of the service. The design explored change at the micro level (exploring the nature of impacts experienced by individual participants over time, how they occur and why they differ) and at the macro level (looking at changes in programme delivery from the perspective of participants using it at different points in time).

Longitudinal studies raise a number of questions that should be considered at the design stage:

- *The number of research episodes and their timing*: the optimal design will reflect the dynamic of the process being observed and the research objectives.
- *Initial sample selection*: in panel studies, the size of the initial sample will need to allow scope for attrition.
- *Fieldwork methods*: in-depth interviews lend themselves more readily to panel designs. Focus groups offer less opportunity for capturing individual perspectives, and thus less opportunity to map change at the micro level (see further below).
- *Selection for follow-up interviews*: in qualitative research studies, follow-up samples can be purposively selected (see Chapter 4) from the initial interview sample. It may be decided that the entire first stage sample should be followed up, particularly if the nature of subsequent change is particularly subtle or complex and thus difficult to use as the basis of purposive selection. However, the follow-up stage can be designed to allow intensive study of particular groups or issues, returning to a purposively selected sub-sample of those interviewed at the first stage.

  This may reflect groups and characteristics which emerge from the first stage of analysis, so that the necessary information for selection is contained in the first round of data collection. Alternatively, it may be important to shape the follow-up sample around events or experiences that have occurred since the first stage fieldwork. In this case, some form of screening – see Chapter 4 – would be required to capture information about change.

- *Analysis*: finally, the analysis of the first stage fieldwork needs to be organised in a way which will make it possible to integrate later stages of data, to make comparisons and identify changes. This means that there is a highly dense and probably quite cumbersome data set to manage and interpret. The process is aided if the same analysis method and thematic framework are used (with new themes added as appropriate), and if new and old data are displayed side by side.

Choosing a data collection method

The fourth issue aspect of qualitative research design we discuss is the choice of data collection methods. These decisions flow from the research questions, but they may also be influenced by the context, structure and timing of research.

Choosing between naturally occurring and generated data

As Chapter 2 described, a key distinction is made between naturally occurring and generated data. The main methods involved in working with naturally occurring data are observation, documentary analysis, conversation analysis and discourse analysis; the main types of generated data in qualitative research are in-depth interviews and group discussions. Choosing between them depends primarily on which type of data will best illuminate the research topic and on practical considerations (see for example Marshall and Rossman, 1999; Mason, 2002; Patton, 2002). But the researcher's own epistemological and ontological positions will also be very relevant (Mason, 2002).

The most basic consideration in deciding which is appropriate for a particular study is whether the required data exist: are there documents, interactions or settings where the phenomenon is displayed?

Assuming there is a real choice to be made, the researcher will need to consider whether it is naturally occurring or generated data which are likely to shed more light on the research subject – whether the research objectives are best met by some form of enactment of behaviour or views, or alternatively by a verbal recounting. Very broadly, the researcher will need to consider:

- *The importance of context*. Context is likely to be an important aspect of any qualitative research study whatever methods are used. Generated data collection methods allow participants to describe the personal or organisational contexts in which the research issue is located and how they relate to it. But if context is such a fundamental aspect of the research phenomenon that observing or experiencing the research phenomenon in its natural context is critical to understanding, then naturally occurring data is likely to be preferred.

- *Whether a recounting of the research phenomenon is likely to be sufficiently detailed, accurate or complete.* There are many subjects about which individual participants are able to give a full account. But this will not always be the case. If the subject of the research is a particularly complex process or interaction, if aspects of it are less obvious or may escape awareness, or if important elements of it are likely to be subconscious or instinctive, then the participant's own account will be partial. Similarly, if people are unlikely to be willing to talk frankly about something, or if it is so bound up with social rules and expectations that they cannot be expected to give a truthful account, then naturally occurring data will be more useful. On the other hand, naturally occurring data may not provide a sufficiently full picture of the research topic, for example if documents present only one perspective on the topic, or if understanding recent history is critical to making sense of an interaction so that existing data will not 'speak for themselves'.

- *Whose interpretation is paramount.* A key distinction between naturally occurring and generated data is the role of researcher and participant interpretation. Naturally occurring data relies on the researcher's interpretation of what is observed or read. While the meaning that the research issue holds for a participant is embedded in their enactment of it, it is the researcher and not the participant who draws out that meaning and makes it explicit. Generated data collection methods, on the other hand, give participants a direct and explicit opportunity to convey their own meanings and interpretations through the explanations they provide, whether spontaneously or in answer to the researcher's probing. The generated data may be further interpreted by the researcher, but the participant's own interpretation is seen as critically important, at least in broadly realist research paradigms (see Chapter 1).

A final practical consideration relates to accessibility. If naturally occurring already exist (in the forms of documents for example) or if there are environments or events where they are displayed, can the research team gain direct access to them? And if generated data would shed more light on the research issue, is it actually feasible – from the point of view of the researcher and potential participants – to carry out in-depth interviews or focus groups?

Choosing between in-depth interviews and focus groups

The key types of generated data in qualitative research are in-depth interviews and focus groups. They serve different roles, and selection between them will turn on three key factors: the type of data sought, the subject area, and the nature of the study group.

THE NATURE OF THE DATA SOUGHT

A key feature of in-depth interviews is their depth of focus on the individual. They provide an opportunity for detailed investigation of each person's personal perspective, for in-depth understanding of the personal context within which the research phenomenon is located, and for very detailed subject coverage. They are the only way to collect data where it is important to set the perspectives heard within the context of personal history or experience; where delicate or complex issues need to be explored at a detailed level, or where it is important to relate different issues to individual personal circumstances.

Focus groups (or group discussions – as Chapter 2 noted, we use the terms interchangeably) offer less opportunity for the detailed generation of individual accounts, and if this is the type of data required then in-depth interviews are preferable. However, they are used where the group process, the interaction between participants, will itself illuminate the research issue. Because they involve discussion, and hearing from others, they give participants more opportunity to refine what they have to say. This can be particularly useful in attitudinal research: explaining or accounting for attitudes is sometimes easier for people when they hear different attitudes, or nuances on their own, described by other people and can better understand, describe and explain their own perspective against this backdrop. The interaction between participants is also useful where what is required is creative thinking, or solutions and strategies.

Focus groups also provide a social context within which the phenomenon is experienced, and they display the way in which context can shape people's views, showing how data are generated through conversation with others. This context also means that they vividly display differences between participants, and create an opportunity for differences to be directly and explicitly discussed.

SUBJECT MATTER

Very complex systems, processes or experiences are generally best addressed in in-depth interviews because of the depth of focus and the opportunity for clarification and detailed understanding. Similarly, understanding motivations and decisions, or exploring impacts and outcomes, generally requires the detailed personal focus that in-depth interviews allow. More abstract, intangible or conceptual topics are well suited to group discussions, where the group can work together to tackle the subject. Group fora are also useful for studies focusing on attitudes and views (as noted above), or for difficult and technical issues where some type of information giving may be required (see Chapter 7).

Even very sensitive subjects can be explored in group settings if people have similar proximity to or experience of the issue, but particular care will be required in group composition and in the conduct of the group (see Chapter 7). Topics which people are likely to see as confidential or where social norms predominate are less conducive to group discussion, unless what is required is a display of those social norms. But often the researcher will be concerned to get beyond what may be seen as socially acceptable, and the more private setting of an individual interview is useful here.

Finally, Chapter 5 describes a range of enabling and projective techniques which can be useful when a high degree of specificity is required, or when more intangible or subconscious subjects are discussed. These tend to work most naturally in group fora and can sometimes seem contrived in individual interviews, but they can be used effectively in either setting.

RESEARCH POPULATION

Because interviews generally take place at a location of the participant's choosing, in-depth interviews are more accessible to potential participants than group discussions and thus are ideal for very busy study groups, or those with mobility constraints. The need to come to a common location will inhibit the attractiveness and accessibility of the research for some populations, and means that the study population needs to be geographically clustered.

Focus groups benefit from some diversity in group composition (see Chapter 7), but it is usually helpful for there to be some commonality between people in their relationship to the research topic or in the socio-demographic characteristics which are most relevant to it. Certainly significant difference in status between participants in the same group should be avoided. In-depth interviews are more appropriate if people have nothing in common or, conversely, if the fact that they know each other is likely to inhibit their contribution, and if there are issues of power or status.

Group discussions can also be an environment which provides 'safety in numbers', and thus make research accessible to people who might, for various reasons, find a one-to-one encounter intimidating or uncomfortable. However, it is also important to think about the extent to which a group forum is one in which participants would be able to communicate fully. These issues are summarised in Box 3.1.

Smaller groups, pairs or triads might provide a good balance between the group and the individual context. They provide more scope for individual depth of focus as well as the opportunity to see how ideas develop. They also allow participants to reflect on, and draw comparisons with, what they hear from others, but they are a more private research forum in which each participant has more time to talk. They are particularly useful in research with younger people, or in studies where participants might feel the subject matter is in some way intimidating (for example, studies exploring views on complex public issues). Interviewing people in friendship pairs or trios can provide a more lively environment in which participants feel safer, with neither the intensity of an individual interview nor the intimidation that a larger and unfamiliar group environment might mean. They are also useful where participants are likely to be particularly articulate with a lot to say, but where some exchange between them is helpful to highlight differences and stimulate contributions – in particular in research with professionals.

Finally, as Chapter 7 notes, there are different types of group research fora which have applications to different types of research topics and objectives.

BOX 3.1   APPLICATIONS OF IN-DEPTH INTERVIEWS AND FOCUS GROUPS

	In-depth interviews	*Focus groups*
Nature of data	For generating in-depth personal accounts	For generating data which is shaped by group interaction – refined and reflected
	To understand the personal context	To display a social context – exploring how people talk about an issue
	For exploring issues in depth and detail	For creative thinking and solutions
		To display and discuss differences within the group
Subject matter	To understand complex processes and issues e.g. – motivations, decisions – impacts, outcomes	To tackle abstract and conceptual subjects Where enabling or projective techniques are to be used, or in difficult or technical subjects where information is provided
	To explore private subjects or those involving social norms	For issues which would be illuminated by the display of social norms
	For sensitive issues	For some sensitive issues, with careful group composition and handling
Study population	For participants who are likely to be less willing or able to travel	Where participants are likely to be willing and able to travel to attend a group discussion
	Where the study population is geographically dispersed	Where the population is geographically clustered
	Where the population is highly diverse	Where there is some shared background or relationship to the research topic
	Where there are issues of power or status	For participants who are unlikely to be inhibited by group setting
	Where people have communication difficulties	

COMBINING IN-DEPTH INTERVIEWS AND FOCUS GROUPS

Chapter 2 discussed the value of mixing qualitative approaches and of combining qualitative and quantitative data. In-depth interviews and group discussions can also very usefully be combined.

For example, focus groups might be used as an initial stage to raise and begin to explore relevant issues which will then be taken forward through in-depth interviews. This would be particularly appropriate in an unfamiliar area to identify issues for coverage. They might involve slightly larger groups than usual and be more flexible in subject coverage giving a freer rein to participants to shape the agenda, to ensure that as full as possible a set of issues are raised (with depth of coverage coming later from the in-depth interviews).

Focus groups could be used after in-depth interviews to discuss the issues at a more strategic level, perhaps focusing on underlying causes and possible solutions. For example, they may be used with professionals who work with population groups involved in earlier in-depth interviews, or with policy-makers or other decision-makers.

They also offer an opportunity to verify or validate research findings (see further Chapter 10). This may involve checking the completeness of the accounts gathered through in-depth interviews, or allowing reflection and comment on the research team's understanding and interpretation of the data. They may be conducted with the same individual participants who took part in interviews, or with other members of the same population, or with people with expertise in the research subject who would be able to comment on what has, or has not, emerged.

Secondary data analysis

A final consideration before leaving the subject of data collection methods is the role of secondary analysis of existing qualitative research data. In the last two decades of the twentieth century, initiatives around archiving meant that more attention was paid to the potential for secondary analysis of qualitative data. It can be a valuable resource, providing an opportunity to bring a new perspective to existing data, to use elements of the data that have not been fully analysed, or to form a base for comparison with newly collected data. However, the adequacy of the original data for the new research aims needs to be considered carefully (Fielding and Fielding, 2000; Hammersley, 1997; Heaton, 1998; Hinds et al., 1997; Mauthner et al., 1998).

First, it may be that certain subject areas were not central to the original objectives, and that this is reflected in the data available. This will limit the depth that secondary analysis can go to and may even lead to misleading results. Similarly, the sample may not be 'comprehensive' for the purposes of the secondary analysis and may have important constituencies missing (see Chapter 4). In addition, the original data needs to be of high quality in terms of the conduct of the original data collection. Although secondary data analysis can be very valuable, careful scrutiny of the quality and relevance of the data for the new research purposes is required.

Negotiating research relationships

Maxwell (1996) notes that research relationships tend to be conceptualised in terms of access and rapport. But he argues that wider considerations about the kind of relationship researchers want to have with study participants are important design and planning issues. This section discusses the issue of negotiating access, but it also looks at how researchers need to make studies accessible to participants, the issue of reciprocity, how researchers' own characteristics impact on the relationship with participants, and ethical issues. Considerations here will also be informed by the political or theoretical perspective of researchers and the tradition or approach within which research is being conducted – see Chapter 1 and Maxwell (1996).

Negotiating access

The issues involved in approaching private individuals about participation in research are discussed below (in reference to informed consent) and in Chapter 4. But research in group or organisational contexts raises some additional considerations, and negotiating access to the setting will be a key part of early stages of the research. It requires patience and sensitivity. Even in commissioned studies where the funder has power to grant access (such as government sponsored research into a government programme), the way in which access is negotiated on the ground can be critical to the success of a study. Engaging effectively with research settings can be aided in a number of ways (Bryman, 2001; Hammersley and Atkinson, 1995; Holloway and Wheeler, 1996; Patton, 2002):

- being sensitive to the hierarchy or organisational structure: particularly getting clearance from senior people who are 'gatekeepers'
- providing clear information about the objectives and purpose of the study and why that setting has been chosen
- being open and consistent about what is required, in terms of the number of visits envisaged, the amount of time required, the range of people the research would involve
- being clear about how the findings will be used – plans for reporting, disseminating and conditions for anonymity and confidentiality (see below)
- anticipating, but more importantly being responsive to, concerns and sensitivities raised
- having a single point of contact within the organisation: to avoid duplication or gaps in communication. Finding someone who will be a 'champion' in the organisation can also help
- being flexible about shaping the study approach in response to the precise setting, and accepting advice
- considering how findings can be shared and at what stage: early discussion of emergent findings; providing copies of reports or papers; dedicated dissemination to research participants (see Chapter 11).

Co-operation is likely to be easier if the research objectives are seen as valuable and relevant by those to be involved. Research in unfamiliar settings can be enhanced by early reconnaisance visits once initial access has been agreed. These contribute to decisions about who should be involved, key research questions, the appropriate timing of fieldwork, and how effective engagement can be secured.

Approval of research with individuals or groups may also be required from an ethics committee, particularly but not exclusively if the research involves sampling through, or contact with, clinical medical settings. The requirements of ethical committees vary considerably. What is important is to establish at an early stage whether ethical approval is required, from which committee(s), and what procedures and requirements are involved. This stage can take several months, so early information and allowing time in the research timetable are vital. Many ethics committees are more used to dealing with quantitative research or randomised control trials. Researchers may therefore find themselves having to provide an explication of qualitative research methods, and dealing with questions or requirements which do not easily transfer to qualitative research. Patience, flexibility and tenacity are key.

Developing research relationships

MAKING RESEARCH STUDIES ACCESSIBLE
TO RESEARCHED GROUPS

Making studies accessible to the groups involved requires consideration of the appropriate language to use in approaching them, anticipation of the possible barriers to participation, and provision to help to overcome them. A sentence in an approach letter such as 'Please let us know if there is anything we can do to make it easier for you to take part in the study' can be a useful starting place, which allows the potential participant to raise issues such as timing; location; practical needs such as childcare and travel; the appropriate language for the interview; or communication or cognitive difficulties. Thought will need to be given to what can practically be provided within the resources available for the study, and suitable arrangements made. Depending on the research topic and population, these issues may need to be raised explicitly by the researcher, so that there can be discussion about issues such as the need for third party facilitation or for an interview to be conducted in the participant's own language. However, researchers will need to be adaptable and to work with whatever situation they find when they arrive for the interview.

How the interviewing strategy might need to be adapted should also be considered. In preparing for data collection, the researcher should give thought to the likely circumstances of participants, their possible value systems and social worlds. The sorts of sensitivities or emotions that might be raised by the research topic, and appropriate strategies for dealing with them, should be considered. The implications for the appropriate presentation, manner and approach of the researcher need to be thought through. For some participants it may be appropriate to make interviews or focus groups shorter, for example for very elderly people, for children, or for others who are likely to find taking part particularly tiring such as people with particular sorts of disability. Or it may be useful to suggest that breaks are taken during the course of the interview, or to conduct the research over more than one session. Participants themselves are, of course, always best positioned to indicate what will be most helpful to them.

The particular questioning techniques that will be required to make the study accessible to the participant should also be considered. For people who may find it particularly difficult to remember factual details or the timing or sequence of events (such as very elderly people, people with learning disabilities or particular cognitive difficulties) it will be necessary to find other ways of accessing this information – another source of information, someone close to them who may know the details, or using a diary to prompt recall. More focused, direct and concrete questions may be necessary if people find very open-ended questions intimidating or difficult to respond to. Enabling or projective techniques (see Chapter 5) may also be helpful if people find it difficult to express themselves directly.

But however considered the researcher's preparation may have been, unexpected situations will always arise and require an appropriate response in situ. Above all, this highlights the need for qualitative researchers to be flexible and adaptable in their approach, to have a commitment to understanding the perspective of the participant, to make research studies accessible to different groups, to be non-judgemental, and to treat participants with respect.

RECIPROCITY

It is also useful, at the design stage, to give some thought to how the researcher can give something in return for the assistance, time and thought given by research participants. Such measures help to encourage participation, but they also go some way to making research more of an exchange, albeit not necessarily an equal one. It is important, however, to be aware of the constraints of the researcher role in considering issues of reciprocity, and the needs to maintain objectivity and neutrality and some distance. Appropriate measures might take the form of a small cash payment, a copy of the report or key findings, or information about relevant support organisations or sources of information (particularly if research on sensitive subjects is conducted with individuals). Larger payments or honoraria may be required by some professional groups. Donations to charity may sometimes be more appropriate than cash, and gift vouchers may be more suitable where participants are children.

Feminist research approaches argue for more intimate reciprocity in the research relationship through researchers sharing information about themselves with interviewees although this approach has been challenged more recently. We discuss this issue in Chapter 6, in the context of in-depth interviewing.

MATCHING INTERVIEWER AND PARTICIPANT CHARACTERISTICS

Qualitative research fieldwork involves interaction between participants and researchers. Researchers make rigorous attempts to present themselves objectively and neutrally, and to minimise the extent to which they themselves intrude on the generation of fulsome and authentic accounts (see Chapter 6). But it is not only a researcher's conduct which is relevant: a broader cross-perception between participant and researcher also takes place. This has led to the argument that ensuring that researcher and participant are 'matched' on key socio-demographic criteria is helpful to the dynamic of data collection.

The issue has arisen particularly in relation to matching on gender. Feminist researchers argue that there is a cultural affinity between women interviewers and participants by virtue of their subordinate social status (Finch, 1984; Oakley, 1981), and that a closer relationship is built up where women interview women, although more recent approaches question how far this is so (see for example Olesen, 2000). But similar arguments have been made for matching on social class or ethnicity, or more generally for researchers having experiences in common with those they interview.

Sharing some aspects of cultural background or experience may be helpful in enriching researchers' understanding of participants' accounts, of the language they use and of nuances and subtexts. The researcher's perceptions here should not be a substitute for the participant's own words, but they can help researchers to make judgements about how to explore issues in more depth. There will also be circumstances where the characteristics of participant and researcher mirror what people may have experienced as oppression or an imbalance in power in other social interactions, based on ethnicity, gender, disability or age. The introduction of power imbalance into the interview setting is unlikely to be conducive to open discussion, particularly if issues of oppression or discrimination are highly relevant to the research question.

There is clearly also a strong argument for matching if interviewers are not fluent in the chosen spoken language of participants – it is difficult to carry out effective in-depth fieldwork without matching on language. And interviewers clearly need to have some knowledge of and insight into the topics they are researching. Finally, matching characteristics may also help in getting access to particular settings or groups or in encouraging people to take part in research (conveying an important implicit message about credibility and openness).

But this does not mean that matching interviewer and participant characteristics is always a useful approach. There is a danger that insufficient explanation or clarification is sought by the researcher because of assumptions created by their shared experience (Burgess, 1984; Hammersley and Atkinson, 1995; Thompson, 2000). Participants too might hold back from giving fulsome accounts, relying on the interviewer to draw on their own background rather than giving a full and explicit account. In studies on sensitive issues, people may find it more helpful to speak with someone who is clearly outside their own community or population group. Moreover, ethnicity, sex and class may also be only part of the way in which participants define themselves and may not be the most important aspects of self-definition or of the participant's 'reading' of the researcher (Hammersley and Atkinson, 1995).

It is important to think through how the researcher's characteristics might enhance or intrude on data collection and to weigh up the relative risk of cultural collusion versus unhelpful power dynamics. Involving people who are from the participant's cultural group or who have direct experience of the research issues in design decisions or in co-moderating interviews and focus groups may be a more useful approach than matching. Ultimately, matching is no substitute for developing high quality fieldwork skills, having empathy and respect for participants, being reflective about participants' social worlds as well as one's own, and being able to listen and understand.

> Unlike some schools of feminist research, our approach to qualitative interviewing emphasises the ability to go across social boundaries. You don't have to be a woman to interview women, or a sumo wrestler to interview sumo wrestlers. But if you are going to cross social gaps and go where you are ignorant, you have to recognise and deal with cultural barriers to communication. (Rubin and Rubin, 1995: 39)

Ethical considerations

The final aspect of the negotiation of research relationships we consider here is ethical arrangements. Any research study raises ethical considerations, and those discussed here are pertinent to other forms of research than qualitative research studies. However, the in-depth, unstructured nature of qualitative research and the fact that it raises issues that are not always anticipated mean that ethical considerations have a particular resonance in qualitative research studies.

INFORMED CONSENT

As in any research study, sample members' informed consent to participate must be obtained. This means providing them with information about the purpose of the study, the funder, who the research team is, how the data will be used, and what participation will require of them – the subjects likely to be covered, how much time is required and so on. Whether participants will be identified or comments attributed to them in any report should be made clear. A balance in the amount of detail given needs to be struck. Giving too much may deter potential participants, or curtail their spontaneous views by being over-specific about the objectives and subject matter. But there is nothing to be gained from people being inadequately prepared for what the interview will require of them or the topics that will be covered.

Informed consent should also be based on an understanding that participation is voluntary – an issue that may require particular emphasis where research is conducted by people who also have a professional relationship with sample members which may lead to feelings of obligation or gratitude (Holloway and Wheeler, 1996).

At this stage, people have consented to take part in an interview and to the researcher using the data in the way described. However, consent is not absolute and needs to be assessed, and sometimes renegotiated, particularly during data collection as we discuss in Chapter 6.

Different arrangements need to be made for some study groups, where consent to approach the potential participant first needs to be sought from a third party. For children and young people aged under 16, consent to approach should be sought from parents, or from a school or other organisation which is in loco parentis; for people with severe cognitive or intellectual impairments consent to approach may be needed from an advocate or carer. Consent to participate should still be sought from the interviewee themselves. In studies taking place within businesses or organisations, arrangements to interview employees may be made via managers or directors, and again consent to participate should be checked with interviewees themselves.

ANONYMITY AND CONFIDENTIALITY

The proposed conditions for anonymity and confidentiality should be given particular thought, and made very clear to participants.

Anonymity means the identity of those taking part not being known outside the research team. It may be compromised if participation is arranged by or through a third party (an employer or organisation) or in case studies or other designs where there is structural linkage between samples. In these cases, absolute guarantees of anonymity cannot be given and the participant should be made aware who will know of their participation.

Confidentiality means avoiding the attribution of comments, in reports or presentations, to identified participants. Both direct attribution (if comments are linked to a name or a specific role) and indirect (by reference to a collection of characteristics that might identify an individual or small group) must be avoided. Indirect attribution requires particular care. It may compromise the extent to which contextual detail can be given in reporting specific comments, and in some circumstances it may be necessary to change minor details to disguise identity, to make a point in a more general way (even if this reduces its power), or to get specific consent from the participant to include it.

These issues also have implications for data storage. Tapes and transcripts should not be labelled in ways which could compromise anonymity, and identifying information (such as sampling documents) must be stored separately from data.

If archiving of qualitative research data is envisaged, there are also issues about whether consent to archive is required, and whether data sets should be anonymised before archiving. Practices in relation to these issues are varied, and consent to archive even non-anonymised material has not always been sought. If archiving is envisaged at the time of the interview, this should be discussed with participants. Certainly if non-anonymised information is to be archived, written consent should be obtained. This is best obtained immediately after the interview so that participants are aware of the nature of the data involved. Where the decision to archive arises only some time after fieldwork, seeking consent is more difficult since it may be impossible to contact the full sample group. In these circumstances it would be inappropriate to archive non-anonymised data. The scale of the task involved in anonymising should not be underestimated, particularly since indirect identification (where sample members' names are deleted but other information may identify them) must be avoided. Anonymising also means that archiving some forms of data – such as video or audio recordings – is not feasible.

PROTECTING PARTICIPANTS FROM HARM

In any study, it is important to give consideration to ways in which taking part may be harmful to sample members, and to take aversive action. This arises most clearly in studies on sensitive topics which might uncover painful experiences and lead people to disclose information which they have rarely or never previously shared. But any study topic can raise sensitive issues for people – such as family relationships, health or sexuality – however remote from the subject matter these may seem. Interviews can have a certain seductive quality: participants may appear comfortable and may disclose information apparently willingly during an interview, but may later regret having been so open. They may also be left with feelings and thoughts stirred up by the interview long after the researcher has moved on.

Participants should be given a clear understanding of the issues a study will address before being asked to take part. Researchers, too, need to be able to make clear judgements about what is and is not relevant and must avoid prurient or irrelevant detail. Sensitive topics, or those which might raise sensitive issues, are best addressed through clear and direct questions, so that people are not drawn through ambiguity or confusion into subjects they would prefer to avoid. It is important to be alert to signs of discomfort, and if these are given to check the participant's willingness to continue or to offer to stop the interview (see Chapter 6). It will sometimes be necessary to stay after the interview has concluded, to respond to any anxieties about confidentiality and to give the participant an opportunity to return to some of the issues discussed, or to turn to more everyday subjects, outside the context of the interview.

But the researcher's role should not be confused with that of adviser or counsellor (see Chapter 6). It is not appropriate to give advice, nor to comment favourably or unfavourably on participants' decisions or circumstances beyond expressions of empathy. Participants' needs for support are better addressed by researchers being equipped with information about relevant services or organisations which they can leave with people. This point is less salient where studies have a deliberately emancipatory orientation, or where the study population is involved in the design, conduct and use of the research. But there are many pieces of research which are not undertaken within these frameworks. Consideration therefore needs to be given to information or advice needs the research process itself may generate, and the best way of meeting them. Although there are different political and theoretical positions on the relationship between researcher and participant, researchers will need to think very carefully about the implications of deliberately straying beyond a position of aspiring to neutrality.

A particularly difficult ethical dilemma arises where information is disclosed during an interview which indicates that the participant is at risk of harm. Should the researcher pass information about this to a statutory authority or to someone else? This may seem an obvious action to take, and indeed may be required by professional codes of conduct (for example if researchers are also clinical practitioners). But it raises clear difficulties. To pass on information without the participant's consent is a profound loss of control for them. The consequences of passing on information may be hazardous for the participant and may increase their vulnerability or harm. The judgement of harm or risk is likely to involve some subjectivity on the researcher's part: their assessment may not be shared by the participant.

If an indication of harm is given during the interview, an appropriate response would be for the researcher to encourage the participant after the interview to report it themselves, or to seek help in some other way. The researcher may want to offer to talk to someone on their behalf, or to support them in seeking help. But if participants have been told that the interview situation is confidential, it would be unethical to report anything disclosed or observed without the participant's consent.

The situation is perhaps more complicated if the suggestion of harm comes not from something disclosed in the interview, but from something observed by the researcher while they are there. Whether or not revealing this would be a breach of confidentiality will depend on the precise way in which confidentiality was described to the participant, and whether assurances related to the content of the interview only or to the researcher's wider interaction with the participant and their household. However, the distinction is unlikely to be clear to participants, and this argues for treating the whole encounter as a private and privileged one unless a contrary message has been given. These dilemmas are difficult ones, and it is important to provide opportunities for debriefing and support for researchers who encounter them.

If researchers do not feel they can adhere to these positions, they must spell out to participants before the interview begins the circumstances under which information would be passed on. The likely consequences of this on willingness to participate, on power dynamics in the interview and on data collection have to be accepted. The research team would then need to be clear about what constitutes risk or harm, and appropriate arrangements for supporting team members in making judgements and taking action put in place.

PROTECTING RESEARCHERS FROM HARM

Researchers who conduct fieldwork also place themselves at risk, and arrangements should be made at the beginning of the study to minimise this. Risk arises in different ways in public places (such as when they are travelling to appointments) and in private fieldwork venues (such as participants' homes). Assessing both is an important part of preparation for fieldwork (Social Research Association, 2001).

In public places, this will involve decisions about (and funding for) appropriate modes of transport. It is helpful to find out as much as possible in advance about how to find the venue, by asking participants or referring to maps. It may be necessary for interviewers to work in pairs, either conducting the interview together or one escorting the other and waiting near the interview venue.

Although fieldwork often takes place in private places, it is in a sense a public engagement – the participant will generally be aware that others know of the engagement and this is likely to offer a degree of protection to researchers. It may be helpful to reinforce this by indicating that others know of the researcher's whereabouts, referring to colleagues or to transport arrangements. Researchers will never be able to predict where risk arises, and the best approach is to be alert in all fieldwork encounters to possible dangers. While stigmatising assumptions should be avoided, background information about participants may help in risk assessment and it is important to be alert to possible risk factors such as criminal histories involving violence or volatile behavioural problems. An alternative venue to participants' homes may be required, and in private homes communal rooms should be used. Working in pairs may be appropriate. If researchers are working alone, there should be arrangements for maintaining contact with others, such as telephone contact between interviews or at the end of the day.

Being aware of ways in which the interview content and dynamic might spark anger or raise risk is also important. Responding to raised feelings may first involve acknowledging them with respect and empathy and if necessary moving to another topic (see Chapter 6), but ultimately researchers may need to end the interview if they feel at risk. Discussing these issues in preparation for fieldwork will help researchers to feel confi-dent about trusting their instincts, and confident that their judgement will be supported by the rest of the team. Opportunities for debriefing and providing support where researchers encounter difficult situations are also very important.

Arrangements to protect researchers from harm have cost implications which should be considered by researchers, and recognised by funders, early in the design stage.

Resourcing and timetabling qualitative research studies

Most research benefits from teamwork. Working as a team provides more obvious opportunities for reflection and review. It helps to keep researchers fresh, injects different perspectives and insights, and helps to maintain vigilance against bias and lowering of standards. It is easy to lose sight of the strategic purposes of a study by becoming embroiled in detail or administration. Conducting a large body of fieldwork, particularly with a single research population, inevitably means that there is repetition in what a researcher hears, and interviewer 'fatigue' can set in. Teamwork also provides some insurance against unexpected difficulties which might otherwise compromise timely completion. The time involved in collabora-tion needs to be considered realistically and built into the research budget, and collaborating across institutes and disciplines is particularly resource intensive.

But there are institutional circumstances in which researchers have to work alone. Here, it is helpful to build in opportunities for others to con-tribute ideas, for discussion of the research question and findings as they arise, and for scrutiny of standards. Supervision, contact with funders and commissioners, steering groups, advisory groups and peer review are important elements of any research set-up, but play a particularly important role where researchers work alone.

Because qualitative research studies and the teams carrying them out will be so diverse, it is impossible to give useful guidelines as to the elapsed time or the financial resources that would be required. Factors such as the volume of fieldwork, the number of different study populations, how they are to be accessed, the scope for iteration between different stages of the research, the outputs required and the nature and working style of the research team – how much collaboration is envisaged within and outside the research team, whether the team is multidisciplinary, whether it has worked together before – will be very influential on both the overall and the elapsed time required.

In general, research budgets in qualitative research are largely driven by the volume of research time required. Although direct expenses can be significant (and are easily underestimated), it is researcher time that will largely determine the budget required. This means that it is vital to put time and effort into thinking through in detail each stage of the study and the particular activities that will be involved. Not being sufficiently clear about how the sample will be identified and accessed, or what method of analysis will be used, can have major implications later for the adequacy of the budget. It is well worth giving a lot of thought to these issues and spending time investigating the feasibility of different approaches before decisions are made about the level of funding and amount of time required. The key stages, and the decisions and activities they can involve, are summarised in Box 3.2, and the chapter that discusses each is referenced.

A final consideration is the importance of managing the timetable and budget once work begins. It is all too easy to spend too much of the available time generating a sample and carrying out fieldwork, or pursuing endless trails of analysis many of which turn out to be dead-ends, only to discover that the time available for writing up is now hopelessly inadequate. A useful management tool is to draw up a detailed timetable at the beginning of the study and to monitor performance against it so that there is early warning of slippage and its implications. A final word of caution is that it is easy to assume that time overspent early on can be made up in the later stages of the study. In practice, if the estimate of time required for early stages is unrealistic, this is likely to be true also of later stages, and more fundamental decisions about the scale of the study, ways of working or the date for completion are likely to be required.

Designing a qualitative research study should be a creative and stimulating process, and doing it well is important preparation for a successful research study which is itself enjoyable to carry out. Although researchers may find themselves impatient to get 'into the field', the combination of systematic planning and imaginative lateral thinking is perhaps symbolic of what is involved in other aspects of qualitative research. It brings the researcher closer to their research questions, understanding them in more nuanced but also more practical terms. It is a process which is inevitably full of anticipation, but one which is also enriching and engaging in its own right.

BOX 3.2   PROJECT STAGES AND PLANNING ISSUES

Framing the research question (see Chapters 3 and 5)

- literature review
- other forms of familiarising e.g. consultation with key groups or experts, reconnaissance visits

Choosing the research method (see Chapters 2 and 3)

- selection of naturally occurring data, generated data or secondary data analysis
- selection of data collection method
- appropriate sequencing: how to provide scope for iteration and interplay between methods
- need for case studies and other structural linkages in samples: implications for sampling, conduct of fieldwork and analysis

Research relationships (see Chapter 3)

- incentives and other reciprocal arrangements
- implications of any need for matching participant and researcher characteristics
- arrangements for informed consent, guarantees of anonymity and confidentiality
- protecting participants from harm
- protecting researchers from harm

Choosing research populations, samples and sites (see Chapters 3, 4 and 10)

- arrangements for access to organisations or groups
- arrangements for ethical approval
- key groups or dimensions to be included in sample
- selection criteria
- options for sample frames
- sources of information about selection variables

Contacting potential participants (see Chapters 3 and 4)

- arrangements for consent for inclusion in sample frame
- arrangements for contact
- arrangements to make research accessible

Designing research instruments (see Chapters 4, 5 and 7)

- instruments required: screening instruments, letters to selected sample members and to participants, topic guide
- involvement of research team in topic guide design
- need for wider consultation or clearance by funder
- requirement for other materials: e.g. information about services to leave with participants; stimulation material to use in interviews or groups; provision of information in consultation exercises; role of projective and enabling techniques

(Continued)

BOX 3.2 *(Continued)*

Preparation for fieldwork (see Chapters 3 and 5)

- assessment of risk to participants and researchers and steps required to avert
- briefing for fieldwork team: objectives; fieldwork strategies

Conduct of fieldwork (see Chapters 3, 6 and 7)

- time allowed needs to reflect sample generation approach (e.g. sampling through organisations, use of snowballing), likely duration of interviews and group discussions, geographic clustering
- requirements for working in pairs
- need to review the composition of the sample
- opportunities for reviewing and refining fieldwork methods
- arrangements for debriefing of research team
- scope for integrating early analysis with later fieldwork
- transcribing

Analysis (see Chapters 8, 9 and 10)

- involvement of team members in development of analytical or conceptual frameworks
- testing and refinement of frameworks
- mapping, ordering, summarising data
- interpretation of data
- scope and need for validation
- types of generalisation likely to be required, implications especially for sample and analysis

Reporting (see Chapter 11)

- assessment of reporting opportunities, audiences and outputs
- time for detailed planning; writing; reviewing; editing and drawing together; responding to comments
- oral presentations

Project administration (see Chapter 3)

- liaison with funders, steering groups, advisory groups
- team meetings
- resource implications of collaboration

KEY POINTS

- A good research design is clearly defined, with coherence between research questions and methods, which will generate valid and reliable data and which can be achieved within the available resources. But social research always involves an element of the unknown, and qualitative research offers the particular advantage of flexibility. In practice, the relationships between study design, theory and data collection are iterative, and each should inform and be informed by the others. Research design is therefore not a discrete stage but a continuing process

- There is some disquiet in the literature about the role of comparison in qualitative research. It can be an effective design element, but its value lies in understanding rather than measuring difference. Case studies involve capturing multiple perspectives which are rooted in a specific setting, and provide detailed understanding which is holistic and contextualised. Both comparison and case studies can be built into research designs, but both have implications for sample size, and can give rise to quite complex analytical tasks

- The detailed nature of its questioning means that qualitative research can be used to collect retrospective accounts, but sometimes a single data collection episode will not be enough. Longitudinal research principally involves panel designs, to capture micro-level change, and repeated cross-sectional designs, to capture macro-level change. Longitudinal studies raise key design issues, particularly regarding the number and timing of data collection episodes, the selection of initial and follow-up samples, the appropriate field-work methods, and the organisation of analysis, which again can become a very complex task

- Research relationships have to be negotiated. Accessing settings and samples requires patience, flexibility, and an understanding of the proposed setting. Research studies also need to be made accessible to those who are intended to participate. Ethical issues also have to be considered, particularly what informed consent will require, arrangements for anonymity and confidentiality, and how participants and researchers can be protected from harm

- Most studies benefit from teamwork, but researchers working alone can build in arrangements such as supervision, the involvement of funders, steering and advisory groups and peer review. Research budgets in qualitative research are largely driven by the volume of research time required, and this requires careful thinking through of what will be involved at each stage.

KEY TERMS

Control groups are used particularly in evaluative studies, where a distinction is made between the 'action' or 'treatment' group which uses an intervention and the control group which does not. They also have a more general application. Building control into the design involves shaping the sample around two groups which are as identical as possible except in respect of specific variables that relate to the central issue being researched or a key aspect of it, so that the effect of those variables can be investigated.

The term **case study** is used in varied ways, but the primary defining features of a case study are that it draws in **multiple perspectives** (whether through single or multiple data collection methods) and is **rooted in a specific context** which is seen as critical to understanding the researched phenomena. The study may involve a single case but more commonly in applied research involves multiple cases, selected carefully to enable comparison.

Longitudinal research designs involve more than one episode of data collection. They may use a **panel design**, where the same people are interviewed more than once, or a **repeat cross-sectional design** in which subsequent waves of fieldwork use new samples. The term **cohort design** is usually used to mean multiple waves of data collection among the same generational group – such as those born within the same week, or those at the same stage of a process.

Secondary analysis means returning to a data set which was collected for one set of purposes, to re-examine it with a slightly different set of objectives – perhaps using it for historical comparison, for more detailed examination of a particular part of the data set, or to look at it from a different theoretical perspective.

Approval of a research design may need to be sought from **ethical committees** either before funding can be sought or before the study can begin. Approval needs to be sought from the network of committees operating within the NHS particularly if the study involves medical records or practitioners, but other institutions such as universities also have ethical committees.

Informed consent is a critical concept in ethical considerations. It involves ensuring that potential participants have a clear understanding of the purpose of the study, the funder, the organisation or individuals conducting it, how the data will be used, and what participation will mean for them.

Further reading

Bechhofer, F. and Paterson, L. (2000) *Principles of Research Design in the Social Sciences*, London: Routledge

Bryman, A. (2001) *Social Research Methods*, Oxford: Oxford University Press

Marshall, C. and Rossman, G.B. (1999) *Designing Qualitative Research*, 3rd edition, Thousand Oaks, CA: Sage

Mason, J. (2002) *Qualitative Researching*, 2nd edition, London: Sage

Maxwell, J. (1996) *Qualitative Research Design: An Interactive Approach*, Thousand Oaks, CA: Sage

Yin, R.K. (1994) *Case Study Research: Design and Methods*, 2nd edition, Beverly Hills, CA: Sage

4

Designing and Selecting Samples

*Jane Ritchie, Jane Lewis
and Gillian Elam*

It is a general feature of social enquiry to design and select samples for study. This is so whether the research is qualitative or quantitative in form. Even if a study involves very small populations or single case studies, decisions still need to be made about people, settings or actions (Burgess, 1982a, 1984). Similarly in ethnographic or field studies, sampling is required simply because the researcher cannot observe or record everything that occurs (Burgess, 1982a; Hammersley and Atkinson, 1995; McCall and Simmons, 1969).

This chapter is devoted to methods for designing and selecting samples for qualitative research. There are a number of different types of sampling strategy in qualitative research, and these are reviewed in the first section. The key questions that need to be considered in sample design are then considered, focusing particularly on sample coverage and sample frames. The following section describes the process of designing a purposive sample – a method that is integral to many of the approaches developed. The final section discusses the practical aspects of implementing sampling selection.

Sampling strategies for qualitative research

Sampling methods

When sampling strategies for social research are described, a key distinction is made between probability and non-probability samples (see for example

Arber, 2001; Bryman, 2001; Greenfield, 1996; Lynn, forthcoming). Probability sampling is generally held to be the most rigorous approach to sampling for statistical research, but is largely inappropriate for qualitative research. We describe it briefly here, however, since it provides helpful context to understanding the principles of qualitative research sampling.

In a probability sample, elements in the population are chosen at random and have a known probability of selection. Often the probability of units being selected is equal in which case groups will be represented in the sample in their true proportions. In other cases, units are selected with unequal (although always known) probabilities. The data then have to be re-weighted during analysis – that is, differential weights attached to adjust for the varied probability of selection, so that the sample is brought back into line with the overall population distribution (Lynn, forthcoming). Either way, the aim is to produce a statistically representative sample – that is a kind of small-scale model of the population from which it is drawn. This approach is essential so that information generated by the sample can be used to provide statistical estimates of the prevalence or distribution of characteristics that apply to the wider population. This kind of sample is also appropriate when the aim of a study is to test hypotheses empirically. There are a number of different types of probability sampling strategies, including simple random sampling, systematic random sampling, stratified random sampling and multi-stage sampling (Honigmann, 1982; Lynn, forthcoming; Moser and Kalton, 1979; Robson, 2002).

Qualitative research uses non-probability samples for selecting the population for study. In a non-probability sample, units are deliberately selected to reflect particular features of or groups within the sampled population. The sample is not intended to be statistically representative: the chances of selection for each element are unknown but, instead, the characteristics of the population are used as the basis of selection. It is this feature that makes them well suited to small-scale, in-depth studies, as we will go on to show. The main sampling approaches that have been developed for qualitative enquiry are summarised below.

CRITERION BASED OR PURPOSIVE SAMPLING

In this approach, the selection of participants, settings or other sampling units is criterion based or purposive (Mason, 2002; Patton, 2002). The sample units are chosen because they have particular features or characteristics which will enable detailed exploration and understanding of the central themes and puzzles which the researcher wishes to study. These may be socio-demographic characteristics, or may relate to specific experiences, behaviours, roles, etc. Burgess (1984) and Honigmann (1982) call this judgement sampling. LeCompte and Preissle (1993) maintain that criterion based is a more appropriate term than purposive because all sampling is purposive, but purposive is the term most commonly used in the literature.

Purposive sampling is precisely what the name suggests. Members of a sample are chosen with a 'purpose' to represent a location or type in relation to a key criterion. This has two principal aims. The first is to ensure that all the key constituencies of relevance to the subject matter are covered. The second is to ensure that, within each of the key criteria, some diversity is included so that the impact of the characteristic concerned can be explored. Taking a very simple example, age is very commonly used as a selection criterion. This is important both to ensure that all relevant age groups are included and to ensure that any differences in perspective between age groups can be explored. The latter requires sufficient representation within each age group for the impact of age and other factors to be disengaged (see further below).

There are a range of different approaches to purposive sampling, designed to yield different types of sample composition depending on the study's aims and coverage. These have been described as follows:

- *Homogeneous samples* (Holloway and Wheeler, 1996; Patton, 2002; Robson, 2002) chosen to give a detailed picture of a particular phenomenon – for example, individuals who belong to the same subculture or have the same characteristics. This allows for detailed investigation of social processes in a specified context.
- *Heterogeneous samples* (Holloway and Wheeler, 1996; Robson, 2002) or *maximum variation sampling* (Patton, 2002) where there is a deliberate strategy to include phenomena which vary widely from each other. The aim is to identify central themes which cut across the variety of cases or people.
- *Extreme case* or *deviant sampling* (Patton, 2002; Robson, 2002). Cases are chosen because they are unusual or special and therefore potentially enlightening. The logic is that learning about phenomena is heightened by looking at exceptions or extremes (for example, ethnomethodologists sometimes use deviant sampling to expose implicit assumptions and norms).
- *Intensity sampling* (Patton, 2002) which employs similar logic to extreme or deviant case sampling but focuses on cases which strongly represent the phenomena of interest rather than unusual cases.
- *Typical case sampling* (Patton, 2002). Cases which characterize positions that are 'normal' or 'average' are selected to provide detailed profiling. This requires prior knowledge about overall patterns of response so that what is 'typical' is known (for example, participants might be selected from their responses to a survey).
- *Stratified purposive sampling* (Patton, 2002), a hybrid approach in which the aim is to select groups that display variation on a particular phenomena but each of which is fairly homogeneous, so that subgroups can be compared.

- *Critical case sampling* (Patton, 2002) in which cases are chosen on the basis that they demonstrate a phenomenon or position 'dramatically' or are pivotal in the delivery of a process or operation. The logic is that these cases will be 'critical' to any understanding offered by the research. Patton sees this approach as particularly valuable in evaluative research because it helps to draw attention to particular features of a process and can thus heighten the impact of the research.

In purposive sampling, decisions about which criteria are used for selection are often made in the early design stages of the research. They will be informed by a range of factors including the principal aims of the study, existing knowledge or theories about the field of study, hypotheses that the research may want to explore or gaps in knowledge about the study population. If, having conducted the fieldwork, additional or supplementary samples are indicated, then these can be selected as described below.

Although 'purposive' selection involves quite deliberate choices, this should not suggest any bias in the nature of the choices made. The process of purposive sampling requires clear objectivity so that the sample stands up to independent scrutiny. So although the researcher or funders may well have hypotheses they want to test, the opportunity for these to be proved or disproved needs to be equal.

THEORETICAL SAMPLING

Theoretical sampling (initially Glaser and Strauss, 1967 and Strauss and Corbin, 1998; see also Bryman, 2001; Finch and Mason, 1990; Mason, 2002; Seale, 1999) is a particular kind of purposive sampling in which the researcher samples incidents, people or units on the basis of their potential contribution to the development and testing of theoretical constructs. The process is iterative: the researcher picks an initial sample, analyses the data, and then selects a further sample in order to refine his or her emerging categories and theories. This process is continued until the researcher reaches 'data saturation', or a point when no new insights would be obtained from expanding the sample further. Theoretical sampling is mainly associated with the development of grounded theory. Glaser and Strauss define theoretical sampling as follows:

> Theoretical sampling is the process of data collection for generating theory whereby the analyst jointly collects, codes, and analyses his data and decides what data to collect next and where to find them, in order to develop his theory as it emerges. This process of data collection is *controlled* by the emerging theory, whether substantive or formal. (1967: 45)

Denzin (1970) distinguishes between two types of sampling: non-interactive (akin to probability sampling) and interactive. Interactive samples, akin to theoretical samples, are flexibly drawn, iterative selections which develop as the research proceeds. They are judged according to the richness of data and the quality of concepts and theories generated.

The key criteria for selection in theoretical sampling are theoretical purpose and theoretical relevance. Sampling continues until 'theoretical saturation' is reached and no new analytical insights are forthcoming. In so doing, the researcher does not look just for confirmatory evidence but also searches for 'negative cases'.

Theory generation proceeds on the basis of comparative analysis and so the choice of comparison groups is extremely important. Glaser and Strauss (1967) distinguish between samples which minimise differences in which the researcher will collect much similar data but also spot the subtle differences which would not be caught in heterogeneous samples; and samples which maximise differences to facilitate the collection of diverse data which may then uncover similarities between groups.

Strauss and Corbin (1998) suggest that different sampling strategies be adopted at different stages of a research project. Initially, while categories are being identified and named, sampling is open and unstructured. As theory develops and categories are integrated along dimensional levels then sampling becomes more purposive and discriminate in order to maximise opportunities for comparative analysis.

OPPORTUNISTIC SAMPLING AND CONVENIENCE SAMPLING

Other authors have identified opportunistic sampling and convenience sampling (Burgess, 1984; Honigmann, 1982; Maxwell, 1996; Patton, 2002) as sampling methods used in qualitative research. Patton draws a clear distinction between them. Opportunistic sampling involves the researcher taking advantage of unforeseen opportunities as they arise during the course of fieldwork, adopting a flexible approach to meld the sample around the field-work context as it unfolds. In field studies, it may be a question of using available encounters and events as they arise. Convenience sampling, on the other hand, lacks any clear sampling strategy: the researcher chooses the sample according to ease of access. Some writers have suggested that convenience sampling constitutes the most common form of qualitative sampling, based on the misunderstanding that small sample sizes do not permit statistical generalisation and therefore it does not matter how cases are chosen. There is, however, much disquiet that this view should prevail and many contemporary authors argue for much more systematic and predefined approaches (Mason, 2002; Patton, 2002).

Before leaving the discussion of sampling methods, it is important to say a further word about why probability sampling is inappropriate for qualitative research. Unlike statistical research, qualitative research does not set out to estimate the incidence of phenomena in the wider population. Qualitative sampling therefore requires a different logic to quantitative enquiry, one in which neither statistical representation nor scale are key considerations

(Holloway and Wheeler, 1996; Mason, 2002; Patton, 2002). The precision and rigour of a qualitative research sample is defined by its ability to represent salient characteristics (see below) and it is these that need priority in sample design. Perhaps more crucially the principles of probability sampling can work against the requirements of sound qualitative sampling.

An example will help to illustrate. Let us suppose that a qualitative study is being undertaken among lone parents about barriers to employment. The population of lone parents contains a much higher proportion of women than men (in the ratio of about 10 to 1). But a qualitative study may well want to explore barriers for men and for women and to see how these might vary with a range of different characteristics, such as the age of the children, age of the parent, working history, educational history, and local labour market. For random sampling to generate the range of characteristics required, it would require a highly complex stratified sample that would test the limits of feasibility, particularly within the scale of sample associated with qualitative research (see further below).

The key differences between the requirements of qualitative and quantitative samples are not always well understood by research practitioners and users. All too often, qualitative samples are criticised for not holding features of quantitative samples (for example scale, national coverage, distributional representation) when these would do nothing to enhance the robustness of the sample for its qualitative purposes. It is crucial that those who want to assess the strength of a qualitative sample apply the appropriate criteria, not ones that belong to a quite different research paradigm.

Key features of qualitative sampling

Although there are some key differences between purposive and theoretical sampling – the two main approaches used in qualitative research – they also have much in common. Both rely on the use of prescribed selection criteria, although prescription takes place at different stages of the research. They also both use samples which are small in scale although with the opportunity to add to or supplement the composition as the research progresses. These three features, which are integral to qualitative sampling, are further considered below.

THE USE OF PRESCRIBED SELECTION CRITERIA
As described in earlier chapters, the aim of qualitative research is to gain an understanding of the nature and form of phenomena, to unpack meanings, to develop explanations or to generate ideas, concepts and theories. Samples therefore need to be selected to ensure the inclusion of relevant constituencies, events, processes and so on, that can illuminate and inform that understanding. Units are chosen because they typify a circumstance or hold a characteristic that is expected or known to have salience to the subject matter

under study. We have termed this principle of qualitative sampling as the requirement for 'symbolic representation' because a unit is chosen to both 'represent' and 'symbolise' features of relevance to the investigation. This terminology also helps to distinguish a crucial difference between sampling for qualitative and quantitative enquiry in that the former is concerned with the purposive representation of 'character' and the latter with statistical representation using random selection to represent population distribution.

A second requirement is to ensure that the sample is as diverse as possible within the boundaries of the defined population. Diversity is needed for two reasons. First it optimises the chances of identifying the full range of factors or features that are associated with a phenomenon. The greater the diversity of characteristics or circumstances, the more opportunity there is to identify their different contributory elements or influences. Second it allows some investigation of interdependency between variables such that those that are most relevant can be disengaged from those of lesser import. Let us suppose for example that differences need to be explored between two groups (say men and women) but it is also known that these groups vary in relation to another variable that is important to the subject of study (say alcohol consumption). Different levels of alcohol consumption will need to be represented among both men and women to explore the impacts of both sex and alcohol consumption, and to allow comparisons to be made between men and women.

These two requirements, for symbolic representation and diversity, mean that 'sampling units' (people, events, organisations etc.) have to meet prescribed criteria in order to be selected for the sample. In addition, because qualitative samples are usually small in size (see below), these criteria have to be applied with optimum efficiency. These principles apply to both purposive and theoretical sampling although, as already noted, the stages at which criteria are defined differ between the two approaches.

SAMPLE SIZE

Qualitative samples are usually small in size. There are three main reasons for this. First, if the data are properly analysed, there will come a point where very little new evidence is obtained from each additional fieldwork unit. This is because phenomena need only to appear once to be part of the analytical map (see Chapters 9 and 10). There is therefore a point of diminishing return where increasing the sample size no longer contributes new evidence.

Second, statements about incidence or prevalence are not the concern of qualitative research. There is therefore no requirement to ensure that the sample is of sufficient scale to provide estimates, or to determine statistically significant discriminatory variables. This is in sharp contrast to survey samples which need to have adequately sized cells to draw statistical inference with the required precision.

Third, the type of information that qualitative studies yield is rich in detail. There will therefore be many hundreds of 'bites' of information from each unit of data collection. In order to do justice to these, sample sizes need to be kept to a reasonably small scale. Finally, and related to this, qualitative research is highly intensive in terms of the research resources it requires. It would therefore simply be unmanageable to conduct and analyse hundreds of interviews, observations or groups unless the researcher intends to spend several years doing so.

There are a number of issues that need to be taken into account in determining sample size:

- *The heterogeneity of the population* – if the population is known to be very diverse in nature in relation to the subject of enquiry, then this is likely to increase the required sample size. Conversely, if the population is reasonably homogeneous, then a smaller sample will include all the internal diversity that is needed.
- *The number of selection criteria* – the number of criteria that are felt to be important in designing the sample will influence the sample size – the more there are, the larger the sample.
- *The extent to which nesting of criteria is needed* – if criteria need to be interlocked or 'nested' (that is, controlling the representation of one criterion within another) for reasons of interdependency or because of the requirement for diversity, then this will increase the sample size. This is discussed further below.
- *Groups of special interest that require intensive study* – if groups within the study population require intensive study, they will need to be included with sufficient symbolic representation and diversity. This will require a larger overall sample.
- *Multiple samples within one study* – it is sometimes necessary to have more than one sample within a study for reasons of comparison or control, and this will have a significant impact on the number of cases that need to be covered.
- *Type of data collection methods* – the overall sample size will be increased depending on whether the methods of data collection involve (roughly in ascending order) single interviews, paired interviews, small or average size group discussions.
- *The budget and resources available* – each sample unit will need intensive resources for data collection and analysis. The scale of the budget available will therefore place some limits on sample size. This may mean that the scope and focus of the study needs to be reviewed – see further below.

Ways in which to handle all these issues in practice are discussed later in the chapter.

As a very general rule of thumb, qualitative samples for a single study involving individual interviews only often lie under 50. If they become much larger than 50 they start to become difficult to manage in terms of the quality of data collection and analysis that can be achieved. Certainly if they reach as high as 70 to 80 the scale should be seriously questioned, and retained only if there are clear reasons, of the sort listed above, for proceeding with a larger sample. For group discussion samples, the equivalent figures are around 90 to 100 (12 to 14 groups) as the point at which the sample will become difficult to manage, and around 140 to 150 (around 20 groups) as the point at which its scale should be seriously questioned. There are occasions where samples have to exceed these limits, because of the considerations listed above. However, if samples are larger, there should be very clear consideration of how it will be possible to carry out the quality of in-depth research required across the whole sample.

It is also important to ensure that samples are not too small. If they are, then they can easily miss key constituencies within the population, or contain too little diversity to explore the varying influences of different factors. It is important to note that small-scale samples only work in qualitative research if good purposive or theoretical sampling has taken place. It is this that supports the use of small numbers because it ensures that the sample will be highly rich in terms of the constituencies and diversity it represents.

ADDITIONAL AND SUPPLEMENTARY SAMPLES

In qualitative research it is perfectly possible to supplement a sample by adding members to it, or to draw a second sample within the scope of the same study. Indeed, as already described, it is an integral feature of theoretical sampling to add to the sample as the research progresses. This may occur when it is found that important constituencies are not sufficiently well represented to derive sound qualitative evidence or when it is clear that the innate diversity of a subgroup warrants further cases or even a separate sample. Unlike statistical enquiries, where information from newly drawn samples cannot easily be 'added' to an original data set unless the probabilities of selection of all the new and old sample cases are known, additional qualitative data can be quite reliably incorporated provided the same form of data collection has been conducted. This is because missing phenomena will add to the completion of the 'map' and frequency of occurrence is not of concern.

To illustrate, let us suppose that one of the selection criteria in a study of service users is ethnic group. Having carried out the initial research, the study evidence shows that there are key differences in experience, assessment and so on, between people from different South Asian communities. However, the sample is not of sufficient size or diversity in its representation of South Asians to explore these differences confidently in any detail. This would then require the selection of a supplementary sample of people of South Asian origin. If resources are not available for this, then the researcher might need to recommend further research, as a separate study, and should acknowledge the limited inference that could be drawn to South Asian populations (see Chapter 10).

In the remainder of this chapter we will be describing how purposive sampling is carried out in practice. An equivalent section could be written on theoretical sampling but there is not the space to do justice to both at the appropriate level of detail – the reader is instead referred to Bryman (2001), Finch and Mason (1990), Glaser and Strauss (1967) and Strauss and Corbin (1998). However, many of the steps and processes involved in purposive sampling are similar if not identical in theoretical sampling because of the shared features described above.

Before leaving theoretical sampling, it may be useful to reflect briefly on the factors that might determine when purposive rather than theoretical sampling is used or vice versa. The choice will be heavily influenced by the purposes of the research, particularly by its theoretical orientation. Theoretical sampling is particularly appropriate for exploratory studies in unfamiliar areas, since it may be difficult to identify in advance the groups and characteristics that need to be included in the sample. This knowledge will instead emerge from the data collected. The choice will also be influenced by the nature of the study population and its complexity. Pragmatic factors such as the time and resources available will also play a part in the decision. Theoretical sampling requires more time, since sample selection, fieldwork and analysis are undertaken iteratively rather than sequentially as in purposive sampling. This also means that it will generally be harder to predict with precision the time and resources that will be required for a study using theoretical sampling. It is perhaps for this latter reason that samples used in applied policy research are often purposive rather than theoretical in their design.

Study populations

Two key decisions have to be made early on that are instrumental to the way sample design progresses. First, who or what is to be sampled? Second, what is the appropriate information source, or sample frame, from which they are to be selected? These questions are relevant to all forms of research whether qualitative or quantitative in form. Here we consider the kinds of issues that need to be addressed in relation to study populations and sample frames, with a particular focus on their implications for qualitative research design.

The first stage in sample design involves identifying exactly what it is that is to be sampled. In social research this will usually involve people at some stage. However, particularly in ethnographic research, what is to be studied might be documents, visual images, events, processes or settings (Hammersley and Atkinson, 1995; Honigmann, 1982; Turner, 1982). In specific kinds of policy related research, it may be dwellings, journeys or environments. Whatever the unit of study, it will be necessary to define the parent population – that is, the population from which the sample is to be drawn.

There are three key questions that need to be addressed in defining the population for study:

- Which group or subpopulation is of central interest to the subject matter of the study? This involves deciding which population will, by virtue of their proximity to the research question, be able to provide the richest and most relevant information. The appropriate population may be obvious, but often it will be necessary to think through the roles, knowledge or behaviour of different groups and their ability to shed light on different aspects of the research question.
- Are there subsets of the central population that should be excluded? This might be because their specific circumstances or experiences set them outside the scope of enquiry, or because it would be inappropriate or even insensitive to include them. For example, in a study about experiences of relationship breakdown it might be decided to focus on couples rather than including children; in a study of healthcare decision-making it might be decided not to include people who are terminally ill.
- Are there additional groups or subpopulations that should be included because their views, experiences and so on would bring contrasting or complementary insights to the enquiry? This defines the supplementary parent population. For example, in a study exploring decisions about working status among lone parents, the study population would be lone parents themselves. If the study were exploring the barriers to work faced by lone parents, it might involve not only lone parents but also employers, to explore demand-side barriers (and perhaps to compare lone parents' perceptions of them with the accounts of employers). If the study were an evaluation of a welfare to work programme targeted at lone parents, it might involve past and current participants in the programme; non-participants; staff involved in delivering the programme; representatives from partnership agencies which provide some aspects of the service, and employers.

It is sometimes necessary to implement a multi-stage design to define the target population. This occurs when the study population is located within a collective organisational unit, such as a workplace, local community or health service. It can also sometimes arise in family or household units where it is not known in advance who the relevant person to include will be. Whichever the case, defining the study population involves two stages, first specifying the characteristics of the 'collective' units required and then specifying those of the individual(s) required within them. For example, in a study of the management of teaching workloads, it would be necessary first to consider which types of schools should be included (primary or secondary; type of funding arrangement etc.) and then which categories of teaching staff within them.

Where the unit is an organisation, there can be uncertainty at this early design stage in defining precisely who will be relevant to include at the individual level. For example, for a study exploring a particular facet of staff recruitment practices there might be a wide choice of people who could contribute relevant information depending on whether the focus is on the nature of recruitment policies and strategies, monitoring their implementation, making decisions about local office staff complement, operationalising recruitment procedures, making appointment decisions, or the suitability of successful candidates. Careful thought will therefore need to be given to which categories of staff or function are closest to the specific questions addressed by the study.

Sample frames

Requirements of sample frames

Once the appropriate study population has been determined, the second key consideration is what is the appropriate sample frame from which the sample can be selected. Samples can be generated in a range of different ways, although not all will be appropriate or feasible for all studies. However, there are some key criteria by which any potential sample frame will need to be judged:

- Does the sample frame provide the details required to inform selection? Since both purposive and theoretical sampling require advance knowledge of potential sample members, the extent to which a sample frame provides the information required for selection is critical. If it does not, a second information-gathering stage (or 'screening' – see below) will be necessary.
- Does the sample frame provide a comprehensive and inclusive basis from which the research sample can be selected? It will need to include the full range of dimensions, constituencies or groups which are of relevance to the research questions. If groups or dimensions might be missing, are there other sample frames that could supplement it? Even if all key groups are included, it will be important to consider whether the sample frame is nevertheless biased in its coverage within those key groups.
- Will the sample frame provide a sufficient number of potential participants to allow for high quality selection, particularly given that not all will be eligible or willing to participate in the study? Here it will be necessary to consider the prevalence of the study population within the sample frame, the level of detail to which selection criteria are to be specified, and the likely attractiveness to the study population of participating in the research. As a general rule of thumb, the sample frame will need to generate a group of eligible potential participants which is around three to four times the size of the required study sample to allow scope for selection (see below). But if attrition is likely to be high or the selection criteria are particularly demanding, this will not be sufficient.

- Finally, there are a number of practical considerations. Can the information easily be manipulated or sorted to highlight the criteria by which the population is defined and selection determined? If the sample frame cannot easily be ordered, the process of selecting individuals to meet particular criteria will be more cumbersome. Is there sufficient geographic clustering for fieldwork to be conducted efficiently, or to bring people together for a group discussion? If the population in the sample frame is highly dispersed, the fieldwork stage will be more resource intensive and group discussions may not be feasible. Does the sample frame provide all the information required to make contact with selected people – full names, addresses and, if appropriate, telephone numbers? And, overall, are the time and costs involved in using the sample frame justifiable? If considerable work will be required to identify individuals who fit the sampling criteria, it may be more appropriate to consider other sample frames instead.

Options for sample frames

There are broadly two key types of sample frames: existing lists or information sources, and sample frames that need to be specifically generated for a research study.

EXISTING SOURCES

Existing information sources will generally be the most convenient type of sample frame. There are a number of key types:

Administrative records   The range of administrative records, management information statistics or databases that can be used as sample frames is very wide, and they can form a very comprehensive and robust sample frame depending on the scope of the study. Their principal shortcoming is that, because they are not generally designed for research purposes, they are unlikely to contain all the information that qualitative research sampling requires, and further screening is therefore likely to be needed. For example, records of social security benefit receipt will not include information about employment histories, which could be an important sampling variable in a study exploring movements between employment and unemployment.

   Access to administrative records will need to be negotiated with their holder. Arrangements will usually need to be made to gain the consent of individuals, either to take part in the study or to their names being released to the research team (see below). Also because they are designed for other purposes, it is always important to check that they contain full contact details for potential participants.

Published lists   Published lists are a particularly useful way of generating a sample of organisations or professionals. It will be important to investigate the criteria for inclusion, and to consider whether the list is sufficiently comprehensive. Contact details will generally be adequate, but there may be relatively little other information so that further screening is necessary. Unless the list is available in electronic format, it may be difficult to order or manipulate the data in a way that aids systematic selection.

For example, as part of a study of the operation of mediation in divorce and separation (Lewis, 1999) a sample of solicitors was selected from a published register of solicitor firms. The register provided details of the size of firms and the date of enrolment of solicitors, but further information about their level of specialism in family law and their experience of cases involving mediation had to be sought in a subsequent screening exercise.

Survey samples   Survey samples can offer a very effective sample frame for a qualitative study if access to such a source is available. This will generally arise when there is some coherence between the survey and the qualitative study in terms of their objectives and coverage, and particularly if the two studies were conceived of together. Although qualitative research samples themselves are not designed to be statistically representative, it can be useful for the sample frame from which they are selected to be so. It will meet all the requirements for comprehensiveness, diversity and lack of bias, provided that the response rate to the original survey did not lead to unevenness in sample coverage.

Survey samples are particularly useful where the required study group is a small or rare population, or where it is defined on the basis of detailed or sensitive information that is more easily accessed in a survey interview than elsewhere. It also offers the opportunity to know how certain variables are distributed within the study population before sample composition decisions are finalised. A survey will also generally be a rich source of data to support quite refined purposive sampling. For example, in a study which explored how solicitors deal with pensions in divorce settlements (Arthur and Lewis, 2000) a survey was used to identify solicitors who had dealt with cases involving pension rights. The survey provided detailed information about the most recent divorce case involving pension rights dealt with by each solicitor. An extensive range of selection criteria could therefore be built into the qualitative research follow-up, including the value of pension rights, how the pension was treated in the settlement, whether the solicitor acted for the party with or without rights, and information about the couple including ages, duration of relationship, and ages of dependent children. Indeed, the information on which sample selection can be based may be so fulsome that it is tempting to be overambitious in designing the qualitative sample, with prescribed criteria that are unmanageable because of their number or detail.

There may be a need for a further screening (see below) to gather more detailed information for selection particularly if the qualitative study is following up a very small or narrowly defined subgroup, or exploring a theme that was not central in the survey. If the follow-up group is a very small one, the sample frame yielded may be very widely dispersed geographically, making fieldwork more time-consuming and expensive, and focus groups unfeasible.

It is also important to avoid over-complex categorisations or making assumptions about likely attitudes or experiences based on survey responses. The different questioning methods of the qualitative research interview may lead to different perspectives on the research question. For example, someone selected because their responses to survey questions suggest they are content with the level of their involvement with grandchildren might, in the course of the qualitative research interview, bring some qualification to their feelings. Derived variables may lose some of their meaning when taken out of the context of the statistical data analysis, and heavy reliance on them as a selection criterion should be avoided.

It is routine practice in large-scale surveys to ask for permission to re-contact participants, and this is essential if a follow-up study is envisaged. If the follow-up study is to be carried out by a different research team, this should be made clear and permission to pass on contact and survey response details should be explicitly sought. If the follow-up study was not envisaged, the funder's consent to return to the sample will need to be sought, and the survey research team will need to gain explicit consent to pass details on. The fact that there is an existing relationship with the research team will often smooth the way to participation in the follow-up study. However, it will be important to consider whether the burden placed on the participant of two interviews is reasonable, and it should be evident to them that there is not undue duplication between the two interviews.

GENERATED SAMPLING FRAMES

If the study population is not one which can be identified through official statistics, a sample frame will need to be specially generated. This is generally more time-consuming than using existing data sources, but will often be the only option. There are a number of methods.

A household screen   A household screen involves approaching households in the study areas and conducting a short interview. The purpose is to identify whether the household contains an individual who belongs to the study group and if so to collect further information relevant to sample selection. The households will be selected without prior knowledge of who lives in them although the characteristics of the area or neighbourhood (tenure of housing; age profile of residents; ethnic composition; level of lone parenthood etc.) may be taken into account in selecting the streets or areas for screening. This can be done through small area statistics or from information obtained from a local authority or other local sources.

The face-to-face encounter means that detailed information can be collected about the potential participant. It also provides a good forum for seeking agreement to participate – a full account of the research study can be given, questions or concerns addressed, and any necessary reassurances or encouragement given. It is also possible to carry out the final selection and arrange an appointment for the research interview at the screening interview. For example, a study investigating women's views about combining work and family responsibilities (Bryson et al., 1999) involved focus groups with younger women without children, women with children who were working, women with children who were not working, and women who were grandmothers. Since a substantial proportion of the female population would thus be eligible, a household screen was a cost-effective sampling method, and one which enabled detailed questions about family composition and work to be asked. Women who met the selection criteria were invited to participate in a focus group on a specified date, and practical arrangements for travel and childcare could be made.

Household screens are generally time-consuming and expensive, particularly if the research population sought is a scattered or rare one, and it is important not to be overambitious in setting selection criteria. Because the interview is fairly short, it is generally not appropriate to ask questions about very sensitive or complex issues.

Because of the time involved, researchers will rarely be able to administer household screens themselves. They will therefore need to engage others to do it on their behalf, either by recruiting interviewers locally or through the use of an agency that specialises in such work. Those carrying out the screen will need to be fully briefed about the study requirements and will need a full set of documentation including:

- a briefing note giving information about the study, setting out clearly the task they are being asked to carry out, the information to be given to participants and the selection requirements
- information about the availability of the research team if interview appointments are to be made
- screening questionnaires to be completed
- 'quota' sheets detailing the number of people to be selected with particular characteristics (see below for an explanation of quotas)
- two versions of letters to be given to people approached. One is for those who agree to take part giving full information about the study and what will be required of them. If interviewers are arranging appointments, these details can be added to the letter. The second version is for people who do not want to take part or who do not meet selection criteria. Its purpose is to leave those approached with a written note of the purpose of the research and the organisation carrying it out.

If the sample population is a small one in terms of its prevalence in the population as a whole, household screens are an expensive way of identifying small populations. However, if the study population has characteristics which are visible – such as having young children, or belonging to a broadly defined ethnic group – a technique known as focused enumeration can be used (Brown and Ritchie, 1984). Here, household representatives are asked whether they know of anyone living, say, within four houses in either direction who might meet the selection criteria. They are not asked to identify the house or to give any details of the household concerned, simply to affirm or otherwise that people within the target group live nearby. The interviewer then acts on the information either visiting the neighbouring houses or bypassing them if no one eligible lives there. There is of course a danger of missing individuals who are not known to their neighbours or whose eligibility is less evident, and this technique needs to be used with care.

Through an organisation   Working through organisations which provide services to or represent particular populations can be a useful way of generating a sample frame for groups which cannot be identified through official statistics or administrative records, and which are too scattered or small to be identified easily through a household screen. However, unless the study is focused around interactions with service providers, it will be important to consider how to include people who are not in contact with organisations. For example, working through Citizens' Advice Bureaux, other advice agencies and solicitors' firms would be an effective way of generating a sample frame of people who have sought advice about housing-related problems. But relying on organisations to provide a sample frame of, say, vulnerable young people would exclude those who are more isolated and marginalised.

A combination of sampling approaches may therefore be required. For example in a study which explored perceptions and experiences of social exclusion (O'Connor and Lewis, 1999) a sample frame was required which included lone parents, disabled people, people from selected minority ethnic groups, vulnerable young people, long-term unemployed people and people with experience of homelessness. Although working through organisations was the optimum way of identifying some of these populations, it was particularly important to the research objectives to include people who were not in contact with relevant organisations. A household screen was therefore also used to add to the groups that could be found through such an approach (particularly lone parents and long-term unemployed people, but this method also identified people in most of the other groups).

When working through an organisation, it will be important to work closely with the staff involved and to be very flexible about the requirements of it. The organisation should be given a clear specification of the types of people sought, and asked to approach people who meet the criteria to tell them about the research study. If individuals are willing to participate, the organisation is asked to pass on a short form for them to complete or seeks their consent to the organisation passing on information from records. It is useful to provide the organisation with a written note to be passed to people they approach, giving information about the research study and the team and setting out what would be required of them.

Although this can be a very effective way of generating a sample frame, the reliance on the organisation requires pragmatism in what is asked of them and in delivery deadlines. There is clearly potential for bias in which individuals the organisation chooses to approach (a particular concern if the study involves exploring views about the organisation), and it will be important to stress the need for diversity. The organisation may lean towards contacting people who are thought likely to give a positive account of it, or those thought to have most to say (perhaps more intensive service users, or those seen as most articulate or with more colourful stories to tell). If the selection criteria are complex or involve information that individuals may not want to disclose to the organisation, it may be necessary to make contact directly with people who are willing to take part in the study to seek further information for selection directly from them.

Snowballing or chain sampling These terms are used for an approach which involves asking people who have already been interviewed to identify other people they know who fit the selection criteria. It is a particularly useful approach for dispersed and small populations, and where the key selection criteria are characteristics which might not be widely disclosed by individuals or which are too sensitive for a screening interview (for example sexual orientation).

However, because new sample members are generated through existing ones, there is clearly a danger that the diversity of the sample frame is compromised. This can be mitigated to some extent, for example by specifying the required characteristics of new sample members, by asking participants to identify people who meet the criteria but who are dissimilar to them in particular ways, and by avoiding family members or close friends. An alternative approach would be to treat those identified by existing sample members as link people, not interviewing them but asking them to identify another person who meets the criteria. Although this is more cumbersome, it creates some distance between sample members.

But these approaches may still not provide the diversity required within the study group. They are also time-consuming, and because sample generation and fieldwork take place concurrently, they make systematic sample selection very difficult. Rather than relying solely on snowballing or chain sampling, it is therefore better to use these approaches to supplement other methods of generating a sample frame.

Flow populations This term is used where samples are generated by approaching people in a particular location or setting – for example, at a Jobcentre, a doctor's waiting room or outside a school. This will sometimes be the most effective way of identifying a specific population where a household screen would be inefficient.

The opportunity to engage with potential sample members will be limited, given the public or quasi-public nature of the location and the fact that people are there for a particular purpose (which may itself be a source of anxiety). This will make it inappropriate to collect detailed information for selection. This method is therefore best used to identify people who are willing to consider taking part in the study, seeking their permission to contact them at their home to describe and discuss the study in detail. For example, in a study which explored how access to income and decisions about expenditure were made within couples whose main income was state benefits (Molloy et al., 1999) the main sample frame used was benefit records but this needed to be supplemented to ensure full coverage of some key groups. A further exercise was therefore set up where potential sample members were approached at selected Jobcentres, and an appointment made to visit them at home to tell them about the research.

CHOOSING A SAMPLE FRAME

There are, then, a range of options for sample frames, and each has its own advantages and potential pitfalls. To summarise:

- For *general population samples*, a household screen will usually be the most effective way to generate the sample frame. It can also be used for smaller subgroups, particularly since quite detailed information can be collected to inform selection. But it is less useful for very rare groups (see below), unless their characteristics are visible in which case focused enumeration should be considered.
- *Groups that have an administrative significance* – such as benefit recipients, property owners, recent divorcees, people on probation – are generally most usefully identified through relevant administrative records.
- For groups which are *rare or otherwise hard to find*, particularly if eligibility involves sensitive information, a survey sample will usually be the most effective source if one can be accessed. Where this is not an option, generating a sample through organisations should be considered, and some snowballing may be useful. If characteristics are visible, focused enumeration may be a possibility.
- For samples of *specific minority ethnic groups*, it is probably most effective to carry out a household screen or focused enumeration in areas with a relatively high density of the ethnic community required. Expanding the sample frame to low density areas could be achieved through snowballing or working through a wide range of organisations (not only those that specifically include people from minority ethnic groups).
- For *samples of organisations or professionals*, published lists are likely to be the best option but further screening will be required.

Ultimately, finding an appropriate sample frame often involves a degree of ingenuity and lateral thinking.

SEEKING CONSENT AT THE SAMPLE FRAME STAGE

If the sample is being generated through an organisation, from administrative records or from a survey undertaken by another organisation or research team, it will be necessary to consider carefully what arrangements will be required for seeking consent from potential sample members for their details to be passed on to the research team. It will be necessary to comply with current data protection legislation and with the specific requirements of organisations, as well as considering other ethical issues pertinent to the particular study.

There are broadly two approaches. An 'opt in' approach requires positive and active consent from the individual for their details to be passed on. An 'opt out' approach gives individuals an opportunity to indicate that they do not want their details to be passed on, but treats inaction as consent. (Of course, there is a further opportunity for those selected to withdraw at the point when they are approached and asked whether they are willing to participate in the study.) In any study, there is likely to be a significant proportion of people who would be willing to take part in the study and to have their details passed on, but who do not take the active step required in the 'opt in' procedure. They may for example be too busy to respond, feel they have nothing to say, or be unconfident about putting themselves forward, but nevertheless be willing to take part if they were specifically invited to. This means that an 'opt out' approach will generate a more comprehensive and representative sample frame. However, an 'opt in' may be a requirement of data protection legislation or of the organisation through which the sample is obtained.

Designing a purposive sample

The previous sections have shown that a purposive or criteria based approach is used in many of the sampling strategies employed in qualitative research. This section describes the key stages in designing a purposive sample and the kind of decisions involved. Alongside each, a continuing example is used to show purposive sample design in practice.

Identifying the population for study

The kinds of questions that need to be addressed in thinking about the population for study were discussed earlier and are not repeated here. But it is important to remember that defining the parent population is, in effect, the first step in determining the criteria for selection since both inclusions and exclusions have to be considered.

BOX 4.1 STUDY ILLUSTRATION (1): DESCRIPTION OF STUDY

The example that will be used to illustrate the practice of purposive sample design is a study about attitudes and behaviours surrounding dental attendance (Finch et al., 1988). The purpose of the research was to identify the factors that affect attendance patterns and in particular those that generate or deter regular attendance.

The original brief for the study required a sample of the general population – that is, there was no specific population to be targeted. An early decision was made to confine the study to adults aged 18 or over. Thus children and young people up to the age of 18 were excluded. This was not because the dental attendance patterns of children were unimportant – indeed quite the reverse – but because the issues of dental attendance are quite different for young people than for adults (in terms of decisions about attendance, accompanied attendance, charging policies etc.). The study was therefore confined to adults in clear recognition that a study among younger people would need to be separately designed and conducted.

A second decision concerning population coverage surrounded the inclusion of people who were non-dentate, that is no longer had their own teeth. It was decided that people with their own teeth were the priority in terms of dental attendance and that the study should be confined to the dentate population.

The choice of purposive selection criteria

The next step is to decide which criteria will be used for purposive selection of the sample. That is, within the parent population or populations, which constituencies need to be represented and with what level of diversity.

The criteria used may be demographic characteristics, circumstances, experiences, attitudes – indeed, any kind of phenomena. But complex criteria make the sample more difficult to select because the information has to be collected before a decision about exclusion or inclusion can be made – and thus before the person has been invited to participate in the qualitative study. Of course, if the information cannot be ascertained in advance of the main data collection, it will be impossible to use that criterion in selection.

The choice of purposive selection criteria is influenced by a review of the aims of the study and the lines of enquiry being pursued. Each of the following should be considered:

- A review of relevant literature or former research will identify characteristics that are known to have an impact on the subject being investigated. These should either be included as selection criteria or used to define the population for study, as described above.
- There will be variables which need to be covered simply to achieve a balanced sample (for example age, socio-economic group).
- There may be hypotheses that the research is exploring that will require coverage of particular subgroups.
- There may be subgroups about which little is known and whose circumstances or views need to be explored.

BOX 4.2 STUDY ILLUSTRATION (2): INITIAL SELECTION CRITERIA CONSIDERED

The criteria that were originally considered for purposive selection were:

- *Age* to ensure a balanced demographic sample
- *Gender* to ensure balance and because patterns of attendance differ slightly between men and women
- *Family unit composition* because it was hypothesised that the attendance of others in the unit (particularly children) may influence the individual's own attitudes or behaviours
- *Ethnic origin* to ensure a balanced demographic sample
- *Employment activity* because it was hypothesised that attendance might be affected by time constraints during working hours
- *Income level* because it was known that the anticipated costs of dental attendance were an inhibiting factor
- *Regional location* because it was known that dental attendance patterns varied in different regions of the country
- *Type of area* because it was hypothesised that issues of access in urban and rural areas might differentially affect attitudes or behaviour
- *Dental health* in order to explore how attitudes varied among people with different levels of dental health
- *Current patterns of dental attendance* to ensure that different types of attenders (regular, irregular, occasional) were all adequately covered for comparative analysis.

Prioritising the selection criteria

It is likely that the list of possible purposive sampling criteria, identified in the ways described above, could contain anything between 10 and 20 variables. It will therefore be necessary to prioritise them in some way rather than apply them all to the same degree of precision. This is because the sample would be driven to a scale well beyond one that is manageable for qualitative research if they were all included with the same level of precision, and given equal importance. This is illustrated below when sample size is discussed.

A first step in prioritising the criteria is to decide which are the most important in terms of achieving a sample that is inclusive of the demographic structure of the population being studied, that contains the key constituencies, and that is sufficiently diverse for comparative analyses to be undertaken. This is no easy task because at first sight everything will seem important – after all they were each chosen because of some expected significance. But gradually by thinking about each one in turn it is possible to assign relative priorities. A good way to do this is to have two or three columns so that variables can be ordered into those that are of primary, secondary and if necessary tertiary importance.

Another consideration in deciding on the priority of individual criteria is the extent to which the variables should interlock, or be 'nested'. That is, is it important that there should be control of one – or more than one – variable within another. For example, if gender and age are purposive criteria, should the sample be controlled for age within sex – that is, the age spread of both men and women controlled. If the answer to this question is yes, then age will be 'nested' within gender. This will mean that both of those variables have to be on the 'top' priority list. The decision about nesting will largely rest with whether or not a strong relationship or interdependency is anticipated between the two criteria in relation to the subject of enquiry. So, for example, in the illustration above, if it is expected that older men will view the subject differently from older women and from younger men – that is, age and gender will each have an independent influence – then a decision to nest should be made. If the answer is unknown, as it often is, then the decision to nest should be avoided as over-nested samples can easily become very large.

When prioritising criteria it is useful to consider whether any of those identified are highly correlated with each other. If this is so then they will probably not both be needed as one will act as a kind of proxy for the other. For example, employment activity is linked with income level and social class and so it would not be necessary to use all three variables in selection. Similarly, the age of parents is highly correlated with the ages of their children so in a study among parents with children, ensuring diversity in the age of the children will also generate a spread in the parents' ages.

Once the priority of the criteria has been considered, it will be possible to assign them as primary, secondary and if necessary tertiary criteria. The primary criteria are those which are considered to be of most importance in relation to the subject and objectives of the enquiry. They will be given first priority in any decisions about the sample structure. Secondary criteria are those of potentially lower importance in relation to the enquiry and will be given less power in the sample composition – that is specified in a less detailed way and with less precision. If there are tertiary criteria, these will not be specified in the sample composition but will be monitored as people are 'recruited' to the sample. In other words, the researcher keeps an eye on them, and if some diversity in their coverage is not naturally being achieved a selection criterion may need to be added. The impact of such assignments in terms of the composition of the sample is explained below when the design of a sample matrix is described.

It is important to recognise that decisions about the relative significance of different criteria are being made on the basis of the best evidence available combined with the hypotheses, theories or issues that are central to the research. A 'perfect' decision therefore cannot be guaranteed and it may well be that the wrong levels of priority are assigned – or even that there are key variables missing. This will not be irretrievable. It is likely that the non-specified variables will nevertheless be present in the sample, quite possibly with sufficient coverage. Certainly the fact that a criterion should have been included or given higher priority will be evident from the data collected: the researcher will be aware from the accounts of those included that a variable they had overlooked is important. Provided there are the resources, supplementary samples can be added if it is found that the sample is very deficient in the representation of a key group.

BOX 4.3   STUDY ILLUSTRATION (3): PRIORITISED SELECTION CRITERIA

The 10 criteria identified above were assigned priority on the basis of their considered importance to understanding the factors affecting dental attendance.

Primary criteria
Dental attendance pattern
Age
Gender
Regional location
Employment activity
Income
Family unit composition

Secondary criteria
Dental health
Ethnic origin
Type of area

Deciding on the locations for the study

Qualitative studies are almost invariably confined to a small number of geographical, community or organisational locations. This is partly so that the context in which the research is being conducted is known and partly for reasons of resource and efficiency. But, equally, the locations selected are usually chosen because of their salience to the subject under enquiry, for example, the levels of employment, nature of the local community or the siting of a specific organisation or service. As such they often contribute to the sample design because of the specific features they hold. For this reason it is always useful to consider sample locations before moving on to the detail of the sample composition.

BOX 4.4   STUDY ILLUSTRATION (4): FIELDWORK LOCATIONS

A decision was made to carry out the research in four different areas. These were sited in four different regions of the country and contained a mix of inner city, urban and rural areas. Through such selection, variation in terms of *regional location* and *type of area* was achieved thus absorbing two of the primary sampling criteria.

Designing a sample matrix

Once the locations have been decided, the most useful way to convert decisions about the remaining sampling criteria into a sample design is to draw up a sample matrix. The matrix will include a number of items (mapped out both vertically and horizontally) relating to the primary sampling criteria. These in turn will yield a number of cells, each of which will be assigned a number of sample units to be selected (a quota – see further below). Other primary criteria that are not accommodated within the body of the matrix are then also assigned quotas. The secondary criteria will then be considered in relation to each of the dimensions or cells to identify ways in which these variables can be controlled.

BOX 4.5 STUDY ILLUSTRATION (5): SAMPLE MATRIX

The sample matrix that was devised for the dental study is shown below. It will be seen that three of the primary sampling criteria – *dental attendance pattern, age* and *gender* – have been used in the body of the matrix and are all nested. This is because they were considered the most important variables to control for the purpose of the study and they are therefore the most highly specified. Two further criteria – *family unit composition* and *employment activity* – are controlled to a lesser degree, but each specified and nested in relation to one of the other variables. For the one remaining primary criteria, *income*, it was thought that other factors (e.g. employment activity and area) would provide the diversity required. Therefore no sample control was assigned although levels of income were monitored (see below).

Age group	Regular attender Male	Regular attender Female	Irregular attender Male	Irregular attender Female	Occasional attender Male	Occasional attender Female	Family unit composition across age group
18–29	1–3	1–3	1–3	1–3	1–3	1–3	3–4 living alone. 4–5 dependent children. 4–5 with other adults.
30–44	1–3	1–3	1–3	1–3	1–3	1–3	2–3 living alone. 6–7 dependent children. 3–4 with other adults.
45+	1–3	1–3	1–3	1–3	1–3	1–3	2–3 living alone. 2–3 dependent children. 6–7 with other adults.
No. to achieve across age groups	5–7	5–7	5–7	5–7	5–7	5–7	

Employment activity across pattern of attendance

Paid empt	7–8	7–8	7–8
Not in paid empt	4–5	4–5	4–5

For the three secondary criteria, the decisions were each different. *Dental health*, although important, could not be established in advance of sample selection without some quite elaborate questioning or cumbersome method of screening. It was therefore decided not to control for this although it was expected that diversity in levels of dental health would naturally occur. *Ethnic origin* was assigned as a variable to be monitored within individual areas, as the density and characteristics of the ethnic minority population was likely to be very varied between the study areas. *Type of area and regional location* had already been taken into account in the nature of the areas selected.

Before placing the selection criteria items in the matrix, each needs to be divided into categories that are meaningful to the subject of enquiry. So, for example, age might be divided into four age ranges, grouped in ways that discriminate important groups for exploration. Thus, if it was a study where greater sensitivity was needed in younger age groups, then the age ranges might be 18–24, 25–34, 35–49 and 50+. Conversely, if it was unknown how age might affect the perspectives of participants, then the banding might be more evenly distributed through the age ranges: 18–29, 30–44, 45–59 and 60+.

Some particular features of the specification of variables in the case illustration should be noted. Both age and sex are nested within pattern of attendance, family unit composition is nested within age, and employment activity is nested within pattern of attendance. Some quotas are specified as ranges – for example, the figures for age within sex and attendance show that some coverage is required within each cell. It will be seen that in some cases (for example, employment activity, family unit composition), the designations are quite crude but geared to the key feature of relevance to the study. The numbers assigned to the three family unit categories differ between age groups, to reflect the likely demographic patterns in each of the age groups concerned.

It will be noted that the numbers in some cells are small. But it is important to remember throughout that the reason for selecting a purposive sample is to achieve symbolic representation and diversity. It is therefore all about controlling sample composition in these terms. It is *not* about trying to produce a cell that is sufficiently large to sustain independent commentary, as would be the case in statistical research. Such a requirement needs to be fully removed from any design thinking.

Setting quotas for selection

Once the sample matrix has been drawn up, it is possible to draw up the quotas that need to be met in sample selection. Quotas specify the precise number of people that will be needed with each of the characteristics set out in the sample matrix. They are used to control the final selection of participants, so that the study sample matches the sample design set out in the sample matrix. So, in a study where a sample of 40 people is to be evenly divided between men and women, the quotas specified will be 20 men and 20 women. Then if age is to be controlled, quotas will specify the number of people required in each of the different age groups, and so on for each of the sampling criteria being used. In each case, the quotas set will directly mirror the sample matrix.

Quotas can be specified as exact numbers but it is more usual – and more realistic – to use ranges. So for example the quotas for men and women discussed above might be specified as 18–22 men, 18–22 women to achieve the broadly even balance required.

BOX 4.6 STUDY ILLUSTRATION (6): QUOTAS

Quotas are needed to achieve approximately three equal groups of different types of attenders. These would be specified as follows:

Age groups	18–29	30–44	45+
Males	11–13	11–13	11–13
Regular attenders	4–5	3–4	4–5
Irregular attenders	3–4	4–5	4–5
Occasional attenders	4–5	4–5	3–4
Females	11–13	11–13	11–13
Regular attenders	4–5	3–4	4–5
Irregular attenders	3–4	4–5	4–5
Occasional attenders	4–5	4–5	3–4

The three main sampling criteria (pattern of attendance, gender and age) are given highest priority in terms of the specification of the quotas. The other criteria listed – family unit composition and employment activity – will also be specified as quotas but not nested within the groups above. They will be listed as specified in the matrix, and separately controlled within each of the three groups of attenders.

The specification of quotas is illustrated below using the matrix for the dental health study. From this, two general features of quota specification can be noted. First, the order in which the variables are listed takes account of the way that data might be collected during screening. This is particularly important for later stages of the screening exercise, when some quotas are beginning to fill up. The most complex criterion to ascertain is pattern of attendance so the screening interviewers would not check for that until they had found a person of the required gender and in the right age group. There would be no point in asking questions to ascertain attendance patterns of someone who was not of the required age on gender.

Second, the ranges given in each of the categories for patterns of attendance are slightly different (either 3–4 or 4–5) so that they add up to achieve the right numbers overall. If they were exactly the same the totals would exceed the numbers required within the different age groups.

Area allocations

If exactly the same sample is required in each geographic area, then an identical set of quotas would be specified for each area. However, if there are features that vary between areas, like for example ethnic origin, then quotas may need to be specified separately for each area. For example, in the dental study, one area had a high proportion of people of South Asian origin, another of African Caribbean origin. A quota was set within each area for the number of people from these communities to be included.

Sample size

If having drawn up the sample matrix the sample size falls outside the manageable range, some important questions need to be addressed. Have too many variables been included or too many given top priority? Is the level of nesting proposed necessary? If having considered these questions the sample size still remains high, then it is necessary to consider whether there are sufficient resources available to achieve high quality information within this scale. If not, it is probably wise to limit the sample in some way in terms of its overall coverage (for example to limit age coverage in some way, or to confine the study to certain types of area). Since qualitative research will be being used because of its in-depth coverage, it is usually better to retain depth of data collection rather than breadth in terms of sample size, even if this means focusing the study on certain parts of the population rather than achieving a more broadly defined sample.

Purposive sampling for group discussions

The design of a purposive sample for research involving group discussions takes exactly the same form as for individual interviews. Although the overall size of the sample will be larger (see above), all the steps described above need to be followed. But there is one further decision to make, which involves specifying the composition of each of the groups. As is discussed in Chapter 7, decisions need to be made about the composition of individual groups, and particularly about how homogeneous or diverse they should be. The optimal approach will depend on the study's aims and the nature of the population being studied. But whatever is decided about group composition needs to be translated into a specification of quotas for each of the discussion groups.

It will be seen that quotas are specified within each individual group to achieve an even balance of patterns of attendance and gender. Other selection criteria (such as family unit composition and employment activity) would also be specified across the group as a whole, and not nested within gender or patterns of attendance. Any decisions made about composition can be translated into quotas within groups in the same way.

Implementing the sample design

Once the sample design has been completed it needs to be translated into action. This final section considers briefly some of the issues that need to be considered in selecting people to take part in a study.

BOX 4.7 STUDY ILLUSTRATION (7): QUOTAS FOR FOCUS GROUPS

Let us suppose that the dental health study described above is being undertaken using focus groups. Decisions would need to be made as to whether different types of attenders should be involved in separate discussions or whether they should be mixed in each of the groups. Alternatively, it may be felt advisable to have separate groups of different ages in the expectation that the issues may be very different for younger and older people. Decisions such as these are then implemented by specifying quotas for individual groups. So if it is decided that age groups should be segregated then the specification for each group might be as follows:

Group 1 18–29	Group 2 30–44	Group 3 45+
4 men	*4 men*	*4 men*
1–2 regular attenders	1 regular attender	1–2 regular attenders
1–2 irregular attenders	1–2 irregular attenders	1 irregular attender
1 occasional attender	1–2 occasional attenders	1–2 occasional attenders
4 women		
1–2 regular attenders	1 regular attender	1–2 regular attenders
1–2 irregular attenders	1–2 irregular attenders	1 irregular attender
1 occasional attender	1–2 occasional attenders	1–2 occasional attenders

Selection to meet quota requirements

Unless the sample frame provides all the information relevant to selection and assignment to quotas, a screening exercise will be needed with a short screening questionnaire – as brief as possible to avoid overburdening people, particularly those who are not subsequently selected, and so as not to jeopardise willingness to take part in the main interview. This can be carried out either over the telephone or face-to-face, the latter being preferable if detailed information is required or if the study is particularly sensitive. It is usually desirable to make practical arrangements for the interview or group discussion at the same time with those who are selected. If further screening is not required, an initial selection of sample members can be made from the information provided from the original sample frame.

In either event, the final selection of sample members will need to be carried out carefully to ensure that the final sample fulfils as closely as possible the quota requirements. As people identified in the initial selection fall out – either because of unwillingness to participate or because they do not meet quota requirements – they need to be replaced by others with as similar as possible characteristics.

Each time a person meets the selection criteria and agrees to participate (or 'is recruited'), a note is made of which quotas they fill. It is important to review the emerging shape of the sample against the quota requirements each time someone is recruited, to identify where gaps may be emerging in the sample and to target the next approach. This should happen for both primary and secondary variables and also for any tertiary level variables where sample controls have not been assigned but where diversity is still important (such as income in the above illustration). For example, even if it has been decided that an interlocking quota of age within sex is not necessary, it will nevertheless be important to check periodically that a good spread of age groups within sex is emerging. Sometimes at the selection stage, monitoring will show that primary criteria are proving difficult to meet in the exact allocations prescribed. In such cases, the quotas assigned may need to be changed slightly or a different selection strategy may need to be adopted.

The complexity of this final stage of sample selection should not be underestimated, and this reinforces the importance of avoiding overambitious sample matrices.

When inviting selected people to take part in the qualitative study, they will need to be given the information noted in Chapter 3 as relevant to informed consent. In practice, selected sample members may also need to be reassured that they have a valuable contribution to make to the study – they may erroneously assume that they are not sufficiently expert or 'would have nothing to say' and reassurance about this may be needed.

Documenting outcomes

It is good practice to record the outcomes of approaches to potential participants. This is essential to understand whether there is attrition among specific groups or constituencies in the sample frame. It is rather different from the calculation of response rates in quantitative research using probability samples, since a substantial number of people in qualitative samples will 'fall out' because they did not meet quota requirements and so were not invited to participate. However, it is nonetheless important to record the number falling into different outcome categories:

- ineligible or out of scope: where they fall outside the detailed definition of the study sample
- non-contacts: where the contact details were wrong or the potential participant could not be contacted for other reasons
- not meeting quota requirements: where they are part of the target study population but fall within quotas that have already been met
- refusals to participate: it is particularly important to try to ascertain (briefly) reasons for non-participation, and to consider how the approach strategy might be improved to overcome this
- agreement to participate: where an interview or attendance at a focus group is arranged.

These steps are important for identifying possible deficiencies or biases in the sample. These in turn might mean that the sample approach needs to be reviewed or the generalisibility of the findings considered at a later stage. They also allow others to assess the rigour of the study methods. We discuss these issues further in Chapter 10, but conclude here by noting the key role that sampling plays in the robustness of qualitative research.

KEY POINTS

- Qualitative research studies use non-probability samples, the most robust approaches to which are criterion based or purposive sampling and theoretical sampling. In both approaches, sample units are chosen 'purposively' for the ability to provide detailed understanding. Purposive samples are designed to be as diverse as possible, including all key groups and constituencies, and units are selected on the basis of 'symbolic representation' – because they hold a characteristic that is known or expected to be salient to the research study. Theoretical sampling is a particular kind of purposive sampling in which units are selected on the basis of their potential contribution to theory development.
- Qualitative research samples are small, for good reasons. There is a point of diminishing return where increasing the sample size no longer contributes to the evidence. The sample does not need to be large enough to support statements of prevalence or incidence, since these are not the concern of qualitative research. It is impossible to do justice to the richness of the data yielded if the sample is large scale. But their small scale only works if good purposive or theoretical sampling has taken place.
- The sample frame used needs to be a comprehensive and inclusive basis from which to select the sample. There are a number of options: existing information sources such as administrative records; published lists and surveys; and frames developed specifically for the study such as through a household screen; an organisation; through snowballing or through screening a flow population.
- Developing a purposive sample involves defining and prioritising purposive selection criteria, designing a sample matrix on which the criteria are mapped and the number of participants sought specified, and setting quotas for selection. Sampling for focus groups additionally involves specifying the composition of each group.
- The selection of participants needs to be monitored carefully to ensure that the final sample meets the requirements for diversity and symbolic representation. The outcomes of screening interviews should be documented.

KEY TERMS

Purposive sampling, also known as criterion based sampling, a key feature of which is that **sample criteria are prescribed**. Sample units are selected on the basis of known characteristics, which might be socio-demographic or might relate to factors such as experience, behaviour, roles etc. relevant to the research topic. Units are chosen to represent and symbolise prescribed groups or characteristics (**symbolic representation**) and to reflect the diversity of the study population as fully as possible.

Theoretical sampling is a particular type of purposive sampling in which units are selected specifically on the basis of their potential contribution to theory. It is mainly associated with grounded theory and involves iteration between sample selection, fieldwork and analysis. An initial sample is selected, fieldwork carried out and data analysed; a further sample is selected to refine emergent categories or theories, and so on until no new insights would be generated by expanding the sample further.

A sample frame is the information source from which the sample is selected. This may be an existing information source (such as administrative records, published lists or a survey sample) or one which is generated specifically for the study.

A sample matrix is a matrix showing the prescribed sample criteria, mapped out vertically and horizontally. Each criterion is broken down into categories, the number of which will vary. Some criteria may be **interlocked or nested** – that is, one criterion controlled within another. **Quotas** are then drawn up, specifying the precise number of people required within each of the categories set out in the sample matrix.

Non-probability sampling is the term given to a range of sampling strategies used in qualitative research. The intention is not to produce a sample which is statistically representative, and the probability of units being selected is not known. This is in contrast to **probability sampling** – an approach to sampling used in quantitative research, and particularly in surveys, to produce a sample which is statistically representative of the sampled population. The sample is selected randomly, and each unit has a known probability of selection. This approach is not generally appropriate for qualitative research.

Further reading

Bryman, A. (2001) *Social Research Methods*, Oxford: Oxford University Press

Burgess, R.G. (1984) *In the Field: An Introduction to Field Research*, London: Allen & Unwin

Glaser, B.G. and Strauss, A.L. (1967) *The Discovery of Grounded Theory: Strategies for Qualitative Research*, Chicago: Aldine de Gruyter

Mason, J. (2002) *Qualitative Researching*, 2nd edition, London: Sage

Patton, M.Q. (2002) *Qualitative Research and Evaluation Methods*, 3rd edition, Thousand Oaks, CA: Sage

5

Designing Fieldwork Strategies and Materials

Sue Arthur and James Nazroo

In-depth interviews and focus groups – the subjects of the two chapters which follow this one – are sometimes grouped together as forms of unstructured data collection. Given their flexible and responsive nature, the use of this term is understandable. But it is also a little misleading. Although qualitative data collection does not involve pre-structured questions, carrying out good in-depth fieldwork requires a high degree of planning, both about the overall shape or structure of the interview or group discussion, and about the fieldwork materials that will be needed. These are the issues with which this chapter is concerned.

We begin by looking at different forms of in-depth interviews and group discussions and at how they can be structured effectively. We then look specifically at the design of topic guides. These are documents which identify the key issues and subtopics to be explored. They are also known as interview schedules or interview guides, but we prefer the term 'topic guide' both because it emphasises the focus on outlining topics rather than questions, and because it is equally applicable to focus groups as to interviews. The following section describes how and why other fieldwork materials might be built into data collection. Finally, we look at how researchers need to prepare for fieldwork and refine their data collection strategies.

Structuring data collection

Level of structure required

All qualitative data collection will have some intention as to structure – even if the intention is to follow entirely the direction taken by participants with the researcher not imposing any structure on the interview or group discussion. But the extent to which the structure and coverage of data collection can usefully be envisaged or planned in advance will vary, depending on the specific purposes of the study. In particular it will relate to how far the researcher can specify in advance the issues to be explored, how much interest there is in issues which they have not anticipated, and how far they are concerned with the way in which issues are raised, approached and conceptualised by people.

A very exploratory study designed to understand underlying values, concepts and norms (akin to what Rubin and Rubin (1995) refer to as 'cultural interviews') is likely to involve a number of very broad questions, encouraging the participant to take the lead and to shape their own narrative. The researcher will probe in depth, aiming to uncover the values and culture of the participant. Although the researcher will have a sense of the key research issues, the agenda will largely be set and the interview shaped by the interviewee. Rubin and Rubin's cultural interviews often involve interviewing the same person more than once, although this is not an essential feature of this very exploratory type of interview.

In other studies, there will be a stronger sense in advance of the issues that need to be explored. The interview or focus group will involve in-depth probing and questioning that is responsive to participants and (particularly in interviews) their individual experiences and context. But there will be a set of issues which need to be covered broadly consistently with all participants, and sometimes a stronger emphasis on factual and descriptive data than in the more exploratory forms of data collection. The researcher will play a more active role in moving the discussion through specific areas about which the people's experiences and thoughts are sought, although there will be scope for participants to move on to these areas spontaneously, and the researcher will still be open to unanticipated issues raised by participants. This type of data collection is closer to what Rubin and Rubin call 'topical interviews' which are 'more narrowly focused on a particular event or process, and are concerned with what happened and why' (Rubin and Rubin, 1995: 28).

Although these issues have tended to be discussed, by Rubin and Rubin and by others, in terms of interviews, similar differences in the degree of structure can be found in focus groups.

Deciding how far the structure and subject coverage should be specified in advance in any particular study requires careful thought about the nature of data sought (Burgess, 1982b; Holloway and Wheeler, 1996; Patton, 2002;

Thompson, 2000). Broadly speaking, data collection is likely to be a little more structured in an evaluative or investigative study looking for example at the operation of a service or policy. If the study needs to provide descriptive evidence of people's experiences of a service or programme, a fair amount of detailed information is likely to be needed to describe the features of the service or programme, and there are likely to be specific issues about which evaluative commentary is sought. Studies with a particular emphasis on comparison will usually also require more structure, since it will be necessary to cover broadly the same issues with each of the comparison groups. It may also need to be more structured where fieldwork is carried out by a team of researchers, to ensure some consistency in approaches and issues covered.

Data collection is likely to be less structured in a very exploratory study – perhaps in an area about which little is so far known, or if a key objective is to understand how participants' conceptions or values emerge through their speech and their narrative. In general, too, focus group data collection is less structured than in-depth interviewing, in part because it is harder to impose a structure on a group discussion but mainly because a key feature of focus groups is that data emerges through interaction within the group (see Chapter 7). The way in which topics are explored will derive very much from how the group responds to what has already been said. There will be less scope to specify, in advance, very specific areas for coverage.

A number of writers (see for example Fielding, 1995; Fontana and Frey, 2000; Mason, 2002; May, 2001; Patton, 2002) distinguish between two main types of qualitative interviews. Unstructured, non-standardised or in-depth interviews involve a broad agenda which maps the issues to be explored across the sample, but the order, wording and way in which they are followed up will vary considerably between interviews. In semi-structured or semi-standardised interviews, the interviewer asks key questions in the same way each time and does some probing for further information, but this probing is more limited than in unstructured, in-depth interviews.

There are different models of semi-structured interviewing, and terms are not necessarily used consistently so that what some commentators describe as 'semi-structured' interviews may be described by others as unstructured or in-depth or, at the other end of the spectrum, open-ended survey interviews. Some approaches are quite flexible, for example allowing interviewers to alter the sequence of questions or the way in which they are phrased. Others lean more to a fixed structure plus probing and are essentially an attempt to combine standardised quantitative questioning with non-standardised qualitative questioning. This latter approach provides more depth than a classic survey interview (Brannen, 1992a; Qureshi, 1992) but has a number of disadvantages (Bryman, 1992). It allows only limited responsiveness to individual personal contexts, and requires interviewer and participant to move between rather different modes of question and answer. Because there is limited probing, the in-depth material is likely to come disproportionately from more confident or articulate people. These features constrain their ability to generate the type of in-depth data that are the hallmark of qualitative research.

Ordering data collection

It is also important to give some early thought to the order in which issues and topics might usefully be approached in an interview or focus group. This involves mentally picturing the interview or group discussion and working out the most natural way to structure it. In the field, the researcher need not stick rigidly to this order – indeed, it is much better to be flexible and to explore issues earlier or later than envisaged if, given the dynamic of the interview or focus group, that is likely to be more effective. But giving some thought to how the various questions in the researcher's mind might be grouped and ordered is helpful, for several reasons.

First, interviews and group discussions are processes with their own dynamic, which means that different issues are best addressed at different stages of the process (see below, and Chapters 6 and 7). The discussion will also feel smoother, more natural and less 'jerky' if issues are discussed in some kind of organised progression. A further issue is that understanding something of the personal context – what, precisely, will depend on the research topic – early in the interview will be important to make sense of what they later say, and to probe effectively. Finally, it will be easier for the research team to become familiar with the topic guide if it has a logical structure.

In practice, the order in which topics are addressed will vary between different interviews or different group discussions, but it is nonetheless worth spending time thinking about a rational order and using this in designing topic guides (see below). There are a number of useful general principles, which are summarised in Box 5.1 below and illustrated in Box 5.2.

- The opening topics should ease participants gently into the interview or focus group situation. They should be relatively straightforward to answer and unthreatening. Their purpose is to get the participant talking and to help them understand the discursive, conversational style of data collection.
- The opening topics are also an opportunity to collect information that will provide important context for later stages of the interview. This might include family or household circumstances, whether the participant is working or not, or any other key background details relevant to the later discussion. This same principle can apply to subsequent ordering of topics – in other words there may be some topics that it is helpful to know about at an earlier stage in order to place other responses in context and to guide follow-up questions.
- Another way to set up an unthreatening atmosphere is to move from general to more specific topics, especially if the subject in question is one which participants may feel is personal, sensitive or demanding.

- On the whole people find it easier to talk about an experience or something they have done (a behaviour), than motivations or reasons for something, or their attitudes or feelings. Generally, therefore, questions about experiences, circumstances and behaviours should precede motivational or attitudinal information.

- However, it can also be helpful to introduce a discussion of definitions or meanings at an early stage in the interview or group discussion, for example what people understand by the term 'satisfaction' in relation to services. Such conceptual questions can be quite challenging for participants, and care should be taken to ask them in a non-threatening manner, to avoid setting up what looks like a test at the start. But it may be useful to hear participants' initial reflections on and definitions of a concept, rather than asking these questions later when their definitions and conceptualisation has been influenced by the discussion that has taken place.

- Towards the end, it is important to wind the interview or group discussion down, partly to end on a positive note but also to ensure that participants have time to move away from any feelings, such as distress, frustration or anger that the discussion may have generated. The kind of topics that are useful towards the end of an interview or group discussion include thoughts about the future, or suggestions for how a programme or service could be improved, or advice or recommendations for other people in similar situations to their own.

- Towards the end, it can also be helpful to include questions which seek an overall summary of somebody's attitudes or experiences. In the interview or group discussion, this will enable participants to provide an overview, which may give a valuable indication of the weight they attach to different factors. It will help to highlight how views have been refined or modified as the discussion proceeded, particularly useful in focus groups. These types of questions may also allow a degree of 'mopping up', to be sure that the researcher leaves with a complete picture of participants' views on the key topics. However, care should be taken in analysis not to overemphasise these summaries of attitudes at the expense of the fuller, more complex data collected earlier on.

Where the subject of the study is an event or a process, it will often be most useful to structure the interview or focus group chronologically. This seems to aid recall. It is also often the case that explaining behaviour or thoughts at one stage requires allusion to something that happened earlier and as a result it can be harder for participants – and researchers – if the discussion keeps moving backwards and forwards in time. Discussing processes broadly chronologically from beginning to end (albeit with some forward and backward referencing) will feel smoother and will often aid in-depth exploration.

BOX 5.1   STAGES OF DISCUSSION IN INTERVIEWS AND FOCUS GROUPS

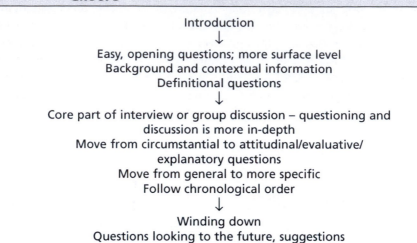

Introduction
↓
Easy, opening questions; more surface level
Background and contextual information
Definitional questions
↓
Core part of interview or group discussion – questioning and discussion is more in-depth
Move from circumstantial to attitudinal/evaluative/ explanatory questions
Move from general to more specific
Follow chronological order
↓
Winding down
Questions looking to the future, suggestions

BOX 5.2   EXAMPLES OF DATA COLLECTION ORDERING

Example 1: interview guide

A study of ethnicity and sexual lifestyles (Elam et al., 1999) which aimed to explore the personal and cultural factors that influence sexual lifestyles, particularly with a view to informing health promotion strategies, approached the key issues in the following order:

• Introduction
• Personal circumstances
• Learning about sex – ways of finding out, what was learnt, influences
• Sexual history and relationships – past and current experiences and behaviour
• Travel abroad and sexual activity – experiences and attitudes
• Safer sex – understanding, awareness and behaviour
• STDs and HIV infection – awareness about diseases and symptoms
• Suggestions for improvements to services and information

Example 2: group discussion guide

A study of an early stage of New Deal for Young People (a welfare to work scheme) (Legard and Ritchie, 1999) using group discussions had the following, broadly chronological, topic guide structure:

• Introduction
• Jobsearch prior to New Deal and perceptions of job readiness
• Initial impressions of New Deal
• Overview of activities under New Deal
• Initial interview
• Subsequent activities on New Deal
• Impact of New Deal on job readiness
• Job search activity
• Future prospects and short- and long-term plans
• Evaluation of New Deal

Designing topic guides

Considerations about the broad structure required will inform the design of the topic guide. A well-designed topic guide will provide flexible direction to field-work process and essential documentation of a central aspect of the research. A poorly designed topic guide at best will be confusing and at worst will restrict the exploratory and reflective nature of qualitative research. Regardless of the nature of the research, the use of topic guides in qualitative research is strongly recommended and careful investment in their design is needed.

The purpose and nature of a topic guide

Even in the most informal and unstructured interviews, the researcher is likely to have identified a broad agenda of topics or themes to explore. A topic guide provides documentation of subjects to investigate that serves as an interview agenda, guide, or *aide-mémoire* (Burgess, 1984).

As an *aide-mémoire*, the topic guide offers a tool to enhance the consistency of data collection, particularly where a number of researchers are involved. It helps to ensure that relevant issues are covered systematically and with some uniformity, while still allowing flexibility to pursue the detail that is salient to each individual participant. But this does not mean asking the questions in the same way or asking the same questions of each individual interviewed. A topic guide should be seen as a mechanism for steering the discussion in an interview or focus group but *not* as an exact prescription of coverage. If it is designed as a kind of semi-structured questionnaire it will limit the degree to which the researcher can interact with interviewees. It will also discourage reflection by both the researcher and the participant, and may prevent the pursuit of unanticipated but nonetheless highly relevant themes that emerge.

The topic guide will often be the only written documentation of the field-work process, apart from transcripts (which generally remain private to the research team, see Chapter 3). As such, the topic guide also serves a function as an important part of the public documentation of the research objectives and process. In the early stages of the research, it is a tool that can be used for consultation and discussion about the direction that the research will take. For the research team, the topic guide will serve largely as documenta-tion of the objectives and concepts that have been developed together during discussions about the study. Displaying topic guides in study reports is an important element of documenting the research approach and making it transparent (see Chapters 10 and 11).

Establishing subject coverage

The process of topic guide design begins by establishing the subjects to be covered in data collection. This will often be clear to the researcher from the stated objectives of the research and the existing literature in the field. These will have been determined at an early stage in the design of the study (see Chapter 3). So, the process usually begins by reviewing the research specification and relevant literature. However, before beginning data collection it is always useful to seek further ideas about the scope of the topic guide through discussion within the team and more widely.

Outside the team, this can involve potential users of the research, including funders or commissioners, other researchers, 'experts' in the field, or those who might be involved in the implementation of the research findings. Throughout the whole of this process though, it is important to maintain clarity about the central objectives of the study and not to allow specific questions or topics to shift the focus too far. Part of this process will therefore involve ruling certain topics as outside the scope of the enquiry.

For research that does not have clearly identified a priori research questions, Lofland and Lofland (1995) and Fielding (1995) describe the initial identification of the scope of a topic guide as the first of four key stages. They term this the 'puzzlements and jottings' stage at which the researcher initially identifies a topic and considers what is problematic or interesting about it:

> Logging data by means of intensive interviewing with interview guides reasonably begins with you, the prospective investigator, taking some place, class of persons, experience, abstract topic and so on as problematic or as a source of puzzlement. (Lofland and Lofland, 1995: 78)

Having identified these 'puzzlements' the researcher then takes each as a topic of investigation and generates a list of problematic or interesting aspects, jotting down questions that will help to explore and clarify each puzzle. At this time, the researcher can discuss with others and consult the relevant literature in order to add to what is already known about the issue.

Whatever initial discussion takes place, it will be very valuable for the topic guide to be generated by all those who will be involved in fieldwork. The production of a topic guide leads to a crystallisation of the research objectives and raises issues about overall fieldwork strategies – how to approach difficult issues, the appropriate order and so on. It will generally be useful for all those involved in fieldwork to contribute to and to learn through the process of designing the topic guide.

An example topic guide

An example of a full topic guide is shown in Box 5.3. This topic guide was used for a study which explored the experience of homelessness among young lesbians and gay men (O'Connor and Molloy, 2001), through in-depth interviews.

The topic guide illustrates a number of points discussed above and below in this chapter. Although this particular guide was developed for use in in-depth interviews, the general features highlighted would also apply to guides for focus groups.

- It will be seen that there are six key sections, each divided into up to a further six subtopics. Each subtopic is broken down in some detail to show the specific issues that will generally need to be covered.
- The order should be noted. Some descriptive information about participants comes first, although the issues of sexuality and homelessness are not listed until later. Some participants might raise them earlier themselves, but they have control as to how early on these are discussed. Having mapped people's personal contexts, the topic guide moves on to look specifically at experiences of housing crisis – ordered broadly chronologically on the guide (cause, nature, sources of help, ending). The next section looks in more depth at sexuality – it is expected that people will feel more comfortable with the subject being discussed by this stage, and its interaction with their experiences of homelessness can be explored. The guide then moves to housing services and particularly their response to sexuality. It finishes with some more general reflections and, on a positive note, with suggestions for the future.
- Items are worded very briefly – almost none goes over one line of text. They are not worded as specific questions but as issues or topics, with an indication of the subtopics to be explored. The researcher is left entirely free to phrase questions as they think best.
- Finally, there are some signposts and instructions, but these are kept very brief – again the researcher is expected to exercise their own judgement about how to use and approach each section in the interview.

The structure and length of the guide

Some general principles around the order of topic coverage were discussed above, and these will inform the structure of the topic guide. The first stage is to establish which topics can be grouped together, and what the logical or natural ordering of the topics will be.

When thinking about the grouping and ordering of topics on the guide, it is important to watch for any repetition that might arise. This may seem an obvious point but a researcher's concern to ensure that key issues are covered can sometimes lead to putting them in several different sections. This makes a guide very hard – and tedious – to use. If there is a lot of probing to be done around one key topic then this should be contained within one section on the topic guide, and its importance emphasised there.

As we discussed earlier in this chapter, the extent to which follow-up issues are prescribed in the guide will vary depending on the purpose of the study, how far topic coverage can be anticipated in advance, and the desired balance between participants and researcher in shaping the structure of the discussion. Rubin and Rubin (1995) distinguish between a 'tree and branch' model (the 'branches' being issues pre-specified for follow up) and a 'rivers and channel' model (where the researcher follows 'channels', or themes, wherever they lead).

BOX 5.3 EXAMPLE OF TOPIC GUIDE

HOMELESSNESS AMONG LESBIAN AND GAY YOUTH

OBJECTIVES
- to explore life histories in detail
- to determine factors which are relevant to becoming homeless
- to gather reflections on their experience(s) of homelessness
- to examine contact of and use of statutory and voluntary agencies
- to understand the needs of homeless lesbian and gay youth.

INTRODUCTION
- introduce National Centre and study; confidentiality; timing

1 PRESENT CIRCUMSTANCES

- Age
- Nature of current housing status
- Summary of current activity (work/education/other)
- Sources and level of income

2 LIFE HISTORY

Encourage detailed coverage of circumstances and key events/periods
Each episode of housing crisis uncovered should be explored fully using
Section 3

- Childhood and family background

    - where born
    - family composition
    - family circumstances (emotional, economic, stability and mobility)
    - extended family (geographic and emotional proximity)
    - any experiences of care

- School life/education

    - where went to school (mobility, stability)
    - experiences of/memories of school
    - whether made friends, whether a happy time
    - any experiences of bullying
    - experiences of exclusion or absence temporary or permanent
    - relationship with teachers
    - when left school/further education
    - any qualifications

- Working history

    - whether worked, when started
    - types of jobs

(Continued)

BOX 5.3 (*Continued*)

- – how long stayed in jobs
- – feelings about jobs

- Leaving home/leaving care

  - – when, what precipitated
  - – experiences and feelings
  - – how well prepared

- Friendships

  - – important friendships and relationships as growing up
  - – whether local network of friends, what based around, how (easily) made
  - – whether still in contact, still important

- Further relationships

  - – boyfriends/girlfriends/partners
  - – living together
  - – relationship breakdowns and separations

- Home moving/stability
  - – experiences of moving
  - – where from/to
  - – what precipitated

3   HOUSING CRISIS

Use this section to explore each period of housing crisis unveiled above

- Cause

  - – how it came about
  - – *explore fully events surrounding the beginning of housing crisis*

- Nature

  - – what was happening
  - – living arrangements
  - – mobility
  - – everyday activities

- Feelings

  - – how felt about themselves
  - – how felt others saw them

- Effect

- – main difficulties experienced
- – how life had changed

(*Continued*)

BOX 5.3 *(Continued)*

- Coping strategies
  - how managed during that time
  - personal resources
  - informal sources of help
    - → who helped them
    - → what role they played in life
    - → whether remained in contact with anyone from home/family background
    - → how made a difference
  - formal sources of help
    - → which services used
    - → why those services (why not others)
    - → how made a difference

- Overcoming crisis
  - ➢ *If in the past*
    - whether/how event or period ended
    - anything they tried to do/managed to do
    - what precipitated change
    - what prevented change
    - what made things worse
  - ➢ *If current*
    - what could bring an end to housing crisis in the future
  - ➢ *If now housed*
    - general feelings about current housing situation
    - if specific housing (i.e. with other L/G/B YP) – views about
    - if generic – views about suitability/need for specific housing

4 SEXUALITY

Use this section to explore the evolution of the young person's sexuality

- First emergence
  - own responses
- Sexual experiences since
- Relationships since
- Identity
  - whether have a particular way of describing sexuality now
  - when formulated
  - how comfortable and for how long
  - how clear
  - any changes over time
  - impact on their lives

(Continued)

BOX 5.3 (*Continued*)

- Coming out

  - out to whom/in what situations
  - situations in which reluctant to come out
  - own feelings about coming out (whether 'fully' out or not)
  - (in situations when have come out) other people's responses to sexuality
  - explore specifically impact of being out on accommodation held

- Housing

  - whether sexuality has impacted on housing at any point in the past

    → security of housing status
    → access to accommodation
    → safety of housing
    → other aspects

5 ACCESSING SUPPORT AND HELP

- Overview of service provision

  - knowledge of different places/services available to help with housing crisis

    → homelessness agencies
    → housing associations
    → local authority housing services
    → lesbian and gay services
    → other services

  - who runs them
  - what do they do
  - attitudes towards/perceptions of different services available
  - how did/can they help
  - what prevents them from helping
  - how felt was treated by services used
  - encourage YP to compare and contrast different services

- Sexuality

  - whether ever asked by agencies about their sexuality
    if asked, explore in what way and responses given
    feelings generally about being asked by agencies
  - if L/G/B, how comfortable being out in services used
    factors that make this easy/difficult

    ➤ *If has a key worker*

  - explore whether the sexuality of key worker is important

6 POTENTIAL HELP AND SUPPORT

- What would have made a difference at times when have experienced housing crisis

(*Continued*)

> **BOX 5.3**   *(Continued)*
>
> - What specifically would they like to see delivered
> - Explore what could/should be done
>
>   - to help people in same situation
>   - to help people avoid being in that situation
>   - what needs to change
>   - what difference would it make
>
> What needs to be learnt from their experiences

In its briefest form, a topic guide simply lists key topics to be covered as a broad agenda for the interview or group discussion. At its most detailed, the topic guide may contain a succession of carefully worded questions. More detailed topic guides can contain information such as:

- suggested wording for opening and closing the interview or introducing particular topics
- specific subjects to be covered within broad topic areas
- suggestions for prompts and directions for probing
- suggested wording for questions addressing sensitive topics.

Topic guides can vary from a single page to several pages in length. The amount of detail will reflect the extent of pre-structuring that is possible or desirable (see above), and thus the type of data sought. But some of this difference in length is also determined by individual styles of creating topic guides and the amount of detail which people feel comfortable with when using a guide. Some researchers are much happier working from a short guide (two to three pages) and feel constrained or overwhelmed by a guide with a large amount of detail on it. Others feel more comfortable with detailed guides, and gain some security from knowing that what they need to cover is written down on the guide in case they lose their way during an interview.

On the whole, it is best to keep the topic guide as short as possible. Shorter guides generally encourage more in-depth data collection, provided the researcher is steeped in the objectives of the study and adept at qualitative data collection. Less detail fosters an approach of responding to each interview or focus group situation, and not reading from the guide in a formal style. If a topic guide is designed with a lot of detail and in a relatively structured style, it may give the impression that the questions on the guide are the only ones that need to be asked (or that they have to be asked in a prescribed way), which will rarely be the case.

At the same time, research commissioners or advisers may want to have a more detailed idea of what is, or is not, going to be covered in the interview. A full topic guide can also act as a good source of briefing for research teams. A useful strategy to meet different people's requirements of topic guides is to have a full detailed guide, which gives a clear steer on relevant topics and areas of interest, and alongside this, a summary topic guide to be used in fieldwork.

It is therefore hard to be prescriptive about the most appropriate length for a guide, although, as a general rule, a guide that is longer than four pages can feel very unwieldy in fieldwork. Another 'rule of thumb' for judging appropriate length is the number of different sections a guide contains – somewhere between six and nine discrete subject sections is probably enough for an interview, for which the optimum duration lies somewhere between one and two hours (see Chapter 6). With this kind of time limit, a topic guide with ten or more sections, or alternatively one which has a great amount of detail in each section, will result in an interview which is only able to provide very surface level information. Depth of information will be lost in favour of breadth of coverage. For focus groups a maximum of five or six key areas is desirable – fewer than an interview to allow time for all group members to be drawn into each topic.

Since on the day participants may have less time than was originally requested, or a great deal to say on some topics, it is important that the team is clear about the issues which are most important, and those that could be sacrificed if time is short.

Language and terminology

In general, topic guides work best when items are not worded as actual questions, but instead use single words or phrases to indicate the issues which should be explored, and leave the formulation of the question up to the researchers themselves. This encourages active interviewing, becoming responsive to the situation and most crucially to the terms, concepts and language used by the participants themselves (see Chapter 6). In practical terms it is very difficult to read carefully a long and detailed question on a topic guide while carrying out interviews or focus groups.

The best way to approach this is to draft topic guides with a simple state-ment of the issues to explore – much more useful in the heat of the moment than a long question. For researchers who prefer a little more guidance, phrasing the question with 'they' rather than 'you' is helpful – for example, 'what do they think are the most important features'; 'how did they become aware of the service'. This encourages more spontaneity in question word-ing, rather than verbatim reading of questions listed on the guide. The guide can also indicate a useful way of approaching a subject that has, perhaps, arisen through discussion in the team: for example, 'ask for description of a typical day at work', rather than 'details of job activity'.

Since the researcher needs to be responsive to the language used by participants, the items should be phrased in language which is as neutral as possible. Sometimes it is easiest to use official or formal language on the guide itself (for example 'sexually transmitted diseases', 'job search activity') provided that it is clear that the actual words used will reflect the language of participants and the terms with which they appear comfortable. The most important thing is to make sure that both the researcher and the participant are using language and specific terms in the same way, and that there is no misunderstanding.

Specification of follow-up questions and probes

In addition to the main subjects of interest, topic guides will usually include some indication of issues for follow-up questions and probing (see Chapter 6 for a full discussion of types of questions and probes). These follow-up questions are an essential feature of qualitative data collection, and vital to ensure full exploration of the issues under investigation. They are used to generate comprehensive accounts of the dimensions or factors involved in an issue, for detailed exploration of a particular attitude, motivation, behaviour and so on, to check views on some feature across the whole sample or to generate examples or illustrations.

One of the ways in which topic guides can vary considerably is the degree to which these are included on the guide or left to the researcher's discretion, and a number of authors discuss the use of probes in topic guides (see for example Rubin and Rubin, 1995, and Fielding, 1995). Again, the optimal amount of detail will depend on the level of consistency sought in coverage, on individual preference and on the level of skill, experience and knowledge of the researchers who will be using the guide. In particular, it may depend on how confident they are at holding in their head the different dimensions of a topic and the key issues to be explored.

Most probes cannot be specified in advance since their wording and use depend on what the participant has just said. The researcher will always need to be developing follow-up questions on the spot. But it is always useful to have a note of the types of issues that could be explored within each subtopic, with as much discretion as possible left to the interviewer as to which in particular they explore, and the questions they formulate to do so. Box 5.4 shows some examples of how this can be approached.

Making the guide easy to use

This section gives a number of practical tips for how to create a guide that is easy to use in an interview or focus group.

- *Objectives*. It can be helpful for the guide to begin with a brief statement of the objectives of the research study – not just a statement of the topics listed in the guide, but a reminder of the underlying purpose of the study.

BOX 5.4   EXAMPLE FOLLOW-UP QUESTIONS AND PROMPTS

Example 1

In a study about sexual health (Elam et al., 1999), the guide contained a section on awareness of sexually transmitted diseases and HIV:

Awareness of infections/diseases which may be picked up through sex

- types of diseases/how spread: risky practices and circumstances
- types of people who catch them: more or less at risk; attitudes towards people with STD/HIV
- how diseases can be avoided
- perception of own risk of catching/passing on
- perception of risk among friends, partners
- experiences: own partners; people own age
- awareness of HIV
- attitudes towards HIV and other diseases

Example 2

In a study about physical activity among disabled people (Arthur and Finch, 1999), people were asked about their beliefs and knowledge about physical activity:

How important is it to do physical activity; why. Explore e.g.

- fitness
- health (how is health different from fitness)
- mental health, general well-being
- social reasons
- reducing risk of injury
- weight control, physical appearance

- *Introduction.* It is often helpful to have a section at the beginning of the topic guide to remind those using the guide about what needs to be said at the start of the interview. This may include summary points about the research objectives, details of the research team or organisation, the commissioner or funder of the research, why the research is being conducted, the policy on confidentiality, on recording data collection, and how the material will be used.
- *Summary of topics.* An overview of the topic guide on a separate front sheet, giving the main section headings, can provide a quick and easy-to-read reminder when it comes to using the guide.
- *Layout.* The layout of a topic guide can make all the difference to how easy it is to use. In particular, making sure that there is a lot of space on the page not only makes the topic guide easier to read at a glance but also allows the user to annotate the guide where they want to (see below).

It is helpful to 'cascade' items as shown in the full topic guide example earlier (Box 5.3), with a heading showing the main topic and a number of subtopics, each broken down further. Other helpful elements of layout are:

- using different levels of bullet points
- highlighting individual words
- distinguishing different sections through colour, boxes or shading, especially where they apply to different subgroups
- italics or text boxes for instructions or for prompts to demarcate them from main topics or subsidiary questions
- font style which is easy to read at a glance (clear, sans serif and not too small).

- *Instructions.* Although ways of using the topic guide should be extensively discussed in briefing sessions (assuming the researcher is not the only person who will be carrying out fieldwork), it can be helpful to include some pointers on the topic guide. The following can usefully be noted on the guide:

  - some suggested wording for questions which are particularly difficult to introduce
  - instructions for how to carry out a task or when to show a visual aid
  - a brief description of the rationale behind asking a particular question
  - an indication of the relative priority of different sections or topics – maybe noting 'key section', 'briefly', or using asterisks
  - instructions for where certain sections are relevant to subgroups only
  - instructions to explore particular dimensions throughout a section or subsection, such as sources of information, influence of others, or how a past experience compares with a current experience.

- *Ending.* It can be helpful to put a reminder at the end of the topic guide to give reassurances about confidentiality and how the data will be used, giving payments or other 'thank yous' for taking part and dealing with any other business, for example sorting out how they will be re-contacted if there is a follow-up element in the research.

- *More than one topic guide.* If a study involves subgroups whose circumstances or experience means that they need to be asked a separate set of questions, it may be easier to create more than one topic guide rather than incorporate all the different areas or wordings on one guide. For example in a study investigating views of continuing service users and of those who had stopped using a service, it might be easier to have a separate guide for each group if a lot of the question areas need to be handled differently. However, in such a case, it would be vital that both guides cover the common areas in the same way, and that both are taken to each interview in case the person has changed status between selection and the interview.

Incorporating other research instruments and materials

At an early stage in considering the topic guide structure, it is useful to think about whether the types of information sought mean that additional research instruments or materials are required. There are a number of options to consider.

Collecting structured data

Sometimes a topic guide will be used in conjunction with a more structured question sheet or proforma. This can be important where relatively complex and detailed background information is needed in order to have a clear understanding of participants' situations. An important example is when detailed financial information (such as sources and levels of income and expenditure) needs to be collected. Because collecting more structured data means breaking the flow and rapport of an unstructured interview, it is usually helpful to do it near to the beginning of the interview. It is also important to be sure that the information is strictly necessary and to think through how it will be combined with the rest of the data.

For example, in a recent study which involved exploring how couples who separate approach division of their financial assets (Arthur et al., 2002) it was necessary to collect detailed information about the couple's financial situation at the end of their relationship. The interviews then involved looking at each asset, debt or source of income and exploring how it was treated, and why. Because how each was treated depended on the existence of other assets, it was necessary to have a full picture of the financial situation early on, but the information involved was much too detailed for the researchers to hold in their heads. A one-sided sheet was therefore designed with space to enter the value and ownership of each type of asset, and this was used as an *aide-mémoire* in the rest of the interview.

Where past events, and particularly their sequence, are important, using specially designed calendars or diaries can enhance data collection. The structure of the calendar or diary acts as a memory jogger and supports greater precision in the dating of events or episodes described. Logging them as they are discussed means that overlaps or gaps between episodes, and the precise sequencing of events, are highlighted for both participant and researchers and their implications or causes can be the subject of further questioning in the interview.

Using case illustrations and examples

Rooting discussion in specific examples can add depth and richness to data collection. It helps to move beyond initial general responses and to achieve a greater level of depth and specificity. Often it will be sufficient for participants to give examples and illustrations as they talk, but sometimes a more structured approach is useful.

In studies of professional practice, looking at detailed case examples can help to ensure that the information collected is not very general or idealised, but a description of actual behaviour. Examples can illustrate how general principles were applied in a specific situation, and the circumstances under which a professional might deviate from what they have described as their general approach.

Participants would usually be asked to draw in examples of cases from their own experience. Some guidance as to the type of case sought is useful, to avoid potential bias resulting from someone selecting an atypical example and to ensure that a varied set of cases is discussed across the sample as a whole. For example, participants might be asked to describe the most recent case, or both a difficult and a more straightforward recent one. To ensure complete confidentiality of client details, the participant would be asked to describe the case without naming the client.

It may occasionally be possible for the researcher to select a case in advance. Details of individual cases might sometimes be available in the data set which is used as the sample frame for the study. For example, court records or medical records would allow prior selection of specific cases. Prior selection will help to ensure that a varied set of cases is discussed and to avoid bias in case selection. But it may be problematic if the participant being asked to discuss the case does not see it as a helpful example, and they will need prior warning of the example selected to aid recall.

In either event, it will be important to allow time for the specific example to be discussed in the broader context of the participant's work (describing features of typicality and atypicality, for example), to discuss other cases, and to describe views or practices more generally.

Enabling and projective techniques

The terms 'enabling' and 'projective techniques' refer to a number of techniques described in this section. They generally require preparation of printed material, and careful thought needs to be given to how they should be incorporated in data collection. The techniques are used to aid expression and refinement of views: perhaps to pinpoint the components' dimensions of attitudes, tease out differences in view, explore boundaries, or prioritise between different options to expose what underpins beliefs or opinions. They can help to focus the discussion following a general debate, enabling people to consolidate their views, or promote further thought.

Enabling and projective techniques tend to be used more in group discussions than in interviews, although they can be used effectively in either forum. They can sometimes seem stilted in interviews, as if the interviewee is being tested or observed, whereas a group can provide a more natural environment in which uncertain participants can take their lead from others who respond more positively to the task.

VIGNETTES

An earlier section described how data collection can be shaped around real cases or examples. Another way of rooting discussion in specific cases or examples involves using prepared hypothetical examples or 'vignettes' (Finch, 1987). These are very valuable both in research with professionals and in general population studies. They are short descriptions of a particular circumstance, person or event, which might be described verbally by the researcher or a written version shown. They introduce an element of consistency which can be useful, allowing comparison between the reactions of different participants to the same hypothetical example. They give a common basis for discussion in focus groups which may be more useful than a case known to one participant only. They can also be a way of getting people to talk hypothetically about what they would do in a particular situation, or to explain how general principles or views they have expressed might be modified in different circumstances. They bring a degree of specificity to the discussion which can be very valuable, for example helping to highlight the boundaries or contingencies of people's beliefs and actions, and can work equally well in interviews as in focus groups.

In a study carried out as part of the evaluation of New Deal for Lone Parents (Lewis et al., 2000), a first stage of in-depth interviews with lone parents was carried out, followed by group discussions with staff delivering the service. A typology of lone parents was drawn up from the in-depth interviews, and vignettes were devised to describe a 'typical' member of each of the key groups. The vignettes were then discussed in the group discussions with staff, and approaches to working with each type of lone parent described. This brought a degree of commonality to the discussion so that all participants were discussing the same cases. It highlighted differences in how staff would work differently with each group, which helped to explain why different groups of lone parents appeared to gain to varying degrees from participating in the service.

A recent study for the Wicks Committee on Public Standards (Graham et al., 2002) explored public attitudes towards the ethical standards that should be expected of public office holders. After general discussion of views, which included asking for and discussing examples of high and low standards of behaviour, a series of vignettes was shown. Each outlined a particular situation, and participants were asked what if any penalty should be imposed. The topic guide showed further issues to probe, particularly changing some of the circumstances to establish the boundaries of people's views and the values underpinning them (see Box 5.5).

BOX 5.5 EXAMPLE OF VIGNETTE

Vignette

A minister announces the appointment of someone to an important government job. The minister insists they were offered the job because they had the most relevant skills and experience. But the person who got the job has donated money to the minister's party, amounting to hundreds of thousands of pounds in recent years. He is also a close personal friend of the minister.

Issues identified for probing in topic guide

- if the case had involved a different type of office holder, such as a local council leader, a university head or an NHS trust director
- if the person had been a family member, rather than a friend and donor
- if the friendship and/or the donation had been made public before the appointment
- if a smaller amount had been involved

CARD-SORTING

Another useful technique is card-sorting. Participants are shown a number of written or visual examples of an issue, and asked to sort them into piles or to order them – perhaps to indicate their priorities, to show which examples do or do not 'belong', or to draw out relationships between different examples. In a study exploring how the term 'training' is understood, group participants were shown cards describing different types of training or learning and asked to indicate which did and did not fall within their own understanding of the term (Campanelli et al., 1994). Such techniques are regularly used in survey research. Their purpose in qualitative research is to facilitate discussion of the reasons for choices and priorities, and their implications, not simply to aid the selection itself.

GIVING INFORMATION OR SHOWING WRITTEN MATERIAL

Although as Chapter 6 describes the researcher will generally want to adopt a neutral and objective role, there may in some studies be a need to introduce information into the interview or group discussion. This might arise for example where reflections on different proposals are required, to stimulate discussion further, or if the topic is one about which knowledge is likely to be particularly limited among participants. (In the latter case, it will usually be desirable for the topic guide to explore knowledge and awareness before introducing information.) For example, in a study of public attitudes to lone parents (Snape and Kelly, 1999) descriptive statistics about lone parents were given to the group after they had aired their own perceptions. This generated more discussion as participants reflected on how it related – or, more particularly, did not relate – to their preconceptions.

Depending on the study objectives, it may be helpful to show other materials. For example, it may be a purpose of the study to consider how far different types of material might address people's information needs, or whether a form is easy to use.

MAPPING EMERGENT ISSUES

Another useful technique, again more appropriate for focus groups, is to map emergent issues as they arise in the session on a flipchart or board. This displays to the group what it has generated, encourages them to take owner-ship of it and to move it forward. The group might be asked to add to the list, but more importantly it will serve as a framework for further discussion. For example, in a study exploring how benefit entitlement adjudication was organised in local offices (Woodfield et al., 1999), descriptions of different organisational systems were mapped diagramatically on a flipchart by one of the co-moderators. This made the differences between systems visible to all participants and meant that the group could elaborate on them and dis-cuss their merits and disadvantages.

Another example comes from a study which was part of a programme of research carried out for the Benefits Agency, looking at the validity of satis-faction measures used in surveys. Qualitative research was used to identify the components that make up satisfaction with aspects of the service, and to understand how broader factors can influence assessments of satisfaction (Elam and Ritchie, 1997). In a series of focus groups, the researchers first logged on a board all the issues raised by the group as satisfactory or unsatis-factory aspects of recent dealings with the Benefits Agency. This formed the basis of the second half of the discussion in which participants discussed how these issues relate to satisfaction: the different ways in which they would contribute to satisfaction, how their importance would vary in different circumstances, and how they would influence their rating of satisfaction.

PROJECTIVE TECHNIQUES

'Projective techniques' are a range of strategies designed to facilitate freer discussion and communication, and to access thinking or beliefs that are less conscious or that may be difficult to speak about. The term derives from the psychoanalytic concept of projection in which, as a defence mechanism, we locate or attribute some part of ourselves, such as our own unacceptable feel-ings, on to something external to ourselves such as someone else. Projective techniques are often used in market research to explore imagery around brands or products or to develop advertising. They can be quite elaborate exercises.

Gordon and Langmaid (1988) identify five different types of projective techniques: association, such as word association or asking participants to describe the 'personality' of brands or organisations; completion, where participants complete sentences, stories or conversations; construction, such as bubble drawings or taking the perspective of a third party; expressive methods, involving drawing and role enactment; and choice-ordering, which involves selecting or ranking items.

Projective techniques also have an application to social research, although they are not appropriate to all subjects. They can provide a means of cutting through self-consciousness and can draw out views that are otherwise less 'acceptable' or 'rational', less conscious, or are based on strong underlying emotions. Because projective techniques involve other forms of communication beyond direct questioning, they are helpful in focus groups with people who have difficulty in articulating their views, such as adolescents. In discussions with younger age groups they are also a good icebreaker or general stimulant to discussion. They are also helpful for enlivening discussion on a subject that people may find less then riveting. For example, a study of political interest (or lack of it) among 14–24-year-olds involved showing participants a picture of the Houses of Parliament and asking them to imagine what it would be like inside, asking them to draw a picture of a politician, and to complete the sentence 'Politics is boring because …' (White et al., 2000).

Although stimulus materials or projective techniques can help the researcher to delve for further information, it is important to be clear whether they are really necessary. Straightforward discussion may be sufficient. Using the techniques does have some disadvantages. The process of introducing and administering materials takes time and is disruptive to the flow of discussion so that for a while the group task becomes more specific or structured and proceedings need to be directed by the researcher. They are also open to misinterpretation: it is important that the participants themselves interpret what they have come up with, not the researcher. There can be resistance within the group to their introduction, and care is needed to avoid trivialising the subject through their use. Finally, it is worth remembering that some people in the group may have difficulties with literacy, or sight problems.

Any materials or exercises used should be kept as simple and short as possible and combined with more free-flowing discussion. They are generally introduced after some warm-up debate or in the latter half of the session. Co-moderation is helpful to handle their administration, particularly if the exercise involves mapping what participants have said and re-playing it to them.

Fieldnotes

Finally, the role of fieldnotes should also be considered. Fieldnotes are long established as a method of data collection in ethnographic research, and particularly in observation form the primary data (Bryman, 2001; Burgess, 1982c, 1984; Lofland and Lofland, 1995). However, in studies using in-depth interviews and focus groups where data are captured through audio-recording, fieldnotes provide an opportunity to record what researchers see and hear outside the immediate context of the interview, their thoughts about the dynamic of the encounter, ideas for inclusion in later fieldwork and issues that may be relevant at the analytical stage. They may simply involve rough jottings, but generally some stimulation of the issues for consideration and some consistency between researchers in the coverage of fieldnotes will be required. It may also be useful, in writing up the research methods, to describe how fieldnotes were used to develop fieldwork and analysis.

All these additional methods of generating data need to be considered at the topic guide design stage and built into it, rather than seen as an add-on feature at a later stage. Clarity about their purpose and prior discussion of how they can be integrated are important if they are to be used effectively and consistently.

Preparing for fieldwork and refining fieldwork strategies

Research team briefing

Because qualitative data collection leaves so many critical decisions and choices to the researcher carrying out the fieldwork, it is essential that a research interviewer is steeped in the research objectives and has a clear understanding of what each section and subsection of the topic guide is seeking to achieve. Assuming the researcher is not working alone, a full briefing for the whole team is one of the most critical elements for successful data collection. This is especially important if any members of the research team have not had the opportunity to be involved in earlier discussions about the objectives and overall design of the research study. The level of briefing required will also partly depend on the interviewing skills and experience of members of the team.

The briefing meeting is often a very good opportunity to discuss how the topic guide will work in practice, to identify any potentially difficult areas, and to think about different ways in which questions might be phrased or issues approached. A briefing meeting should be interactive and lively, encouraging questions, discussion, and pooling ideas or worries. Following this meeting, the topic guide may need to be revised. The research team for example may suggest modifications to the order or grouping of subjects, identify gaps in coverage, have views on the length and amount of subject coverage, or want to suggest ways of dealing with sensitive question areas.

Written information will also be an important aspect of the briefing of team members. This might include, for example, background information about the aims and coverage of the research, a summary of the aims of each section of the topic guide or notes about technical terms used. Where there is a complex policy or a programme to be discussed in the interview, it is particularly important that the research team has a good understanding of what is already known about the nature and operation of the system under review.

It may also be necessary to obtain comments on or approval of the topic guide from a research commissioner or advisory group. This can be a very helpful process, especially where the advisers are highly knowledgeable about the research area or very clear about what they are seeking from the research. However, it can also sometimes need careful management, particularly if commentators are not familiar with qualitative research methods. It is common for people who are unused to qualitative research to feel a little nervous about the 'loose' structure of a topic guide compared with a survey questionnaire and to want to add follow-up questions or standard probes to the guide.

Preparation for fieldwork

After the briefing, it is important to spend time studying the guide, becoming really familiar with its structure and detailed contents, thinking about how different issues might be addressed, the type of responses they might yield and how they will need to be followed up. This sort of preparation is not designed to pre-empt what will come up in the interview or focus group, but it is helpful for the researcher to begin to think about the sort of direction the interview or group might take.

It has already been noted that the topic guide serves an important function in the documentation of the research. But in terms of what shapes the conduct of fieldwork, it should really be seen as just one element only – a written aid to take to and guide the interview. The individual researcher's skill at interviewing and their understanding of the research requirements will overlay the written guide. This will be evident in their working copies of the guide. Each researcher will want to customise their copy of the guide in ways that suit their own personal preferences and style. This will help them to memorise key areas and think about ways they want to approach a subject.

Before fieldwork begins, this would include highlighting or underlining different sections, writing key words in the margin, or noting how they plan to introduce particular subjects. This personal customisation is a valuable stage in thinking about how to use the written document in practice. As fieldwork progresses, they may also note ways of asking questions or probes they have found useful, or incorporate issues that have been raised by earlier participants that would be useful dimensions to explore with others.

Initial use and testing the topic guide

Initial interviews and focus groups will be an important test of the scope of the topic guide, and carrying out initial test fieldwork, or 'piloting' a topic guide is a critical part of research. When assessing the scope of the guide, it is important to review whether it allows participants to give a full and coherent account of the central issues and incorporate issues they think are important. In other words, it should not constrain what participants want to say in relation to the research questions. If a research instrument is not working, because it is not generating the clarity, scope or depth of data sought, then it needs some revision. This is as true of qualitative research as it is of quantitative research. The difference is that 'pilot' interviews do not need to be excluded from the data set unless a very radical change of direction or coverage occurs. The data collected will still contribute to the research findings even if the emphasis changes slightly. However, if the first few interviews or group discussions suggest a revision of the research objectives, or a radical change in the way in which the data are collected, then there may be more reason to consider whether or not to keep the initial interviews or discussions.

A useful aid in the refinement of fieldwork strategies and topic guides is for members of the team to conduct initial interviews or focus groups working in pairs. This is helpful for discussion of how well the guide is working, how to respond to unanticipated issues or circumstances, and how to incorporate them in later data collection. It is also a useful check that there is consistent understanding of the research objectives and of the purpose of each section of the topic guide.

It is in any case very valuable for the research team to meet to review the topic guide after perhaps four or five interviews or the first couple of focus groups. This provides researchers with a chance to 'fine tune' the guide before the bulk of the fieldwork takes place. Revisions may include creating a more natural order of topics, adding (or removing) minor topics or follow-up questions, or thinking about language or ways of addressing topics that may have been problematic. It is also worth, at this stage, reflecting on the duration of interviews and focus groups and the amount of time spent on different topics, and considering whether this needs to be modified to ensure the appropriate depth is reached on key topics. Finally, an obvious point but one perhaps easily missed in the heat of fieldwork, is the importance of reflecting on whether the type of data being collected is what will be required to meet the research objectives.

To some degree, the first few episodes of data collection are also part of the briefing and familiarisation process, as it is not until a topic guide has been used in the field that it is possible to understand how it will work in different situations. Researchers will become less and less dependent on the topic guide as the study proceeds, using it more as an occasional prompt or guidance, or moving to a summary version of the guide as familiarity with the issues to cover increases.

The key roles of the topic guide, then, change as the study proceeds. Initially its creation helps to crystallise the researcher's conception of the study topic and shape their consideration of the fieldwork strategies that will be required. In the field it acts as an *aide-mémoire,* helping to ensure that key issues are explored systematically but supporting flexible and responsive investigation. At the end of the study it is salient because it documents the fieldwork approach, and thus gives some insight into a stage of the research process which it can otherwise be difficult to describe.

KEY POINTS

- Despite the use of the term 'unstructured data collection', any qualitative research study requires some early consideration of the structure and content of data collection. The degree to which subject coverage and order can be specified in advance will vary, depending on the objectives of the research and the nature of data required.
- The topic guide is an *aide-mémoire* which guides the researcher during fieldwork and ensures some consistency in fieldwork approaches. However, it should be used flexibly and should enhance rather than inhibit responsive questioning. It is also an important public document of the approach to fieldwork. In practice, the order in which topics are addressed will be responsive to the fieldwork situation, but starting with a logical or 'natural' order will aid the researcher.
- The length and style of the topic guide will be shaped not only by the research questions but also by the size and experience of the research team, the type of fieldwork envisaged and the requirements of funders. It is helpful to list items as issues rather than as questions, identifying the subtopics to be explored and any follow-up questions that can be anticipated. Topic guides for group discussions need to be shorter than those for in-depth interviews. Fewer topics should be included, and there will be less scope for identifying specific areas for detailed exploration since these will also flow from how the group members respond to what other participants have said.
- Thought also needs be given to the value of using other fieldwork materials or enabling or projective techniques. These can be useful to aid expression and refinement of beliefs, and to understand the boundaries or contingencies of views.
- The whole research team should be involved in the creation of the guide where possible. A thorough briefing on the research objectives, the guide and fieldwork strategies is critical. Early fieldwork will be an important test of the guide, and it is helpful for the team to meet and review the guide after the first few episodes of data collection.

KEY TERMS

Unstructured data collection refers to the responsive, flexible and interactive questioning techniques used in in-depth data collection. It is sometimes compared with **semi-structured data collection**, where there is more pre-specifying of order and question-wording.

Topic guides are also known as interview schedules or interview guides. They list the key themes to be explored, broken down into topics and subtopics.

Enabling and projective techniques are a range of approaches to facilitate data collection. Enabling techniques include using **vignettes** (or short hypothetical examples or 'stories'), **card-sorting** (where written examples are ordered or sorted by participants), giving information, or mapping emergent issues for subsequent discussion. Projective techniques draw on the psychoanalytical concept of projection and are used to access material that is less conscious or more difficult for participants to articulate.

Fieldnotes are notes made by researchers 'in the field' and more typically used in ethnographic research, where they often form the primary data. However, in studies where data capture is by audio-recording, fieldnotes can usefully record feelings about the dynamic of data collection, information acquired outside the immediate context of an interview or focus group, or ideas for analysis.

Further reading

Fielding, N.G. (1995) 'Qualitative interviewing' in N. Gilbert (ed.) *Researching Social Life*, London: Sage

Lofland, J. and Lofland, L.H. (1995) *Analyzing Social Settings*, 3rd edition, Belmont, CA: Wadsworth

Patton, M.Q. (2002) *Qualitative Research and Evaluation Methods*, 3rd edition, Thousand Oaks, CA: Sage

Rubin, H.J. and Rubin, I.S. (1995) *Qualitative Interviewing: The Art of Hearing Data*, Thousand Oaks, CA: Sage

Spradley, J. (1979) *The Ethnographic Interview*, New York: Holt, Rinehart & Winston

6

In-depth Interviews

Robin Legard, Jill Keegan and Kit Ward

In-depth or unstructured interviews are one of the main methods of data collection used in qualitative research. Classic ethnographers such as Malinowski stressed the importance of talking to people to grasp their point of view (Burgess, 1982a), and personal accounts are seen as having central importance in social research because of the power of language to illuminate meaning:

> [T]he expressive power of language provides the most important resource for accounts. A crucial feature of language is its capacity to present descriptions, explanations, and evaluations of almost infinite variety about any aspect of the world, including itself. (Hammersley and Atkinson, 1995: 126).

The in-depth interview is often described as a form of conversation (Burgess, 1982a, 1984; Lofland and Lofland, 1995). Indeed Sidney and Beatrice Webb described the method of the interview as being 'conversation with a purpose' (Webb and Webb, 1932: 130). As such it reproduces a fundamental process through which knowledge about the social world is constructed in normal human interaction (Rorty, 1980). But there are some obvious differences between normal conversation and in-depth interviews – their objectives, and the roles of researcher and participant, are quite different (Kvale, 1996; Rubin and Rubin, 1995). In reality, although a good in-depth interview will appear naturalistic, it will bear little resemblance to an everyday conversation.

This chapter begins with a brief review of the various perspectives on the interview raised by different traditions of qualitative research. We then look at the key features of in-depth interviews and the professional and personal skills they require. The chapter examines the nature of the 'contract' between participant and researcher, and the 'staging' of an interview. We then set out some key principles in asking questions and probing, and the techniques that inform good interview practice. We also cover how researchers can respond to difficult situations that may arise in interviewing. The chapter concludes with coverage of practical issues in organising interviews.

The in-depth interview

Perspectives on the interview

The different traditions of qualitative research described in Chapter 1 have resulted in a diversity of perspectives on in-depth interviewing. In particular, there are debates about how far knowledge is constructed in the interview or is a pre-existing phenomenon, and about how active or passive the role of the interviewer should be. As Chapter 5 describes, there is also diversity in how structured interviews are, and in how far the content is set by researcher or participant.

Two alternative positions on in-depth interviewing are put forward by Kvale (1996). The first, which he summarises as the 'miner metaphor', falls broadly within a modern social science research model which sees knowledge as 'given':

> knowledge is understood as buried metal and the interviewer is a miner who unearths the valuable metal … [T]he knowledge is waiting in the subject's interior to be uncovered, uncontaminated by the miner. The interviewer digs nuggets of data or meanings out of a subject's pure experiences, unpolluted by any leading questions. (Kvale, 1996: 3)

The second, which Kvale calls the 'traveler metaphor', falls within the constructivist research model in which knowledge is not given but is created and negotiated. The interviewer is seen as a traveller who journeys with the interviewee. The meanings of the interviewee's 'stories' are developed as the traveller interprets them. Through conversations, the interviewer leads the subject to new insights: there is a transformative element to the journey.

> The traveler … asks questions that lead the subjects to tell their own stories of their lived world, and converses with them in the original Latin meaning of *conversation* as 'wandering together with'. (Kvale, 1996: 4 emphasis in original)

The researcher is thus an active player in development of data and of meaning. Holstein and Gubrium (1997) stress that the researcher is not simply a 'pipeline' through which knowledge is transmitted. They, too, see knowledge as constructed in the interview, through collaboration between interviewee and researcher.

This emphasis on knowledge as something that is created within the unique situation of the interview has led to concerns among some authors about the stability and validity of interview data (see Chapter 10 for discussion of validity generally). But other writers, while they acknowledge the influence of postmodern thinking on the nature of interviewing, nevertheless see the interview as meaningful beyond its immediate context. Interviews can:

> provide access to the meanings people attribute to their experiences and social worlds. While the interview is itself a symbolic interaction, this does not discount the possibility that knowledge of the social world beyond the interaction can be obtained. (Miller and Glassner, 1997: 100)

The influence of postmodernism, constructionism and feminism has also led to new perspectives on in-depth interviewing, and new forms of interview (Fontana and Frey, 2000; Kvale, 1996). Postmodern approaches emphasise the way in which a reality is constructed in the interview, and the relationship that develops between researcher and interviewee. In creative interviewing the researcher moves away from the conventions of interviewing, with lengthy or repeated interviews taking place in people's everyday world situations, and an emphasis on free expression (Douglas, 1985). In dialectical interviewing, the interview focuses on contradictions in the social and material world and on the potential for action and for change, with an emphasis on the transformative aspects of an interview. Heuristic approaches emphasise the personal experience of the interviewer, and see the process of interviewing as a collaboration between researcher and participant, sharing reflection and enquiry (Douglass and Moustakas, 1985).

Feminist research approaches have particularly raised issues about the form and features of in-depth interviewing (Finch, 1984; Nielsen, 1990; Oakley, 1981; Olesen, 2000; Reinharz, 1992), although as Olesen in particular has stressed there are many different feminist approaches. Feminist interviewing attempts to be more reflexive and interactive, aiming to take a non-hierarchical approach which avoids objectifying the participant. The distinction between the roles of researcher and participant becomes less stark: the interview is seen as a collaboration between them as they share in the process of negotiating coverage, language and understanding. Reciprocity is emphasised. The researcher feels free to step outside the formal role of the neutral asker of questions, expressing their own feelings and giving information about themselves (an issue discussed later in this chapter). Some feminist approaches emphasise the value of women interviewing women (Finch, 1984; Oakley, 1981), although the issue of cultural affinity is also discussed in relation to other characteristics and patterns of characteristics (Olesen, 2000; Rubin and Rubin, 1995). This has led to questions about whether people should be interviewed by researchers who have similar socio-demographic characteristics, or who have experiences in common with them (see Chapter 3).

Finally, biographical, narrative, life history and oral history approaches (see Chamberlayne et al., 2000; Miller, 2000; Thompson, 2000) also bring different perspectives to the interview and have yielded different forms of interview. These methods are concerned with understanding cultural milieux and social worlds through personal accounts and narratives, with life history or biographical interviews covering an individual's whole life and oral history approaches concentrating on specific events or periods. The approaches involve intensive and extended data collection with several interviews with each participant, and participants are given a fairly free rein to shape their own narratives.

These different perspectives and traditions thus lead to different priorities, emphases and practices. But there are a number of features of in-depth interviewing which remain broadly consistent.

Key features of the in-depth interview

The first key feature of the in-depth interview is that it is intended to combine structure with flexibility. As Chapter 5 noted, even in the most unstructured interviews the researcher will have some sense of the themes they wish to explore, and interviews will generally be based on some form of topic guide (or interview schedule or guide) setting out the key topics and issues to be covered during the interview. However, the structure is sufficiently flexible to permit topics to be covered in the order most suited to the interviewee, to allow responses to be fully probed and explored and to allow the researcher to be responsive to relevant issues raised spontaneously by the interviewee.

A second key feature is that the interview is interactive in nature. The material is generated by the interaction between the researcher and interviewee. The researcher will ask an initial question in such a way as to encourage the interviewee to talk freely when answering the question. The next intervention by the interviewer will usually be determined by the participant's answer. (How much of themselves researchers offer in this interaction is discussed below in this chapter.)

Thirdly, the researcher uses a range of probes and other techniques to achieve depth of answer in terms of penetration, exploration and explanation. An initial response is often at a fairly 'surface' level: the interviewer will use follow-up questions to obtain a deeper and fuller understanding of the participant's meaning. The in-depth format also permits the researcher to explore fully all the factors that underpin participants' answers: reasons, feelings, opinions and beliefs. This furnishes the explanatory evidence that is an important element of qualitative research.

Fourthly, the interview is generative in the sense that new knowledge or thoughts are likely, at some stage, to be created. The extent to which this is so may vary depending on the research questions, but it is likely that the participant will at some point direct themselves, or be directed by the researcher, down avenues of thought they have not explored before. Participants may also be invited to put forward ideas and suggestions on a particular topic and to propose solutions for problems raised during the interview.

The emphasis on depth, nuance and the interviewee's own language as a way of understanding meaning implies that interview data needs to be captured in its natural form. This means that interview data is generally tape recorded, since note taking by the researcher would change the form of data.

Finally, these key features together mean that qualitative interviews are almost always conducted face-to-face. It would be extremely difficult to conduct really detailed in-depth interviewing over the telephone. The interview is an intense experience, for both parties involved, and a physical encounter is essential context for an interview which is flexible, interactive and generative, and in which meaning and language is explored in depth.

Requirements of a qualitative interviewer

The success of the interview depends, to a large extent, on the personal and professional qualities of the individual interviewer. In contrast to quantitative interviewing, qualitative research interviewers are, themselves, research instruments, and there are some key requirements of them (Kvale, 1996; Marshall and Rossman, 1999; Rubin and Rubin, 1995; Thompson, 2000). So what are the qualities that go to make up a successful depth interviewer?

In-depth interviewing makes a number of demands on the mental and intellectual abilities of an interviewer. First, the ability of the researcher to listen is fundamental to the art of interviewing. The researcher must hear, digest and comprehend the participant's answers in order to decide how to probe further. Second, good in-depth interviewing requires a clear, logical mind. The researcher needs to be able to think quickly to distil the essential points of what the participant is saying, exercise judgement about what to pursue, and simultaneously formulate the relevant question. Third, a good memory is an important attribute. It is often necessary to make a mental note of a point made earlier on by the participant and return to it at a judicious moment in the interview to seek further clarification or elaboration.

Curiosity – an enquiring mind – is an essential asset in an in-depth interviewer. It greatly helps if the instinct of the researcher is to want to know more about what they have been told. Thompson (2000) stresses that in-depth interviewing requires interest in and respect for people as individuals, and is not for people who cannot stop talking about themselves. Patton (2002) argues for patient curiosity:

If what people have to say about their world is generally boring to you, then you will never be a great interviewer. Unless you are fascinated by the rich variation in human experience, qualitative interviewing will become drudgery. (Patton, 2002: 341)

However active or passive the role of the interviewer, an in-depth interview is based around the ability of the interviewer to establish a good rapport with the participant. Researchers have to be able to establish a good working relationship with people from all walks of life, from people living in difficult circumstances to those in positions of power and influence. A good working relationship is achieved where the researcher seeks to put the participant at ease and to create a climate of trust. This involves demonstrating a real desire to understand from the perspective of the interviewee. It also involves the researcher displaying the confidence that comes from being professional, having a job of work to do and knowing how to do it. Trust is strengthened where the researcher appears to be comfortable with the interview situation, and with everything the interviewee has to say.

Creating the right rapport also involves demonstrating interest and respect, being able to respond flexibly to the interviewee, and being able to show understanding and empathy (Thompson, 2000). Adaptability is therefore a key requirement. This does not mean attempting to be like the interviewee; rather it involves respecting the individuality of the other person while retaining one's own identity.

Interviewees also respond positively where the interviewer displays a sense of 'tranquillity' – an inner stillness which communicates interest and attention and which is accompanied by a feeling of being comfortable with the interviewee and the situation. Humour also has its place in helping to foster a sympathetic interviewing environment: the ability to share a joke made by the interviewee or to lighten a situation with humour can facilitate the interviewing process.

Researchers need to establish their credibility with participants by asking relevant questions which are seen as meaningful by the participant and which are based on an understanding of the research subject. But equally the interview is not a forum for the researcher to make a show of their own knowledge. This can be particularly challenging in interviews with senior professionals or with peers. Researchers need a degree of humility, the ability to be recipients of the participant's wisdom without needing to compete by demonstrating their own.

Efficiency and careful preparation are also essential. This means, for example, being fully conversant with the objectives of the research and with the topic guide. It means planning an itinerary that allows for punctuality in keeping appointments, and ensuring that recording equipment is in good order.

Mason (2002) stresses the range of tasks that interviewing involves. At any one time the researcher needs to listen to what is being said and understand it; assess how it relates to the research questions; be alert to contradictions with what has been said earlier; decide what to follow up or explore in more detail now and what to return to later; decide how to phrase the next question; pick up on nuances, hesitation, emotion and non-verbal signals; pace the interview; keep an eye on recording equipment, and deal with any distractions or interruptions that arise. Concentration and stamina are essential qualities for coping with these simultaneous demands.

One task that can be omitted from this list – and indeed that is best deliberately set aside during interviews – is analysis. During the interview, the researcher needs to be totally dedicated to interviewing. Their attention should be focused on listening and responding. It is deleterious to be thinking about analytical constructs, or considering how what is being said sits within analytical themes, during the interview since this means that the researcher will not be giving their full attention to what the participant is saying. It can lead to questions that are rooted in the researcher's over-hasty interpretation of what they are hearing, rather than questions which seek to understand the interviewee's interpretation and the meaning something holds for them.

The staging of an interview

Although the purpose of the interview is to understand the perspective of the interviewee, the researcher will nevertheless have a clear sense of the issues they wish to hear discussed. The researcher therefore has an important role to play in directing the interview process, and must be clear about how to 'stage-manage' the interview effectively so as to meet the purposes of the research.

A number of aspects of the process need to be considered for effective stage-management. Firstly, the researcher needs to be aware of the various stages that an interview passes through during the course of its existence and know how to direct the interview through each stage. Secondly, the researcher has to understand the terms of the contract between researcher and participant and know how to make them work for the benefit of the research. Thirdly, it is up to the researcher to make clear what the role of the participant should be during the interview.

Interview stages

An in-depth interview involves a number of stages (Robson, 2002; Rubin and Rubin, 1995; Spradley, 1979). In broad terms, the researcher's task is to ease the interviewee down from the everyday, social level to a deeper level at which they can together focus on a specific topic or set of topics. Towards the end, the researcher needs to signal the return back to the everyday level. The process needs to be fully completed before the researcher leaves the participant.

The stages of an interview, and the ways in which researchers can help to direct the participant through them, are as follows:

STAGE ONE: ARRIVAL

The interview process effectively begins the moment the researcher arrives on the participant's doorstep. The first few minutes after meeting can be crucial for establishing the relationship between researcher and participant which is a prerequisite for a successful in-depth interview. The researcher therefore needs to be aware that the participant may be feeling anxious or even slightly hostile initially. It is important at this stage for the participant to feel that they have control on their own territory, but the researcher should take responsibility for putting them at their ease. The researcher therefore needs to play the role of the guest while at the same time being quietly confident and relaxed, making conversation but avoiding the research topic until the interview begins. Once the participant seems comfortable with this stage of the process, it is time to move on.

STAGE TWO: INTRODUCING THE RESEARCH

This is the stage at which business begins. The researcher starts to direct the interaction by introducing the research topic. This involves providing a clear reiteration of the nature and purpose of the research, reaffirming confidentiality, and seeking permission to record the interview. It also involves making sure the environment is suitably quiet, private and comfortable for the interview to proceed without distraction (see below).

STAGE THREE: BEGINNING THE INTERVIEW

As Chapter 5 noted, the opening questions are an opportunity to collect important contextual information. Although it may be thought that beginning with a neutral topic is better than asking personal details, such as the interviewee's age or relationship status, having such information at the beginning is important to help with question formulation. For example, it may be useful to know that the participant has young children when it comes to exploring influences on their views and experiences. Asking for factual background information in the middle of the interview can break the flow. In addition, it is at the beginning of the interview that interviewees realise that their role is to 'open up' and give full answers. They can begin to do this most easily where the subject matter is something with which they are familiar.

In an informal way, the researcher thus asks for background information about their age, who they live with, whether they go out to work and so on. These questions are asked in a way that makes it clear they are not being read from a pre-formulated list. Follow-up questions (for example about how long the interviewee has lived in the area, brief details about their job) help to set the scene of an interview in which the participant will be required to give detailed and spontaneous answers, and in which the researcher will probe and respond. The researcher can also judge from the initial reply how easily the interviewee will take to this role and can adapt their approach accordingly.

STAGE FOUR: DURING THE INTERVIEW

Chapter 5 described some general principles in shaping the main body of the interview. Here, the researcher is guiding the participant through the key themes – both those anticipated by the researcher and those which emerge from the interview. Each subject is explored in depth with a series of follow-up questions and probes. At this stage, the interviewee will be working at a deeper, more focused level than normal, discovering ideas, thoughts and feelings that may be dormant in daily life.

STAGE FIVE: ENDING THE INTERVIEW

About five to ten minutes before the end of the interview, the researcher can signal the approach of the end of the interview to allow the interviewee gradually to return to the level of everyday social interaction. Phrases such as 'the final topic …' or 'in the last few minutes …' are useful here. It is also important to check that the participant has not been left with any unfinished business: for example, feelings unexpressed or issues of burning importance left unmentioned.

STAGE SIX: AFTER THE INTERVIEW

What happens when the tape recorder is switched off is also important. The researcher thanks the participant warmly, and begins to help the participant to move out of interview mode by saying something, fairly briefly, about how their contribution will help the research. Any reassurances about confidentiality or the use of the interview data should also be given. This is the time to answer any questions raised by the interviewee during the interview (see further below), or to give any information about support groups or services (see Chapter 3). Moving away from the interview sometimes sparks some final reflections, or even new information, from interviewees. If these are significant, the researcher may feel it is appropriate to ask the interviewee to repeat them with the tape recorder running again, or may make a note of them after the interview.

The researcher should take their cue from the participant – if the participant seems to want to talk, either about the interview subject or more generally, it is important to be prepared to stay a little longer. By the time the researcher takes leave of the participant, the process of coming out of the interview should be fully completed and the participant, it is hoped, left feeling 'well'.

The interview 'contract'

Researchers need to feel confident that the participant has freely given their consent to be interviewed. While the researcher clearly has obligations to the participant (discussed in Chapter 3), they also have permission to interview the participant within the terms on which consent has been given. In a sense, the participant has entered into a type of 'contract' by agreeing to take part in an interview. The terms of the contract are that the participant has agreed to be interviewed for a predetermined length of time, at a particular venue, on a particular topic, and under clear conditions of confidentiality.

Nevertheless, the researcher should also be aware that participants have the right to change their mind at any time. It is therefore advisable to take nothing for granted and to ensure that the terms are agreed. At the beginning of the interview the researcher restates the aims of the research and reaffirms confidentiality. Should the contract need to be changed for any reason during the interview, for example if extra time is required, the terms should be negotiated and agreed – never assumed.

Researcher and participant roles

Researcher and participant have different roles in the interview process. The researcher needs to be clear about his or her own role in the process, and needs to help the participant to understand what their role is to be at an early stage in the interview.

The role of the researcher is that of a facilitator to enable the interviewee to talk about their thoughts, feelings, views and experiences. However, the role of the facilitator is an active, not a passive, one. It does not mean sitting back and just letting the interviewee talk. On the contrary, it means managing the interview process to ensure that the required subjects are covered to the required depth, without influencing the actual views articulated.

Managing the interview process involves ensuring coverage of the agenda to be discussed within the interview, steering the interviewee back to topics from which they stray. It means exercising judgement about the length of time that should be devoted to any given topic and when to move on to the next one, and about how to respond if the interviewee moves on to unanticipated topics. The researcher has to decide what questions are asked and how they are phrased, and how to follow up until a satisfactory answer has been obtained.

Another important part of the researcher's function is to help interviewees to see what their role is in the interview process. The interviewee's role is to give fulsome answers, to provide more depth when probing questions are asked, to reflect and to think, and to raise issues they see as relevant but which are not directly asked about. By using open questioning techniques, demonstrating interest and actively encouraging the interviewee to talk, the researcher is intimating to participants that their role involves opening up and talking as opposed to giving simple answers. It is quite usual for people to start anticipating follow-up questions like 'why?' and start supplying the information without prompting. Participants also need to make judgements about whether to include a subject not yet raised by the researcher or about how much detail to give. The researcher helps them to make those judgements by providing a clear articulation of the objectives of the research, and by asking questions which can clearly be seen to relate to those objectives.

Asking questions to achieve breadth and depth

The aim of the in-depth interview is to achieve both breadth of coverage across key issues, and depth of coverage within each. A number of writers describe different types of questions which are used to achieve this (Kvale, 1996; Rubin and Rubin, 1995; Spradley, 1979).

A distinction can be made between content mapping and content mining questions. Content mapping questions are designed to open up the research territory and to identify the dimensions or issues that are relevant to the participant. Content mining questions are designed to explore the detail which lies within each dimension, to access the meaning it holds for the interviewee, and to generate an in-depth understanding from the interviewee's point of view. Any interview involves a combination of these question types and they are not confined to distinct parts of the interview. A content mapping question is asked to raise issues; content mining questions are used to explore them in detail; content mapping questions are used to raise further issues, and so on.

Both types, but particularly content mining questions, also involve probes. Probes are responsive, follow-up questions designed to elicit more information, description, explanation and so on. They are usually verbal, but non-verbal probes – such as a pause, a gesture, a raised eyebrow – are also highly effective. In content mapping questions, probes are used to help in mapping out the territory; in content mining questions, they are the essential tool through which depth is achieved.

Content mapping questions

There are a number of types of content mapping questions.

GROUND MAPPING QUESTIONS
Ground mapping questions are the first questions asked to 'open up' a subject. They are generally widely framed questions designed to encourage spontaneity and to allow the interviewee to raise the issues that are most relevant to them. With, at this stage, minimal probing, they will often generate a rich list of dimensions which will need to be followed up.

> ➢ Have you ever applied for a benefit?
> – No, I haven't, I wouldn't want to.
> ➢ Why is that?

- I've always managed to be self-sufficient all my life and I couldn't bear to ask for money I wasn't entitled to.
- ➢ What makes you say you are not entitled to it?
- Well, I haven't paid towards it at all so I am not really entitled to anything, am I? I would feel very uncomfortable. It would feel like I was having to accept charity.

DIMENSION MAPPING QUESTIONS

Dimension mapping questions are used to focus the participant a little more narrowly on particular topics or concepts: they are used to signpost, structure and direct the interview. They may be used, for example, to structure a participant's account of a process or experience, perhaps in broadly chronological order, where they may be as simple as 'What happened next?' Or, as in the example above, they would be used to focus on each of the dimensions or topics raised by the interviewee in response to the initial ground mapping question, encouraging the participant to talk about each in turn (self-sufficiency, entitlement, contribution, charity) and uncovering the elements that make up each concept. The researcher might refer directly to the fact that the participant mentioned, for example, 'managing to be self-sufficient' and ask what they meant. More detailed probes (see below) would then be used to ensure that each of the elements that makes up the interviewee's conception of self-sufficiency is explored in depth.

PERSPECTIVE-WIDENING QUESTIONS

To understand the interviewee's perspective fully, they need to have an opportunity to give more than their first thoughts on a subject. Encouraging them to look at issues from different perspectives will uncover more layers of meaning and greater richness. The third type of content mapping questions are therefore ones through which the researcher widens the interviewee's perspective, stimulates further thought or ensures comprehensive coverage.

They may be questions which invite the participant to consider dimensions or subtopics which the researcher wishes to hear explored, rather than ones which have been generated by the interviewee. These are sometimes described as 'prompts' – items to which the researcher explicitly directs the interviewee's attention rather than ones raised by the interviewee through more open questioning. Such questions need to be raised with a light touch, so that dimensions which are not of relevance to the participant are not given undue emphasis and the unique perspective of the participant lost.

- ➢ Are there any other factors that would influence your decision? I'm thinking of things like whether the client has a job, their family commitments and so on.

Perspective-widening questions might also involve stimulating thought by putting to the participant issues or perspectives that have emerged in earlier interviews or in other research. Again, it is important that this is done in a way which leaves the participant to answer freely:

> ➤ People talk a lot about the doctor–patient relationship. Do you see that as being relevant here?

A further technique involves checking out all sides of the interviewee's perspective, to ensure that the answer obtained is a comprehensive and fully rounded one – asking for other views or factors, encouraging them to think about positive as well as negative issues and so on.

> ➤ You've said you were delighted with it, but was there anything that fell short of your expectations?
> ➤ Are there other cases where your decision would be different?

Content mining questions

Content mining questions are the tools used for exploring what has been raised by the interviewee through different types of content mapping questions – obtaining a full description of phenomena, understanding what underpins the participant's attitude or behaviour and so on. Although some probes may have been called into play in content mapping, it is in content mining that they are used much more extensively. There are four broad groups: amplificatory, exploratory, explanatory and clarificatory.

AMPLIFICATORY PROBES
Participants rarely provide the level of depth of articulation that qualitative interviewing requires without further probing, and amplificatory probes are used to encourage them to elaborate further. They are important for obtaining full description and in-depth understanding of the manifestation or experience of a phenomenon.

Examples of amplificatory probes – each of which would be followed up with further probes until the researcher is satisfied there is nothing else to add – are:

> ➤ You said you have a very varied patient group. Can you tell me a little more about the types of patients you see?
> ➤ Can you give me an example of a case that was difficult in the way you've described?
> ➤ When you say he was on your side, what gave you that impression?
> ➤ What was it exactly that you liked about her manner?
> ➤ What was she saying or doing that made you feel she was ill-informed?

EXPLORATORY PROBES
A key role of qualitative research is to explore the views and feelings that underlie descriptions of behaviour, events or experience, and that help to show the meaning that experiences hold for interviewees:

> ➤ How did you respond when ...?
> ➤ What did you feel when ...?
> ➤ Why did you think it was important to ...?

Exploring impacts, effects and consequences also helps to illuminate experiences and behaviours, and to create a more rounded understanding of them:

> ➤ What effect did that have on you?
> ➤ Did that help you in any way?
> ➤ How did your approach change when you found that out?

EXPLANATORY PROBES

One of the hallmarks of the in-depth interview is probing for reasons – asking 'why?' Explanations are repeatedly sought for views, feelings, behaviours, events, decisions and so on. There is often an initial reluctance to do this among new researchers since it seems to be contravening social norms, to be impolite, to do so. Nevertheless it is fundamentally important for the researcher to understand the reasons for a participant's views and behaviours. Explanations are often multi-layered, and it is a key value of qualitative interviewing that responsive, iterative probing can uncover these layers. Where a simple 'Why?' feels too bald, there are a number of ways of softening the question:

> ➤ What was it that made her go up in your estimation?
> ➤ What makes you say that?
> ➤ What was it about the case that made you decide to ...?

CLARIFICATORY PROBES

Exploring issues in depth requires a high degree of precision and clarity. Clarificatory probes are therefore important, and used in different ways:

- *To clarify terms and explore language.* It is all too easy to assume the researcher understands the meaning of terms used by the interviewee. But exploring the language used will often show that the assumptions differed from the interviewee's reality, and will add real depth and richness to the researcher's understanding of the interviewee's perspective. It is therefore important to be alert to the use of emotive or descriptive words. In some cases, it is sufficient to repeat the word in the interrogative: 'Dodgy?' Other examples of probes to clarify language are:

  > ➤ How was it scary?
  > ➤ Could you just explain what you mean by it being a classic case of ...?
  > ➤ You said it was really special to see your granddaughter for the first time. In what way was it really special?

- *To clarify details, sequences etc.* There will be points in any interview where details, dates or sequences need to be clarified – whether someone is talking about the same colleague or a different one, whether they saw the solicitor before they began mediation or only after, whether descriptions of a client's manner related to the same encounter or to different meetings, and so on.

- *Clarifying through testing an expressed position.* Asking clarifying questions which gently challenge or test the participant's account, without being confrontational, can encourage them to elaborate further:

  > You said you were resigned to it, but did you *ever* think about leaving?
  > Some people might have thought about leaving at that point. Did those sorts of feelings ever come into it for you?

- *Challenging inconsistency.* Finally, it is also important to be alert to conflicts or inconsistencies in the interviewee's account. These may arise because an issue that involves social norms is being addressed and the interviewee is gradually gaining confidence to express their real view. Or they may occur where someone is being encouraged to think about something for the first time so that their view is developing as they speak. Again, it is important to find a non-confrontational way of drawing the participant's attention to inconsistency or contradiction, and asking them to clarify:

  > Earlier you were saying that you were delighted with how the project went but you've also said quite a lot about what didn't go so well. What are the main feelings you're left with?
  > You began by saying that disability means not being able to do things physically, but you've just been talking about it as being what *other people* stop you from doing. Is it always both those things equally, or do you sometimes see it as one more than the other?

In-depth, iterative probing

Probes are not meant to be used in isolation. It is not sufficient to move on to the next point having asked just one probe ('why', for example). The response to that probe will then require another, and so on. This will reveal a whole mine of information around the particular point that would otherwise remain unexplored, and probing needs to continue until the researcher feels they have reached saturation, a full understanding of the participant's perspective.

This kind of iterative probing involves asking for a level of clarification and detail that can sometimes feel unnatural or artificial. It goes far beyond what is usual in everyday conversation. The researcher is putting aside their own knowledge and their own intuitive understanding, and asking for explanations of things they might think they comprehend. But this is essential to achieve the depth of understanding that is the aim of qualitative research. Questions which may feel obvious or banal, or even ridiculous, can reveal a layer of complexity or detail that the researcher would otherwise have missed. They can if necessary be prefaced by a phrase which recognises that an unusual level of clarification is being sought, such as:

> ➤ This may sound like an obvious question, but why …?'
> ➤ I just want to make sure I've really understood you. What was it exactly that …?'

Good probing is a little like detective work. The researcher is alert to clues that they have not yet heard the full answer, that something does not quite 'ring true' or 'add up', that the interviewee may be rationalising after the event, or giving what they perceive as the 'correct' answer. For example, an interviewee talking about reasons for not taking up physical activity may refer to lack of time. The researcher may have a hunch that time is not the only barrier to physical activity and may, through careful probing, elicit that other factors are also at work:

> – really don't have any time to do any sort of activity except walking to the bus stop on my way to work. I'd love to if I could, I really would. But I don't finish work till after 6 and then I have to help my wife with the three children. I am also a school governor which takes up a lot of my time.
> ➤ What sort of things do you do at weekends?
> – Well, there is the shopping and then I have to mow the lawn and generally look after the garden and ferry the kids around, take them to friends, swimming, you know.
> ➤ Do you go swimming with them?
> – No. I have a couple of times but I don't usually.
> ➤ Why is that?
> – I suppose if I'm honest I am really quite lazy physically and I have never much cared for swimming or any other kind of sport.

With further probing, it transpires that the interviewee's aversion to physical exercise dates back to being teased about his physical aptitude at school.

Question formulation

Using broad and narrow questions

It is often said that good in-depth interviewing involves open questions. These are contrasted with dichotomous yes/no questions which call for affirmation rather than description (Patton, 2002). Certainly, in-depth interviewing does not involve a series of yes/no questions, and researchers have to work hard to ask questions which encourage a fulsome response. Although short, open questions look deceptively easy, they are much harder to implement in practice. Asking closed questions is a habitual aspect of ordinary social intercourse and one has to make a conscious effort to think in an 'open' way in an interview. For example, rather than asking 'So did you then make an appointment to see your doctor?', a question like 'What happened next?' would allow the interviewee to mention all the actions they took, their discussions with other people and their feelings, as well as whether they did indeed make an appointment to see their doctor.

However, to suggest that in-depth interviewing involves only open questions is to understate the specificity that good interviewing requires. Both content mapping and content mining involve asking questions which vary in terms of how broad or narrow they are. For example, content mapping as we have described involves very wide questions to map the territory or a dimension. But it might involve asking whether a particular motivation or view was relevant – a question which could be answered by a simple 'yes' or 'no', and which would then need further probing. Content mining, similarly, primarily involves broad and open questions but may also require narrow questions. In fact, understanding the interviewee's perspective in depth can require a high degree of specificity. For example, in a study looking at impacts of a welfare to work programme it would be essential to know whether someone was looking for work before they used the service, and whether they were doing so after, as well as understanding broader issues like their feelings about work, the meaning work holds for them, and their perceptions of barriers or difficulties.

Closed questions can also play a role in controlling the interview process. They are useful, for example, where the participant's answer is straying from the question and the researcher needs them to focus on the particular topic. They are also helpful where a participant is extremely voluble and the researcher needs to structure their response by asking narrower questions to ensure an issue is discussed in the detail required.

Avoiding leading questions

The researcher's questions in an in-depth interview are designed to yield a full answer: they are not intended to influence the answer itself. However, it is all too easy to ask a question that suggests a possible answer to the interviewee, such as 'Were you furious when he said that?' or – even worse – 'You must have been furious when he said that.'

A much better version of the question, which allows the participant to supply the response and will reveal what they actually felt, would be:

➢ How did you react when he said that?

The participant is then free to supply whatever responses he or she chooses. In this case, possible responses might be:

– I was shattered
– Oh, I didn't take any notice of him
– I hit him and threw him out of the house

If necessary, a question which might seem to invite a particular response can be 'neutralised' by adding 'or not?':

➢ Would you like to have done that, or not?

Asking clear questions

The most effective questions are those that are short and clear, leaving the interviewee with no uncertainty about the sort of information sought. There are various pitfalls to avoid here. First, it is sometimes tempting to preface a question – perhaps to make it seem less intrusive if it covers a delicate issue, or to link it with something said earlier by the participant, or to explain how the question was prompted by the researcher's understanding of the subject. Although some explanation will occasionally be necessary to clarify the relevance of the question, preambles can easily become so convoluted that the question itself gets lost or obscured. Where this temptation arises, the most effective solution is usually to 'think simple' and ask the question in as straightforward a way as possible.

Double questions too should be avoided. In the heat of the moment, it is very easy to ask two questions in one: 'How old were you when that happened and what effect did it have on you?' This is a relatively simple example of a double question. However, where they are more complex it becomes very confusing for the participant to remember or to answer both halves. People's inclination is generally to answer the easier part, and the one that would generate richer data will be lost. It is much more effective to ask one question at a time, follow it up with whatever probes are appropriate, and then ask the next question.

Third, it is important to avoid questions that are too abstract or theorised. The most effective questions are those to which the interviewee can relate directly and which are clearly pertinent to their own views or circumstances. Although the researcher's question may derive from their understanding of relevant social theory, it is important to find a way of translating it into a simple, concrete question phrased in everyday language. It is, paradoxically, these questions that are most likely to generate the rich data that actually further theoretical understanding (Kvale, 1996).

Finally, it is important to be sensitive to the language and terminology used by people, and to 'mirror' it as far as possible. Using official or bureaucratic language where someone has used more colloquial language can set up a barrier which might impede the interview process. It is also, of course, important to explore the specific terms used by people where this might shed light on their underlying perceptions, values or attitudes.

Further techniques for achieving depth

As well as the ways in which questions are asked, there are some further techniques that are central to achieving depth of coverage.

Listening and remembering

A fundamental principle of in-depth interviewing is to listen. This does not just mean listening to the words but really trying to hear the meaning of what the participant is saying, understanding where there is a subtext that needs to be explored, and hearing the nuances in the participant's account. Indeed, Herbert and Irene Rubin subtitled their 1995 book on qualitative interviewing: *The Art of Hearing Data*. The interactive nature of the in-depth interview means that the researcher's next question should be determined by the interviewee's answer, not determined in advance. It is important to find a way of clearing one's mind of plans for conducting the rest of the interview and concerns about how things are going, to listen really acutely. Although it may seem a passive role, listening is in fact an active part of interviewing (Hammersley and Atkinson, 1995), and it is listening to which a good interviewer's energies and attention will be most directed.

One of the spin-offs from really hearing what someone is saying is that it helps the interviewer remember points that need to be followed up at a later stage in the interview. One response from an interviewee may trigger four or five points to probe in the researcher's mind. However, a swift decision has to be taken about the immediate issue that needs to be followed up. In such cases, the researcher should make a mental note to return to the other issues raised, either once they have dealt with the immediate issue or later in the interview when they are dealing with a relevant topic:

> Can I take you back to something you said earlier ...
> You said earlier that you felt embarrassed about ... why was that?

Facilitating the relationship with the participant

The importance of the researcher establishing an effective working relationship with the participant has already been stressed. The following are some of the ways in which the researcher can assist the relationship during the interview:

EXPRESSING INTEREST AND ATTENTION
This is achieved by maintaining eye contact with the interviewee, giving the odd smile and the occasional nod designed to express attention (not approval), and by asking follow-up questions which demonstrate that the researcher has heard what has been said and wants to know more. These are signals to the participant to continue giving full answers and that what they are saying is relevant and valuable.

ESTABLISHING THAT THERE ARE NO RIGHT
OR WRONG ANSWERS
It is sometimes useful to say this at the start of the interview, but it is important to convey it throughout the interview through a non-judgemental

manner. It also means not correcting mistakes or misunderstandings. A participant may be misinformed about their entitlement to a particular social security benefit, for example, or about the designated procedure for assessing a claimant's eligibility. Rather than correcting them and running the risk that they would feel foolish and clam up, the researcher's task is to find out how they formed this impression and what its consequences were.

BEING SENSITIVE TO TONE OF VOICE AND BODY LANGUAGE

People often convey their state of mind through their tone of voice, manner or body language. The researcher should be constantly receptive to these clues. So, for example, if the interviewee sounds doubtful about a view, this should act as a signal to the researcher to explore further. This might involve simply allowing them to continue talking, or asking whether they have other views or experiences, or saying 'you look (or sound) a little doubtful' and giving them an opportunity to reflect or clarify further.

Body language and speech patterns can be important clues that there is more depth to be found. They also add a context and flavour to the interview that a researcher may feel has enriched their understanding during the interview – for example, where a participant was particularly emphatic about a point, or seemed angry or frustrated. But this context will be lost if it is not verbalised and explained, and thus captured in the recording. The researcher needs to ensure the underlying feeling is made explicit, and then explained, for example by saying 'You sound very certain about that – what makes you so certain?', or 'You look a little uncomfortable as you're talking – why is that?' These emotional contexts can also be usefully recorded in fieldnotes (see Chapter 5) although this is no substitute for directly addressing it in the interview, since the researcher's interpretation of it may simply be wrong.

ALLOWING THE PARTICIPANT TIME TO REPLY

In an in-depth interview, people are asked to think and give views about issues that are not necessarily top of mind for them. They require time to think about a particular point and then formulate their response. It can be tempting for interviewers to fill these pauses with explanation or supplementary questions. However, moments of silence in in-depth interviews are usually very productive and it pays dividends for the research if the interviewer can hold the pause until the participant is ready to speak. Contemplative silences or those that indicate the participant is thinking should never be filled.

PACING THE INTERVIEW

It is important to ensure that sufficient time is allowed to cover all the topics on the topic guide. If it seems that extra time may be needed, this should be negotiated with the participant as early as possible.

HANDLING EXTRANEOUS INFORMATION

Depending on the sampling and selection methods (see Chapter 4), the researcher may have fairly detailed information about the participant relating to the subject matter. This information may be of some use in preparing for the interview, although it is important not to over-plan since additional – or contradictory – information may emerge during the course of the interview. But it is usually more effective for the dynamic of the interview to approach the subject fresh with the participant, rather than to introduce information that has not come from the interview.

A different approach might be appropriate if someone has already taken part in a survey interview as part of the same research programme, which has generated detailed factual information. Here, it may be appropriate to refer to and check the information known, to avoid undue repetition. This would be less useful, however, in relation to information about attitudes or feelings collected by the survey, where approaching these issues fresh in the in-depth interview would be more likely to unlock the detailed account required.

Turning assumptions and interventions into questions

The aim of an in-depth interview is to obtain as full and unbiased an account as possible of the participant's perspective on the research topic, and the researcher's task is to use every means at their disposal to aid this. Assumptions, comments or other interventions can inhibit the interview process, and such reactions should be turned into a question.

- *Never assume.* It is easy to assume an understanding of what someone means by the terms they use, but it is surprising how often the assumption turns out to be incorrect when the interviewee is given an opportunity to explain what they mean. Similarly, it is essential not to assume that the reason for a particular course of action or belief is clear, or that it can be implied from what has already been said. It is surprising how often what seems clear takes on a deeper and richer meaning – or sometimes an altogether different meaning – when the interviewee is asked for a little more explanation. A very useful rule of interviewing is to turn an assumption into a question.
- *Refrain from commenting on an answer.* While it may be thought to help in establishing rapport, commenting on an answer by saying for example 'that's interesting', can introduce an element of judgement into the interview and interrupt the flow, inhibiting active listening and probing.
- *Refrain from summarising the interviewee's answer.* Summarising what people have said is rarely helpful. It is difficult to capture the full meaning relayed by the participant in a short summary, and attempts to do so may seem glib or patronising to the participant. The likelihood is that the summary will be partial or inaccurate, which will not aid the interview.

Summarising also prevents the interview moving on, halting the flow when a better response would be a question which seeks more depth, such as asking the participant to explain further or to give an example. If it seems important for the researcher to check that they have understood a response, they should do so in the form of a question which makes it easy for the interviewee to provide further clarification:

> ➢ Can I just check that I have got this right? Is what you are saying ...? Have I understood that right or have I missed something?

- *Refrain from finishing off an answer.* It is important to avoid 'putting words into the interviewee's mouth', however tempting it may be to finish off their answer. It is always better to allow them time to finish, asking a further question if this will help them to make their point, or gently pointing out that they have left a sentence unfinished. For example:

> – I felt angry, you know, really –'
> ➢ You felt really –?

> – There are lots of factors I take into account in deciding what sort of financial settlement might be appropriate: Each party's needs, their resources, the length of the marriage –'
> ➢ Are there any other factors?

- *Avoid extraneous remarks.* Extraneous remarks such as 'Right', 'okay', 'yes' or 'I see' can encourage the participant to close down, to see what they have already said as sufficient. They are sometimes used by nervous interviewers as a prelude to moving to a new question, where a follow-up question is actually what is required. For example, if a participant said: 'It isn't really up to me to decide where we go on holiday', a nervous interviewer might say: 'Oh right. So where did you last go on holiday?' A more relaxed researcher will find out who does take the decision, why this is, and how the participant feels about it. Prefacing questions with 'And' or 'So' is another habit of new and nervous interviewers, but it results in a tone which is less spontaneneous and relaxed.

Neutrality and avoidance of self-disclosure

As noted earlier, a key area where different theoretical perspectives on interviewing are manifested is the issue of how far the researcher should enter into a two-way exchange with the participant, giving information or views as well as seeking them.

Rubin and Rubin (1995) stress that qualitative interviewers should aim to achieve empathy without becoming over-involved. They must learn to empathise with different points of view, and if this is unacceptable to them they may need to draw boundaries around the kind of research they undertake. Retaining an objective and neutral approach may be particularly challenging if a researcher is personally drawn to or involved in their research subject. But considering how these challenges might arise and how they might be met is an essential part of their preparation for fieldwork. While complete objectivity and neutrality may ultimately be a chimera, it is important to be vigilant in striving for balance in interviews.

If the participant expresses a view with which the researcher strongly agrees or disagrees, their task is always to find out what underpins the participant's view rather than to express their own or to enter into debate. Even views or comments which are offensive to the researcher should be explored. This is undeniably difficult if the researcher feels that to let a view go unchallenged might be seen to imply collusion with it. However, a question such as 'How did you come to that view?' or 'Why do you see it that way?' is a useful vehicle for exploring unattractive views in a way that avoids collusion and challenges the assumption that the view is widely held or shared by the researcher. This is likely to be a more effective strategy than a direct challenge. Equally, it is important for the researcher to remain detached and calm where people use language or become emotional in ways which the researcher might find shocking or distressing.

People sometimes seek approval of their views, or of their actions, from researchers. Again, both favourable and adverse comments should be avoided. Neutrality is a more effective response, and more in keeping with the researcher's role as independent questioner rather than counsellor or adviser.

Since qualitative interviews are essentially aimed at encouraging participants to talk about their personal views and experiences, there is a debate in the research community about whether or not researchers should also disclose some details about themselves. Earlier writers on feminist approaches such as Graham (1984) and Oakley (1981) saw the interview as a reciprocal exchange in which the interviewer will show feelings because there is 'no intimacy without reciprocity' (Oakley, 1981: 49). Ann Oakley's research with women before and after they became mothers has been particularly influential. Her study involved four interviews with women before and after their child was born, and she was often present at the birth too. Perhaps understandably, given the intensity of the research and the experience it was exploring, she felt that the prevailing rhetoric of the researcher as a depersonalised extractor of data was wrong. She felt that not to answer women's questions, which often sought information about the medical or physiological aspects of childbirth but also asked about her, would be exploitative, and would inhibit rapport and be inconsistent with the way in which feminist researchers wanted to treat other women.

But answering questions and giving personal views or details is also problematic, and can inhibit the objective of obtaining a fulsome, open response which is as free as possible from the researcher's influence. For instance, a participant being interviewed about her use of childcare may ask whether the researcher has children. Indicating that she has may temporarily create a reciprocity or intimacy, but can also begin to hinder the participant's account. The participant may give less detailed responses on the grounds that the researcher 'knows what it's like'. It may colour their perceptions of the researcher and cause them to censor their own views or comments (did the researcher make different choices about work and childcare; do they spend more time with their children; might they disapprove of the choices made by the interviewee). The interviewee may want to maintain the intimacy by staying on common ground, reluctant to raise experiences or views they think the researcher may not share. Equally, for the researcher to disclose that she does not have children may create distance between them, perhaps making the interviewee reluctant to talk about more difficult aspects of parenting.

Once one question has been answered, it is difficult to avoid answering further questions and the researcher loses time that could be spent more valuably hearing from the participant. A better response would be to say that the researcher wants to focus on the participant and their experience during the interview, but to offer to answer questions – and to ensure the participant has the opportunity to ask them – once the interview has ended. Maintaining a warm and interested, but neutral, presence is certainly a delicate balance, and one that becomes harder where research is more intense or, as Oakley says 'where there is least social distance between the interviewer and interviewee' (1981: 55).

Responding to different interviewing situations

The interviewing situation is to a certain extent always a venture into the unknown in that it is impossible to predict the precise course the interview will take. Situations arise in the course of an interview which may require special handling on the part of the researcher. In some cases, the situation can be anticipated in advance. In others, it may suddenly present itself without warning.

Conducting sensitive interviews

Sensitive interviews come in two forms. First, the nature of the topic itself may be intrinsically sensitive. Obvious examples are topics relating to issues like sex, financial problems, bereavement, relationship breakdown or serious illness, which deal with very private and emotionally charged issues. The researcher can anticipate this in advance and be mentally prepared in various ways:

- It is helpful for researchers to remind themselves that the participant has consented to be interviewed on the subject, and the researcher therefore has permission to address it – sensitively and appropriately – unless that consent is withdrawn or comes into question.

- Reassurance about confidentiality at the outset of the interview will help to put the participant at ease about disclosing potentially sensitive information.
- Any unease or embarrassment on the part of the researcher will communicate itself to the participant and may make them reticent about discussing the topic. Even questions that appear to be somewhat intrusive or sensitive should be asked in a matter-of-fact way. Researchers will often be surprised at how willing people are to talk about sensitive subjects, and at how their own discomfort seems to be greater than that of the interviewee.
- It is helpful to acknowledge the sensitivity of the area and that the participant is being asked to bare their soul:

  ➢ I know this may be difficult for you, but how did you feel when you found out that you wouldn't be able to have children?

- As noted in Chapter 3, it is helpful to have details of local or national support groups or sources of information relevant to the research subject for people who may be distressed about their experiences. But the researcher should not step outside their role and become a counsellor or adviser.

The second type of sensitive interview arises where a topic that appears fairly innocuous becomes highly sensitive because some aspect of the discussion triggers a strong emotional response in the interviewee – perhaps because it raises a particular incident in someone's past that the researcher could not have anticipated. These situations draw on more general strategies for dealing with strong emotions in interviews, which the next section addresses.

RESPONDING TO EMOTION

Where a strong emotional response, such as anger, distress or embarrassment, occurs in the interview situation, the first signs are often expressed through facial expression, tone of voice or body language. At this stage the researcher should register the fact mentally but not interrupt the interviewee if they continue talking.

If the participant becomes very distressed or upset it is important to acknowledge this and respond appropriately:

- It is important to be guided by the participant as to what they are and are not willing to address. People may want to continue to talk about subjects even though they find them distressing. However, if this is not clear, consent to continue the interview, and to continue to cover the issue that prompted distress, needs to be reaffirmed by asking whether the participant is happy to continue with that topic.
- Even if a participant becomes tearful, they may want to continue. The researcher should not make this decision for them, but should check

whether they would like to take a break, and if so switch off recording equipment. However, if a participant is so distressed that they are unable to indicate whether or not they want to continue, the researcher should stop recording and give the interviewee a chance to recover before asking whether they want to continue.

- The interviewee's distress should be acknowledged by the researcher's body language – maintaining eye contact and communicating an empathetic willingness to listen – or by comments such as 'It sounds as if that was a difficult time for you' which indicate empathy but an interest in hearing more. More direct comments of sympathy that convey the researcher's own emotional reaction or feelings should be avoided.
- Whatever the researcher's own reaction to the situation, they should not display their own emotions during the interview but deal with them later.

In some cases, people may display anger and hostility. Here it is important to remain calm and not take the anger personally, to acknowledge that the interviewee has strong feelings about the topic and ask them to say more about it.

> It sounds as if that was something you felt very strongly about. Can you say a bit more about how it affected you?

It may be helpful to explain why the line of questioning is relevant to the research topic if this may not be clear to the interviewee. And, again, it may be necessary to reaffirm consent by checking whether the participant is willing to continue. The researcher should be prepared to move on to another topic, and should seek permission to return to it if necessary.

RESPONDING TO ANXIETY OR RETICENCE

Some people may seem particularly anxious about the interview, or reticent in their responses. If the researcher senses this before the interview begins, it is helpful to spend more time trying to put them at their ease by chatting generally before beginning the interview. Taking time over the introductory information about the nature and purpose of the study, confidentiality, and how the study findings will also be used will be particularly important. It should be stressed that there are no right and wrong answers and that the researcher is interested in everyone's views.

Strategies for addressing reticence or anxiety during the course of the interview include:

- spending more time on the opening subjects to give the participant an opportunity to feel more at ease
- spending more time earlier on more factual, concrete and descriptive topics before moving on to their feelings and emotions. Intangible or conceptual questions should also be left until the participant seems more at ease

- using very open questions that require more than a 'yes' or 'no' answer to encourage the interviewee to talk
- speaking clearly and calmly, ensuring that questions are clear and straightforward
- showing interest and attention and giving plenty of positive reinforcement by maintaining eye contact, nodding and smiling encouragement
- stressing that the researcher is interested in everything they have to say, even if it is something the interviewee has not thought about before
- acknowledging that other people have sometimes found it a difficult topic to talk about
- if necessary, stimulating ideas by referring to what other participants have said and asking for their view.

RESPONDING TO DOMINANCE OF THE INTERVIEW AGENDA

There is a delicate balance to be struck between allowing the participant to speak freely and raise issues of relevance to them, and ensuring that the key research issues are addressed. Getting this balance right becomes more difficult where a participant is particularly dominant. This may arise because they are in a position of authority and used to setting the agenda or see themselves as an expert in an area, or because for some other reason they find the interview situation difficult. Their behaviour may arise in a number of ways:

- Saying they have very little time: the time required for the interview should always be reaffirmed at the beginning of the interview. If this is very curtailed, the researcher will need to decide whether to focus on a few key topics only, or to try to rearrange the interview.
- Asking the researcher questions: questions about the conduct or purpose of the study should be answered by giving factual information but not entering into a discussion. But the researcher should be polite but firm about not answering questions about their own views, until the interview is over.
- Returning repeatedly to the same point: the importance of the point should be acknowledged, but the need to cover other subjects stressed.
- Answering the question of their choice rather than the one asked by the researcher: it is important to bring them back to the original question.
- Giving very brief answers or saying they have no view or relevant experience: this should not always be accepted at face value. The same question can be asked in different ways, or returned to later in the interview.

Again, it is helpful for researchers to remind themselves that the participant has agreed to be interviewed, and to persist with the interview.

RAMBLING RESPONSES

People sometimes ramble, become very repetitive, or get side-tracked by tangential issues when answering a question. The researcher's task is to try and bring the participant back on track. Ways of doing this without causing offence are:

- at the first available opportunity, to ask a question which re-routes them to a relevant point
- to use body language to indicate that the researcher wants to interrupt (leaning forward, beginning to voice a question, raising a hand slightly)
- to acknowledge that what they have said is important and has been noted – they may be returning repeatedly to a point because they feel it has been ignored
- if they continue to return to the same point, to move the interview on to a completely different part of the required subject matter, or to return to a relevant issue they raised earlier
- if necessary, to withdraw signs of encouragement and approval – removing eye contact, looking down at the topic guide and other ploys designed to indicate less than rapt attention
- to ask more direct, structured questions which give less scope for long replies, at least until the participant seems more willing to remain on relevant topics
- if they are digressing and talking about other people, to bring the topic back to themselves: 'what about you?'
- mentioning that time is moving on and that there are a few other topics that need to be addressed. Rambling responses are sometimes an indication of tiredness or loss of concentration on the participant's part, and saying that only a little more of their time is required or that there is one remaining issue for discussion will often reinvigorate them.

Every interview situation is unique, and every interview a step into unknown territory. What is important is to be alert to changes in the dynamic of the interview and in the participant's demeanour, to ponder what might be bringing about this change, and to shape the response accordingly. Addressing a dominant or rambling participant needs to be done with grace and humour, avoiding confrontation. The researcher needs to show their respect for the participant, but at the same time to respect their own right to carry out the interview so long as the participant consents.

Practical considerations

Scheduling appointments

The length of interviews will vary between studies, and between participants. It should not be constrained by the researcher, but should reflect how long the interviewee wants or needs to spend in the interview. Generally, at least an hour is required, but it will be difficult for both researcher and interviewee to concentrate if the interview lasts for more than two hours. In scheduling appointments, it is important to bear in mind the degree of mental concentration required to conduct qualitative interviews. It is important to allow time between interviews to assimilate what has been heard, to prepare for and travel to the next appointment, and to rest so the researcher feels calm and alert when he or she arrives. Allowance should be made in the work schedule for interviews starting late or over-running, and for participants asking questions or needing reassurance and an opportunity to come out of the research topic after the interview. In practice, this means it is rarely possible to carry out more than three interviews in a day – and even then only if long journeys are not involved.

It is not uncommon when interviewing professionals in particular to find that the agreed time is no longer available, and the researcher will need to decide whether to try to rearrange the appointment. As Chapter 5 noted, it is useful to consider which areas of the topic guide should be seen as key if time remains short.

Venues

The choice of venue for in-depth interviews is often left to the participant. It will usually be their home, or (if they are interviewed in their professional capacity) their workplace. But some participants may prefer to be interviewed away from their personal surroundings, and researchers need to be willing to find another venue if this is what the participant wants. The environment needs to be conducive to concentration: private, quiet and physically comfortable. Researchers therefore have to develop strategies for adapting the environment for this purpose. It may be necessary to ask whether there is a space where the interview can be carried out without disturbing other household members, to ask for a radio or television to be turned off, and to ask whether a chair can be rearranged to allow interviewee and researcher to face each other comfortably with recording equipment appropriately positioned. In professional interviews, it is helpful if telephones can be directed to another extension or to voicemail to avoid interruption.

Recording

It is highly desirable to audio-record the interview and for the researcher to take few if any notes during the interview. This allows the researcher to devote his or her full attention to listening to the interviewee and probing in-depth. It provides an accurate, verbatim record of the interview, capturing the language used by the participant including their hesitations and tone in far more detail than would ever be possible with note-taking. Audio-recording also becomes a more neutral and less intrusive way of recording the interview. Note-taking can give participants unintended cues – that they should slow down or pause if the researcher is writing; that they have said enough if the researcher is not. It is rare for participants to refuse to be taped so long as the researcher provides a clear, logical explanation about its value, reassures about confidentiality and explains what happens to tapes and transcripts.

Being comfortable with the operation of recording equipment, checking it works before and immediately after the interview, and having spare tapes and batteries on hand is essential.

Other people attending the interview

There are times when it is helpful for two members of the research team to attend an interview, particularly at the beginning of fieldwork when it allows the interviewing strategies and the topic guide to be reviewed (see Chapter 5) or for training purposes. The reason should be explained and the participant's consent sought when the appointment is made, and the second person's presence explained again at the beginning of the interview. If the second person is a representative of the funding organisation, this should be made clear: confidentiality will need to be stressed. It is generally more effective for the interview to be conducted largely by one researcher only, with the second invited to ask further questions at specific points or at the end of the interview. It is difficult to develop a line of questioning and to probe in depth if the interviewing role is being shared, and dealing with two interviewers at once can become confusing for the participant. More than one additional person would be intrusive to the interviewing relationship.

Overall, being interviewed provides what is likely to be, for many people, an unusual experience in which someone else is dedicated to listening to them, encouraging them to reflect and speak freely, and reinforcing the value and worth of what they have to say. People seem generally to find some satisfaction in the experience – they are sometimes surprised at how much they had to say, and they are very receptive to the idea of being interviewed again where studies involve a longitudinal element. The end of the interview is not the time to ask for reflections or feedback on the process, unless this is specifically relevant to the interview (for example, if part of the purpose of the study was to explore how far a very sensitive issue can be pursued). This can otherwise feel to the interviewee like a request for reassurance for the researcher. But there is a dearth of research into what the experience of being interviewed is really like for participants, and this subject merits much more investigation.

Finally, a well-conducted interview will seem a very precious thing to the researcher. They will feel privileged to have been given access to the participant's social world, to their meanings and experiences. That richness will be a joy when they move on to analysis. But a poor interview, with issues only half explored, will be a hindrance, and even the finest analysis will not be able to retrieve it.

KEY POINTS

- There are a number of different theoretical perspectives on in-depth interviewing, and different types of interview. But the features which are broadly consistent across research models are their flexible and interactive nature, their ability to achieve depth, the generative nature of the data and the fact that it is captured in its natural form.
- In-depth interviewing calls for a diverse and challenging range of qualities in researchers. A key skill is the ability to listen and to hear, but their role as facilitator is an active rather than a passive one.
- Achieving breadth and depth involves asking a combination of content mapping questions (to map territory and identify the component elements of dimensions) and content mining questions (to explore them in detail). Both types of question, especially the latter, require probing questions of which there are a range of types. Clear, non-leading questions are key. Dichotomous questions are of little value, but to suggest that only open questions have a role is to understate the specificity that good in-depth interviewing achieves.
- Assumptions, extraneous comments and a temptation to summarise should all be turned into questions. An empathetic but neutral stance is required, and sharing personal information during the interview can hinder the in-depth interview process.
- Any topic can raise sensitive issues or strong emotions. There are a range of strategies for dealing with these, but recognition and acknowledgement of the participant's reactions are key.

KEY TERMS

Probes are responsive questions asked to find out more about what has been raised. Their aim is always to obtain greater clarity, detail or depth of understanding – for example to elicit further description, an example, an explanation, and so on. Their key feature is that they relate directly to what has already been said by the interviewee, often referring to the exact phrase or term that they have used. Probes are a crucial element of any in-depth interview.

Prompts are questions which come from the researcher rather than directly from what the interviewee has said. They are used where the researcher wants to ask the interviewee to reflect on something else – perhaps something raised in other interviews, or that the researcher thought might be relevant from their own reading or thinking.

Leading questions are those which could be perceived as indicating a preferred, expected or acceptable response, and should be avoided.

Open questions are questions which require more than a single word, or a handful of words to be answered. **Closed questions** are those which can be answered with a simple 'yes' or 'no'.

Reciprocity is the idea of researchers giving something back to those they interview by sharing their own views, experiences, or reflections on what has been said. It is a feature of some approaches to feminist research in particular, but carries some cautions with it.

Further reading

Kvale, S. (1996) *InterViews: An Introduction to Qualitative Research Interviewing*, Thousand Oaks, CA: Sage

Lofland, J. and Lofland, L.H. (1995) *Analyzing Social Settings*, 3rd edition, Belmont, CA: Wadsworth

Rubin, H.J. and Rubin, I.S. (1995) *Qualitative Interviewing: The Art of Hearing Data*, Thousand Oaks, CA: Sage

Spradley, J. (1979) *The Ethnographic Interview*, New York: Holt, Reinhart & Winston

Thompson, P. (2000) *The Voice of the Past: Oral History*, 2nd edition, Oxford: Oxford University Press

7

Focus Groups

Helen Finch and Jane Lewis

The use of focus groups in social research increased considerably over the last two decades of the twentieth century. (We use the phrase 'group discussions' as being synonymous with focus groups, as we described in Chapter 2.) They originated among social scientists working in applied and academic research settings. Fontana and Frey (1993) trace the origins of focus groups back to the 1920s, when they were used mainly in the development of survey instruments. Paul Lazarsfeld and Robert Merton (Merton et al., 1956) adopted them in the 1940s and 1950s as an aid to the development of training and information materials, and Lazarsfeld originally used them for radio audience research (see Morgan, 1997).

Since the mid-twentieth century, focus groups developed as a research technique most strongly in market research (Bloor et al., 2001), where they have been used extensively for exploring issues such as brand images, packaging and product choice. They have also been adopted enthusiastically in political, and particularly party political, research. Their use here has perhaps been somewhat overenthusiastic, and they have sometimes been used and interpreted inappropriately, without due regard to their qualitative and group-based nature. But they are now well established as a mainstream method across the fields of social research, where they are widely used and are an extremely valuable research approach.

This chapter begins by exploring the unique features of focus groups, and describing different types of groups. We then look at the processes groups go through and the stages of conducting focus groups. We look at the techniques involved in handling discussion, and at how the group process can be harnessed to enrich data collection. Finally, we consider the context in which the discussion takes place, in terms of group size and composition, the physical environment and the organisation of focus groups. The chapter should be read in conjunction with earlier chapters, particularly Chapters 2 and 3 which distinguish the features and uses of focus groups from in-depth interviews. Much of the discussion in Chapter 5 (designing fieldwork strategies) and Chapter 6 (asking questions in in-depth interviews) will also be relevant.

Features and types of focus group

Key features of the focus group

The group context of focus groups creates a process which is in some important respects very different from an in-depth interview. Data are generated by interaction between group participants. Participants present their own views and experience, but they also hear from other people. They listen, reflect on what is said, and in the light of this consider their own standpoint further. Additional material is thus triggered in response to what they hear. Participants ask questions of each other, seek clarification, comment on what they have heard and prompt others to reveal more. As the discussion progresses (backwards and forwards, round and round the group), individual response becomes sharpened and refined, and moves to a deeper and more considered level.

A focus group is therefore not a collection of individual interviews with comments directed solely through the researcher. This is better described as a 'group interview', and lacks both the depth of individual interviews and the richness that comes with using the group process (Bloor et al., 2001; Bryman, 2001; Kitzinger and Barbour, 1999). Instead, focus groups are synergistic (Stewart and Shamdasi, 1990) in the sense that the group works together: the group interaction is explicitly used to generate data and insights (Morgan, 1997), as we describe below.

A further feature of focus groups is the spontaneity that arises from their stronger social context. In responding to each other, participants reveal more of their own frame of reference on the subject of study. The language they use, the emphasis they give and their general framework of understanding is more spontaneously on display. As all this emerges from discussion within the group, the perspective is less influenced by interaction with the researcher than it might be in a one-to-one interview. In a sense, the group participants take over some of the 'interviewing' role, and the researcher is at times more in the position of listening in.

> The focus group presents a more natural environment than that of the individual interview because participants are influencing and influenced by others – just as they are in real life. (Kreuger and Casey, 2000: 11)

This stronger social context offers an opportunity to see how ideas and language emerge in a more naturalistic setting than an in-depth interview, how they are shaped through conversation with others. It reflects the social constructions – normative influences, collective as well as individual self-identity, shared meanings – that are an important part of the way in which we perceive, experience and understand the world around us (Bloor et al., 2001). But this does not lessen the researcher's load: focus groups need to be carefully managed for this to happen.

> Focus groups are naturalistic rather than natural events and cannot and should not be left to chance and circumstance; their naturalism has to be carefully contrived by the researcher. (Bloor et al., 2001: 57)

Types of focus groups

Typically, focus groups involve around six to eight people who meet once, for a period of around an hour and a half to two hours. This format can be used for a wide range of population groups and research objectives. As with in-depth interviews, there will be variation in the extent to which discussion is structured, if the researcher has a strong sense of the issues to be explored; or flexible, allowing the group itself to shape the agenda and the flow of discussion (see further Chapter 5). Chapter 3 also noted that group discussions can be used in combination with in-depth interviews, either before or after interviews, and with a different size and structure depending on their purpose within the overall research study.

There are further variations in the application of group-based discussion methods and the form that groups may take. Although focus groups generally meet just once, reconvened groups can be valuable when studies address issues that are intangible or unfamiliar to respondents. The group is reconvened perhaps a week or two after it first meets. The intervening period provides an opportunity for group members to reflect on what they have heard and for the issue to become more familiar to them. They may be asked to carry out tasks between the sessions (looking at materials, keeping a diary, discussing the issues raised with others) to aid this process.

Some group discussion settings may take the form of a workshop, implying a larger group, meeting for a longer session, with a more structured agenda involving specific tasks or activities, perhaps with small group work as well as the group coming together as a whole.

Since the last decade of the twentieth century there has been an emphasis on using research for consultative purposes, particularly as the shortcomings of traditional public consultation techniques (such as public meetings and written consultations) for reaching all social groups were recognised. This led to some innovations in the application of research methods, and particularly of group discussion methods.

For example, citizens' juries bring together groups of between 12 and 20 people who, over the course of several days, hear from 'witnesses', deliberate, and make recommendations about courses of action (Coote and Lanaghan, 1997; Davies et al., 1998; Stewart et al., 1994; White et al., 1999). Deliberative Polls (Fishkin, 1995) focus on measuring how views and attitudes change as the study group becomes better informed. They involve a baseline survey, followed by small group discussions and the opportunity to hear from expert panels over several days. The survey is repeated at the end of the deliberative session. Consultative panels have been conducted in different forms, and involve drawing people together in a series of sessions to deliberate and contribute to decision-making.

The common features of these methods are that they combine opportunities for accessing information with discussion and deliberation. Citizens' juries and consultative panels generally also require some sort of recommendation as an output. These new forms of groups are not without their difficulties. Making consultation accessible and attractive to people remains a challenge, particularly given the substantial commitment of time and thought required, and the validity of data is compromised if decisions or recommendations are forced by pressure of time or pressure to reach agreement. However, they are an interesting application of focus group research methods to decision-making, particularly useful in more unfamiliar, technical or complex areas where information provision is important.

Although group-based research usually involves a physical coming-together of participants this is not always the case. Nominal groups have been used for some time. Here, views are gathered from group members individually and collated and circulated for comment – the group may or may not meet at a later stage. The Delphi technique is a particular application of this. A panel of experts is asked individually to provide forecasts in a technical field, with their views summarised and circulated for iterative forecasting until consensus is reached (Stewart and Shamdasi, 1990; Barbour and Kitzinger, 1999).

Advances in technology are also leading to growing interest in virtual groups, where again participants do not physically meet. Teleconferencing technology allows telephone groups to be conducted, particularly with less mobile or particularly time-pressed populations. Online focus groups are also being used more (see Bloor et al., 2001). They may involve synchronous discussion, in which participants can log on at the same time and exchange views in real time, using online chat software. Alternatively, discussion may be asynchronous with people logging on to make comments as and when they want to. Clearly, here and in nominal groups the role of the researcher will be quite different from their moderation of a live group, an issue discussed by Bloor and colleagues.

Group-based research can, then, take many different forms. Although this chapter is primarily concerned with more typical forms, in which a small number of participants come together once only, it is important to consider whether other forms may be more appropriate, and how the techniques described below can be applied to other group contexts.

Group processes and the stages of a focus group

The group process

An understanding of group processes and models of small group behaviour is helpful to offer insight into what can happen in focus groups, and why. From this can be implied appropriate strategies to facilitate the group as it goes through different phases.

Based on an examination of studies of small groups, Tuckman (1965) in collaboration with Jenson (Tuckman and Jenson, 1977) identified five stages in small group development which demonstrate a sequence that groups tend to pass through. The model was based on examination of studies of small groups which were mainly therapy and training groups. However, it also resonates with the process of small groups assembled for research, and has proved valuable in informing moderation techniques (see Figure 7.1).

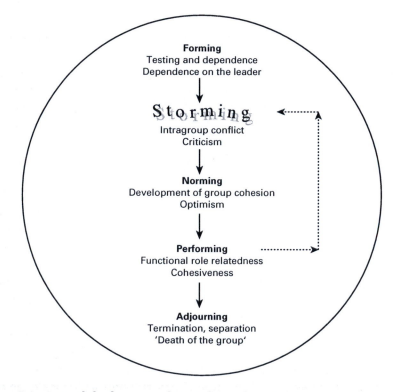

Figure 7.1 **A model of group phases (Based on: Tuckman and Jenson, 1977)**

In the 'forming' phase, individuals may be guarded, tense and anxious, and concerned about inclusion and acceptance. They tend to address comments solely to the moderator, not yet engaging with other group members. Occasionally, people respond to anxiety by overstatement, perhaps seeming confrontational or dismissive of the subject matter. In a group discussion, this is the stage at which background information is usefully collected so that participants are on familiar ground, introducing themselves to each other and beginning to get the measure of the researcher and the rest of the group. If substantial research topics are introduced in this phase it can be illuminating to see where people begin in addressing them, but it is important to bear in mind the possible influence of their uncertain feelings about the group environment on what they say.

'Storming' is a period of tension or criticism that may be shown up in a number of ways. It may be typified by dominance or one-upmanship from some individuals, by silent aloofness from others, or by the adoption of particular roles – the 'expert' perhaps – as a defensive position. Strong differences may emerge in this phase of the group which may provide useful material to return to, but these differences may diminish later as people express themselves with more complexity and subtlety. Again, it is important not to place too much reliance on strong statements made at this stage without reflecting on how the views expressed are articulated later in the discussion.

This is followed by the group settling down to a calmer phase of sharing, similarity and agreement, or 'norming', in which the norms of the group are established. The group begins to work cooperatively and may be particularly keen to find common ground, to agree with each other and to reinforce what others say. Participants may in this phase begin to put into practice the 'ground rules' that the researcher has set down (see below) – giving way to others, not speaking all at once. This is the stage at which social norms will be most influential, revealing what are seen as socially acceptable views or behaviours. These may be a valuable part of the research data although again it is important to reflect on how what is said compares with views expressed later, as group members gradually become more comfortable with the environment and feel able to express less normative views. But the researcher will need to find ways to prevent the 'norming' from masking attitudes and diversity (see below).

The 'performing' phase which follows finds the group working interactively in open discussion on the research issues. This is likely to be with energy, concentration, enjoyment and a less guarded stance, allowing both agreement and disagreement between participants. At this point the researcher can almost sit back, observe and listen, and let the group get on with the task in hand. The group will often return in a more reflective environment to points discussed earlier. They will be able to tackle the most challenging topics, working together with a synergy developing which achieves greater depth of insight. This is the most productive phase of the group process, but it takes time to reach it.

Finally, in the 'adjourning' phase, the group works towards ending. Participants may take the opportunity to reinforce something they have said earlier or to give their final thoughts. The researcher will thank them for what has been achieved. The group, or at least some members, may feel reluctant to leave – the stage is sometimes called 'mourning'.

The phases will be apparent by the mood and energy level of the group, indicated by both verbal and non-verbal behaviour. But as with all models, it does not always work out precisely like this in practice. Not all the phases will necessarily be discernible though it is likely that elements will be noted. Nor do the phases necessarily remain in this linear sequence, although it would probably be unhelpful to let the group move too far through the process without some 'norming'. There may be a circular process, with the group dynamic perhaps reverting back from 'performing' to 'storming' behaviour, for example on introduction of a new topic of discussion or a specific task. The essential point for the researcher, however, is to recognise that the phases are a normal part of the group process, to allow them to happen, to help them along, and to structure the discussion appropriately taking them into account.

The stages of a focus group

This section focuses on the stages that moderating a group discussion involves and the tasks for the researcher within each, reflecting the group development phases described above.

STAGE ONE: SCENE SETTING AND GROUND RULES
Management of the start of the session is of vital importance. Preparation on the part of the researcher for the handling of this stage can pre-empt difficulties later in the discussion. As participants arrive, the researcher thanks them warmly for coming, welcomes them and tries to put them at their ease by friendly conversation, avoiding the research topic. When the group is complete the researcher makes a more formal start to the session, with a personal introduction, outline of the research topic, and background information on the purpose of the study and its funder. Confidentiality is stressed, and an explanation is given of what will happen to the data and of proposals for reporting.

The researcher's introduction should not be too lengthy or too technical, but sufficient to reassure that this is a bona fide research study to which participants are invited to contribute. It should also emphasise points that may increase participants' motivation to take an active role in the discussion.

These might include more specific details on why the research is being undertaken or how it will be used; perhaps with emphasis on the opportunity that the forum provides for active consultation, or for involvement in decision-making.

The researcher also includes an indication of expected roles, and reassurance. It is explained that the session will be in the form of a discussion and that group participants should not wait to be invited before they step in. The researcher stresses that there are no right or wrong answers, that everyone's views are of interest, that the aim is to hear as many different thoughts as possible. They may add that there are likely to be different views or experiences among the group, and that people should feel free to say what they think, and if they agree or disagree with other participants' views, to say so. Explanation is given of the need to record the discussion in order to provide a full account of everything that is said. Participants are asked not to talk over each other. Depending on the subject area, it may also be helpful to ask the group to treat what other people say as confidential and not to be repeated outside the session. This will be particularly important if people know each other and are part of a wider network – colleagues or co-residents, for example.

At this stage, participants are likely to be feeling both curiosity and concern. Their unspoken fears – 'What's this all about?', 'Might there be a hidden agenda?', 'Might I be shown in an unfavourable light?' – need to be put to rest. The style and content of the introduction will need to be adapted to the type of people in the group though it will be necessary for all groups to take time over this important initial stage.

STAGE TWO: INDIVIDUAL INTRODUCTIONS

Switching on the tape recorder, the researcher asks the group to introduce themselves in turn by saying their names and giving other simple background information (items usually specified by the researcher – see Chapter 6). As each individual speaks, the researcher might decide to probe a little, to draw out a fuller response and begin to set the tone of an in-depth discussion.

These background points serve a number of purposes. They allow participants to introduce themselves to each other, beginning to build up a degree of familiarity. They provide a chance for each individual both to speak and to listen, to rehearse two roles essential in the process of discussion. The information provided by individual participants may be used by the researcher during the discussion, for example as part of a probe to draw people out or to ensure that what might be different perspectives are drawn in. They also serve to link a voice (and its spatial location) with a name and other personal characteristics, on the recording tape. This is useful in the transcription process, particularly in research studies that require individual response to be tracked as far as possible through the discussion.

The researcher jots down a spatial diagram of participants' names (and perhaps brief background details) as the individual introductions proceed, for their own use as an *aide-mémoire* to refer to throughout. For some groups, name-cards or badges can be useful, if participants are accustomed to this rather more formal set-up.

When the personal introductions are complete, the researcher may choose to make a brief comment about the composition of the group as a whole. They may highlight differences that have just been revealed, pointing out the benefit of this for contrasting views and experiences in the forthcoming discussion. Or they may note similarities, particularly as a prelude to exploring a sensitive issue in depth. This can reinforce the feeling of now being 'a group' and one in which all the group members are included, whatever their situation.

STAGE THREE: THE OPENING TOPIC

After the individual introductions, the researcher starts off the general discussion by introducing the opening topic. This may be something fairly neutral, general and easy to talk about, or it may be a more conceptual or definitional issue about which group members' spontaneous thoughts are sought (see Chapter 5).

The researcher's aim at this point is to promote discussion and to use the opening topic to engage as many of the participants as possible. At first their response may be faltering, between silences, perhaps with just one or two people speaking, directing their comments to the researcher. Or one individual may speak at length about their own personal views or situation; or a spirited discussion may start straightaway, spanning a range of topics.

The researcher continues to be verbally active, asking further questions (or rephrasing the same question) around the particular topic and enquiring generally about other people's views to open out the response. It is beneficial to get everyone to say something at this early stage in the group, as an individual's silence can become harder for them to break as the group proceeds and they feel more and more left out. Widening the discussion at this early stage also helps to wean off dependence on the researcher. But it can take time before individuals respond to each other rather than referring their comments directly to the researcher. The researcher encourages group interaction by allowing short silences to invite thought, or draws links between issues that different people have raised, perhaps highlighting differences and similarities in views. Non-verbal cues are also employed, for example maintaining eye contact around the group, leaning forward in an interested fashion, and perhaps gesturing with hands in a manner to invite the group to continue.

Issues will be raised early in this initial discussion that relate to key topics requiring full debate – indeed sometimes it can seem as if the entire topic guide has been covered within the first five minutes. The researcher might interject if this occurs, noting the points made, and explain that this important issue is something to return to later for fuller discussion. Or the researcher might judge that it would now be appropriate to select one of the issues mentioned and move the discussion on to it.

STAGE FOUR: DISCUSSION

At this point, following initial discussion, the researcher new to group discussions may feel things are getting out of control. Now what? Their role is one of juggling: balancing the need to promote group interaction against the need for some individual detail, and the value of free-flowing debate against the need for coverage of specified topics.

Through active listening and observation, the researcher will keep a mental note of what is being said and will probe both the group as a whole and individual members, using open questions expressed in simple language. The researcher listens to the terms used by respondents, explores their meaning to respondents and mirrors that language in formulating further questions or comments. It will be necessary to direct the flow over other relevant topic areas if they are not raised spontaneously by the group, and to keep the discussion broadly focused on the research subject. At the same time, attempts are made to include everyone and to balance the contributions of individual members, and the group process is engaged to generate new insights and thoughts. All these tasks are described in more detail in the sections which follow. The discussion will generally be lively at this stage, but if there are short silences it is best to avoid the temptation to fill them. Holding back usually means that someone in the group will take responsibility for keeping the discussion going.

STAGE FIVE: ENDING THE DISCUSSION

The final topic will have been decided in advance, with an eye to how it fits in with the overall shape of the discussion and group developmental phases. It is advisable to try to finish on a positive and completed note, as with individual interviews – for example covering ideas or suggestions about what might be done to improve a situation, following a discussion about problems (Chapter 5). This is particularly important if emotionally difficult material has been raised during the discussion.

Attention needs to be paid to pacing the end of the discussion in order to allow time for the group to prepare for it and to avoid too abrupt a finish. The researcher therefore signals its approach, for example with mention of 'the final topic', and finally, with questions that enquire about '– anything else to say before we finish?' or '– anything we've left out, or that people feel they haven't had a chance to say?'

Finally, the researcher ends the discussion and thanks the group, stressing how helpful the discussion has been. In some studies it may be advisable to reaffirm confidentiality, especially if sensitive issues have been covered, and to reiterate the purpose of the research and how it will be used. The researcher should be prepared to stay awhile after the tape recorder has been switched off. People often seem to enjoy the experience of a group discussion and, having become part of it, can be reluctant to leave.

Conducting the discussion

An overview of the researcher's role

The researcher uses the group process to encourage open, interactive discussion, but also controls it to bring everyone in, prevent dominance, and steer the group away from irrelevant areas. Yet the process in which the researcher is engaged remains one of gathering information on a specific topic of enquiry. The role of the researcher in relation to a focus group is therefore something of a hybrid. Partly it involves the role of a moderator with its connotations of restraint, as one who 'restrains or presides over a meeting'; partly it involves the role of a facilitator, as one who 'makes easy' or 'assists the progress of' a process. This section describes the techniques used by researchers in conducting the discussion, and the following section looks at some further strategies for making effective use of the group process.

The necessary level of researcher interventions will vary between groups, and will depend on both the dynamic in an individual group and the nature of the research subject, particularly how much interest it holds for participants. Some groups are taciturn and unforthcoming (just as some individual respondents are) and require the researcher to maintain a more verbal presence: questioning, probing and drawing out. Others are lively. It is as if the group is the respondent.

The researcher's role is critical to the success of the group discussion. It requires energy and can be demanding and challenging. The sort of people who are good at it are able to relate well in groups and possess qualities to put people at ease, though the skills are able to be learned and come with practice. Many of the skills are those that are required for in-depth interviews (see Chapter 6), but also important are adaptability, confidence, the ability to project oneself in positive ways to encourage the group, and a combination of assertiveness and tact.

Flexibility or structure: controlling the discussion

How much the researcher needs to intervene to structure the discussion will depend partly on the type of research study. It will be necessary to impose some structure to ensure that issues are covered, but the balance between imposed structure and flexibility of discussion, in which the issues are generated from within the group, will vary between different studies (see Chapters 3 and 5).

The researcher's aim is to allow as much relevant discussion as possible to be generated from within the group while at the same time ensuring that the aims of the research are met. There is more scope in a focus group than in an individual interview for spontaneous emergence of issues, prompted by the variety of different people's contributions. This means that discussion is further removed from researchers' directions and led more by respondents. The way participants introduce topics is itself interesting and revealing – it is more 'grounded', or 'naturally occurring'.

The researcher will therefore remain as non-directive as possible but will nevertheless be pacing the debate to ensure that all the key issues are covered as fully as possible (though not necessarily in a predesignated order) within the allotted time. This will involve deciding when to move on to another topic; making a mental note of issues that arise early and which will need to covered later in more depth; keeping the discussion relevant and focused; and choosing when to allow more free-ranging discussion with minimal intervention, and when to use silence as a means of promoting further reflection and debate. All of this becomes easier for the researcher when the subject matter and the way groups relate to it becomes more familiar, after the initial groups of the study have been conducted.

It is not uncommon for a group discussion to divert into irrelevant tangents, and this happens more easily than in in-depth interviews. At times the researcher will therefore need to steer it back by reminding the group of the topic, if it meanders too far into less relevant territory. For example, participants may dwell on an alternative topic, one that they would perhaps prefer to discuss, or they may relate repeated and lengthy anecdotes. Some tangential discussion will be inevitable, and necessary as it may contain nuggets of new information. It should therefore not be cut off too abruptly. But because time is limited, decisions will need to be made by the researcher about what is and is not relevant and when to move on.

Introducing a question linked to the relevant subject area will help to steer the discussion back. It may be necessary to draw attention to the fact that talk has veered away, and perhaps to remind people of the purpose of the research. A gentle touch, humour and perhaps an apology can be helpful here.

Probing for fuller response

As in individual interviews, the researcher probes to ensure issues are covered in depth. The aim is to clarify, to delve deeper and to cover all angles, rather than accepting an answer at its face value. Group members also play a part in this, questioning each other, but an additional purpose in probing in a group is to open out discussion and widen the range of response. A distinction between probing of the group as a whole rather than of individuals within the group therefore needs to be borne in mind. It is likely that both types of interventions will be needed, though too much of the latter can interrupt the flow of discussion. After probing an individual's comment if this is needed to understand it fully, the group researcher would then open out the discussion. There are a number of ways of doing this:

- asking generally 'How do other people feel?' or 'What does everyone else think?'
- repeating the question, or a fragment of it
- highlighting a particular comment that has been said and asking for thoughts on it
- asking the group directly, 'Can you say a bit more about that?'
- looking around or gesturing to the rest of the group to come in
- maintaining an expectant silence, to allow the group time to reflect further on the issue
- highlighting differences in views and encouraging the group to discuss and explain them.

Noting non-verbal language

Throughout the discussion, the researcher will be alert to group participants' body language. This important communication, additional to their verbal response, is noteworthy from two points of view. First, it adds views or emphasis relating to the discussion topic. People will often demonstrate their agreement or disagreement by nodding or shaking their head, or by utterances which may not be picked up by the person who transcribes the tape. They need to be encouraged to verbalise these indications of view – otherwise episodes of unanimity or strong agreement, which the researcher notes clearly at the time, are lost from the data. The researcher may, for example, say 'Everyone's nodding vigorously – why is that?' or 'You've all gone rather quiet! Why is this subject harder to talk about?' Secondly, body language provides an indicator of participants' feelings relating to the group process at any particular time. The researcher can see who is trying to inter-ject, who is looking worried or lost, who is looking bored – and from this discern an appropriate way to bring them into the discussion.

Controlling the balance between individual contributions

CREATING SPACE FOR EVERYONE TO CONTRIBUTE
Part of the researcher's role is to ensure that every participant gets a chance to contribute to the debate. While it is unlikely that each individual will con-tribute equally, there will at times be a need to exert a degree of restraint or of encouragement, and to some extent to 'orchestrate' the flow of contribu-tions. This can involve addressing dominance from one or more participants,

reticence from others, or simultaneous over-talk within the group (see further below). Like the conductor of an orchestra, the researcher's use of non-verbal communication will be significant here, often with powerful effect. In facilitating the discussion, the role of the researcher is quite physical, far more so than in one-to-one interviews. Their body language – facial expression, glance, gesture and body posture for example – can often pre-empt the need for verbal intervention to control the balance between participants.

It can be tempting for the researcher to intervene too soon. By holding back awhile the group participants may regulate the balance themselves. It depends which phase the group is in. One individual's overbearing manner, or another's lengthy silence, may be a characteristic of the 'storming' phase of the group for example, which in time will probably settle down. Only later might the researcher need to take action, proceeding from indirect to increasingly direct means of addressing the problem if it persists, in ways described below. Until then, the maintenance of eye contact with each individual around the group will probably suffice, together with general requests for new contributions to the discussion.

ADDRESSING DOMINANT PARTICIPANTS

There will be occasions when it is necessary to restrain the contributions of an individual participant if they are dominating the discussion – for example, always the first to respond to a question, or making very lengthy or repetitive comments. The other participants may become increasingly silent and perhaps begin to look directly at the researcher, implicitly appealing to them to step in.

The researcher could try a range of strategies, first finding indirect ways to shift attention away from the dominant participant so that others may speak, but adopting a direct approach if this is unsuccessful. Non-verbal attempts might include withdrawing eye contact from the dominant person; leaning away; looking at others in the group, and gesturing to others to speak. If this still has little effect, verbal interventions would similarly first be general, inviting others to speak ('Let's hear some other opinions'), before becoming more specific, requesting that they be given an opportunity ('It's helpful to have heard your experience but I want to hear from others too').

It is important to avoid a confrontation. The public nature of the group means that, perhaps more than in an in-depth interview, respondents may feel rebuked. The researcher might therefore take pains to emphasise the value of the dominant person's contribution but also the importance of hearing from all participants, perhaps employing humour in the exchange, or apologising for having to curtail a response.

DRAWING OUT RETICENT PARTICIPANTS

It can be difficult to judge the cause of a silent group member's reserve, although if possible the response would be tailored to this. The person may be naturally quiet, or lack confidence in groups, or perhaps be uncomfortable due to the group composition, feeling significantly different in some way from other participants (see further below). It could be that he or she is just not able to get a word in edgeways during a voluble discussion, particularly in larger groups. But reticent participants often have viewpoints or experiences that are perhaps different from the main and therefore of particular interest to the research.

People who are shy or anxious will be encouraged by the researcher's reassurance, to the group as a whole or specifically to them, that anything people have to say would be useful. But this may not be sufficient. Although it would be counterproductive to pressurise an individual to contribute, it will sometimes be necessary to take more active steps, initially in an indirect manner, to provide encouragement.

Eye contact alone can give confidence. The researcher could ask the group as a whole, though looking in the direction of the silent individual, for further thoughts or ideas, or could look expectantly in their direction during a pause in the discussion. It may be possible to link a specific question with something that is already known about the person, from the introduction perhaps or from anything else that they may have indicated so far, that would make the question relevant to them. For example, the researcher might ask 'What about people here who have children?' – remembering from the introduction that the silent person does indeed have children. In a more direct way, a question would be put to the silent individual: 'You haven't had a chance yet to say what you think' or 'How did your experience compare with what's been said so far?' Any questions posed in this situation would need to be open questions rather than ones that might elicit a mere 'yes' or 'no' or a factual response.

If, having tried these strategies several times, the person remains uncommunicative, the researcher might decide to leave matters as they are and focus instead on the other discussants, especially if the group is quite large in size. The researcher would continue to look encouragingly towards the silent member of the group from time to time and include them in questions addressed to the group as a whole, but not use more direct approaches to try to draw them in.

AVOIDING SIMULTANEOUS DIALOGUE

At times it can be necessary to stop group participants talking over each other, in order to distinguish different views on the recording tape and to allow time for everyone to express themselves. This might be done by addressing one individual among those talking and asking for their view, or by asking the group directly to stop so that *each* point of view can be heard. It can be sufficient to look very attentively at just one person who is talking, and simply pointing to the tape recorder can sometimes work. Whatever tactic is used, it is important to make time to return to the individuals who were silenced, to hear their views.

Focusing on participants' personal views

A particular type of behaviour that emerges more in group discussions than in in-depth interviews is avoidance of expressing personal views, and this can be a type of resistance or 'storming' behaviour. It might be easier for group respondents to take a more distant or second-hand standpoint, such as that read in the media for example, or to present views known to be politically acceptable, than risk expressing a personal view. The researcher needs to get the focus back on the participant by asking them directly what *they* think. A gentler approach is needed if a participant is referring to third parties to introduce subjects that have an element of taboo (talking about 'other people's' experience of debt or relationship violence, for example). Here, rather than asking that person directly about their own experience, the group as a whole could be asked whether they have personal experience of these issues.

Using the group process: some further strategies

A good focus group is more than the sum of its parts. The researcher harnesses the group process, encouraging the group to work together to generate more in-depth data based on interaction. This section looks at some further ways in which the group process can be used to stimulate new thinking and reflective discussion.

Encouraging in-depth exploration of emergent issues

The researcher helps the group to create a reflective environment in which the group can take an issue, approach it as they choose and explore it fully. It is important to allow time for this, and to let the discussion flow. But the researcher also needs to be actively helping the group to achieve greater depth, encouraging them to focus on emergent areas that they think will be illuminating to explore. The researcher does this by engaging with the substance of what is being said, probing for more detail and depth, sometimes reframing what is said, or asking the group to reflect on a different angle of it. In doing so the researcher tries to stay close to the data as it emerges and to encourage the group to build on what they have generated.

There are a number of useful approaches here:

- If a potentially interesting issue has been raised by one group member, the researcher may allow discussion to continue, seeing whether others will pick up on it.
- The researcher may decide to draw attention more directly to the point, asking for more comments on it or asking a specific question about it of the group.

- They may encourage the group to reflect on the links or relationships between what individual participants are saying. For example, if respondents have given examples of poor service, the researcher might ask what the examples have in common, whether they stem from the same causes.
- If divergent views are being expressed (for example about the priorities a service should address), the researcher may ask whether these are in conflict with each other or can be reconciled; or what the appropriate priority within or balance between them is; or why such differences of view arise.
- They may encourage respondents to focus on the implications or consequences of what has been raised in individual examples.

An example of this comes from a study of concepts and experiences of disability in which a series of groups were held with non-disabled people (as well as groups and in-depth interviews with disabled people) (Woodfield et al., 2002).

One group of non-disabled people began by describing their images of disabled people, focusing on serious, visible, physical conditions and particularly wheelchair users. The researcher commented on the fact that this is what they had raised, and asked whether they had other images. The group began to discuss mental health and intellectual impairments. People also mentioned temporary conditions and long-term illness. The researcher commented on how diverse these examples now were, and asked how useful the umbrella term of disability was. The group began to question the appropriateness of administrative definitions of disability (for example in relation to benefit entitlement) given the broader way in which they were now understanding it.

The researcher then asked what the different conditions that had now been mentioned had in common. This led to respondents raising concepts of 'otherness', 'difference', 'incompleteness'. They then commented that these concepts could also apply to sexual orientation, ethnicity and gender, and began to discuss how these issues linked with disability. Without further questions from the researcher, the group moved on to discuss how disability and other forms of 'otherness' are reinforced by society through discrimination. The researcher asked whether this process works differently for disability in any way, and they talked about discrimination being further entrenched through the physical inaccessibility of buildings and facilities. The group began to talk about legislation as the key to tackling discrimination and about the need to enforce physical access and employment rights through regulation. To return to the issue of the social construction of disability, the researcher asked whether the label 'disability' was meaningful or useful. The group talked about the way in which labels might impact on disabled people's self-image, and lead to reactions of pity among non-disabled people. This led several people in the group to a shared conclusion that social constructions and perceptions of disability are important, that wider social change is required and that legislation alone is not sufficient.

Having begun with images of wheelchairs, the group moved to a discussion of disability that was more layered. The researcher's questions sharpened the focus on different concepts or themes which emerged from the discussion. The resulting data was probably much richer than what would have emerged from in-depth interviews. With the researcher encouraging the group to work together and to build discussion from individual people's contributions, the group achieved more insight than they could have gained individually.

If the group is working well together they may deepen the commentary themselves, through asking questions of each other, reflecting and refining their own views, building on what others have said and developing more in-depth discussion of the issues that emerge. This happens when group members are really engaged with the research subject, and also if they are particularly articulate and informed about it. It may seem in these circumstances as if the researcher's interventions are relatively minor. However, the researcher will be making decisions all the time about what to probe to focus and deepen the discussion, and to include other participants or issues.

For example, in the study referred to in Chapter 5 which explored linkages between sexuality and homelessness among young lesbians and gay men (O'Connor and Molloy, 2001), group discussions with representatives of housing services were carried out after a series of in-depth interviews with young people. The groups were used to look at how organisations providing housing can respond to the needs of young lesbians and gay men, and key findings from the in-depth interviews were presented to the group. This, and the fact that participants were articulate and knowledgeable about the subject area, meant that the group largely carried itself through an in-depth discussion of a complex set of issues. The researchers probed to ensure that each issue was explored in detail, following up new points that emerged, and asking questions about the linkages between issues. The group began by discussing whether young gay and lesbian people could or should be housed together and moved through the following areas:

- the advantages and disadvantages of housing young lesbians and gay men together in designated housing, or making housing provision generic so that different groups live together
- the organisational difficulties involved in creating designated housing
- other ways of meeting young people's needs, such as housing lesbians and gay men in areas of towns where they are less likely to experience offensive treatment from neighbours
- questioning the assumption that lesbians and gay men are two groups that should be seen as similar, discussing how they differ and how sub-groups within each have specific and different needs (reflecting age, ethnicity etc.)
- how the individual circumstances of different young lesbians and gay men can make it difficult for them to make contact with housing services in the first place

- concluding by stressing the need for multiplicity in provision (of which designated and generic housing was just one part), for diversity in staffing, better outreach work, more effective networking between providers and better signposting of young people to specific providers who can meet their needs.

Although all these issues could have been raised by the researchers, the fact that they emerged from the internal reflections of the group made for a richer discussion, one in which the energy and ownership of the group, and the connections they made between different issues, was displayed.

Exploring diversity of view

The group context provides a key opportunity to explore difference and diversity. It is not only that differences will be displayed as the discussion progresses (and thus more immediately than across individual in-depth interviews). There is a particular opportunity in group discussions to delve into that diversity – to get the group to engage with it, explore the dimensions of difference, explain it, look at its causes and consequences.

   The diversity of views may be quite apparent, in which case the researcher can draw attention to it and ask why it has arisen, or what underlies it. But sometimes difference is more subtle, and people in the group agree with each other's positions or statements although they are actually inconsistent or contradictory. Here a little theatre may be required: the researcher can look puzzled, say they are confused, and ask the group to clarify things. This encourages the group to confront and acknowledge diversity and to refine what is being said in the light of it.

Challenging social norms and apparent consensus

A common criticism of focus groups is that the group exerts a pressure on its participants to conform to a socially acceptable viewpoint and not to talk about divergent views or experiences. As the discussion unfolds, the group participants may focus on their similarities or present just one side of the issue, or their contributions may reflect prevailing social norms. This can be linked to the dynamics in the group, and is a particular characteristic of the 'norming' phase (see above), though it could happen at any time throughout the discussion. The researcher needs to be alert to what is going on, and to find ways of challenging social norms and apparent consensus. There are a number of ways of approaching this:

- asking whether anyone has a different view, or deliberately drawing out an individual respondent who the researcher thinks may feel differently

- stressing that disagreement or difference in view is both acceptable and wanted. This would be said in the researcher's introduction (see above), but might be reiterated during the debate
- trying to find the boundaries of social norms by asking whether there are circumstances or situations under which the group would feel differently
- playing the role of devil's advocate, or challenging unanimity by presenting an alternative viewpoint (though taking care not to present this viewpoint as the researcher's own): 'Some people might say …' or 'So are you really all saying that you would *never* …'.

It can also be helpful to encourage the group to recognise and confront the normative view, and in doing so implying that other views are permitted. For example a study looking at public perceptions of the appropriate priority of first and subsequent families in the child support payment levels set out by the Child Support Agency (O'Connor and Kelly, 1998) involved group discussions with women whose partners had children from previous relationships. The group was stressing the importance of encouraging their partners to stay in touch with their children and to support their ex-partners, and suggesting that this was more important than providing for new partners and children. The researcher commented on how supportive they were all being, said that the Child Support Agency might be surprised by it, and asked whether that was how they always felt. The group began to acknowledge that their feelings were actually more complex and described occasions when they felt their partner had leant too far towards their first family. Some highlighted the particular circumstances that meant their partners were able to support the first family without compromising the second, and talked about how their views would change in other circumstances.

In practice, if the researcher is able to create an environment in which people feel safe and comfortable with speaking frankly, group-based research can be very effective for discussing topics which involve social norms. Once one person expresses an unusual or non-conformist view, others will often be emboldened to do the same, and there can be a more frank and open exchange than might happen in an individual interview.

Enabling and projective techniques

Finally, enabling and projective techniques – described in detail in Chapter 5 – can be used very effectively in group discussions. People respond well to them in a group, and they can seem less contrived than in an individual interview. The techniques help to focus discussion and to refine the formulation and expression of views. The material they generate can highlight variation in imagery and perspective, leading to fruitful discussion of similarities and differences and why they occur. The group process thus creates a particularly useful forum in which to use them.

Group composition and size

The size and composition of a group will be critical in shaping the group dynamic and determining how, and how well, the group process works. Features that are relevant here are the degree of heterogeneity or homogeneity within the group, existing relationships between group members, and the size of the group.

Heterogeneity versus homogeneity

As a general rule, some diversity in the composition of the group aids discussion, but too much can inhibit it. An element of diversity is like the grit in an oyster, important for the production of a pearl. Participants tend to feel safer with, and may prefer being with, others who share similar characteristics, but this does not necessarily make for the fullest discussion. Although it can facilitate disclosure, things can become too cosy and the researcher will need to work hard to tease out differences in views. Recognising their shared experience, participants can also assume that others know what they mean rather than articulate it fully.

Conversely, a very heterogeneous group can feel threatening to participants and can inhibit disclosure. If the group is too disparate, it is difficult to cover key topics in depth. In studies researching sensitive subjects, the shared experience of 'everyone in the same boat' is particularly important to facilitate disclosure and discussion. Sensitive topics therefore leave less scope for diversity, although some difference between group participants is nevertheless desirable. For example, in a study of women's decisions about terminating a pregnancy, it would be essential that a group involved only women who had had abortions. It would be advisable to have separate groups for younger and older women, and perhaps also for those who had already had children at the point when they made their decision and those who had not. But within these parameters, it would be helpful to construct the group to ensure some diversity in circumstances such as age, social class and relationship status, and experiences of different healthcare providers in the public and charity sector.

The ideal is therefore usually a point of balance between the two extremes of heterogeneity and homogeneity, with as much diversity as the group can take but no more.

As well as the sensitivity of the subject, three further issues need to be considered in weighing up the extent of diversity to build into group composition. First, it is usually necessary for respondents in each group to have broadly the same proximity to the research subject. There needs to be a degree of commonality in how they relate to the research topic – something similar in their experience of it or their connection with it. For example, in a study about attitudes to the environment it might be decided to exclude from some focus groups people who are active in environmental groups, since other group participants might hold back in discussing particular views or behaviours or may defer to them as 'experts'. A group discussion might usefully combine users and non-users of a particular service if the purpose was to discuss the various types of help or services people had used and the reasons for using different types. But if the particular service itself, and experiences of it, were to be a key topic, non-users would have little to contribute to significant parts of the discussion.

Second, the socio-demographic makeup of the group can influence how frank and fulsome discussion will be – particularly in relation to characteristics such as age, social class, educational attainment, gender and ethnicity. People are likely to feel more comfortable among others who they see as being from the same broad social milieu, and it is unhelpful if there are significant imbalances in social power or status within the group.

A third consideration is that it may be a specific requirement of the research to look at differences between subgroups within the sample (see further Chapter 3) – for example, differences between age groups, between people with and without children, or between current and past service users. Although this could be addressed in a focus group which cuts across these sample categories, too much diversity would make it difficult to see subgroupings among participants and to ensure that the differences are drawn out in the discussion. The influences of particular circumstances or experiences can sometimes be explored with more subtlety and insight if they are reflected in focus groups of different composition, with for example past and current service users, or people with and without children, involved in separate group discussions. Diversity in other characteristics represented within each focus group would still, however, be desirable.

Token representation should be avoided – for example, one man in a group which otherwise comprises women, or one person from a particular minority ethnic group. If one participant is markedly different from others in the group then any discomfort they feel is likely to influence how much they disclose. They may feel that their own experience is too remote from that of the other participants and remain silent, or they may resent the implication that they alone are expected to speak for the broad group they represent. For these reasons, at least three people would generally be required to represent a particular subgroup, characteristic or circumstance which is likely to be significant within the group's structure.

However carefully group composition is planned, it is not always possible to achieve the balance planned: not everyone who says they will attend will actually do so. The researcher will need to be alert to possible feelings of 'difference' and should make special efforts to include participants who might feel they do not belong.

Strangers, acquaintances and pre-existing groups

Focus groups are typically held with strangers as this facilitates both open questioning and disclosure. People often speak more freely in front of others who they do not know and whom they are unlikely to see again: there is little fear of subsequent gossip or repercussion.

However, groups with people who already know each other are also common. For example, the purpose of the study might be to investigate a work-related issue among colleagues, views about institutional accommodation among co-residents, or attitudes towards an activity among people who carry it out together. In these situations it can be beneficial to work with a pre-existing group.

Kitzinger and Barbour see pre-existing groups as generally very helpful:

> These are, after all, the networks in which people might normally discuss (or evade) the sorts of issues likely to be raised in the research session and the 'naturally occurring' group is one of the most important contexts in which ideas are formed and decisions made. (Kitzinger and Barbour, 1999: 8–9)

Pre-existing groups can trigger memories of shared situations and are valuable for exploring shared meanings and contexts such as how an organisation understands a policy objective and how this translates into practice, or how the use of illegal drugs within a group of friends is shaped by their shared values. They can also provide an atmosphere in which participants can feel safe enough to reveal shared subversive behaviour which might be unsayable in front of strangers.

However, there is a danger that shared assumptions mean issues are not fully elaborated because their meaning is taken for granted, or that the group norms dominate in the session. The researcher may have to work hard to move discussion into new territory. Certainly substantial differences in status between group members who know each other should be avoided – an important consideration particularly when research is carried out in people's workplace.

What is more difficult is where the researcher finds, unexpectedly, that some participants are acquainted. The researcher would then be on the lookout for shared views and assumptions and might need to probe particularly fully to draw out differences. If the researcher becomes aware of the relationship before the group begins, asking acquaintances not to sit next to each other during the discussion might also help.

Group size

Focus groups typically involve around six to eight participants, but the optimum group size will depend on a number of issues:

- *The amount that group participants are likely to have to say on the research topic.* If they are likely to be highly engaged with or interested in it, or particularly articulate, a smaller group is desirable (for example, among professionals discussing an aspect of their practice).

- *The sensitivity or complexity of the issue*. Sensitive or complex issues are better tackled in smaller groups.
- *The extent to which the researcher requires breadth or depth of data*. If breadth is key, for example to reveal quickly the range or diversity in opinions on an issue, a larger group will be more effective. If depth is critical, a smaller group is better.
- *The population group involved*. Some are likely to feel more comfortable in a smaller group, such as children or, conversely, older people. A smaller group is also more accessible to people with communication difficulties.
- *The structure and tasks involved in the session*. A workshop approach, with specific tasks and subgroup work, is more effective with larger numbers.

If the group is larger – above about eight participants – not everyone will be able to have their say to the same extent. With less opportunity to speak, active participation will be uneven. There are more likely to be some participants who say very little, and there is greater potential for subgroups to emerge which can be unhelpful for group dynamics. This can make things harder to manage for the researcher who will need to be more of an active presence in controlling the balance between contributions. It may result in a somewhat faltering discussion or one that remains at a superficial level. Identifying individual speakers' voices on the recording tape also becomes more difficult.

In groups that are smaller than about five or six, the researcher may similarly need to be more active, but in the sense of energising or challenging the group (in the way that other members might, if they were there). If the group is smaller because some people did not attend on the day, the composition of the group may be skewed away from what was originally planned, perhaps with just one individual representing a certain subgroup or characteristic. The researcher will need to be alert to this, and may also need to put across other points of view to stimulate discussion.

If the group is very small, with fewer than four participants, it can lose some of the qualities of being a group, particularly if there is a lot of difference between respondents. However, paired interviews and triads (see Chapters 2 and 3) can be an effective hybrid of in-depth interviews and group discussions, useful for example for in-depth discussion among colleagues or people who know each other well. Here, more commonality between participants is likely to be necessary to avoid the process becoming a collection of interviews.

Practicalities in organising the group

The organisational details of the focus group need to be sorted out at the planning stage of the study, and before potential participants are approached, since they may affect willingness to attend. Decisions will always be informed by the proposed composition of the group and by the subject matter of the discussion. Rather than prescribe general rules therefore, this section highlights a checklist of points to bear in mind (summarised in Box 7.1). The guiding principle behind these decisions is to organise a setting to which the specially selected group of people will be happy to come, in which they will feel sufficiently at ease to take part in discussion, and where the discussion can be adequately recorded.

BOX 7.1   ORGANISING A FOCUS GROUP: A CHECKLIST OF PRACTICALITIES

Timing
  Time of day
  Day of the week
  Time of year
  Number of groups per day

Venue
  Type of establishment (ethos)
  Building (access)
  Location (proximity, safety)
  Room (size, comfort, privacy, quiet, ambience)
  Availability of second room if needed
  Physical arrangement (seating, table)

'Hosting' the group
Management of:
  Transport/childcare
  Refreshments
  Incentives (cash, vouchers)
  Other people who come with participants

Observers and co-moderators
  Role
  Seating

Recording
  Quality of equipment
  Familiarisation
  Checking before and after group

Time and place

The time of day and day of the week when the potential participants are likely to be available to attend the group needs to be thought through in advance. Competing activities which could discourage attendance also need to be thought about (such as major sporting events) and certain times of year would be avoided – around Christmas or other peak holiday periods. Because it is not possible to suit everyone's timetable, especially for studies which involve mixed populations, the overall design of the study is likely to include group discussions at different times of day to accommodate a variety of schedules.

The researcher's own working schedule is a further factor to be taken into account. If more than one group per day is planned, sufficient time is required between each to allow for dispersal of the first group's participants, arrival of the next group, and for recovery time in between. It is rarely feasible to conduct more than two group discussions in succession per day unless they are very brief.

Choosing the venue involves thinking about its location and the type of place that it is: the type of establishment, building and immediate environment. The venue should be appropriate to the participants and to the subject of study in terms of its ambience or any likely associations that it may hold. For focus groups that are held with members of a pre-existing group, the venue may be the place where the group is already located and as such has the advantage of being familiar. Otherwise, options such as a hotel, a hired room within a pub or a community centre should be considered.

A further characteristic for consideration is the room in which the discussion takes place: its size, comfort and privacy. It is important to check out potential distractions such as background noise (as the group who competed with bell-ringing practice from a nearby church would testify). A second room may be necessary. If participants are accompanied by a family member or friend, these people would ideally wait outside the group room. It is also helpful to have a second room if two consecutive groups are scheduled, as a place where early arrivals for the second group can wait.

Provision at the discussion venue

The physical arrangement of the room needs to facilitate discussion, with chairs positioned in such a way that participants can all be seen by the researcher and can see each other – a circle or oval. A table in the middle of the group confers the practical advantage of a base on which to stand the tape recorder and refreshments and can also offer participants a feeling of psychological protection of sorts. It should be no larger than is necessary.

Simple refreshments, such as tea, coffee or other drinks are usually served before the discussion starts, as group members arrive. Although the researcher moderating the group may be able to perform this role, it is ideally undertaken by a second person, such as the person who recruited participants for the group, or a co-moderator or observer. This person acts as a host to welcome people, to serve refreshments, and deal with any incentives or arrangements for transport or childcare (see Chapter 3) that may have been agreed beforehand.

Co-moderation is useful if exercises or projective techniques are to be used, and in the early part of fieldwork to test and review fieldwork strategies and the topic guide (see Chapter 5). If more than one person is moderating the discussion, they would sit beside each other in the circle. It is generally more effective to agree in advance which researcher will be responsible for leading the discussion, or for each to take responsibility for different parts, to avoid confusion over the flow of questioning and discussion. Any observers would be outside the circle and out of eyeshot of the majority of the participants, for example in a corner of the room. Observers should be introduced at the start and should maintain an unobtrusive presence. Any written notes they make (for example about the dynamic of the group, issues to take to other groups, reflections on the topic guide) should be kept to a minimum.

Recording

A good quality tape recorder is essential, with a remote multidirectional microphone, and is far more important in focus groups than for individual in-depth interviews. Otherwise, sections of the discussion, or softer voices, or the contributions of people sitting further away from the microphone may be lost. The tape recorder is usually positioned adjacent to the researcher, with the microphone in the centre of the table. The researcher should be familiar and comfortable with its use (see Chapter 6). People starting out often find that their biggest disappointment is not the way the discussion went, but that their recording of it has failed because they were unfamiliar with the equipment.

Before the participants arrive it is essential to check that the tape recorder is functioning: that the recording level is appropriate, the batteries charged, tape inserted, and that a spare tape is to hand. After the discussion has ended, checks should be made as soon as possible that no technical problems have prevented recording.

Focus groups, to conclude, call on a wide range of expertise, from the practical organisational skills described in this section to the ability to put people at their ease, respond sensitively to group dynamics and create a sense of joint endeavour. But the skills come with experience, and with that experience researchers will find focus groups a research technique which is highly stimulating and can bring real insight.

KEY POINTS

- Focus groups are more than a collection of individual interviews. Data are generated by interaction between group participants. Participants' contributions are refined by what they hear others say, and the group is synergistic in the sense that it works together. The group setting aids spontaneity and creates a more naturalistic and socially contextualised environment.
- The researcher needs to be aware of the different phases through which groups can pass, and to make use of each. A useful model identifies five sequential phases: forming, storming, norming, performing and adjourning.
- The interaction between participants is important in determining the flow of discussion, but the researcher guides it, probing both the group as a whole and individuals, trying to ensure that everyone has their say, that the research issues are covered, that discussion stays on track, and picking up on body language. Group participants take on some of the interviewing role, asking questions of each other.
- The group process is harnessed to enrich the discussion. This involves making time for reflection and refinement of views; focusing on and reframing emergent issues to encourage the group to go deeper into them; highlighting diversity within the group and encouraging people to explore its dimensions and causes, and challenging apparent consensus where this is led by conformity to social norms.
- Diversity in group composition enriches the discussion, but there also needs to be some common ground between participants – based on how they relate to the research topic or their socio-demographic characteristics. The ideal group size will be affected by how much people will have to say, the sensitivity of the issue, the balance required between breadth and depth of coverage, and the participant population. The role of the researcher will vary in groups of different sizes and degrees of diversity.
- Practical arrangements are also key to the success of group discussions: the time, the venue, the layout of the room and the quality of recording equipment are all important.

KEY TERMS

Group dynamics refers to the relationships between group members which change during the course of the group and influence the energy and direction of the group. They are shaped by **processes** which may be evident in any small group and which vary depending on the **stage**

of the group, and are also influenced by the **composition** of the group, the subject matter, the broader environment and the behaviour of the researcher.

Non-verbal communication refers to the physical behaviour of the researcher or participants: their facial expression, where their gaze is directed, their hand gestures and their posture. It gives the researcher important clues as to the possible feelings of individual participants, and is a useful tool employed by the researcher to control the discussion.

Norms are behaviours or beliefs which are required, desired or designated as normal within a group, shared by that group or with which members believe they are expected to conform. It is important to be alert to the ways in which adherence to social norms within a group might inhibit disclosure and open discussion.

Further reading

Barbour, R. and Kitzinger, J. (eds) (1999) *Developing Focus Group Research: Politics, Theory and Practice*, London: Sage

Bloor, M., Frankland, J., Robson, K. and Thomas, M. (2001) *Focus Groups in Social Research*, London: Sage

Casey, M.A. and Kreuger, R.A. (2000) *Focus Groups: A Practical Guide for Applied Research*, 3rd edition, Thousand Oaks, CA: Sage

Morgan, D.K. (1997) *Focus Groups as Qualitative Research*, 2nd edition, Thousand Oaks, CA: Sage

Stewart, D.W. and Shamdasi, P.M. (1990) *Focus Groups: Theory and Practice*, Newbury Park, CA: Sage

8

Analysis: Practices, Principles and Processes

Liz Spencer, Jane Ritchie and William O'Connor

Analysis is a challenging and exciting stage of the qualitative research process. It requires a mix of creativity and systematic searching, a blend of inspiration and diligent detection. And although there will be a stage dedicated to analysis, the pathways to forming ideas to pursue, phenomena to capture, theories to test begins right at the start of a research study and ends while writing up the results. It is an inherent and ongoing part of qualitative research.

Until the latter part of the twentieth century, the analysis of qualitative data was a relatively neglected subject, both in the literature and in researchers' accounts of their methods. As a result, it was often hard to decipher what people had done with the rich, unwieldy and often tangled pile of data they held in the transcripts, fieldnotes and documentary evidence collected. At one level, it appeared an almost esoteric process, shrouded in intellectual mystery. At another, it appeared largely haphazard with discovery falling from the evidence as if somehow by chance. Either way, the processes that had occurred in carrying out qualitative analyses were largely obscure.

Fortunately, this has changed and there is now much better documentation of the different approaches to carrying out qualitative analysis that have developed. Nevertheless, while such accounts explain how to sift, label, order or even reduce qualitative data, many stop short of explaining how classification or explanation is achieved or how theories or hypotheses are generated. In other words, there is now much greater visibility about how qualitative data analysis is 'managed' but rather less about the intellectual processes involved in 'generating findings' from the evidence collected.

It is our aim to open the doors on such processes with two chapters devoted to analysis. This first chapter describes different approaches to, and practices of, analysis; the features that analytic methods need to hold for effective and penetrative investigation; and the stages and processes involved in analysis. In the following chapter we consider the forms of analyses that might be undertaken in a qualitative study, irrespective of the tool used to aid the analytic process. It displays the different levels and types of analysis that can occur and how these are developed and pursued. It is illustrated with a detailed description of one analytic method, Framework, showing how it is used to aid the analytic process through all its key stages.

Traditions and approaches within qualitative analysis

Unlike quantitative analysis, there are no clearly agreed rules or procedures for analysing qualitative data. Approaches to analysis vary in terms of basic epistemological assumptions about the nature of qualitative enquiry and the status of researchers' accounts (see Chapter 1). They also differ between different traditions in terms of the main focus and aims of the analytical process. These include:

- *ethnographic accounts* which are largely descriptive and which detail the way of life of particular individuals, groups or organisations (Hammersley and Atkinson, 1995; Lofland and Lofland, 1995)
- *life histories* which can be analysed as single narratives, as collections of stories around common themes, or quarried to construct an argument based on comparison between different accounts (Thompson, 2000)
- *narrative analysis* which identifies the basic story which is being told, focusing on the way an account or narrative is constructed, the intention of the teller and the nature of the audience as well as the meaning of the story or 'plot' (Riessman, 1993)
- *content analysis* in which both the content and context of documents are analysed: themes are identified, with the researcher focusing on the way the theme is treated or presented and the frequency of its occurrence. The analysis is then linked to 'outside variables' such as the gender and role of the contributor (Berelson, 1952; Robson, 2002)
- *conversation analysis* which focuses on the structure of conversation and classifies interaction in terms of key linguistic systems such as turn taking and adjacent pairs (Atkinson and Heritage, 1984; Silverman, 2000a)
- *discourse analysis* which is concerned with the way knowledge is produced within a particular discourse through the use of distinctive language (for example, legal discourse, medical discourse) or through the adoption of implicit theories in order to make sense of social action (for

example, poverty, power, gender relations). Discourse analysis may also focus on what is going on in an interaction in terms of performances, linguistic styles, rhetorical devices and ways in which talk and text set out to convince and compete with alternative accounts (Silverman, 2001; Tonkiss, 2000)

- *analytic induction* which aims to identify deterministic laws and the essential character of phenomena, involving an iterative process of defining a problem, formulating and testing an hypothesis, then reformulating the hypothesis or redefining the problem until all cases 'fit' the hypothesis (Robinson, 1951)
- *grounded theory* which involves the generation of analytical categories and their dimensions, and the identification of relationships between them. The process of data collection and conceptualisation continues until categories and relationships are 'saturated', that is new data do not add to the developing theory (Glaser and Strauss, 1967; Strauss and Corbin, 1998)
- *policy and evaluation analysis* where analysis is targeted towards providing 'answers' about the contexts for social policies and programmes and the effectiveness of their delivery and impact (Ritchie and Spencer, 1994).

Several writers have distinguished between analytical approaches according to their primary aims and focus. For example, Tesch (1990) claims that some approaches, such as conversation analysis, discourse analysis, symbolic interactionism and ethnomethodology focus on the use of language. Others adopt a descriptive or interpretative approach which aims to understand and report the views and culture of those being studied. Tesch includes life histories and classic ethnography in this latter category. A third category involves theory building, through such approaches as grounded theory, for which specific analytic approaches have been developed (see for example Strauss and Corbin, 1998)

Kvale (1996) identifies three different contexts of interpretation in qualitative analysis: self-understanding where the researcher attempts to formulate in condensed form what the participants themselves mean and understand; critical common sense understanding where the researcher uses general knowledge about the context of statements to place them in a wider arena; and theoretical understanding where the interpretation is placed in a broader theoretical perspective.

Distinctions are not always clear cut, however, and qualitative traditions, and indeed individual studies, often cross boundaries. For example, Bryman and Burgess (1994) have questioned Tesch's typology, arguing that theory building may be part of both language based and descriptive or interpretative approaches. Similarly, some writers would argue that there is no such thing as purely descriptive, a-theoretical analysis, since all description involves selection and interpretation of meaning according to implicit, informal theories-in-use (Hammersley and Atkinson, 1995; Mason, 2002; Williams, 1976).

Key features of different approaches

Approaches to qualitative analysis can usefully be compared and contrasted according to the way they address a number of different issues. These include:

THE STATUS OF THE DATA
Data may be treated as referring to and representing phenomena (in terms of feelings, perceptions, experiences or events) which exist apart from the data and the setting in which the data were captured or generated, and the analyst is concerned with the accuracy of the data and of his or her account. Alternatively, data (in terms of 'narrated', and 'situated' accounts) may be treated as *the* phenomena under study, in which case the analyst seeks to understand the way in which 'plausible accounts of the world' (Silverman, 2000b: 123) are constructed.

THE PRIMARY FOCUS OF ANALYSIS
While some analytical approaches, for example discourse analysis, conversation analysis, and some forms of narrative analysis, focus primarily on language, and the construction and *structure* of talk, text and interaction, others such as content analysis, grounded theory and policy analysis are mainly concerned with capturing and interpreting common sense, substantive meanings in the data.

THE WAY DATA ARE REDUCED
Qualitative data are usually voluminous, messy, unwieldy and discursive – 'an attractive nuisance' (Miles, 1979). They may take the form of extensive fieldnotes, hundreds or thousands of pages of transcripts from individual interviews or focus groups, documents, photographs or videos, and the researcher must find a way of getting a handle on the data. Consequently, data reduction is a central task in qualitative analysis, but one which is achieved in a number of different ways. It may involve paring down statements to their core meaning, as in phenomenological analysis; thematic summaries or précis of content, for example in descriptive accounts; collective analytical categorisation which subsumes a wide array of data under each category; identification of an overall structure in the data; or graphic displays of synthesised data as in the work of Miles and Huberman.

THE KINDS OF CONCEPTS GENERATED
A common procedure in the analysis of qualitative data is the identification of key themes, concepts or categories. The nature of these concepts, however, and the way in which they are generated varies a great deal between different approaches. Concepts may refer to the substantive meaning of the data, or to the structure of an account as in discourse or conversation analysis. Concepts also vary in their source and level of abstraction. While some

labels, known as 'in vivo' concepts, are based on the language and terms of those being studied, others are chosen by the researcher and may include common sense terms, terms influenced by the literature, or concepts devised by the researcher to capture the essence of talk and interaction. Some researchers argue that initial labels will, and should, be rather loosely defined and mundane, possibly using participants' own terms, or what Blumer (1954) termed 'sensitizing concepts' which give a general reference to empirical instances, later developing into more analytical, definitive concepts which 'refer precisely to what is common to a class of objects, by the aid of the clear definition of attributes or fixed bench marks' (1954: 7). By contrast, in some later versions of grounded theory, the aim is to develop and introduce more abstract and theoretical, albeit emergent, concepts at a very early stage of the analysis (Strauss and Corbin, 1998).

THE WAY CONCEPTS ARE APPLIED TO THE DATA

Labels and categories can be used to organise and analyse qualitative data in two main ways: cross-sectional 'code and retrieve' methods, and in situ, non-cross-sectional analysis (Mason, 2002). In cross-sectional code and retrieve methods, the researcher devises a common system of categories which is applied – manually or with a computer – across the whole data set and used as a means of searching for and retrieving chunks of labelled data. This approach is felt to offer a systematic overview of the scope of the data; to aid finding themes or examples which do not appear in an orderly way in the data; to aid locating conceptual, analytical categories in the data; and to help getting a handle on the data for making comparisons or connections.

Non-cross-sectional data organisation involves looking at particular parts of the data separately each of which may require a different conceptualisation of categories. This approach is seen by some to offer better opportunities than cross-sectional analysis to gain a sense of the distinctiveness of particular sections of the material; to understand complex narratives or processes; to organise the data around themes which do not appear in all parts of the data; and to identify overall structures within each case or interview. Mason (2002) cites case studies, narratives and biographies as examples where this type of approach is considered more appropriate. Also included within non-cross-sectional approaches are cross-referencing systems which do not segment text but enable the analyst to browse and create pathways through the data, mainly through the use of hypertext links available in computer software packages (Coffey and Atkinson, 1996; Hammersley and Atkinson, 1995). This approach is discussed later in this chapter where computer assisted methods of analysis are described.

THE EXTENT TO WHICH DATA ARE RETAINED IN CONTEXT

Approaches to qualitative data analysis vary in their treatment of context and in the importance they place on retaining links to the original data. Code and retrieve approaches discussed above are sometimes criticised for grouping and comparing chunks of data outside the context in which they occurred (Coffey and Atkinson, 1996). By contrast, some researchers positively commend the breaking up and reconstituting of data as the only way to further analytical understanding. Perhaps the most forceful proponent of this approach is Anselm Strauss who argues that coding: 'fractures the data, freeing the researcher from description and forcing interpretation to higher levels of abstraction' (1987: 55).

Richards and Richards (1994), however, are concerned about the way some forms of grounded theory treat data, maintaining that this type of analysis 'takes off' from the data, jettisoning them once they have informed the development and refinement of categories. They emphasise the importance of retaining links to the original data and revisiting them constantly as an integral part of the analysis process.

THE WAY 'ANALYSED' DATA ARE ACCESSED AND DISPLAYED

Researchers are not always explicit about how they view and access their data throughout the analytical process. Some appear to work directly from raw data or from annotated transcripts and fieldnotes, and one imagines them locked away, 'immersed' in their data until an interpretation emerges. With code and retrieve methods, the analyst views data in textual chunks which have been sorted according to category or theme or have been collated in relation to another category or variable. Some researchers write accounts of the way in which the data have been interrogated, categories have been developed and relationships between them noted. These accounts or memos are formally logged and viewed as part of the interpretative process. Finally, some researchers organise and display summarised and sorted data in diagrammatic form, in matrices or figures, in order to spot connections and interrelationships which are difficult to see in an ordinary text based format. (See Miles and Huberman, 1994, for an extensive discussion of this kind of data display.)

THE EXPLICIT LEVEL OF ABSTRACTION

Another way of differentiating between approaches is the level of abstraction at which the researcher chooses to operate and the extent to which she or he sets out to portray rich and descriptive detail, find patterns, develop typologies, offer 'local' explanations or consciously develop more general theory (Hammersley and Atkinson, 1995). While some researchers acknowledge the legitimacy of different levels of abstraction, and maintain that the type of analysis will depend on the nature of the research question and the purpose of the study (Mason, 1996: Patton, 2002), others are committed for epistemological reasons to different kinds of analytical output. For example, Whittemore and colleagues (1986) argue for narrative analytical methods which portray people's subjective experience, faithfully reflecting the way in which they give meaning to their lives, rather than 'pointillistic' and selective interpretations, or accounts which subordinate the reality of people's lives to the aim of wider generalisation. By contrast, other researchers argue for the primacy of wider inference and the generation of theory. For example, Strauss (1987) is critical of researchers who remain descriptive and just précis data under broad themes, dismissing this as careful journalism because the analysis is not taken through to abstract concepts and themes. Richards and Richards claim that 'The main task of qualitative research is always theory construction' (1994: 170), and Miles and Huberman maintain

> Just naming and classifying what is out there is usually not enough. We need to understand the patterns, the recurrences, the *whys*. As Kaplan (1964) remarks, the bedrock of inquiry is the researcher's quest for 'repeatable regularities'. (1994: 67 emphasis in original)

THE STATUS OF CATEGORIES AND THE LOGIC OF EXPLANATION

Qualitative researchers vary in their treatment of categories and the way in which they use them within an explanatory framework. Some writers treat – and refer to – categories derived from qualitative data as variables (Miles and Huberman, 1994; Robson, 2002). That is, they see certain categories as entities that can be uniformly conceptualised and captured in a way that will change in relation to other phenomena. Others are critical of this approach arguing that qualitative data cannot be reduced to such standardised categorisations. They also reject the notion of any causality in the sense of X leads to Y. They prefer instead to see categories as ways of grouping, displaying and discussing data thematically such that comparisons between conceptual content can be made or further lines of enquiry pursued. Yet others talk about using a quasi-variable approach in which certain variables (such as demographic characteristics) are used in combination with conceptual categories to investigate patterns within the data (Richards and Richards, 1994).

THE PLACE OF THE RESEARCHER IN THE ANALYTICAL ACCOUNT

Approaches also vary in the extent to which the analytic role of the researcher is considered as part of the evidence, with some accounts omitting or making only passing reference to the researcher and others treating the role of the researcher as an integral part of the interpretation offered. Mason outlines the implications of a reflexive approach:

> A reflexive reading will locate you as part of the data you have generated ... You will probably see yourself as inevitably and inextricably implicated in the data generation and interpretation processes, and you will therefore seek a reading of data which captures or expresses those relationships (2002: 149)

The discussion above has shown how approaches to qualitative analysis vary in terms of the ways data are used and analytic concepts constructed. There are also many different approaches to more practical issues surrounding data handling and management so that these processes can take place. Until the latter part of the twentieth century, all the methods used to do this were manually based involving a range of different 'tools' for organising and displaying raw or summarised data. These included 'scissors and paste' techniques, whereby the data were cut up and collated within broadly similar subject areas; 'mapping' methods where thematic or cognitive maps were made of linkages or constructions within the data; 'index cards' or 'document summary forms', ways of summarising 'whole' cases thematically; and matrices in which themes were retained in the context of cases and brought together within a two-way matrix. By the 1970s a number of qualitative analysts were developing computerised methods to carry out these tasks, either by using existing software or by developing specialist software for qualitative analysis. Because of the ever widening use of computer-assisted methods, the next section provides a brief account of their functions and the impact they have had on the way analysis is conducted.

Computer-assisted qualitative methods

There is much existing literature on computer-assisted methods for qualitative data analysis which charts the development of computer approaches (see Fielding and Lee, 1998; Kelle, 1997a; Tesch, 1990; Weitzman, 2000) and appraises the process and outputs they generate (see Barry, 1998; Burgess, 1995; Kelle, 1997a; Seale, 1999; Weitzman and Miles, 1995). The reader is strongly advised to refer to these texts for further detail; our purpose here is simply to highlight some of the main features of computer approaches and the debates that surround their use.

There have been several attempts within the literature to classify the different types of computer-assisted qualitative data analysis software or CAQDAS (a term coined by Fielding and Lee, 1991) that have come into existence since the early 1980s. The most notable are those constructed by Tesch (1990) and Weitzman and Miles (1995). However, rapid development in software used for qualitative data analysis, as well as progressions in the operating systems and environments of personal computers, have all but rendered these classifications outdated. Weitzman (2000) provides the most up-to-date categorisation of CAQDAS software, building upon earlier work with Miles (cited above), which categorises software into five types:

- *text retrievers* – which facilitate the searching of large amounts of data for instances of words or phrases
- *textbase managers* – data management packages which provide a structure to the data stored and are usually searchable in a similar way to text retrieval programs
- *code and retrieve programs* that allow you to label or 'tag' passages of text that can later be retrieved according to the codes applied

- *code based theory builders* which are recent additions to many code and retrieve programs. These support the conceptualisation of data by the analyst and may also have extended hyperlinking facilities which allow the analyst to create links between different aspects of the data set
- *conceptual network builders* – programs which facilitate the graphic display and investigation of conceptual, cognitive or semantic networks within a data set.

Others, such as Fielding and Lee (1998) support this classification but add that text retrievers or textbased managers are sometimes no more than generic software which has been adapted to suit the needs of the qualitative researcher (such as conventional word processing and spreadsheet/database programs), while the other three types of packages are usually designed specifically for the analysis of qualitative data. There is also software that cuts across this classification and some of the more popular CAQDAS packages like Nudist, Atlas/ti and WinMAX fulfil most or all of the functions described above.

Within existing literature, there is much emphasis placed on finding the 'right' package to suit the analytical task, rather than allowing the structures and processes of a particular piece of software to dictate how the researcher carries out qualitative analysis (Coffey et al., 1996). This is important because as Weitzman (2000) has claimed 'there is still no one best program'. He and other commentators (for example Burgess, 1995; Fielding and Lee, 1998) urge potential users to interrogate packages to see if they fit their approach to qualitative research before embarking upon their analytical journey. Weitzman and Miles (1995) suggest that the most important functions to investigate in a CAQDAS package are coding, memos or annotation, data linking, search and retrieval, concept/theory development, data display and graphic editing. Two other features deemed important by Weitzman and Miles are flexibility and user friendliness, qualities that cannot be under-estimated when encountering a new computer package.

There appears to be general agreement among commentators that the advent of CAQDAS methods has been beneficial to the analytical process, though not without reservation by some. Discussions continue in the literature and through cyberspace newsgroups about the general pros and cons of using computers for qualitative data analysis and about the merits of individual software packages. In comparison with manual methods, the main benefits are seen to be the speed that CAQDAS methods offer the analyst for handling large amounts of (textual) data; the improvements in rigour or consistency of approach; the facilitation of team research; the ability of computer software to assist with conceptualisation of data and theory building; and the relative ease of navigation and linking (or 'consolidation' (Weitzman, 2000)) of data.

Unfortunately, these benefits are seen by others with somewhat different epistemological assumptions to constitute the primary shortcomings of

CAQDAS methods. As Weitzman concludes 'the very ease, speed and power of the software have the potential to encourage ... the researcher to take shortcuts' (2000: 807–8). Initial reservations about *any* use of computers in qualitative data analysis (Hesse-Biber, 1995) have largely been replaced in more recent times by concern about the implications of different software types for analytical process and output. An example of this is Coffey and Atkinson's (1996) objection to the way some computer packages encourage tagging and retrieval of segments, removing them from their context. They suggest that there is a misguided view that coding and computing give a scientific gloss to the analytic process. They favour teasing out meaning within its context, or looking for the overall structure in the data, techniques that are used in discourse analysis or in the analysis of formal narrative structure. These and other researchers recommend an alternative use of computers to aid qualitative data analysis, namely the use of hypertext links which do not segment text, and permit the analyst to browse and create complex pathways through the data. Clearly, there is much of importance in these continuing debates and readers are referred to texts such as Coffey and Atkinson (1996) and Fielding and Lee (1998) for further discussion.

What appears to attract most agreement in the debates so far is the view that computer-assisted analysis software should not obviate the crucial role of the researcher within the analytical process. Concern is expressed about the dangers of assuming that CAQDAS software will provide data in a form that is ready for analytic commentary in the way that packages like SPSS, SAS and Quantime do for quantitative data (Weitzman, 2000) – particularly for those new to qualitative analysis research. This leads to warnings that 'using software cannot be a substitute for learning data analysis methods' (Weitzman, 2000: 805). Likewise, Coffey and Atkinson assert that:

> Coding data for use with computer programs and the retrieval of coded segments of text is not, in our view, analysis. At root, it is a way of organising data in order to search them ... qualitative research is not enhanced if researchers decide they will take their data and 'put it through the computer', as if that substituted for the intellectual work of analysis'. (1996: 172)

> None of the computer programs will perform automatic data analysis. They all depend on researchers defining for themselves what analytic issues are to be explored, what ideas are important and what modes of representation are most appropriate. (1996: 187)

Instead, Coffey and Atkinson argue that computer software is but an 'analytic support'. Others go so far as to reject the view that such software can in any way be seen to perform analysis. Kelle (1997b), for example, suggests that the role of the computer in the analytic process, though important, is sometimes 'overemphasised' and that rather than being viewed as tools for data analysis, CAQDAS packages are more appropriately described as 'software for data administration and archiving'.

The introduction of new software packages or new features for existing ones means that it is impossible to anticipate the way in which CAQDAS will affect the conduct of qualitative analysis in the future. At present, however, it seems that certain approaches to analysis are better supported by CAQDAS than others. As discussed above, cross-sectional code and retrieve methods are very well catered for, and some packages such as ETHNOGRAPH, Atlas/ti and WinNAX were specifically designed with grounded theory approaches in mind. The search functions in most CAQDAS packages are invaluable for content analysis, and the capacity to retrieve word strings in large data sets can assist discourse analysis. Those wishing to carry out certain forms of non-cross-sectional analysis can make use of hyperlinks to find connections and strands in the data which would be extremely difficult and time-consuming to do manually. On the other hand, few CAQDAS packages support analysis of the formal structure of narratives (Coffey and Atkinson, 1996; Seale, 2000), and are generally considered not worth setting up for very small data sets.

Debates about the impact and value of CAQDAS will no doubt continue as long as qualitative researchers employ and develop computer-assisted approaches to data analysis. It seems likely that the role of the computer will increase as technological advances are made and new packages emerge. This leads some to argue that manual methods of qualitative data analysis will soon be as extinct as slide rule calculations are in quantitative research (Fielding and Lee, 1998).

The key requirements of analytic tools

In order to carry out a robust analysis that allows all the different levels of investigation to be achieved, researchers need certain aids and tools at their disposal. Similarly, whatever method of analysis is chosen, certain features are necessary in order to produce a refined and complete synthesis and interpretation of the material collected. If it has been properly collected, the data will be rich in descriptive detail and full of explanatory evidence. But, almost inevitably, the data will be unwieldy and tangled in its raw form. The analyst therefore needs certain facilities not only to do full justice to the evidence collected but also to make the task one that is manageable within the resources and time scales that will be available.

It is important to note that in the remaining part of this chapter, we are describing principles and processes that are relevant to qualitative analyses concerned with understanding and interpreting substantive meanings. As described in the previous section, other forms of analysis, such as narrative analysis, discourse analysis and conversation analysis, may have a different focus, concerned primarily with the construction and structure of talk and interaction. Consequently, some of the features discussed would be applicable to such methods, others would be irrelevant or would be replaced with processes with a different analytic function.

As the previous discussion has indicated, many writers have emphasised the pivotal role that analysts themselves play in carrying out qualitative research analysis (see for example Coffey and Atkinson, 1996; Weitzman, 2000). It is the analyst's conceptual skills that will be needed to read, sift, order, synthesise and interpret the data. No methods of analysis or CAQDAS packages will replace these skills but are simply facilitative 'tools' to aid the analytic process.

Nevertheless, because of this, it is important that researchers choose a 'tool' or 'analytic support' that will help, not distract, them during their analytic searches. As already indicated, there are numerous methods to choose from but certain features are needed to maximise the potential of a full qualitative analysis. We select the following as important 'hallmarks' to look for in any system or method used to interrogate qualitative data:

- *Remains grounded in the data*: It is essential that the analytic ideas and concepts that are developed are rooted within the data, rather than simply superimposed. To achieve this, the method needs to provide a structure that allows emergent ideas, concepts and patterns to be captured and revisited. It is also vital to have quick and easy access to the original data at any stage of the analytic process.
- *Permits captured synthesis*: At some stage, the original data will need to be reduced from their raw form of verbatim text, observation notes, documentary evidence or whatever it may be. This reduction is an inherent and essential part of the analytic process, without which the analyst will not be able to make sense of the evidence. But it also needs to be carefully handled so that the original terms, thoughts and views of the study participants are not lost. It is therefore important that the synthesis is captured, partly to ensure that it can always be checked back against the original material but also to have a record of the conceptualisation or interpretation that is taking place.
- *Facilitates and displays ordering*: A similar point concerns the ordering, or sifting, of the evidence. Almost certainly, the data will not come in neat subject related packages – if they do, it would suggest that the data collection lacked the penetrative and exploratory questioning needed. So again, at some stage, the data will need to be organised and sorted so that they can be inspected in largely related blocks of subject matter.
- *Permits within and between case searches*: Part of the analytic process requires searching through the data set for defining characteristics, clusters, associations and so on. This means that the analyst has to be able to move through the whole data set quite easily so that the essential patterns can be found. This requires facilities for three different types of search

  - *thematic* categories and patterns *across* different cases
  - *associations* between phenomena *within one case*
  - *associations* in phenomena *between groups* of cases

The ways in which such searches are conducted are discussed in the next chapter. However, we would note here that this is a crucial feature to look for in any computer-assisted package. Too many code and retrieve packages fragment the data to the point that the overall narrative is lost and linkages between different aspects of an individual case or story are difficult or impossible to re-create.

- *Allows systematic and comprehensive coverage of the data set*: It is important to allow each unit of analysis (i.e. interview, group, observation, document etc.) to be given the same analytic 'treatment'. If they are not, then certain forms of analysis will be precluded. (For example, it is not possible to look for associations between groups if only part of the sample has been analysed in a particular way.) This means that the analysis undertaken needs to be systematically applied across the full data set. In the latter context, the only exceptions would be if a decision has been made *not* to analyse part of the data at all; or in certain forms of non-cross-sectional analysis where specific conceptual frameworks are being applied.
- *Permits flexibility*: New ideas, refinements, puzzles can occur at almost any stage of a qualitative analysis, almost up to the last page of a transcript or set of case notes. It is therefore important that the method of analysis allows some flexibility to add and amend features as it progresses.
- *Allows transparency to others*: It is increasingly the case that the content of qualitative analyses needs to be made accessible to people other than the main analyst. For example, it may be important to discuss the developing stages of an analysis with research colleagues or collaborators, supervisors or even funders. Similarly, there are occasions on which secondary analysis may be warranted, or a follow-up study is planned, where the workings of the original analysis need to be revisited. For such purposes, the method used needs to allow others to review the analytic building blocks as well as the final outputs.

All these features are desirable qualities to look for when choosing a 'tool' to aid the analytic process. All of them are required if the full potential of a qualitative data set is to be gained without disproportionate amounts of research time being spent. In the latter context it is important to emphasise that qualitative analysis is a very time-consuming process, whatever approach is used. Indeed, it is likely that the time and resources required to analyse a unit of data will far exceed those needed to generate the data in the first place. Resources are never unlimited and it is therefore important that the activities in which analysts are engaged are moving them towards an understanding and interpretation of the evidence.

BOX 8.1   THE ANALYTIC HIERARCHY

A depiction of the stages and processes involved in qualitative analysis

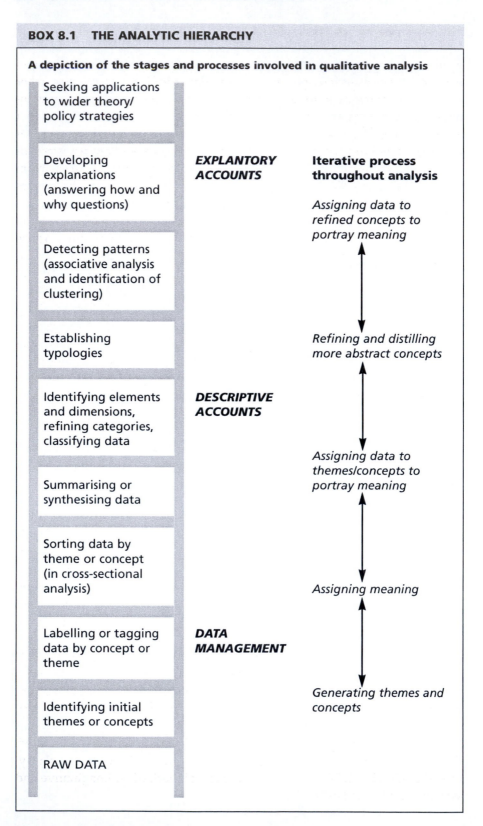

Seeking applications to wider theory/ policy strategies

Developing explanations (answering how and why questions)   **EXPLANTORY ACCOUNTS**

Detecting patterns (associative analysis and identification of clustering)

Establishing typologies

Identifying elements and dimensions, refining categories, classifying data   **DESCRIPTIVE ACCOUNTS**

Summarising or synthesising data

Sorting data by theme or concept (in cross-sectional analysis)

Labelling or tagging data by concept or theme   **DATA MANAGEMENT**

Identifying initial themes or concepts

RAW DATA

Iterative process throughout analysis

Assigning data to refined concepts to portray meaning

Refining and distilling more abstract concepts

Assigning data to themes/concepts to portray meaning

Assigning meaning

Generating themes and concepts

The analytic hierarchy

Whatever approach a researcher uses, there is a need to capture, portray and explain the social worlds of the people under study, and so the researcher must initially stay close to the original data. But the data are usually voluminous and messy, and researchers can often feel 'bogged down' in what appears to be a muddy field, unable to see any form, pattern or structure. It is therefore tempting to move directly from the raw data to more abstract or analytical accounts in order to make the task more manageable. In the main this should be resisted as it is important to build a structure of evidence within which the building blocks of the analysis can be seen.

We describe this analytic structure as a form of conceptual scaffolding and refer to it as the analytic hierarchy (see Box 8.1). The hierarchy is made up of a series of 'viewing' platforms, each of which involves different analytical tasks, enabling the researcher to gain an overview and make sense of the data. In similar vein, Miles and Huberman describe qualitative analysis as a process of 'moving up a step on the abstraction ladder' (1994: 224).

The concept of an analytic hierarchy could be applied to many different approaches to qualitative analysis but the version described here relates to thematic, largely cross-sectional analysis based on interpretations of meaning. Within this, the first stage of analysis involves data management, sorting and synthesising the data so that the analyst can then move on to more interpretative work, making sense of the findings through the production of descriptive and explanatory accounts. These three stages are further described below.

The analytic process, however, is not linear, and for this reason the analytic hierarchy is shown with ladders linking the platforms, enabling movement both up and down the structure. As categories are refined, dimensions clarified, and explanations are developed there is a constant need to revisit the original or synthesised data to search for new clues, to check assumptions or to identify underlying factors. In this respect, the platforms not only provide building blocks, enabling the researcher to move ahead to the next stage of analysis, they also make it possible to look 'down' on what is emerging, and to reflect on how much sense this is making in terms of representing the original material. How well does it fit the data, does it paint a coherent picture or are there missing or untidy bits? These questions will almost certainly require a trip back to the original or synthesised material to unpack more of the detail or to find the more subtle shades of influence or definition. This movement between the data and the analytic concepts, repeatedly going backwards and forwards, will help to produce greater refinement in the analytic account developed. The ability to move up and down the analytical hierarchy, thinking conceptually, linking and nesting concepts in terms of their level of generality, lies at the heart of good qualitative analysis. Indeed, the 'capacity to shuttle between levels of abstraction with ease and clarity' was identified by C. Wright Mills as 'the signal mark of an imaginative and systematic thinker' (1959: 43).

Data management

At the beginning of the analytic process, the researcher is faced by a mass of unwieldy, tangled data and so the first task is to sort and reduce the data to make them more manageable. This stage involves generating a set of themes and concepts according to which the data are labelled, sorted and synthesised. Initially, these themes and concepts should remain close to participants' own language and understandings, though later these may be replaced by more abstract analytical constructions.

Data management may be carried out manually or, more commonly nowadays, using one of the many CAQDAS packages available.

Descriptive accounts

> Qualitative analysis asks such questions as: what kinds of things are going on here? What are the forms of this phenomenon? What variations do we find in this phenomenon? That is, qualitative analysis is addressed to the task of delineating forms, kinds and types of social phenomena; of documenting in loving detail the range of things that exist. (Lofland, 1971: 13)

Having generated and applied a set of themes and concepts at the data management stage, the analyst makes use of the synthesised data to prepare descriptive accounts, identifying key dimensions and mapping the range and diversity of each phenomenon. In this context, it is important to emphasise two features of qualitative data which are central to descriptive analyses. The first is language – the *actual* words used by study participants. It is these that portray how a phenomenon is conceived, how important it is and about the richness or 'colour' it holds. Second, the substantive content of people's accounts, in terms of both descriptive coverage and assigned meaning, forms the nucleus of qualitative evidence. This needs to be sensitively reviewed and captured so that the fineness of detail in different perspectives or descriptions is understood.

Once the nature of phenomena have been clarified and the data classified according to a set of substantive dimensions, refined categories or more abstract classes, the analyst may go on to develop typologies. Typologies are specific forms of classification that help to describe and explain the segmentation of the social world or the way that phenomena can be characterised or differentiated. They may apply to groups of people within the population or to sets of phenomena like beliefs, circumstances or behaviours. Patton describes typologies as 'classification systems made up of categories that divide some aspect of the world into parts along a continuum' (2002: 457).

Writers have distinguished between different forms of typologies. Patton (2002), for example, differentiates between two forms that may arise from an analysis, which he terms 'indigenous' and 'analyst constructed'. The former are classification systems devised by participants themselves, for example, terms such as 'chronics' or 'borderlines' which have been used by teachers to label and distinguish between different kinds of truanting and lateness among pupils. The latter are created during the analytical process, and classify patterns, categories or themes emerging from the data. Lofland (1971) distinguishes between typologies based on static analysis (at a particular time) or phase analysis (a process over time).

Explanatory accounts

Explanatory accounts tend to be developed at the later (or higher) stages of analysis when most of the descriptive and typological work has already been undertaken. In order to move from descriptive to explanatory accounts, the analyst will usually try to find patterns of association within the data and then attempt to account for why those patterns occur. Again, there are different ways in which linkages may be found. There will be explicit associations that occur in the text or notes; linkages between sets of phenomena; and associations between experiences, behaviours and perspectives and certain characteristics of the study population.

The ability to explain, or build explanations, lies at the heart of qualitative research. Most qualitative data sets are rich in the levels of explanation they can offer. They enable the analyst to explain why the data take the forms that have been identified, to account for why patterns, recurrent linkages, processes or apparent contradictions are found in the data.

When people explain their behaviour overtly or when a researcher infers an explanation, however, what is the status of the explanation that is offered? While some qualitative researchers seek explanations in terms of universal deterministic causes, for example this was an aim within analytic induction, others increasingly reject the possibility of identifying these kinds of causes, arguing that the social world is not governed by laws in the way that the physical world is thought to be. However, if human behaviour is not law-like, neither is it chaotic; it displays regularities which can be identified through careful analysis. How can these regularities be explained? Can any kind of causal explanations be developed in qualitative research? What is meant by the idea of cause within a qualitative context?

Because qualitative research is particularly concerned with the way in which people understand and give meaning to their social world, some writers believe that the concept of cause is not necessarily helpful. For example, Hughes and Sharrock (1997) argue in favour of explanations at the level of meaning rather than explanations at the level of cause (in the narrow deterministic sense). Giving the example of traffic behaviour in the vicinity of traffic lights, they argue that an explanation of this behaviour can be developed by understanding the meaning the lights have within a particular setting, group or culture, rather than by attempting to specify the necessary and sufficient conditions and causal mechanisms which produce a given pattern.

Other qualitative writers, for example Patton (2002), suggest that causal explanations may be developed within qualitative research but use the term cause in a loose sense to refer to conjectures, rather than narrowly deterministic laws. They claim that qualitative researchers use a different kind of logic: rather than specifying isolated variables which are mechanically linked, in qualitative analysis the analyst tries to build an explanation based on the way in which different meanings and understandings within a situation come together to influence the outcome.

Some writers maintain that universal deterministic causes are not achievable in either qualitative or quantitative social research. Giddens (1984) argues that causes may be sought for social phenomena, and that reasons are causes, but not in a Humean (X always follows Y) sense. He distinguishes between doing things for a reason, where the actor has an 'understanding of "what is called" for in a given set of circumstances in such a way as to shape whatever is done in those circumstances' (1984: 345), and reasons for things happening which may include a range of situational factors over which the actor has no control. According to Giddens, social research will never be able to specify invariant, deterministic causal relations because any causal mechanism will be inherently unstable: people differ in their ability to make things happen and actions often have unpredictable and unintended consequences.

It is our view that qualitative explanations attempt to say why patterns and outcomes in the data have occurred. These explanations may use a causal logic in a loose, non-universal, non-deterministic sense, but the logic is not based on linear variable analysis. They rarely cite a single cause or reason, but set out to clarify the nature and interrelationship of different contributory factors or influences – such as personal intentions, patterns of understanding, norms and situational influences. Sometimes explanations will be offered with some certainty because of the strength of the evidential base. Other times they will be suggested as hypotheses which need to be tested in further research. But essentially the 'building blocks' of qualitative explanations need to be made clear so that others can view the sources and logic of the construction, judging for themselves the 'validity' or 'credibility' of the findings (see Chapter 10).

In the following chapter we describe how all the different steps involved in data management and descriptive and explanatory analyses are carried out in practice. But it is important to reiterate here that qualitative analysis, albeit exciting, is not without its challenges. Popper once likened theory development to 'building on piles driven into a bottomless bog' (cited in Campbell, 1977) and such a description could well be applied to the process of qualitative data analysis. It is therefore important to have a strong analytic structure within which to carry out all the investigative and creative tasks that are required. With this, there is some hope that what initially appears to be a muddy field or 'bog' will begin to transform into firm pasture with clear borders, landscape and rich colour.

KEY POINTS

- There are many different traditions and approaches for analysing qualitative data which vary with epistemological assumptions about the nature of qualitative enquiry, the status of researchers' accounts and the main focus and aims of the analytic process.
- There are a number of different 'tools' available for analysing qualitative data. Originally these were manual methods but the latter part of the twentieth century saw a rapid growth in computer-assisted qualitative data analysis software (CAQDAS). These offer a variety of functions. There is strong advice that these should be seen only as an 'analytic support' to aid the process of analysis and not as a replacement for the intellectual role that is required of the researcher.
- Whatever method of analysis is used, it needs to offer certain facilities to the researcher in order to maximise the potential for a full and reflective analysis. These include features that facilitate and display ordering; permit within and between case searches; allow flexibility and transparency to others; and allow emergent ideas, concepts, patterns etc. to remain rooted within the original data.
- Analysis requires an organisational and conceptual structure that allows the researcher to gain an overview of the data, carry out different analytic tasks and make sense of the evidence collected. This structure needs to permit continuing and iterative movement between the original data and the conceptualisation, abstraction and interpretation derived from them.

KEY TERMS

The **analytic hierarchy** refers to the process through which qualitative 'findings' are built from the original raw data. It is described as a form of conceptual scaffolding within which the structure of the analysis is formed. The process is iterative and thus constant movement up and down the hierarchy is needed.

The analytic process requires three forms of activity: **data management** in which the raw data are reviewed, labelled, sorted and synthesised; **descriptive accounts** in which the analyst makes use of the ordered data to identifying key dimensions, map the range and diversity of each phenomenon and develop classifications and typologies; and **explanatory accounts** in which the analyst builds explanations about why the data take the forms that are found and presented.

Further reading

Bryman, A. and Burgess, R. (eds) (1994) *Analyzing Qualitative Data*, London: Routledge
Coffey, A. and Atkinson, P. (1996) *Making Sense of Qualitative Data*, Thousand Oaks, CA: Sage
Fielding, N.G. and Lee, R.M. (1998) *Computer Analysis and Qualitative Research*, London, Sage
Seale, C. (ed.) (2000) *Researching Society and Culture*, London: Sage
Strauss, A.L. and Corbin, J. (1998) *Basics of Qualitative Research: Grounded Theory Procedures and Techniques*, 2nd edition, Thousand Oaks, CA: Sage
Weitzman, E.A. (2000) 'Software and qualitative research' in N.K. Denzin and Y.S. Lincoln (eds) *Handbook of Qualitative Research*, 2nd edition, Thousand Oaks, CA: Sage

9

Carrying out Qualitative Analysis

*Jane Ritchie, Liz Spencer
and William O'Connor*

In this second chapter on analysis, we consider in more detail the various activities that are involved in carrying out qualitative analysis. We describe all the stages and processes involved in the analytic hierarchy (see Chapter 8) and the different forms of output that might arise. The activities discussed here will be needed in any analysis concerned with the substantive content of qualitative data, irrespective of which method is being used as a facilitative tool.

The processes involved in analysis are not easy to convey solely in abstract form and examples are given to illustrate the processes described. In addition, in the Boxes that are interleaved in the text, we have illustrated all the steps involved with reference to Framework, a matrix based method for ordering and synthesising data. The Boxes provide a detailed demonstration of the kind of activities that actually take place during analysis as well as describing one method that analysts might use.

Analysis is a continuous and iterative process, as was described in Chapter 8, but two key stages characterise its course. The first requires managing the data and the second involves making sense of the evidence through descriptive or explanatory accounts. Although this distinction is not clear cut, since interpretation and the assignment of meaning take place throughout the analytical process, it is useful to disengage the two stages for the purposes of unravelling the different activities required. Certainly one stage needs to precede the other since, without data management, it will be almost impossible to collate, review or understand the material collected. The main sections of this chapter work through these two stages step by step.

Making sense of the data relies, in part, on the method or tool that is used to order and categorise data, but it is more dependent on the analyst and the rigour, clarity and creativity of her or his conceptual thinking. Therefore, any guidance about how to move through the analytic hierarchy must not only focus on the tools used, but also on the conceptual and intellectual processes engaged in by the analyst. Again the following sections describe these processes through both commentary and illustration.

The analysis method framework, which is used to illustrate throughout this chapter, was developed during the 1980s at the National Centre for Social Research (Ritchie and Spencer, 1994) and is now widely used by qualitative researchers. It is a matrix based analytic method which facilitates rigorous and transparent data management such that all the stages involved in the 'analytical hierarchy' can be systematically conducted. It also allows the analyst to move back and forth between different levels of abstraction without loosing sight of the 'raw' data.

The name 'Framework' comes from the 'thematic framework' which is the central component of the method. The thematic framework is used to classify and organise data according to key themes, concepts and emergent categories. As such, each study has a distinct thematic framework comprising a series of main themes, subdivided by a succession of related subtopics. These evolve and are refined through familiarisation with the raw data and cross-sectional labelling. Once it is judged to be comprehensive, each main theme is displayed or 'charted' in its own matrix, where every respondent is allocated a row and each column denotes a separate subtopic. Data from each case is then synthesised within the appropriate part(s) of the thematic framework. These processes are described in more detail in the boxed illustrations.

When Framework was first developed, it was usual for charts to be drawn up manually on large A3 sheets of paper. However, most spreadsheet 'worksheets' can be adapted in a matter of minutes to accommodate a thematic chart. Extra worksheets can be created within a spreadsheet file to store additional thematic charts, so that one file can host synthesised data for an entire study.

Framework is currently being developed into a standalone CAQDAS package. It will (initially at least) run on IBM compatible PCs and operate using Microsoft Windows. The package will facilitate the synthesis of data (in much the same way described above) and will store each piece of data within a thematic matrix – which can then be printed out. In addition, it will contain search facilities for interrogating either individual cases or themes within the thematic matrix.

Data management

Qualitative 'raw' data come in various forms but most commonly comprise verbatim transcripts of interviews or discussions (or audio tapes if they have not been transcribed), observational notes or written documents of other kinds. Whatever form they take, the material is likely to be highly rich in detail but unwieldy and intertwined in content. Indeed, it is often at this first stage that several hundred pages of transcript or fieldnotes, hours of recordings or piles of original documents can seem quite daunting. It is precisely for this reason that organised steps to 'manage' the data are essential.

Identifying initial themes or concepts (Boxes 9.1 and 9.2)

In most analytical approaches, data management initially involves deciding upon the themes or concepts under which the data will be labelled, sorted and compared. (In the case of fieldnotes, of course, the data are not strictly 'raw' and entries are selective, having already been filtered according to the particular focus of the study or interests of the researcher.) In order to construct this thematic framework, however, the analyst must first gain an overview of the data coverage and become thoroughly familiar with the data set. The amount of familiarisation required will depend on a number of factors but is likely to vary in inverse proportion to the analyst's involvement in previous stages of the research.

Familiarisation, though it may seem an obvious step, is a crucial activity at the start of analysis. To re-employ the analogy of 'conceptual scaffolding' used earlier, the process of familiarisation is akin to building the foundation of the structure. If that foundation is ill conceived or incomplete, then at best it could jeopardise the integrity of the construction, or at worst bring the whole structure crashing to the ground.

It is not necessary to include the entire data set in the familiarisation process, nor would time or resources usually permit, so the researcher needs to make a careful selection of data to be reviewed. In doing this, it is generally wise to review the proposal on which the research is based, with particular attention to the stated objectives of the research. Re-examining the sampling strategy and the profile of the achieved sample is also worthwhile as it will highlight any potential gaps or overemphasis in the data set, but also in the diversity of participants' characteristics and circumstances. If applicable, the analyst should also incorporate the work of different interviewers or data gathered from different sources such as from focus groups or in-depth interviews. The familiarisation process should continue until it is felt that the diversity of circumstances and characteristics within the data set has been understood.

When reviewing the chosen material, the task is to identify recurring themes or ideas. These may be of a substantive nature – such as attitudes, behaviours, motivations or views – or of a more methodological ilk, such as the general atmosphere of an interview or the ease or difficulty of exploring particular subjects. Once these recurring themes have been noted, the next step is to devise a conceptual framework or 'index', drawing both upon the recurrent themes and upon issues introduced into the interviews through the topic guide. Themes are then sorted and grouped under a smaller number of broader, higher order categories or 'main themes' and placed within an overall framework. Once the index has been devised, numbers are sometimes assigned to differentiate the individual categories. An alternative is to use textual terms to capture the essence of the theme or subtheme.

BOX 9.1 BUILDING A THEMATIC FRAMEWORK

Identifying initial themes or concepts

A thorough review of the range and depth of the data is an essential starting point to analysis. Such a review is likely to yield a long list of what appear to be important themes and concepts within the data. Most people tend to use sheets of paper (one very large sheet is sometimes best) or a notebook to log such concepts as they emerge during reading or listening.

Constructing an index

Once an initial list has been generated it is important to construct a manageable index. This is achieved by identifying links between categories, grouping them thematically and then sorting them according to different levels of generality so that the index has a hierarchy of main and subthemes. Here it may be helpful to write each theme on a small piece of paper or a 'post it' note, as these can be sorted and resorted until the researcher feels he or she has a workable structure. This structure is not necessarily permanent and can be changed at a later time. Its function at this early stage is to ensure that there is conceptual clarity within the framework, that no obvious areas of overlap or omission exist at the level of conception used.

Box 9.2 shows an example of a conceptual framework or 'index' developed in a study which aimed to examine the causes of homelessness among young lesbians and gay men.[1] Although the overall index contains 44 subthemes, they are grouped under just 6 main substantive headings with an additional 'Other' category. This means that the researcher can 'hold' the overall structure in her or his head, rather than becoming lost in a proliferation of more specific categories. It should also be noted that there is an 'other' category in each subset to provide an identifier for any uncovered issues that arise within the broad subject area concerned.

In the analytic approach described in the main part of this chapter, we see it as important that, at this stage, themes or topics emerging from the data are described in terms that stay close to the language and terms used in the data set. Imposition of concepts from existing literature related to the research topics, or broader social or political theories, will distract analytical thinking at this stage. Furthermore, by introducing more abstract concepts at this early stage, the analytical process ceases to be grounded in the data. The time for theory building or constructs introduced from other literature or research comes later in the analytical process.

The content of the index will vary depending on the type of qualitative analysis being undertaken. For example, it may be very semantically based concerned primarily with the use of language, involve descriptive categories that remain close to the data or contain more abstract classifications.

---

[1] This study is used for illustration throughout the demonstration boxes. It involved a number of strands of research activity, including interviews with young lesbians and gay men who were, or had been, homeless. A total of 33 such interviews were conducted for which the analytic framework described here was used. The study was funded by a grant from the Community Fund Health and Social Research Programme (O'Connor and Molloy, 2001).

BOX 9.2 EXAMPLE OF A CONCEPTUAL FRAMEWORK OR INDEX INDEX FOR STUDY OF HOMELESSNESS AMONG LESBIAN AND GAY YOUTH

1 Personal details (current)

1.1 Demographic/partnership status
1.2 Accommodation/household/living arrangements
1.3 Employment/educational activity; income
1.4 Health
1.5 Other

2 Life history

2.1 Childhood/family relationships
2.2 School life/education
2.3 Home moving/stability/disturbed parental care
2.4 Experiences of care
2.5 Employment
2.6 Significant relationships: friendships/partnerships
2.7 Leaving parental home/care
2.8 Abuse physical/sexual
2.9 Drug/alcohol use
2.10 Criminality
2.11 Ethnic/cultural/religious issues
2.12 Mental health/self harm/suicide
2.13 Physical health
2.14 Other issues

3 Housing crisis

3.1 Causes and nature
3.2 Effects/difficulties experienced/feelings about
3.3 Coping strategies – personal
3.4 Coping strategies through help received
3.5 Changes and how occurred
3.6 Views/ feelings about current housing arrangements
3.7 Connections/relationship with family/home
3.8 Other issues

4 Sexuality

4.1 Early recognition/feelings about
4.2 Coming out
4.3 Sexual experiences/relationships since
4.4 Sexual identity/feelings about now/openness about
4.5 Impact on housing/living arrangements
4.6 Involvement in lesbian/gay scene
4.7 Other issues

5 Existing help, support and services

5.1 Knowledge about
5.2 Experience/use of; views about

(*Continued*)

BOX 9.2 *(Continued)*

5.3 Reasons for not using
5.4 Sexuality and services/support; experiences/views about
5.5 Other issues

6 Potential help/support/services

6.1 What is needed/would have made a difference
6.2 Views about specific/generic services for lesbians/gay men
6.3 Other suggestions for change

7 Other key issues (not covered above)

7.1 Personal
Service related

Labelling or tagging the data (Box 9.3)

Having constructed an initial conceptual framework, the next task is to apply it to the raw data. In common with some other analysts (Richards and Richards, 1994) we refer to this process as 'indexing' rather than 'coding' because this more accurately portrays the status of the catogories and the way in which they 'fit' the data. When applying an index, it simply shows which theme or concept is being mentioned or referred to within a particular section of the data, in much the same way that a subject index at the back of a book works. The term coding, on the other hand, often refers to a process of capturing dimensions or content that has already been more precisely defined and labelled, as in coding open-ended answers in a questionnaire. This level of precision is neither intended nor often appropriate at an early stage of thematic allocation which is why the term indexing is seen as preferable.

With textual data, indexing involves reading each phrase, sentence and paragraph in fine detail and deciding 'what is this about?' in order to determine which part or parts of the index apply. Indexing can be a manual operation, where references are noted in the margins of transcripts, fieldnotes or documents. Alternatively, it can be carried out electronically using one of the many CAQDAS packages now available. Either way, the index is usually applied systematically to the whole data set, certainly for any cross-sectional analysis.

The assignment of index categories is illustrated in Box 9.3, and this example demonstrates some important features of indexing. First, in just three pages of transcript, 15 different index categories have been applied involving three different major themes. When the content of description is complex, emotional or has high significance, as in this case, it is common to find a number of important themes are mentioned in close proximity. On other pages of transcript, where a single issue is discussed in detail or where a less emotive event is being described, fewer index categories will be used although usually a minimum of two or three.

A second important feature is that subjects weave in and out of each other, such that two or three index numbers are repeatedly interspersed. This is usually a sign of some interconnection between themes or issues that should be noted for later associative analyses. In this case, some of the interconnections are to be expected because of the innate content of the subject matter. For example the respondent was describing 'coming out' to her parents and their reaction, so it is not unexpected to find 2.1 (childhood/family relationships) interlinked with 4.2 (coming out) and – because this was heavily influential in her departure from home – to categories concerned with the impact on living arrangements (categories 2.7, 4.5). But it can also be seen in this short passage that the participant's health and employment have been mentioned on more than one occasion, a connection that may have significance in later analysis.

The other key point concerns how alert the analyst has to be to short references to subjects buried within a discussion about other issues. In this case for example, there are very brief references to the early awareness of her sexual identity (4.1) and her expression of it (4.4). There is also a passing reference to her father's religion and, very tangentially, to cultural expectations (2.11). Although these subjects will have been covered in much greater depth in other parts of the interview, their very presence in the context of 'coming out' and the causes of leaving home is likely to hold significance for subsequent analyses.

It is likely that the preliminary thematic framework or 'index' will need some refinement after an initial application. It may be for example that there are important missing categories to add; categories that need subdivision to reflect recurrent distinctions in the material; or categories that need collapsing because they are too refined for this initial stage of labelling. Refinements of this kind can be made at an early stage of indexing but this then requires revisiting the material already indexed to make the labelling consistent. It should also be remembered that labelling at this stage is intended only as a first step in sorting the data for later retrieval. There will be many later opportunities to refine or add categories to the conceptual framework that is being developed. Indeed, if indexing proves too time-consuming because of subtleties in the index being applied then it is worth considering some revisions to reduce its complexity. However, the revisions made during indexing should be clearly recorded by the analyst as it is likely that they will be relevant to the later stages of analysis.

There are studies where it may be decided *not* to index but to move straight to sorting and synthesising the data. This is possible if the data are very orderly in their structure either because of the form of interview conducted, or because of a very precise structure within the topic guide. It can also happen for reasons of expediency when there simply is not enough time to carry out indexing before the next stage. While all these circumstances are recognised, it is important that indexing is not abandoned lightly because it may well speed rather than slow down, the analytic process.

BOX 9.3   LABELLING THE DATA

When applying an index the analyst must make a judgement about which part or parts of the thematic framework apply to each passage of the data. It is often the case that a passage will contain references to more than one theme and, consequently, will be 'multi indexed'. The following excerpt shows the indexing process in more detail.

   The text that follows is a small part of an interview with a young women in her early twenties. She is describing what happened when she first told her parents that she was a lesbian. Some details have been changed to preserve anonymity and some small passages have been removed for reasons of space.

How can you be, you're letting down the family, how do you know for sure, I mean you're only young, you know, it could be a phase, all the rest of it. And my dad was basically saying that   **4.2**
how no daughter of mine is going to be a lesbian, no daughter of mine, I'll never accept you. Because the thing about it really, because I was even closer to my dad, I've always had things   **2.1**
from my dad, I've always been closer to my dad than my mother and he was really upset by this because I'd always been daddy's girl basically and he said he felt really sick, you know, and stuff like and he says why, do you want to be a man or   **4.2**
something, yes. So all this abuse really basically.
Abuse?
Yes, verbal abuse. No, he wouldn't, it was verbal abuse.
What about your mother's reaction?
I think she has always known basically. She was really quiet, she didn't say anything, she has always known, I know that now,   **(4.1)**
she has always known. It's my dad and his mouth goes into like overdrive really but she has always known really and she accepts me for who I am really which is good, so I haven't lost her. I mean I still go and see her, you know, when dad's not   **2.1**
there because he does night shifts anyway so he has gone by 10 o'clock so I can go like after 10 and see her and my sister. My sister just thinks that we just had a big family argument kind of thing and she has no idea what it's about. And I'm not   **4.2**
going to tell her quite yet anyway, I'll have to wait a bit.
What about – you said you think your mother always knew?
Yes
Is that something that she has told you or is that something that you've ...
No, I just get that impression because when I said what I said, she didn't react to it at all, you know, she wasn't shocked or   **4.1**
anything like that, you know, and I mean I don't talk about any of it, I mean my sexuality with my mother or anything like that because I think she has been through enough, I don't see that –
I feel uncomfortable about that anyway but, you know, I just,   **4.4**
I've always felt that way, I don't know, I mean because of the way I dress and stuff like that, I think she has kind of picked up on something as well. I think it's specifically that bond between,

(Continued)

BOX 9.3 *(Continued)*

you know, mother and the child, you know, it has like been there anyway, I just feel …

Has she said that to you or –

Not in so many words but she says, she has turned round and says that she loves me. My parents don't actually say that, I don't think they've ever said that to me but she says I love you and I know that's love … yes, she does, she's quite affectionate towards me so – yes.

So you stayed with your parents for I think you said about a month?

It was about a month and sort of that's the problem I had so I had to get out.

How were you feeling during that month? I realise it's a while ago.

Yes. Well, it didn't help matters, I was depressed anyway because of my job because I'm one of those people who has to be on the go and I have to be working otherwise I'm just not happy and I just felt that I was, because I was smoking heavy as well, I've got asthma as well so I was totally out of it anyway, seriously I was actually out of it, I mostly on a high anyway so I kept in my room and completely dodged my dad, it's not really hard because he does night shift so he's like asleep during the day anyway and honestly, I don't know how I got through that, I don't know, I really don't, I just did, I just did really.

Sorry, when you were saying you were smoking heavily …

Yes.

… are you talking about cigarettes?

Cigarettes, yes, sorry. I mean B&H, B&H for me is really, really strong … And plus when you've got asthma as well, it doesn't actually help but, yes, so I was smoking that way, yes.

So you went on for a month and then your father was bringing …

Yes, these men.

… young men round.

Yes. I didn't twig what he was doing at first, I mean, he was trying in a way, because my dad is like really Catholic and he was trying to set me up … I confronted him, why are you doing this, you know, … , I was so angry, I went ballistic … I put my hands round his neck … its not like me to get like that but he really drove me to it. I just went for him, I don't know what I was thinking, I just did, and it was an unconscious thing as well, I had no idea what I was doing, just did. And he collapsed as well, I know it was tight because I was really hurting him and he was choking and I thought no. My sister said to me when you're angry you have this strength anyway and it was as though I had no idea how I did that, how I overcome his strength like that because he's quite a strong man, I don't know how I did it …

So you left and went to Jackie's, you said?

I just went over because she lives literally like, OK, across, not quite opposite but like just up the road so I didn't go very far to

(Continued)

Right margin codes:

2.1

4.5/
2.7

2.12
2.5

2.13

2.1

2.13

2.1

2.11
2.1/3.1

2.7/3.1

BOX 9.3 *(Continued)*

her, and she goes, well, you can stay here, you know, you can stay as long as you want. What happened then basically, I think I stayed, I think I overstayed my welcome really because she was, you know, she was going out with someone and she thought there was something going on between us and I thought I've got to get out of this place, like I felt that no one wanted me, you know, the suspicion and stuff, because I thought I need some space and I have to get out. She had always said to me, you know, phone XXXX (lesbian and gay housing agency), even from the age of 18 said to me, phone XXXX, they'll help you to find a place, and I've always said, well, I can't do that, you know, leaving my mother, you know, my sister, so that it has always been everyone else, not myself. So, yes, I just phoned XXXX and they referred me to ——— (hostel).	**3.4/** **3.2** **4.1** **2.1** **3.1**
So how long would you have been with Jackie, can you remember?	
Oh, stayed there, about 7 months, I think, something like that anyway, yes.	**3.1/2.6**
And how did that change things for you, moving in with Jackie?	
Well, I thought it was impossible because my parents were just in the next road, they had no idea, they had no idea about Jackie at all. Oh sorry, they did know where she lived, they knew about her because she used to phone the house and everything but they had no idea that she was gay so they didn't think anything of it really … , even though I knew I was in a place that I would be accepted for who I was but I still felt uncomfortable, … because me and her are very good friends and that's it, you know, nothing else, and that made me feel really uncomfortable as well so I just felt I just had to go, you know, at some point. I mean I wasn't ready though, I just felt that I had to first like find a job … I wasn't even thinking about a hostel or anything like that, I was just thinking, you know, maybe try – I actually wanted to find a place of my own so I was saving up money, I was working, you know, shifts, 7-day weeks, things like that, you know, and totally exhausted.	**2.6** **3.2** **2.5** **3.3** **2.5**

Where data are in the form of tape recordings which have not been transcribed, indexing is more difficult. The researcher may use the tape counter to identify passages which refer to particular themes, or skip this stage and move straight to a thematic summary of the data as described below.

Sorting the data by theme or concept (Box 9.4)

The next step is to sort or order the data in some way so that material with similar content or properties are located together. The purpose of sorting the data is to allow the analyst to focus on each subject in turn so that the detail and distinctions that lie within can be unpacked. Although the ordering may well be altered at a later stage, this initial physical clustering of material allows an intense review of content that will be needed at subsequent stages of analysis.

Analysts use different ways to sort their data as was described in Chapter 8. Using index categories, some will bring material together in thematic 'sets', either manually or more usually electronically. Others will develop a thematic structure within which data can be located and explored, often using a matrix format as is illustrated in Boxes 9.4–9.6. However, whatever method is used, it is crucial that sections of material are not removed from their context in a way that is irretrievable. While sorting is needed to concentrate on each subject in turn, there will be later stages of analysis that require placing these segments alongside other subjects or back in their original setting. On this point, it is perhaps worth reflecting that the 'cut and paste' method which, at one time, was widely used to sort data into subjects holds a real danger of losing the context or location of the material. The same dangers exist with some of the code and retrieve CAQDAS packages.

It is also important when sorting data to ensure that there is the opportunity to assign material to multiple locations. There are two reasons for this. First it may be that a single passage will have relevance to two conceptually different subjects and carving it up would destroy both its meaning and its coherence. Second, the juxtaposition of two apparently unrelated matters may give the very first clues to some later insight or explanation. This is further discussed later in this chapter (see Explanatory accounts).

Summarising or synthesising the data (Boxes 9.5 and 9.6)

The final stage of data management involves summarising or synthesising the original data. This not only serves to reduce the amount of material to a more manageable level but also begins the process of distilling the essence of the evidence for later representation. It also ensures that the analyst inspects every word of the original material to consider its meaning and relevance to the subject under enquiry.

Again, analysts use different ways to reduce their data as discussed earlier. But it is our view that three requirements are essential if the essence of the original material is to be retained. First key terms, phrases or expressions should be retained as much as possible from the participant's own language. Second, interpretation should be kept to a minimum at this stage so that there is always an opportunity to revisit the original 'expression' as the more refined levels of analysis occur. Third, material should not be dismissed as irrelevant just because its inclusion is not immediately clear. It may well be that issues that make little sense at this early stage of analysis become vital clues in the later interpretative stages of analysis.

BOX 9.4   SORTING AND SYNTHESISING THE DATA

Creating thematic charts

The process of indexing may well lead to a refinement of categories. The next step within Framework is to use the index, and the learning gained through indexing, to construct a set of thematic matrices or charts. Here each main theme and its associated subtopics are plotted on a separate thematic chart. Thus, the number of thematic charts will be dictated by the number of main themes the study presents. Each case or respondent is allocated a row in the matrix, while each subtopic is displayed in a separate column.

In the homelessness study five subject charts were developed, covering around 50 subthemes. Box 9.6 shows an example of one of these. It demonstrates how section 3 from the thematic framework for the homelessness study described above has been developed and translated into a thematic chart or matrix format. For reasons of space, it is possible only to show a selection of the material that actually appeared on this chart. This is because charts are normally designed for larger A3 paper which allows both *more columns* and *more rows* in each main thematic area. However, the example will allow the main principles of chart design to be seen.

The chart headings shown replicate the index on some items but not on others. This is a result of the further development of analytic themes that occurred during the process of indexing, on the basis of which decisions are made about how to construct the charts. This can happen in a number of different ways. For example, there are likely to be issues or themes that are thought to hold particular significance for analysis and which thus require a separate thematic column. The chronology of mobility/housing disruption (column 3.1) was one such issue which derived from a number of different index categories. Alternatively, it may be decided to split an index category into different parts with a structure suited to the analysis intended. In the study illustrated this happened with index category 3.1 which was first split into 'The nature of housing crisis' (Chart heading 3.2) and 'causes', with a further subdivision of causes between factors 'Unconnected to sexuality' (Chart heading 3.4) and 'Connected to sexuality' (Chart heading 3.5). Another decision that may be made (not illustrated here) is to chart two or more index categories within one chart heading either because the subject matter is heavily interconnected or because it is planned that the subjects need to be considered alongside each other for more detailed unpacking.

Once the main themes to be used are decided, each is allocated a column on the chart. Each case is then assigned a particular row on the chart and will stay in this same location on every chart. The first column of each thematic chart is reserved for case identification. Generally, the main demographic or other characteristics used in selecting the sample are included here – in this case age, gender, ethnicity and sexuality – but as the analysis develops, more conceptual constructs could also be inserted – for example the typological category to which the case belongs (see Box 9.9). Each column is assigned a number to enable easy referencing between columns. If it is useful, the index numbers that relate to particular columns can also be shown (not illustrated here). Column 3.8 is reserved for charter's comments only and facilitates the analyst in logging interpretative observations even at this early stage in the analysis process. These are placed in a separate column to clearly distinguish them from the data collected from the respondent. It

(Continued)

BOX 9.4   *(Continued)*

is useful practice to reserve a blank column at the end of a thematic chart to pick up further emergent themes and as a place where the analyst can make a note of hunches to be investigated at a later time (a process similar to memoing).

Although it seems a small detail, it is important that the matrix has consistent space and order. Within any given thematic chart, the width allocated to an individual subtopic should be identical for each case, otherwise looking down the column, across all cases, at the data summarised for a subtopic will be difficult, if not impossible. The relative width allowed for each subtopic, however, will depend on the anticipated amount of data to be included, so that different columns on a thematic chart will be allocated varying widths. Finally, the row height on all thematic charts must be consistent, and each case allocated the same chronological position on each thematic chart. This allows comparisons to be made between separate parts of the thematic framework at the individual case level.

BOX 9.5   SORTING AND SYNTHESISING THE DATA (CONTINUED)

Thematic charting

Thematic charting is a process which refers to the summarising of the key points of each piece of data – retaining its context and the language in which it was expressed – and placing it in the thematic matrix. With Framework, the analyst will usually work from already indexed material, but it is possible for some projects to work directly from the raw data, for example un-indexed transcripts or tape recordings.

The key question in charting is 'how do I summarise the content to best retain the context and essence of the point and without losing the language or voice of the respondent?'. In general, the process requires extreme care and requires a finely tuned judgement about the amount and content of material to chart. The general principle should be to include enough data and context so that the analyst is not required to go back to the transcribed data to understand the point being made, but not include so much that the charts become full of undigested material, which can make them very unwieldy. In this respect, the emphasis is on appropriate synthesis – that is summarising without losing content or context – rather than transcribing the point or piece of data exactly as expressed in the transcript. It cannot be overstated how important it is to achieve the right balance in synthesising data. Over-condensed data lack the richness to properly describe or explain, while including too much data can mean that the analyst remains 'bogged down' in the raw data, bereft of a 'viewing platform', from which to see it. Other guidelines for effective charting include:

- *Note the page reference of each piece of data*. Applying a page reference to each piece of synthesised text is important because, in so doing, the charts become a window into the data set. If required, a point can be investigated in more detail and the context in which it was made

(Continued)

BOX 9.5 *(Continued)*

interrogated for further meaning. Failure to include page references may require re-reading an entire transcript to find the original point. If tapes rather than transcripts are being used, then the tape counter can be used to reference the location of the passage concerned.

- *Retain the language of the respondent.* While clearly data is paraphrased in the process of synthesis, it is important to retain as much as possible the words used by the respondent during the interview or group discussion. These have both illuminating and explanatory power for later analytical tasks.

- *Mark but do not recite quotations.* It is tempting to include in the charts large sections of verbatim material where a respondent gives a vivid description of a particular phenomenon or indicates the relationship between two or more events or circumstances. To transcribe verbatim on to the charts will mean that the analyst will soon run out of space within individual cells. To avoid this, it is advisable to indicate on the charts in some way where such quotations exist – usually with an asterisk next to the page number – so that the analyst can return to the transcript at the reporting stage.

- *Use agreed abbreviations and conventions.* When working in a team, synthesis can be aided by using agreed abbreviations or acronyms for common words or phrases, in a sense, a type of analytical shorthand. Similarly, there needs to be consistency between the different styles of fonts used to denote different types of text. As well as the two types of text described earlier – verbatim text and synthesised text – cells can all include interpretative text, such as analytical observations that occur to the researcher while charting; and instructive comments, which may be notes to see related points in another part of the thematic framework, or indicate that summary of a particular point is continued in an adjacent cell (particularly useful where a cell becomes too full). It is important that both these types of text are distinguished from others in the cell, particularly the more interpretative comments that clearly are of a more tentative nature.

It is important for analysts to review the charted data when the end of a transcript is reached. Starting at the first subtopic of the first thematic chart and reading across the case to the end will help an analyst to see any gaps that have occurred in the transfer of data – for example, where a cell is empty when the analyst knows there are data in the transcript. It can also highlight what subtopics are missing from a particular transcript and notes can be inserted on the chart at this point to indicate the reasons for the absence of data. For instance, the topic may not have been relevant to the experience of that particular respondent, the interviewer may not have probed sufficiently or the respondent may have been resistant to discussing that particular topic. Finally, it is at this point that many of the more interpretative comments or hunches which occur to an analyst during the charting process are added to the charts. Such comments can be invaluable in highlighting implicit and explicit relationships between different subtopics or themes at the individual case level, which then form the basis of analytical questions that can be asked of the entire data set once charting is completed and the descriptive and explanatory stages are under way.

(Continued)

BOX 9.5 *(Continued)*

In general, an analyst will move through a transcript chronologically beginning at the start of a transcript and summarising each piece of data within the appropriate part of the thematic framework. However, when the entire data set has been indexed, the analyst can choose to concentrate on one main theme at a time. This is done by revisiting only the parts of the transcripts with appropriate numerical or textual references and then synthesising them within the correct part of the thematic framework. Each approach has relative merits. The former is useful in gaining a thorough understanding of individual cases, and for identifying relationships between different themes and subtopics across the data set. It also clearly avoids the possibility of any part of the transcript remaining uncharted. The later is beneficial in a research team where there are a number of different objectives which require different forms of analysis or in studies with different populations. It is also beneficial where the topic in a particular chart is very complex as it allows deep immersion in subject matter across the whole data set. However, one person in the team should keep an overview of the entire data set, to ensure that data are not missed and that linkages and relationships are being identified.

When examining material to summarise or reduce it, it is useful to work through the data systematically to ensure that all the content has been considered. Again, this can be done by bringing together all the data on a specific theme so that it can be studied and synthesised across all cases. Alternatively, the analyst can work systematically through a transcript, dealing with each theme in turn. However, once the data is synthesised, it should have coherence in terms of the content displayed such that its essence can be understood without recourse to seeing the original material.

Some general features of data management

The steps involved in data management may take place in a different order depending on the analytic tool being used. For example, in Framework sorting and synthesising take place almost simultaneously after each labelled piece of text has been examined for its content. In other methods, synthesising may take place before the data is sorted, to aid a more refined form of ordering.

Some analytic 'tools' do not offer a systematic method for synthesis, other than through the construction of abbreviated tags, concepts or analytic notes. If this is so then it is important to introduce a stage that allows the formulation and expression of the original material to be seen in reduced form. Without this there is a danger that too much abstraction will occur at too early a stage such that the analyst can only revisit either conceptualised categories or the full text at the later stages of analysis. Neither of these will be satisfactory – one too abbreviated, the other too unwieldy – for aiding the processes of description and explanation that will be taking place.

BOX 9.6   EXAMPLE OF A THEMATIC CHART

HOUSING CRISIS	3.1	3.2	Factors causing housing crisis		3.6	3.7	3.8
Serial No., Gender, Age, Ethnicity etc.	Chronology of mobility and housing disruption	The nature of housing crisis	3.4 Unconnected to sexuality	3.5 Connected to sexuality	Nature of connection with family/ home during HC and once overcome	Feelings about and impact of housing crisis	Notes/ comments
NO. 34, Male, 17, Gay, White UK	ran away at 14 for 2 weeks (1st HC) but found & went into to care – when left there after 2 yrs went to mums, left there cos of bro's abuse, then to hostel for 3 months (2nd HC), then left there cos of harassment, then moved back to mums, left again cos of bro's abuse (3rd HC–early 2000); then	1 – was here, there & everywhere, on streets, doing best to get money, stealing (4) 2 – not seen as housing crisis tho was resident in a hostel (called it 'own place' cos had his own room) big building with loads of separate flats (20) 3 – went and stayed in hostel 4 – stopping here there and e'where – treating him like	1. physical abuse from brother (THO POSS CONNECTED TO S COS BRO WLD CALL HIM POOF ETC. BUT ABUSE ALSO APPEARS UNRELATED TO S) 2. Again physical abuse from bro (20) 3. Physical abuse from bro – this time beating with metal bar but this time also beat sister 4. ran away from hospital cos were	went to [city] in 3rd period of HC because gay and liked the village – THO REASON FOR RUNNING AWAY UNCON-NECTED TO S, MORE CON-NECTED WITH ESCAPING FROM HOSPITAL (22–23)	Loves mum to bits, treats him really bad, but every time he was away and she said come back he would cos loved her – always had a close rel, went e'where together (13)	didn't like sleeping on streets, v afraid (26) hasn't got a place to call home, that's been awful, cos thinking where am I going to put my head down tonite – awful being on the street (26–27) made him change from being a little tearaway to keep-ing out of trouble with the police (29)	MULTIPLE PERIODS OF HOUSING CRISIS – STILL ONGOING – LIKELY TO HAPPEN AGAIN ALTHO VIO-LENCE FROM BROTHER NOT EXPLICITLY TO DO WITH S, IT DOES APPEAR TO FEATURE AS PART OF THE REASON FOR ONGOING ABUSE SEE 3.4 *(Continued)*

BOX 9.6 (continued)

	went to hostel; got put in hosp from there after suicide attempt; (4th) ran away from H to [city] slept rough for 3 mths – now in hostel – may move on soon	had £200 and a bag of clothes (22–23) stayed with men in exchange for place to stay and s'times ££ too (25)	'mad person', ended up sleeping in streets in [name of town]			been good to get away from mums – feels a lot better in himself – dressing nicer, spending £ on what he wants, mum never got him nout, she always took his £ from jobs (30)
No.40, Female, 18yrs, Lesbian, White UK	Lived with mum and stepdad and bros and sisters until 15 – THEN RAN AWAY (THOUGH HAS RETURNED A FEW TIMES) – NO STABLE ACCOMMODATION SINCE THEN – A SUCCESSION OF	When sleeping rough, it was not so bad in the summer. Did not like it cos did not like waking up and feeling all dirty all the time. Would go to her mate's house and he would sometimes give her something cos she	Left home cos not allowed to do what her friend's did. Sick of arguing with parents (6) Wanted to go home and tried several times, but once there always wanted to be doing her own thing. Mum didn't want her	Would get into trouble to hurt her mum (SEE 2.2) wanted to hurt her mum cos of her response to her S. mum did not accept it and that made her feel that she did not belong to	was in contact with mum when sleeping rough. Went back few times but it did not work (8) Now is lot happier in self. When rings mum and tells her she is still	HC and upheaval messed her head up more. Thinking of getting her head straight and now feels a lot happier than has in a
						V MOBILE – SAYS SHE CANNOT REMEMBER WHERE SHE HAS BEEN IN PAST FEW YEARS

(Continued)

BOX 9.6 (Continued)

CRISES BEEN IN HOSTELS THROUGHOUT NORTHEAST, ALSO PRISON & DRUG REHAB V DIFFICULT INTERVIEW TO UNRAVEL START AND END OF HC	was starving, but always pretended had somewhere to stay cos was too ashamed to admit she slept rough (22/23)	smoking and drinking. Got fed up cos couldn't do without drinking (10) Thrown out of several hostels for taking drugs. Got a smack habit (18) Part of reason for leaving home was wanting her own space. Felt alone at home anyway so thought might as well just not be around them (34)	that family. If mum had accepted S would have stopped trying to get into trouble cos would have known that her mum loves her for who she is **(32) Leaving home was connected to S cos her sister was blackmailing her – had seen her kissing some girls. Was worried, didn't want to face it, so that was part of reason for leaving home (33)	off drugs, mum says oh good. When used to tell her that, she would say you'll be back on it. Wanted encouragement from mum and someone to believe in her (24) Mum is OK about her S now. They are in contact. Mum and sister want to visit her, but she stopped them. Will see them when she has a flat, something to show them (42)	long time (23) When moving about and sleeping rough got real depressed and started hating herself, wasn't bothered what she looked like or where she was. Felt it wasn't a life, but then thought she deserved it cos she was a worthless person (26)**

It is important to recognise that through all the stages of data management, 'meaning' is being attributed to the original material. As each piece of data is inspected, the analyst will be deciding what is being said and what the content is conveying. Thus the construction and assignment of labels, the bringing together of similar material, the summarising of original text all require an interpretation of what has been said or observed. It is for this reason that clear documentation of the data management stage is needed so that there is some record of what took place in the conceptualisation and assignment of different parts of the evidence. Such records might include what is included in different categories in an index, or where less common subject matter is located, or notes on as yet unclear subjects. It is also important that there is always access back to the original material for cases where earlier interpretations come under question as the analysis becomes more refined.

These steps in data management are very time-consuming and can even feel tedious. But the very process of labelling, sorting and synthesising brings deep familiarisation with the evidence available. This gives the analyst a full and detailed picture of what has to be portrayed in the later analyses. In particular, the process of actually writing a summarised or synthesised account begins to trigger the vital insights into, or questions about, the data that will lead to the later interpretative stages of analysis. Only by working through the raw material at this level of intensity do the lines of enquiry to pursue, or the puzzles posed by the data begin to emerge. The time invested is therefore worth every moment since the 'jewels' that await the analyst will certainly begin to glimmer.

Descriptive accounts

Defining elements and dimensions, refining categories and classifying data (Boxes 9.7 and 9.8)

An initial stage in descriptive analysis refers to unpacking the content and nature of a particular phenomenon or theme. The main task is to display data in a way that is conceptually pure, makes distinctions that are meaningful and provides content that is illuminating. There are three key steps involved:

- *Detection* in which the substantive content and dimensions of a phenomenon are identified
- *Categorisation* in which categories are refined and descriptive data assigned to them
- *Classification* in which groups of categories are assigned to 'classes' usually at a higher level of abstraction.

Detection involves looking within a theme, across all cases in the study and noting the range of perceptions, views, experiences or behaviours which have been labelled or tagged as part of that theme. Once this range has been noted, the analyst then sets out to sort and distil the key dimensions within the range, identifying broader, more refined categories which can both incorporate and discriminate between the different manifestations of the data. Data are then assigned to the new categories. Descriptive accounts may be based at this level of categorisation, or the analyst may further refine the categories, identifying fewer classes by which to sort, encapsulate and present the data.

The process of moving from synthesised or original text to descriptive categories is explained and illustrated in Boxes 9.7 and 9.8. Some important points relevant to all descriptive and classificatory analyses are demonstrated by the process shown in Box 9.8.

At the first stage of abstraction (Column B), the descriptions have stayed close to the original data. This is because it will not necessarily be clear at this stage how the more abstract classification will be constructed and it is important that the initial elements can be seen. However, the very process of studying each piece of charted data – and assigning a description to it – will start to clarify the higher level categories that might be used.

In the more abstract categorisation, shown in Column C, three different things are happening. First, the analyst has now begun to assign 'labels' to the data that have moved beyond the original text and has begun to 'interpret' the data in a more conceptual way. For example, 'felt hopeless/useless' has been categorised as 'Affected feelings of self worth'. Second, the categorisations being used show that the same features are appearing in different cases, even though they were differently described originally. For example, cases 40 and 44 have both mentioned feelings about themselves that have been categorised as 'self worth'; cases 34 and 38 have both mentioned the 'uncertainty/unpredictability' of their lives during the housing crisis. Third, other categories are emerging that are very similar in conception and which could be collectively described under a slightly broader heading. For example, it is possible that 'loss of a home' (No. 34) and 'loss of a life' (No. 40) might be more broadly classified at a later stage as a 'sense of rootlessness'.

Another feature to note about the derived description is that two quite separate classifications are emerging. The first concerns feelings or emotional responses that arose during the housing crisis; the second, the changes that occurred as a result of it. This is a very common occurrence when a charted column is investigated. There will often be two, three or even more separate sets of issues to describe, each related to a different phenomenon. It is for this reason that each column has to be interrogated or 'creamed' until there is nothing of any substance left to describe or classify. Sometimes in doing this, phenomena that connect closely with another column may emerge and these might be put together with that other data.

BOX 9.7   USING FRAMEWORK FOR DESCRIPTIVE ANALYSIS

Defining elements and dimensions, refining categories and classifying data

Using Framework to define elements and constructs, refine categories and classify data involves the analyst in understanding 'what is happening' within a single subtopic – that is, within a column on a thematic chart. This entails the analyst reading down the particular column across cases to understand the range of data that exist. It is advisable to do this a number of times but, once the analyst is familiar with the data within the chosen subtopic, he or she can then begin identifying different elements, constructs and categories that are emerging. The first step often involves using different coloured highlighter pens to label pieces of data in that particular column which suggest different representations of the phenomenon. Having done this, it is helpful to log and categorise different elements and categories on a separate sheet of paper, along with examples of each as presented within the data. While going about this task, it is important to question whether each piece of data provides a category, or is merely a characteristic or component of one already recorded. This is why extracting data from the thematic charts and summarising it on a separate sheet helps as similarities and differences become clearer. Throughout the process, the analyst should continually question the categorisation of each piece of data.

This task is not complete until all of the data in that column or subtopic have been fully inspected and a decision made about where it belongs. Sometimes everything in the column will be judged as relevant to the categorisation and thus the data within the column will have been exhausted. But other times there will be material there that does not belong in the conceptualisation of the descriptive categories but which is nevertheless clearly linked. This may be dealt with in a separate categorisation or may be considered alongside other material in another column. Either way it should not be ignored unless a clear decision has been made that it is irrelevant.

Once the analyst has extracted all of the definitions, elements, constructs etc. summarised in the charts, it will then be possible to classify them by grouping them under one or more higher order labels. The aim of this task is to construct a coherent and logical structure within which to display the content of the descriptive elements. This can take various forms since differently constructed categorisations can be derived from the same data, but would all encompass the same range of phenomena. However, with clarity about the elements and without over-interpretation of the data at this stage, the underlying conceptualisation of the categorisation should remain evident.

The process of identifying elements and categories from a Framework chart is illustrated in Box 9.8.

The example in Box 9.8 illustrates only four cases. In the study concerned, 33 people were interviewed and each described the impact of a housing crisis on them. As a consequence, there will be literally hundreds of 'elements' to consider for description and classification of the kind described above. But as the number of cases interrogated increases, so too does recurrence or similarity in the elements being identified.

BOX 9.8   USING FRAMEWORK FOR DESCRIPTIVE ANALYSIS

Column A	Column B	Column C
Data charted in column 3.7 Feelings about and impact of housing crisis	Elements/dimensions identified – in order identified in chart	Categories/classes
No. 44 Uncomfortable while at friends, really wanted find place of own so was saving money, working 7 day weeks and was totally exhausted (19) Was doing care work for agency (20) Felt totally hopeless, *useless*. Cld have fallen out with [friend] and she cld have kicked her out. Don't know how homeless ppll do it, Know I wldnt survive on streets, that's not me, like my comforts hot water, clean clothes etc. Was terrified*(25)	Discomfort staying with other people Wanted place of own Needed to save/get money Felt hopeless/useless Potential tension with friend staying with Like home comforts Frightened	Difficulties of temporary accommodation Increased motivation to get own accommodation Affected feelings of self worth Affected friendships (permanently/ temporarily) Missed comforts of home Felt frightened/fearful
No. 38 moving from place to place not a bad experience – taking on the world that's where the excitement was, you didn't know what was going to happen (14) didn't find sleeping rough that difficult – started drinking a lot – all 3 of them were going to bed pissed – so it didn't matter (17)	Felt like 'taking on the world' Excitement No knowledge of what would happen Started drinking a lot	Felt energised Uncertain/ unpredictable Alcohol dependence
No. 34 didn't like sleeping on streets, v afraid (26) hasn't got a place to call home, that's been awful, cos thinking where am I going to put my head down tonite – awful being on the street (26–27) made him change from being a little tearaway to keeping out of trouble with the police (29) been good to get away from mums – feels a lot better in him-self – dressing nicer, spending £ on what he wants, mum never got him nout, she always took his £ from jobs (30)	Afraid No place to call home Uncertainty about where would sleep Changed behaviour – kept out of trouble with police Good to be away from mother Dressing better Can spend money on what wants More money for himself Mother can't take money away	Felt frightened/fearful Loss of having a 'home' Uncertain/ unpredictable Avoided criminal activity Liked being away from parent(s) More self care Freedom to spend money as likes More personal spending money

(Continued)

BOX 9.8 *(Continued)*

No. 40 HC and upheaval thinks messed her head up more. Is thinking of getting her head straight and now feels a lot happier than has in a long time (23)	Got depressed	Depression
	Hated herself	Affected feelings of
	Wasn't bothered what looked like	self worth
		Less self care
	Wasn't bothered about where she was	Lost interest/aimless
When moving about and sleeping rough got real depressed and started hating herself, wasn't bothered what she looked like or where she was. Felt it wasn't a life, but then thought she deserved it (26)**	Wasn't 'a life'	
	Felt she deserved what had happened	Loss of having a 'life'
		Felt difficulty was deserved

Once the charted data have been investigated, as described above, numerous categories will have been identified, the number depending on the complexity of the issue being considered. Each of these will be considered to see if they link with or are similar to others identified. At this stage it is likely that higher levels of abstraction will take place, to yield sets of categories within a broader classification. But all the time the connection between the original data and the classification taking place should remain visible so that the elements that have been aggregated can be seen – and if possible – revisited. This might be done in the form shown above – or it might be carried out on a large sheet of paper with all the different elements listed in sets or blocks of a similar kind. Whatever approach is used, it is likely that a lot of reassignment of elements will take place as the most meaningful classification develops.

Because of the crucial importance of descriptive and classificatory analyses in qualitative research – they will be needed in *every* study whatever its methods or purpose – another example will be given here to illustrate the process and the kinds of categorised outputs that are achieved. The data used come from a study which aimed to understand the factors that underpin and influence appraisals of services, in the context of claiming and receiving social security benefits (Elam and Ritchie, 1997). In the study, people who had had recent contact with a social security office were asked about their experiences and how they assessed them. This generated an extensive 'descriptive' list of factors that had affected people's judgements about the services they had received.

Having investigated this list, they were then grouped into eleven sets, categorised as follows:

Categories

Staff – Attitude and manner, communication and competence
Amount of claimant effort required
Speed of dealing with claim or enquiry
Accuracy of assessment or process
Benefit procedures and regulatory requirements
Information available
Office – access and condition and facilities
Outcome of claim or transaction

Examples of descriptive items included

Staff being polite
Being talked down to
Not being told what is happening
Talking to someone who listens
Talking to someone who knows what they are doing
Being passed from person to person
Having to repeat information already given
Having to phone back several times
Length of time spent waiting in the office
Quick decisions about claims
Mistakes in amount of benefit paid
Benefit payments arriving on time
The length of application forms
Easier systems for challenging decisions
Clear explanation of how benefit is calculated
Leaflets that are easy to read
Easy to get to by public transport
Inconvenient opening hours
Uncomfortable seating
Good system for organising queuing
The amount of benefit received
Feeling that the matter is being dealt with

The ten main categories were then re-sorted into five groups, at a slightly higher level of abstraction as shown below.

Approach of benefit officials
Staff attitude and manner

Efficiency
Claimant effort, speed, accuracy, procedures and requirements, staff competence

Communication
Information available, staff communication

Offices
Access, condition and facilities

Outcomes
Outcome of claim or transaction

From the beginning to end of this analysis, an array of around 100 factors had been described, categorised and then grouped into five main classes. These levels of classificatory reduction are quite typical but it is important for the analyst to have a clear conceptual structure within which they occur. It will also be noted that certain categories could have been differently classified under a different conception of the final classification. For example, it would have been possible to classify all the staff categories under a broader head of 'Benefit officials' rather than assigning them to those concerned with 'Efficiency' or 'Communication'. There will often be this potential to conceptualise classifications in a different way and it is for this reason that the internal composition of the classes needs to be clearly identified.

It is commonly advocated that, at the first level of description categorisation should remain close to the data, as in the example shown (see 'Examples of descriptive items included'). As has been said, this is so that the basis of more abstract or theoretical classification, which may occur at later stages of analysis, is clear. A useful test is to consider whether the initial categorisation that has been used would be easily recognised by the study participants. The construction of other concepts derived from research, literature or theory can easily pull the 'meaning' of the descriptive categories too far away from the spirit of the data. As the analysis progresses, however, and the analyst groups items into more abstract conceptual classes, new categories are likely to become increasingly summative, abstract or theoretical. As such they will move further away from the language and forms of presentation of the original contributors although they should retain their overall meaning.

A second consideration is the level of detail at which responses should be captured. Inevitably, when different participants speak about a subject they do so from the perspectives of their own values and experiences. This means that they might highlight different features even though they are discussing a common issue. There are therefore different levels at which the data can be described and this will apply to all descriptive analysis. A decision about the level of detail captured in the categorisation will depend on the objectives of the study and the centrality of the phenomenon being described within those objectives. It will always be possible to illuminate the content of categories, either through amplificatory text, through examples or through verbatim quotations (see Chapter 11).

Finally it is important that the categorisation is comprehensive. In generating a description of content, all cases should be included and all the elements of relevance should be incorporated. Although the recurrence of individual elements or categories has certain relevance in conveying the collective content of the data, it is the itemised content, not the frequency with which items occur, that matters in descriptive mapping. Even if a descriptor is mentioned only once it still contributes to the full set of elements that form the whole picture.

In the context of discussing description and categorisation it is important to say a word about recurrence. There is much discussion in the research literature about whether frequency counts should be used as part of the evidential base of a qualitative data set. While there is no doubt that recurrence and numerical counts of recurrence should not be ignored, they should not be presented as primary findings in themselves since they will have no statistical value at all. Rather, they should be used to find the significance of the recurring phenomena through other means. If, for example, a particular subgroup of a population – or even a majority of the population as a whole – mention a particular issue, then the qualitative researcher will use this information when seeking to explain why this is the case, as will be discussed in more detail later in this chapter.

Categorisation and classification can be used to describe the form or nature of any social phenomena. These may concern specific phenomena such as circumstances, events, attitudes, beliefs, norms, systems and so on. Alternatively the classification may relate to the characteristics of different groups within the study population. Because of such wide applications, it is likely that all qualitative studies will contain some descriptive and classificatory analyses. But as suggested at the start of this section, it is essential that the categorisations and classifications developed are conceptually coherent. It is a very poor sign of the interrogative powers of the analyst if the descriptive and classificatory analyses are ill defined, meaningless or tangled.

Establishing typologies (Box 9.9)

THE NATURE OF TYPOLOGIES

Typologies have two important characteristics. First they are usually, although not inevitably, multidimensional or multifactorial classifications. That is, they combine two or more different dimensions so that a more refined or complex portrayal of a position or characteristic can be identified. Second, they offer a classification in which categories are discrete and independent of each other. In other words, a feature or individual can only be assigned to one category. It is this latter property that gives them particular value in 'dividing' or 'sectoring' the social world.

DETECTING AND DEFINING TYPOLOGIES

There are a number of steps to be taken in the detection of a typology. The first task is to identify the relevant dimensions of a typology. Lazarsfield and Barton (1951) describe this as the 'dimensions which underlie the discrimination' made by the typology. For this, it is important for the analyst to have a strong familiarity with the data set and that tasks further down the analytic hierarchy, such as identifying the elements of a phenomenon and refining categories, have been completed. This process is illustrated in Box 9.9 that without having fully understood a single phenomenon and then its relationships with other phenomena, it will be difficult to identify or construct meaningful and robust multidimensional groupings. Moreover, by conducting such analyses, the analyst will undoubtedly find clues about the existence of possible typologies. It will also be worth investigating hunches developed in earlier analytical tasks or those that emerged during the course of fieldwork. Through such investigations, it should be possible to identify the dimensions that 'discriminate' in the typology and to rule out others.

Once this initial construction is developed, the analyst needs to ensure that all the cases can be assigned to each of the dimensions being used in the typology. Unless the sample fits into each of the dimensions, and fits uniquely, the dimensions will not operate effectively within the typology. Once the dimensions of the typology have been checked in this way, then their cross-fertilisation into typographical categories can be made. Once this has been done the whole process of testing needs to start again to ensure that all cases can now be allocated to one, and only one, of the typological categories. The power of a typology lies in its ability to locate all cases in a series of related but independent categories. If there are people or cases that cannot be uniquely assigned, then the conception of the typological construction, or the dimensions on which it is based, need to be revisited.

The investigation of 'fit' to each of the typological categories is clearly a very iterative process. It will involve constant checking and tweaking of the assumed dimensions of the typology and the typological categories developed. It is the cases that fall between categories or do not seem to fit neatly into any of the categories that are the key to developing a strong typology. Interrogation of these may bring to light a missing dimension from the typology or suggest an extra typological category. The analyst should continue to allocate and reallocate cases to the available typological categories until all cases have been assigned. This process undoubtedly requires adherence to an 'analytical conscience' in ensuring that all cases do fit and fit one category only. If they do not then the typology will need to be rejected as a method of sectoring although it still may be useful as a form of classification.

A final point about typologies concerns the internal coherence of the categories. While the categories themselves need to be discrete from each other, some variations within categories may occur in relation to the dimensions used for construction. Indeed, capturing any variation within categories will form part of the descriptive account of the typology. For example, in the typology cited above the 'action takers' ranged from people who had discussed a plan of action with a professional or agency to people who had already made arrangements for other accommodation. It was the fact that members of this group had taken action, rather than the nature of the action itself, that uniquely distinguished them from people in the other categories.

BOX 9.9   CONSTRUCTING A TYPOLOGY

Developing a typology using charted data may be carried out within one chart or across two or more. It will involve cross-case analysis so that dimensions on which the study population divides have been identified. These will form the main dimensions of a typology.

Having identified the dimensions, the next step is to test them across the data set. It has to be possible to apply one, and only one, category to each participant for that dimension to work within the typology. Once the dimensions have been tested in this way, and if necessary revised – the next step is to decide how they combine to form typological categories. Multidimensional typological groupings are then constructed, and usually assigned some working title.

Once these newly constructed, multidimensional, categories have been devised, they then need to be tested across the whole sample. Each case is then inspected as a whole (that is looking horizontally through the set of charts) checking each of the phenomena that form the typology. On the basis of this, one of the typological categories is assigned and then clearly annotated on the chart

The construction and testing of a typology can be partially illustrated from the example chart shown earlier (Box 9.6) The data detailed in Columns 3.1 (Chronology of mobility and housing disruption) and 3.2 (The nature of housing crisis) show different experiences of housing crisis in terms of its severity on two key dimensions:

- the number of different episodes of housing disruption that had occurred
- the consequences in terms of the nature of the housing 'accommodation' in which it resulted.

These two dimensions were felt to be of central importance in describing the nature of homelessness that the young people had experienced.

Each of these dimensions had been categorised during the descriptive and classificatory analysis as follows:

Episodes of housing disruption	*'Accommodation'*; resulting
Single period	Rooflessness
Multiple periods	Moving between friends/other people's accommodation
Continuous	Hostel or other accommodation for homeless people

On the accommodation dimension, more than one category could be applied to a single case so this was reduced to a two-way categorisation identifying whether or not rooflessness had been experienced. It was also found that 'continuous' disruption invariably included a period of rooflessness. Although single periods could last a few weeks or a number of years, the fact that it had now ended was of significance to the study. The typology thus developed was as follows:

Severity of homelessness history

HH 1 Single period – no rooflessness
HH 2 Single period – involving rooflessness

(Continued)

BOX 9.9 *(Continued)*

HH 3 Multiple periods – no rooflessness
HH 4 Multiple periods – involving rooflessness
HH 5 Continuous homelessness

It will be noted that these are ordered broadly in terms of their assigned severity. They were not given titles but labelled classifiers were assigned so that they could easily be viewed when looking at other data in the charts.

It is not possible to display the testing and assignment of the classification across the whole data set. However, the four cases illustrated were 'typologically' classified as follows:

No. 44 HH1   No. 38 HH4   No. 34 HH5   No. 40 HH5

Finally it should be noted that, in the illustration above, the two columns from which the typology was drawn were on the same chart and next to each other. This is unusual – more commonly the different dimensions used to construct a typology will not be so closely located. This will not cause any problems because, within Framework, cases are always found in the same location on each chart (see Box 9.5). This means that it is quite easy to use two or more columns in combination, simply by looking along rows in the same location.

In order to illustrate the power of typologies within qualitative analysis a further example of a typology is given below. The study was carried out among parents who had an adult son or daughter with learning difficulties and explored the reasons why the son or daughter had continued to live in the parental home and what thought had been given to the future when the parent(s) may no longer be able to provide appropriate care (Richardson and Ritchie, 1989). In the course of the study, a typological classification was established to capture the parents' current perspectives on their son or daughter leaving home. Two dimensions were used in the designation of categories – recognition of the need to consider alternative arrangements and the likely immediacy of action. The four categories established were:

- *Evaders*: people who felt 'leaving home' will never have to happen and that their sons or daughters will always be taken care of
- *Delayers*: people who recognised that action will have to be taken at some stage but felt it was too early or too difficult at the present time
- *Debaters*: people who felt torn between the need to take action and difficulties of implementing change, but trying to begin the process
- *Action takers*: people who had already taken some action or made a specific plan to find alternative living arrangements for their sons or daughters.

It is important to note that, although typologies often do relate to groups of people, they may be used to describe any type of phenomena. For example they may relate to sets of beliefs or to types of experience. Alternatively they may be used to describe different systems, for example for delivering a service; the structures of organisations; the nature of environments, for example in inner city areas; or the forms of events.

It is also possible in analysis to use predefined typologies that are established prior to the study. Indeed it may well be that an important typology is used as a key criteria in sampling. For example, in the study used in Chapter 4 to illustrate purposive sampling, a primary sampling criterion had been the previous pattern of dental attendance. People were identified as 'regular', 'irregular' or only 'occasional' attenders prior to sample selection. This typology was used in the purposive selection of the sample but also in much of the qualitative analyses.

Although typologies are very powerful analytical tools, it is important to remember that they are not always appropriate or required. Not every qualitative study will lend itself to the creation of a typology, and it is possible to waste a lot of precious analysis time searching in vain for tenuous links between groupings of phenomena. Put simply, there is no value in creating a typology just for the sake of it. Hammersley and Atkinson (1995) argue that to be effective, a typology should give good purchase on the data, and help explain differences – rather than be a purely conceptual exercise. Similarly Lofland and Lofland (1995) advise that there is no point devising arbitrary typologies as they are only worthwhile if they aid systematic understanding.

Explanatory accounts

Detecting patterns; associative analyses and identification of clustering (Box 9.10)

Associative analysis is a lucrative form of qualitative data investigation as it almost invariably brings a deeper understanding of the subject under review. Such analyses involve finding links or connections between two or more phenomena. These connections may be in the form of linkages between one or more sets of phenomena, or attachments to subgroups. This section describes how such connections are identified and then verified.

LINKAGES BETWEEN SETS OF PHENOMENA
(MATCHED SET LINKAGES)
It is common in qualitative analysis to find that linkages repeatedly occur between sets of phenomena. We have termed these matched set linkages. The connections can occur between two phenomena of the same kind (for example, two sets of attitudes), between two phenomena of different kinds (for example, experiences and decisions, circumstances and behaviours, beliefs and attitudes) or there may be multiple associations (for example, beliefs, attitudes and behaviours). Sometimes there is a clear explanatory connection between the two sets of phenomena. Often, however,

it is not clear that one phenomena explains the other but only that they tend to co-exist.

An example of matched set linkages comes from studies which aimed to understand why people who were entitled to social security benefits had not claimed them. It is consistently found that some of the non-claimants hold very negative attitudes towards many of the people who did claim benefits, an attitude that was often accompanied by the view that benefits should some-how be earned (that is, through paying taxes or National Insurance, through having 'worked for a living' through being deserving – for example having a long-term illness or disability – or even having 'fought in the war'). This is not necessarily an explanatory connection since one does not necessarily account for the other. Rather, the two sets of attitudes tend to go hand in hand.

Matched linkages cannot be verified until the full data set is reviewed although they may begin to emerge at a much earlier stage of analysis. When the data set is complete they can be found by looking across a range of different phenomena across all the cases. Such searches are rarely random – they may well be led by something that one of the participants has said, evidence or theories from other research or by a hypothesis which is being tested.

ATTACHMENT TO SUBGROUPS

It is often important in a qualitative study to investigate whether there are any patterns occurring in the data within particular subgroups of the study population. The groups concerned may be those determined by primary sampling criteria or by other socio-demographic characteristics or may have been established as important subgroups or typologies during the analysis. Typologies and other group classifications are extremely useful in displaying associations in qualitative data by showing how particular views or experi-ences may attach to particular groups or sectors of the population (Hammersley and Atkinson, 1995).

For example, in a study noted earlier examining attitudes towards going to the dentist, a primary sampling criteria had been the previous pattern of dental attendance (that is, whether regular, irregular or only occasional attenders). This criterion was used to examine whether – and how – views about dental health, inhibitors to going to the dentist and views about receiving dental treatment differed with actual attendance. Similarly the typology of parents, cited earlier, was used to find a number of important differences between the four groups. For example, one group of parents (the 'evaders') were found to be avoiding the question of whether their sons or daughters should leave or remain in the parental home by 'just hoping' that the dilemma would never have to be resolved. Some of these parents noted that they had 'never spent a day apart' from their son or daughter with a learning difficulty. This led to an inspection across the whole data set which showed that this 'evading' group of parents had much less experience than other parents of separation from their son or daughter. This link proved pivotal in helping to explain why some parents wanted to avoid any decision about their sons or daughters leaving the parental home.

BOX 9.10   ASSOCIATIVE ANALYSES

Constructing a central chart

When the thematic charts have been analysed the analyst may decide to construct an overall, or central, chart. A central chart is one that displays a mixture of demographic data and classifications developed during the descriptive stage of analysis. A useful analogy is that of an analytic logbook. The analyst works through a data set, understanding the emerging phenomena and then logging the results on the central chart for each case in the data set. Entries are generally highly summarised, displaying the key substantive areas and the more abstract classifications that have been developed.

A central chart would typically contain anything up to thirty or forty items. A few of these will be demographic characteristics, as noted above, but most will be abstracted classifications or typologies developed in the descriptive and classificatory stages of analysis. A central chart of this kind is extremely helpful for detecting patterns of association for further investigation and for trying to piece together different parts of the data for a more summative review. It may also be useful for generating a higher level – or 'meta' – classification or typology, involving different parts of the data set.

It is not possible to display the central chart for the homelessness study because it would require considerable explanation to make all the summarised items meaningful. However, the kind of information contained included:

Age, gender, ethnic group, sexuality, employment history, sources of income
Categorisations of episodes of housing crisis, accommodation resulting, current accommodation
Housing prior to housing crisis and nature of departure from home (categorised)
Summary of factors causing housing crisis
Coping strategies (summarised)
Nature of interventions (summarised)
Outcome of interventions (summarised)

… and so on with selected key phenomena or issues from each subject chart.

Detecting patterns of association or clustering

When deciding where to search for linkages or clusters within the data, the researcher will already have hunches and hypotheses he or she wishes to evaluate. It may be necessary to return to individual thematic charts where connections or links mentioned by respondents may be recorded, or where the researcher's own preliminary hunches or observations have been noted in the more interpretative columns.

Whatever the source of the lead, the analyst should begin the search for associations at the individual case level. By reading across charted data for each individual case, similar and different linkages between phenomena may emerge. By moving through the cases, reading down two or sometimes three columns at the same time, the analyst should be looking out for patterns between phenomena and whether or not these are replicated across the data set. A useful tool in the search for matched set linkages is to plot, for each case, the various phenomena in summary form on the central chart (if one already exists) or to create a simple summary chart. By interrogating this, it is possible to identify patterns that may escape the analyst's eye in the

(Continued)

BOX 9.10   *(Continued)*

larger set of thematic charts. These patterns can then be confirmed within the main set of charts. Summary or central charts can also be a useful way to investigate whether there are any patterns that exist which are unique to particular subgroups. The data set should be interrogated until all relevant patterns and associations – including contradictory ones – have been identified and explored.

For example, in the homelessness study, an important relationship was found between the nature and severity of the housing crisis, the coping strategies that people had used to deal with it and the factors that had led to it ending (if it had done so). All this information was on one chart (Chart 3) although in different thematic columns. In another example from the same study, connections were found between ways in which young people – and other people – had responded to their sexuality; the factors that had perpetuated the housing crisis; and the resulting impact on the young person, both practically and emotionally. In this case, the information that led to finding these connections was in four different thematic columns on three different subject charts. In both examples it was necessary to investigate the charts, first within cases and then across all cases within the selected themes. The matrix structure of Framework makes such two-dimensional searches possible and relatively easy to carry out.

The search for patterns or differences takes place exactly as described for matched set linkages. However, in this case, the focus of the search is known in advance (that is, to detect differences between identified groups) so the data can be ordered in a way that makes inspection easy to undertake. This can be done manually through summaries of the data (see Box 9.10) or by reordering the data set on the computer.

VERIFYING ASSOCIATIONS

Having found what appear to be linkages and associations in the data, it is necessary to then explore why they exist. This is because the relationship itself – that is, that there is a connection between X and Y – is not verifiable within the small, purposively selected samples used in qualitative research unless the explanation for their occurrence can also be found. The methods used to verify associations are the same for each of the types of associative analysis described above.

A first step is to check exactly how the level of matching between the phenomena is distributed across the whole data set. This is one of the few occasions when numerical distributions are used in qualitative research – but as a means, not an end, to gaining understanding. The counts will show how many times phenomenon A links with phenomenon B – and within which subgroups in the sample. It will also show where there is *no* matching of the kind under study.

A second step is to interrogate the patterns of association. Unlike large-scale quantitative surveys where a correlation may be presented as an output in its own right, in qualitative research a pattern of association is used as a pointer towards further stages of analysis. As noted in Chapter 8, the evidential base of a qualitative data set is a rich resource in offering explanations of why phenomena are occurring. Now is the time to use it. A pattern has been found and appears significant – why is it occurring?

The way in which explanations are developed is discussed below, but it is important to stress that in the search for explanations the analyst looks not only at cases that fit the pattern, but also at cases that do not. In qualitative analysis, 'outliers' as they are sometimes termed, should never be ignored. This is partly because a qualitative analysis is not complete until all the scenarios discovered have been examined, even if they cannot be fully explained in the testing of explanations. For example, they may show that the original pattern was perhaps a false lead; or that other factors also have an influence on the phenomena under study such that a more refined or complex analysis can be developed. Search continues until all those that are out of pattern have been examined. This either brings further refinement to the tiers of explanation – or it leaves some individual cases as unexplained puzzles. Either way the continued search has a payoff in terms of deepening understanding of what is occurring in the data set.

Developing explanations (Box 9.11)

The search for explanations is a hard one to describe because it involves a mix of reading through synthesised data, following leads as they are discovered, studying patterns, sometimes re-reading full transcripts, and generally thinking around the data. It involves going backwards and forwards between the data and emergent explanations until pieces of the puzzle clearly fit. It also involves searching for and trying out rival explanations to establish the closeness of fit. In essence, it is a stage at which the data is interrogated in a number of different ways to further understanding of what is causing or influencing phenomena to occur.

Explanations rarely just emerge from the data. As Richards and Richards comment, they are more often

> … actively constructed, not found, as Miles and Huberman nicely put it, like 'little lizards' under rocks. They will continue to be constructed by human researchers. They are 'mental maps', abstracted webs of meaning, that the analyst lays over bits of data to give them shape without doing violence to them (1984: 83). The researcher must weave these webs … see the links and draw the threads together, often by creative leaps of imaginative analogies. (1994: 170)

There are a number of ways in which the researcher can build an explanation, depending in part on the nature of the study, the emergent patterns within the data, and the researcher's own theoretical or epistemological perspective. To unpack the way in which explanations are developed, it is helpful to distinguish between different types of explanation. At an analytic level, explanations may be based on the explicit reasons that are given by participants themselves, or alternatively implicit reasons that are inferred by the analyst. Within these two approaches, explanations may be dispositional – that is, they derive from the behaviour and intentions of individuals; or they may be situational – that is, attributed to factors from a context or structure which are thought to contribute to the outcome (Layder, 1993; Lofland and Lofland, 1995).

It is important to note a difference in the nature of the evidence used to generate and support explicit and implicit accounts. For explicit accounts, the evidence appears overtly in the reasoning within the participants' responses (see below). For implicit accounts, on the other hand, the researcher may draw on patterns within the data, for example the matched set linkages and attachment to subgroups described above, or the interweaving or juxtaposition of apparently unconnected themes which nevertheless occur in close proximity within the interviews. Alternatively, the researcher may deliberately put together different pieces of evidence in order to develop or construct an explanation. Where reasons are implicit and inferred by the researcher, the process may entail searching for a possible underlying logic within what people have said; using common sense to search for explanations; applying powerful analytic concepts; comparing findings with those in other studies; or relating findings to a more theoretical framework. Again, each of these is discussed below.

USING EXPLICIT REASONS AND ACCOUNTS

During an effective in-depth interview, participants will always be asked why they feel, act and believe as they do and these explicit accounts are of immeasurable value in understanding motivations and intentions. The researcher may decide to simply present the recurrence, range and diversity of explanations given by participants themselves, or to look for patterns among and offer explanations for these explicit accounts. These may be dispositional – for example, the aspirations and requirements that lead to the choice of a particular vocation or career; or situational, for example, the features of dental surgery delivery that have put people off going to the dentist.

INFERRING AN UNDERLYING LOGIC

It may be the case that deeper explanations of a phenomenon are not immediately conveyed, or even clearly understood, by the individuals themselves and the researcher will want to identify factors which are not initially evident in the data. For example, in the benefit take up study, some of the reasons given directly by participants only went so far towards explaining why there was such reluctance to claim a financial entitlement. In the course of discussing their benefit claiming behaviour, however, it was common for participants to make adverse remarks about, or to have very negative images of, 'other people who claim', as described above. This also suggested that there was a wish to dissociate from other claimants – to not be identified with them – and further explanations were built around this inference.

Three approaches are possible on the basis of such evidence. In the first, the researcher may tease out an explanation based on the juxtaposition or interweaving of two apparently unconnected themes. Here, the analyst makes a connection between the negative perceptions of benefit claimants and reasons for not claiming which appear in close proximity in the interview, even though one is not explicitly cited as an explanation for the other. The analyst then hypothesises that fear of identification with 'other benefit claimants' was one of the factors inhibiting a claim among some non-claimants. Although this still leaves unanswered questions (such as why some people have such negative images of benefit claimants), it provides a level of explanation that rarely emerges directly from non-claimants themselves.

Alternatively, an explanation may be based on the repeated coexistence of two sets of phenomena although they do not necessarily appear in proximity in the interview. Using the example above, it has been shown in the analysis that there were very negative images of benefit claimants among some groups of non-claimants. However, without the help of seeing these images intertwined with reasons for not claiming, it would not necessarily be evident that any kind of explanatory link existed. The search for an explanation would therefore need to be more circumspect since the two phenomena may just be coexistent rather than related factors.

It is also possible to use the absence of phenomena to inform the underlying logic of an explanation. This can arise, for example, when a feature that is formative in some people's accounts is entirely missing from others. This raises an important question as to why this is the case which then needs to be investigated. This can be done through examining the accounts of people who have *not* mentioned a factor or reason to see if an explanation for its lack of relevance or influence can be found; or comparing the two sets of accounts to see what differences might explain its presence or absence.

USING COMMON SENSE TO SEARCH FOR EXPLANATIONS

The researcher may follow common sense assumptions when attempting to explain patterns within the data. These premises or assumptions may either fit a pattern commonly known to exist or simply make straightforward 'sense' through something seen in the data. However, once they have been made explicit, they will need to be fully interrogated across the whole data set to ensure that their explanatory base is supported.

For example, in a study of factors affecting dental attendance, it would be 'common sense' to assume that access to the dental surgery, in terms of opening hours and location, may raise different issues for people who are in employment than for those who are not. This 'assumption' can legitimately give lead to investigation but not to what the outcomes of that investigation might be. It may well be for example that there are inhibitors to dental attendance surrounding access for both groups but that these differ in terms of their nature. Thus the 'common sense' assumption is a spur to investigation which then continues with interrogation of the data.

DEVELOPING EXPLANATORY CONCEPTS

Sometimes a powerful analytical concept which is developed in the course of the study can itself explain a phenomenon. Often these are underpinning or 'meta' concepts that make it possible to place important emergent themes within a broader explanatory framework. For example the concept of 'social loss' was developed by Glaser and Strauss (1967) to refer to estimations made by nurses about the social value of patients and the degree of impact a patient's death would have on his or her family or occupation. Glaser and Strauss found that the greater the social loss of the patient the better the standard of care he or she received. Thus the concept of social loss was used to explain variations in the data. Another example comes from Wiener's (1975) study of people with rheumatoid arthritis. She developed the concept of 'normalisation' to refer to the attempts people made to carry on with their lives. Not only does the concept draw together seemingly diverse behaviour, normalisation also depicts an overall strategy for coping with the disease and helps explain why people behave in particular ways.

DRAWING FROM OTHER EMPIRICAL STUDIES

Ideas and hunches about possible explanations can also come from comparing the researcher's own study with others which have been carried out in the same or a similar field. Here the researcher may 'borrow' concepts or explanations to see how well they fit his or her findings. For example, studies that have examined systems for allocating and managing money within households have consistently shown that adherence to traditional 'gender roles' have an important influence on the systems developed (see for example Pahl, 1989). This concept was adopted in a study which explored ways in which couples in receipt of benefits manage their income. It was found to have significant power in explaining differences in the money management models found (Molloy et al., 1999).

USING THEORETICAL FRAMEWORKS

Where researchers are interested in a particular field or body of literature, or where they are committed to a particular theoretical perspective, they may wish to relate their local findings to a broader context and develop 'local' explanations in accordance with their chosen theoretical or analytical framework. For example, the researcher may employ established theoretical concepts such as 'socialisation', 'gender stereotyping' or 'deviance career' to explain patterns within their study. Alternatively, researchers may decide that their study is a particular case of a broader phenomenon and apply theoretical explanations to account for the findings of their own research.

BOX 9.11   USING FRAMEWORK TO BUILD EXPLANATIONS

The use of Framework in the search for explanation is difficult to illustrate because it depends on looking at and investigating the complete data set. It is necessary to see how different bits of data fit together, either across the main themes or within groups of cases to explore links, connections and explanatory routes. Since it is not possible to display the full data set, a brief account of how the Framework charts can be used in these stages of analyses is given below.

There are three general features of Framework that aid explanatory analysis:

- easy access to the synthesised data so that it can be continually revisited
- the ability to be able to look within cases across a range of different themes or phenomena
- the ability to move rapidly between thematic and case based analysis because of the matrix display.

Each of these features allows the analyst to move up and down the 'analytic hierarchy' as described in Chapter 8.

The search for explanations within charted data involves very similar practices to those involved in the investigation of associations (see Box 9.10). It begins by selecting individual cases and reviewing the charted data in the columns relevant to the linked phenomena. Through repeated interrogation of cases at the individual level, explanations can be generated and assessed. Alternatively, explanations can lie in subgroup analysis – for example where different relationships or patterns between two or more phenomena relate to their place in a particular typology or group within the study population. Such explanations can be aided by the use of central charts to reveal clusters of cases with similar attributes or characteristics. Hypotheses built upon such clustering can then form the basis of interrogation within the main set of charts.

However, when no obvious explanations exist, the charted data will need to be interrogated in a different way. As discussed in the main part of this chapter, common sense often plays a part here in directing the analyst towards possible hypotheses, as do explanations derived in other studies or from theoretical frameworks. Such hypotheses can help the analyst to select the appropriate parts of the data set for in-depth investigation (i.e. which columns to select to review for all respondents). Summary or central charts can again be a very useful tool in facilitating this kind of analysis. By examining the fit of hypotheses in summary form across all cases, potential explanations can be confirmed or abandoned. If confirmed, explanations can then be further explored in the full set of thematic charts. However, it is important to retain analytical integrity when searching for implicit explanations within the charted data. Although the analyst's substantive knowledge of a topic can be put to great use, this should not be imposed upon the data for explanations that they will not support.

In the homelessness study, the piecing together of information across both cases and themes led to the development of a number of strategies for service delivery. One of the key strands of explanation on which these strategies was based concerned the need for recognition of the origins of homelessness – and hence for interventions appropriate to the individual to be made. The development of both the explanation and the strategy came about through a number of different routes but the ability to look at both causes and outcomes, and across cases where interventions had and had not been appropriately gauged, was crucial in supporting the basis of the recommendation.

Explanations developed in this way must be carefully checked to ensure that they reflect the uniqueness and diversity of the data and do not 'bully' the findings to fit preconceived ideas. We have argued that, at the beginning of the analytical hierarchy, the researcher should stay close to the participants' own language and accounts and then, later in the analytical process, introduce theoretical concepts or theories in as far as they actually match the data. If a theoretical framework is applied to the data too early in the analytic process, much of the detailed richness of the data will be lost.

Seeking wider applications

The final tier of analysis involves a consideration of whether evidence from the study has some wider application. This might be a contribution to theory or to a theoretical debate, suggested strategies for the formulation or realignment of a social policy, or recommendations about practices within a public service. The next chapter is devoted to a discussion of how qualitative data can be generalised and the different kinds of wider inference that can be drawn. But, at the end of this analysis chapter, it is important to recognise that any consideration of the wider applications of research findings forms part of the analytic output from a study. As such it needs to be strongly supported by evidence with a clear exposition of how the inferential or explanatory arguments have been developed.

Analysing group data

The principles, processes and outputs described above relate to all forms of qualitative analysis concerned with interpreting meaning, irrespective of the type of data collection methods used. But there are some additional features that need to be considered when data have been collected through group discussions rather than individual interviews. We briefly consider these below.

The nature of group data

There are a number of ways in which group data differ from individual interview data but the following have particular significance for analysis:

- *Group dynamics.* A dynamic will occur within each group that will affect the way in which the subject is discussed. This will partly be manifest through what is said, or how it is delivered, but there will also be many non-verbal communications. The latter is additional evidence that the researcher will need to make explicit so that it is captured on tape or noted immediately after the discussion (see Chapter 7).

- *Interactions.* There will be interactions between group members that may take the form of affirmations, disagreements, conflicts, or simply continuation of a previous contribution from another member. These are part of the 'data' and the way in which such interactions take place are a useful source of information. But they will also result in some incomplete or fractured elements in the discussion.
- *Uneven coverage.* The level and coverage of data available for each participant is likely to be uneven. This will occur within one discussion where each member of the group will speak at varying lengths on different topics, depending on the salience of that subject to them; and across different groups because each group will shape a slightly different agenda depending on the contributions of individual members and the dynamic between them.
- *Less extensive coverage.* Whatever the level of contribution, there will be less coverage/depth of information for each participant than in an individual interview because time has to be 'shared' between the different discussants.
- *The influence of other views.* Group members have the opportunity to hear different or opposing views or other ways of expressing their own arguments. As a consequence, they will modify, refine or extend what they say in the light of the other contributions. This process needs to be investigated in the group forum so that the ways in which views develop can be traced in analysis. It is for this reason that each contribution needs to be attributed to their originator in the verbatim transcript, although obviously in anonymised form (see Chapter 7).

Approaches to group analysis (Box 9.12)

There are two main ways in which group data can be analysed, the first of which is most commonly practised:

- *Whole group analysis* which treats the data produced by a group as a whole without delineating individual contributions. The group therefore becomes the unit of analysis and will be treated in the same way as a unit of individual data. Additional information (in the form of notes) about group interactions or the balance of individual contributions may be added to the data as part of the evidence.
- *Participant based group analysis* where the contributions of individual participants are separately analysed within the context of the discussion as a whole. This allows the information of each participant to be retained and for interactions between individual members to be noted as part of the recording of the group dynamic.

Methods for carrying out these two different forms of analysis are described in more detail in Box 9.12.

BOX 9.12   USING FRAMEWORK TO CHART GROUPS

Many of the principles for charting data from in-depth interviews also apply to group discussions. However, there can be some differences in the way a data set is structured depending on whether the analyst chooses a 'whole group analysis' or 'participant based group analysis' – as described in the main text. While the appearance of thematic charts remains the same for both types of analysis, what is treated as a 'case' varies.

In whole group analysis – each row on a thematic chart is designated for a separate group discussion. For each piece of data charted for that group, there needs to be a note of which respondent made the contribution (using an identifier – see below) as well as a page reference. Conversely, for participant based group analysis, each group is allocated a different matrix or chart. Each person within the group discussion would then be allocated a unique row in that chart, again designated with some identifier. The identifiers are usually the gender of the contributer followed by a number to indicate their order of speaking at the start of the group (e.g. M1, F2, F3, M4 etc.).

The guidelines for entering data in charting groups are identical to those for entering data from depth interviews. In addition, it is useful for later analysis to keep a record on the charts of dynamics that occur within the group process. This would include:

- *The interactions between group members* so that specific interchanges about, or the elaboration of, a point can be followed. With whole group analysis this can be made clear as text is recorded. For participant based analysis, the flow of the text can be indicated by comments like 'Disagrees with M3 because ...' Or 'intercepts/follows F2 with ...'
- *Non-verbal communications* which should have been picked up and captured on tape during the discussion or through notes made by the researcher at the end (see Chapter 7). These will be things like assent or dissent being shown through the nodding or shaking of heads, people looking doubtful or puzzled about what someone else is saying or the stridency, not to mention volume, with which points are expressed. These should again be entered on the charts in the form of notes like (general agreement with this view) or (strong exchange between M1 and F5 about this). Again, these notes should be used to consider why this dynamic has occurred in the context of the group.
- *The levels of participation by different group members* so that the characteristics of people who have contributed above or below the average can be identified. The reasons for this can then be considered in relation to the subject matter under study. This is particularly important when 'whole group analysis' is undertaken where the contributions of individuals will not be evident from an inspection of the charts alone.
- *The formulation and evolution of views* will occur as the group progresses, as was described in Chapter 8. This is a vital element of group evidence because it shows how people move on in their thinking in the light of new or different information. In the main this should be captured through the order in which points appear on the transcript, which is likely to be the same in the charted material. But it may also require some notes from the analyst, when listening to the tape or reading the transcript. It will certainly require some revisiting and reflection at later

(Continued)

> **BOX 9.12** *(Continued)*
>
> stages of analysis so that the evolution of views and perspectives can be interpreted in the later analysis.
> - *Suggestions and ideas* because groups are very productive forums for generating new ideas and solutions there is often much material of strategic value embedded in the text. It is sometimes helpful when charting to delineate this – through the use perhaps of underlining or a coloured font. Another possibility is to have a column in each chart to capture the specific suggestions that have been made by the group. This can include suggestions that are implicit as well as those expressed as recommendations.
>
> *The use of screening information.* It is never possible in a group discussion to collect very detailed information about the circumstances or histories of each individual attending. It is sometimes useful therefore to use information collected during screening to provide additional background. This can be recorded in summary form in group based analysis or as part of the data if participant based analysis is being carried out. However, this requires having the screening information for those who attended the group carefully matched to their group identifier.

The advantage of participant based analysis over whole group analysis is that it allows more detailed evidence about similarities and differences between group members to be determined. It also allows certain types of analysis (such as associative analysis) to take place at an individual as well as a group level. The main disadvantage is that it may remove the immediate context in which the contribution was made, although there are ways to deal with this during the data management stage of analysis. It is also much more time-consuming than group based analysis because the contributions of each member have to be traced throughout the discussion. A decision about which approach to use will therefore depend in part on resources but will also be determined by the objectives of the research and the kind of analytical outputs that are required.

It is important to note that certain forms of analysis are more limited with group than with individual data. The identification of sectors and typologies has to happen at a more general level of assignment because different levels of information will be available about each individual. It cannot be carried out at all if group based analysis has been undertaken unless the groups themselves are very homogeneous in representing previously defined sectors of the population. Similarly, associative analysis is likely to be less refined than with individual data as it will have to take place either at the more global level of the group; or will be incomplete because of missing evidence.

Nevertheless, group discussions also have additional ingredients that are missing from individual data brought about through the interactions between group members. They can be extremely creative and may therefore be a rich resource for developing new strategies or generating hypotheses. They can also help in the understanding of diversity by engaging people with different perspectives in debate and can thus have additional explanatory power. These analytic advantages and limitations have to be weighed in the context of the aims of the study when a choice about data collection methods is being made (see Chapter 3).

KEY POINTS

- Data management may involve the identification of initial themes or concepts within a data set; labelling or tagging the data; sorting the data by theme or concept; and summarising or synthesising the verbatim material. Although there are many analytic tools or supports available to aid these tasks, data management is generally a laborious process. Nevertheless, working through the raw data material at this level of intensity is worth the investment. Only by doing so will the lines of enquiry to pursue, or the puzzles posed by the data, begin to emerge.
- Descriptive accounts which involve detection, categorisation and classification of the substantive content and dimensions of phenomena, are frequently used in qualitative analyses. They require exploring the data to generate descriptions that are conceptually pure, make distinctions that are meaningful and display content that is illuminating.
- Typologies are specific forms of classification that help to describe and explain the segmentation of the social world or the way that phenomena can be characterised or differentiated. They are usually multidimensional or multifactorial classifications in which categories are always discrete and independent of each other. Establishing typologies involves identifying relevant dimensions, testing the fit of the dimensions, establishing cross-fertilised typological categories and testing the fit of the newly defined categories.
- Explanatory accounts tend to be developed at the later (or higher) stages of analysis when most of the descriptive and typological work has been undertaken. They may derive from finding patterns of association within the data and then attempting to explain why those patterns occur; or building explanations from other evidence or interrogations of the data. These might involve using explicit reasons and accounts; inferring an underlying logic; using 'common sense'; developing explanatory concepts; drawing on other empirical studies; or using theoretical frameworks. These, in turn, are likely to lead to consideration of how the study evidence has wider application, either to theoretical debate or to the formulation or realignment of social policy.

KEY TERMS

Framework is a matrix based method for analysing qualitative data. It facilitates data management such that all the stages involved in the analytic hierarchy can be conducted. The name 'Framework' comes from the '**thematic framework**' which is a central component of the method. The thematic framework, as in other analytic tools, is used to classify and organise data according to key themes, concepts and emergent categories.

Indexing concerns the process of labelling or tagging the original data to identify the theme or concept to which it relates. Some analysts or software developers refer to the same process as 'coding'. Indexing usually occurs at an early stage of the analytic process as a first step in identifying the content of the data.

Charting refers to the process of synthesising the original data and locating it within the thematic framework or matrix that has been developed. It involves the inspection of every piece of data and depends on accurate retention of the original terms, concepts and language used by the study participants. It encompasses both reduction and ordering of the data, two of the key stages in data management.

Further reading

Hammersley, M. and Atkinson, P. (1995) *Ethnography: Principles in Practice*, 2nd edition, London: Routledge
Mason, J. (2002) *Qualitative Researching*, 2nd edition, London: Sage
Miles, M.B. and Huberman, A.M (1994) *Qualitative Data Analysis: An Expanded Sourcebook*, London: Sage
Richards, L. and Richards, T. (1994) 'From filing cabinet to computer' in A. Bryman & R.G. Burgess (eds) *Analyzing Qualitative Data*, London: Routledge
Strauss, A.L. (1987) *Qualitative Analysis for Social Scientists*, Cambridge: Cambridge University Press

10

Generalising from Qualitative Research

Jane Lewis and Jane Ritchie

The issue of generalisation – that is, whether the findings from a study based on a sample can be said to be of relevance beyond the sample and context of the research itself – is an important one. However, there is much diversity among authors in the meaning attached to the term and in conclusions about whether qualitative research findings are capable of supporting wider inference. This is largely because perspectives on generalisation are strongly influenced by the epistemological and ontological orientations of the contributors (Seale, 1999). As was discussed in Chapter 1, debate about whether it is valid to draw wider inference from a single study depends on how the 'meaning' attached to qualitative research evidence is conceived; and whether it is seen to have any 'reality' beyond the context in which it was derived.

Partly as a consequence of such differences, writers vary in the attention they pay to the issue of generalisation; some give it serious attention within the epistemological framework within which they work; some dismiss it as having no relevance; and some ignore the subject completely. But this, in turn, means that there is not a clear and agreed set of ground rules for the conditions under which qualitative research findings can be generalised or what this process involves.

It is our view that the findings of qualitative research can be generalised but that the framework within which this can occur needs greater clarification. This chapter is therefore devoted to generalisation and the circumstances under which it is possible. We begin by discussing definitions of generalisation and their particular meaning in the context of qualitative research. This leads on to a discussion of validity and reliability and their relationship with generalisation. We then set out some suggested principles for drawing wider inference from qualitative research and the conditions under which it can occur.

Definitions of generalisation

Generalisation is often discussed in two linked but rather different contexts. These have been described by Hammersley (1992) and others as 'empirical' and 'theoretical' generalisation.

Empirical generalisation concerns the application of findings from qualitative research studies to populations or settings beyond the particular sample of the study. Some authors prefer the terms 'transferability' or 'external validity' to describe this. The nature of the 'receiving context' to which findings are applied is varied, and again authors are not always explicit about the types of context to which findings can be 'transferred'. They may be the wider population from which the sample is drawn, other populations, or settings or 'treatments' outside the precise subject of study.

The second context within which generalisation is discussed is theory-building. This involves the generation of theoretical concepts or propositions which are deemed to be of wider, or even universal, application. Conclusions are drawn from features or constructs developed in a 'local' or single study which are then utilised in developing wider theory.

One of the difficulties in understanding the issues surrounding generalisation is that the distinctions between empirical and theoretical generalisation are not universally or consistently applied. As a result it is not always clear with which aspect of generalisation writers are dealing. But an additional confusion arises because empirical generalisation incorporates two separate constructions of inference that require different conditions – that is, generalising to the population from which the sample is drawn, and generalising to other settings and contexts.

To help with clarification, therefore, we suggest that generalisation can be seen as involving three linked but separate concepts:

- first, what we have termed representational generalisation: the question of whether what is found in a research sample can be generalised to, or held to be equally true of, the parent population from which the sample is drawn
- second, the question of whether the findings from a particular study can be generalised, or inferred, to other settings or contexts beyond the sampled one. We have called this inferential generalisation
- third, theoretical generalisation which draws theoretical propositions, principles or statements from the findings of a study for more general application.

For many research studies, and particularly those carried out in the social policy arena, a first concern is usually representational generalisation. That is, there is a primary concern to know how far the findings from a study can be generalised to the specific population from which the study sample was drawn. But this application of generalisation receives much less coverage in existing literature on qualitative research methods than theoretical and inferential generalisation, by whatever names they might be called.

This is particularly frustrating given that representational generalisation involves very different issues in qualitative research than in quantitative research. In the absence of clear understanding of this, the quantitative research paradigm is sometimes inappropriately applied to qualitative research, with unsatisfactory results. As Platt notes:

> It is curious how often criticisms of case studies as a basis for 'generalization' use ideas of representative sampling, appropriate only for estimating the prevalence of a characteristic in a population, to dismiss their adequacy for making contributions to theoretical explanation. (1988: 17)

The issues involved in inferential and theoretical generalisation are also applicable, of course, to quantitative research, although it is striking that they are discussed rather more thoughtfully in texts on qualitative methods than in those concerned with survey research.

The three forms of generalisation described above can be illustrated by a qualitative study undertaken as part of an evaluation of 'personal adviser' services within an employment programme for disabled people (Loumidis et al., 2001). Briefly, pilot projects, run variously by statutory, voluntary and private sector organisations, were set up to provide advice and support to people receiving out-of-work disability benefits who wanted to work, or to take steps towards paid employment. One element of the evaluation was a qualitative study among participants, which involved in-depth interviews exploring experiences of participation and movements into, or towards, work.

In the context of this study, representational generalisation raises questions about whether the findings from the interviews with the sample of participants can be generalised to the total population of pilot programme participants. This is clearly of immediate relevance: if the findings can only be said to be of relevance to the individuals sampled, this will affect the reliance that can be placed on them in developing the employment programme. Representational generalisation involves two key issues. First, whether the phenomena found in the research sample (for example, views, experiences, behaviours or outcomes) would similarly be found in the parent population. Second, whether other additional phenomena (or different perspectives on them) would be found in the parent population which are not present in the study sample.

Inferential generalisation raises questions as to whether the findings can be inferred to other settings – that is, to services beyond those operating within this pilot disability programme. The most immediate concern was the relevance of the findings to a second wave of pilot projects which were to be set up in the months after the evaluation concluded. These were likely to be different in structure, focus, philosophy and funding from those examined in the original evaluation and it was important to consider how far the findings of the first evaluation could be used to inform their design and operation. But there are also questions about how far the findings can be applied or transferred to other services providing support to disabled people who wish to move into or towards work, or even to settings where other types of services are provided to disabled people.

There may additionally be questions about how far the study evidence can be transferred to populations other than disabled people – for example, other populations to whom welfare to work programmes are targeted. This question of transferability to other populations is a further aspect of inferential generalisation although perhaps a more difficult one. As is discussed below, inferential generalisation requires congruence between the 'sending' and the 'receiving' contexts. This makes it necessary to have knowledge of both the sending and receiving contexts before a 'transfer' of the findings can occur with any certainty.

Finally, theoretical generalisation involves the contribution of the evaluation to social policy or theory more generally. These might be inferences of relevance to policy, such as requirements for effective welfare to work programmes or models of service delivery. Alternatively, they might be contributions to wider social theory, such as discrimination and disability, or paid work as a normative concept.

Although the scope for generalisation is an important criterion by which the utility or quality of a research study is judged, there may also be value in individual studies which cannot be generalised. A study which cannot support representational generalisation may still generate hypotheses which can inform and be tested in further research. It may yield material about a particular individual case which is of interest in its own right; in this context, Platt (1988) uses the example of studying how Darwin arrived at his theory of evolution. And in certain settings, the findings of a single study, which can be representationally generalised, will be of value even if they cannot be inferred to other populations or if they make little or no contribution to wider social theory. Nevertheless, whether a study can support generalisation is rightly seen as one of the criteria by which it will be judged. The next section thus looks at how these different applications of generalisation are approached in the context of qualitative research.

Approaches to generalisation

Theoretical generalisation

The classic concept of generalisation, as defined by writers such as Kaplan (1964), involves statements of causal relationships which are of universal application. Kaplan provides a definition of 'nomic' generalisation, the most important characteristic of which is that

> ... generalisation must be truly universal, unrestricted as to time and space. It must formulate what is always and everywhere the case, provided only that the appropriate conditions are satisfied. (1964: 91)

Generalisations are thus assertions which are context-free, and their value lies in their ability to achieve prediction.

As was discussed in Chapter 1, many writers have been unhappy with the transposition of concepts from the natural sciences to the social sciences. This has particular relevance for the basis on which wider theoretical inference is drawn in social enquiry. Different interpretations of theoretical generalisation have therefore been developed in social research related to the ontological base from which they derive. These lie somewhere between the law-like universal theories of the natural sciences on the one hand, and the assertion that there can be no meaning outside the individual context on the other.

As has already been indicated, our own position lies somewhere in the midst of these. It is our view that qualitative research studies can contribute to social theories where they have something to tell us about the underlying social processes and structures that form part of the context of, and the explanation for, individual behaviours or beliefs. The particular value of qualitative research lies in its ability to explore issues in depth and from the perspectives of different participants, with concepts, meanings and explanations developed inductively from the data. The degree to which the data from a study support existing theories can be assessed, by comparing how well different cases 'fit' within an established theory and how far it is able to explain behaviour in individual cases. Those theories can then be developed and refined so that they accommodate any newly found variations in behaviours or circumstances identified through research.

Ultimately, we would argue, like Seale (1999), that the relevance of a new or refined theory needs to be established by further empirical inquiry. Rather than seeing theory as fixed and immutable, it is perhaps better understood as a fluid collection of principles and hypotheses. The relevance of these can only be asserted with varying degrees of certainty depending on the extent to which research or other empirical evidence exists to support them.

Inferential generalisation

Lincoln and Guba have been particularly influential in positions on inferential generalisation – generalising from the context of the research study itself to other settings or contexts. They talk about 'naturalistic generalisation', a concept introduced by Robert Stake (1978) in his discussion of case study methods. This offers a more intuitive and empirical form of generalisation, based on the researcher's own experience and feelings, rather than one that is rationalistic and law-like. As Stake says:

> What becomes useful understanding is a full and thorough knowledge of the particular, recognizing it also in new and foreign contexts. That knowledge is a form of generalization, arrived at by recognizing the similarities of objects and issues in and out of context and by sensing the natural co-variations of happenings. (1978: 6)

In discussing the transferability of data, Lincoln and Guba agree with Cronbach that there will always be factors that make a particular setting unique but that, taking these into account, judgements about transfer to other settings can be made (Cronbach, 1975). Cronbach argues that generalisations should be seen as working hypotheses or extrapolations rather than as conclusions. Patton, discussing this, sees extrapolations as

> ... modest speculations on the likely applicability of the findings to other situations under similar, but not identical conditions. Extrapolations are logical, thoughtful and problem-oriented rather than statistical or probabilistic. (2002: 584)

Building on these views, Lincoln and Guba argue that transferability depends on the degree of congruence between the 'sending context' within which research is conducted, and the 'receiving context' to which it is to be applied. The researcher must provide 'thick description', a concept first introduced by Geertz (1993). Thick description has been translated in many ways but essentially requires the researcher to provide sufficient detail of the original observations or commentaries – and the environments in which they occurred – to allow the reader to gauge and assess the meanings attached to them. This, it is argued, will allow the degree of similarity, or congruence, between the two contexts to be assessed by others. Although, as Kennedy (1979) notes, researchers may not like the ambiguity of this, it is difficult to see how researchers could predict the potential for inferential generalisation from their studies. It would be impossible for any researcher to anticipate, and to understand in depth, the range of other populations or settings which might hold appropriate resemblance, or for which the transfer of findings might have relevance.

Inferential generalisation in social research must similarly be a matter of judgement, and the role of the researcher is to provide the 'thick description' of the researched context and the phenomena found (views, processes, experiences etc.) which will allow others to assess their transferability to another setting. As with theoretical generalisation, the inference must rest as a hypothesis until proved or disproved by further evidence.

Representational generalisation

Representational generalisation, as we have termed it – the extent to which findings can be inferred to the parent population that was sampled – is generally dealt with by other writers in discussions of generalising to 'other' or 'wider' populations but receives surprisingly little specific coverage.

Where it is addressed, some writers see the particular methods of qualitative research studies as undermining the scope for representational generalisation. These arguments are generally based on the fact that qualitative research involves relatively small samples which are not selected to be statistically representative (see for example Miles and Huberman, 1994; Arksey and Knight, 1999), or on the use of responsive and non-standardised interviewing (see for example Holloway and Wheeler, 1996). Other writers see the existence of confirmatory evidence from other research conducted with the parent population as being necessary to assert that a study's findings can be generalised (see for example Hammersley, 1992), and the role of quantitative research data here is particularly stressed (Seale, 1999).

Lying beneath these perspectives appear to be concepts of representational generalisation which are derived from quantitative research paradigms, with an emphasis on probability samples and measurement. When these are simply applied to qualitative research, it is hard to avoid the conclusion that representational generalisation cannot be supported.

However, the basis for representational generalisation in qualitative research is very different from quantitative research. Qualitative research cannot be generalised on a statistical basis – it is not the prevalence of particular views or experiences, nor the extent of their location within particular parts of the sample, about which wider inference can be drawn. Rather, it is the content or 'map' of the range of views, experiences, outcomes or other phenomena under study, and the factors and circumstances that shape and influence them, that can be inferred to the researched population. Although individual variants of circumstances, views or experiences would undoubtedly be found within the parent population, it is at the level of categories, concepts and explanation that generalisation can take place.

Other research evidence can help in assessing how far the findings from a study can be generalised to the parent population, but it is not a requirement for representational generalisation. Assessing representational generalisation turns on two broad issues. The first is the accuracy with which the phenomena have been captured and interpreted in the study sample. This will depend on the quality of fieldwork, analysis and interpretation. The second issue is the degree to which the sample is representative of the parent population sampled. Here, as we have argued in Chapter 4, representation is not a question of statistical match but of inclusivity; whether the sample provides 'symbolic representation' by containing the diversity of dimensions and constituencies that are central to explanation.

Establishing representational generalisation thus draws in issues of validity and reliability, although with different formulations than they hold in statistical research. Indeed, the validity and reliability of data have a crucial bearing on whether any wider inference can be drawn from a single study, of whatever form the inference might take. This is because, in different ways, they are concerned with the robustness and 'credibility' of the original research evidence. However, as with the broader issue of generalisation, doctrines about the nature and importance of these concepts within qualitative research differ with the 'school' to which the writer belongs. The following section provides an overview of these differing perspectives, and discusses how reliability and validity link with different forms of generalisation.

Reliability and validity

The concepts of reliability and validity were developed in the natural sciences. Because of this, and the very different epistemological basis of qualitative research, there are real concerns about whether the same concepts have any value in determining the quality or sustainability of qualitative evidence. Certainly, tests or measures of reliability and validity, as used in mathematical or physical sciences, are wholly inappropriate for qualitative investigation and cause considerable confusion when applied. But in their broadest conception, reliability meaning 'sustainable' and validity meaning 'well grounded' will have relevance for qualitative research since they help to define the strength of the data. This is of particular concern in the context of generalisation where the ability to transfer findings to other contexts or wider theory will be circumscribed by the soundness of the evidence. It is for this reason that we have devoted this section to an exposition of how reliability and validity can be interpreted and understood in the conduct of qualitative enquiry.

Reliability

Reliability is generally understood to concern the replicability of research findings and whether or not they would be repeated if another study, using the same or similar methods, was undertaken. The extent to which replication can occur in qualitative research has been questioned on a number of counts. The 'constructivist' school, for example, argue that there is no single reality to be captured in the first place so replication is an artificial goal to pursue (for example Hughes and Sharrock, 1997; Marshall and Rossman, 1999). There are also concerns that the concept of 'replication' in qualitative research is naïve given the likely complexity of the phenomena being studied and the inevitable impact of context (Lincoln and Guba, 1985). Similarly, those who believe that qualitative research is dynamic and can only be conducted effectively in a responsive manner argue that studies can never be, nor should be, repeated (Holstein and Gubrium, 1997).

Because of such concerns, the idea of seeking reliability in qualitative research is often avoided. Instead, writers discuss similar issues using terms and concepts that are felt to have greater resonance with the goals and values of qualitative research.[1] For example in discussing reliability (and also validity) a number of authors talk about the 'confirmability' of findings.

Others talk in similar vein about the 'trustworthiness' (Glaser and Strauss, 1967), the 'consistency' (Hammersley, 1992; Robson, 2002) or the 'dependability' (Lincoln and Guba, 1985) of the evidence.

All of these features lie at the heart of reliability in its broadest sense and are key to appraising the soundness of a study. But as with reliability they raise important questions about how researchers can ensure that these qualities exist and how they can measure or demonstrate them.

A first requirement is to have a clear understanding of what features of qualitative data might be expected to be consistent, dependable or replicable. Essentially, it is the collective nature of the phenomena that have been generated by the study participants and the meanings that they have attached to them that would be expected to repeat. In other words, there needs to be some certainty that the internal elements, dimensions, factors, sectors and so on, found within the original data, would recur outside of the study population. A secondary consideration is whether the constructions placed on the data by the researcher have been consistently and rigorously derived. Thus the reliability of the findings depends on the likely recurrence of the original data and the way they are interpreted.

It is in the latter context that in discussions about reliability, or its equivalents, an important distinction has been drawn between external and internal reliability. The first concerns the level of replication that can be expected if similar studies are undertaken; the second relates to the extent to which assessments, judgements, ratings and so on, internal to the research conduct, are agreed or replicated between researchers, judges etc. (sometimes termed inter-rater reliability). Both of these matter in assessments of quality although the value placed on inter-rater reliability (often seen as synonymous with internal reliability) is often given more attention. Equally, both have salience if concepts other than reliability are preferred – for example, notions of external and internal confirmability or consistency make equal sense.

Some authors are of the view that reliability and replication have direct relevance to qualitative research (LeCompte and Goetz, 1982; Silverman, 2000a). They may also prescribe precise ways in which this can occur. Seale (1999), for example, sees the expectation of complete replication as 'a somewhat unrealistic demand' but argues that this is more a consequence of practical problems associated with qualitative research than 'insuperable philosophical problems' concerned with conceptions and measurements of 'reality'. His view is that good practice in relation to reliability and replication can be achieved through an aspect of reflexivity, that is 'showing the audience of research studies as much as is possible of the procedures that have led to a particular set of conclusions' (1999: 158). This enables readers imaginatively to 'replicate' studies, and also helps to ensure that claims are supported by adequate evidence.

---

1 There are also other terms suggested as equivalents for reliability, such as credibility, that are more closely related with validity.

We share the view that reliability should not be seen as an alien concept in qualitative research. Certainly this is true for applied policy research where some notion of replicability has to matter if any wider inference from the data is to be drawn. For example, a qualitative research study might show that certain groups of young people within a sample require a modified 'slow track' through an employment programme, and why this was so. Unless it was believed that this was a finding that would be replicated if other studies were carried out – that is, it was not simply a 'quirk' of this particular sample – there would be little incentive to act on this evidence.

It is this need to be reassured about the sturdiness of a finding, beyond just the study sample, that links questions about reliability to those surrounding generalisation. Unless there is some belief that a finding would be repeated if another similar sample were studied (and another, and another) then there must be some doubt about the significance of the 'phenomena', as identified in its original form. This is not to question the existence of the phenomena itself but rather to acknowledge that other factors may exist which will affect its potential for replication (for example, some bias within the original sample or a 'location bound' phenomena). This would also mean it had no potential for transferability of the kind described by Lincoln and Guba (1985).

Some attention has been paid to how to ensure that qualitative research is reliable, or has one of the qualities associated with potential replication (see for example Kirk and Miller, 1986; Perakyla, 1997). There are two levels on which it is suggested that this should happen. First there is the need to ensure that the research is as robust as it can be by carrying out internal checks on the quality of the data and its interpretation. Second, there is the need to assure the reader/enquirer of the research by providing information about the research process.

In this context, questions surrounding the appropriate design and conduct of the research are crucial and need to be asked throughout the research process. For example:

- Was the *sample design/selection* without bias, 'symbolically' representative of the target population, comprehensive of all known constituencies; was there any known feature of non-response or attrition within the sample?
- Was the *fieldwork* carried out consistently, did it allow respondents sufficient opportunities to cover relevant ground, to portray their experiences?
- Was the *analysis* carried out systematically and comprehensively, were classifications, typologies confirmed by multiple assessment?
- Is the *interpretation* well supported by the evidence?
- Did the design/conduct allow equal *opportunity for all perspectives* to be identified or were there features that led to selective, or missing, coverage?

These questions are of the same order as those that might be asked in quantitative research if the reliability of a study was being assessed. But the content of the questions is very different and it is a clear understanding of such differences that is often missing. Those who have a poor understanding of the qualitative research paradigm often judge reliability by criteria that are applicable only to quantitative measurement. By such criteria the soundness of qualitative research will inevitably fail, just as any quantitative study would fail by assessment through qualitative criteria.

Validity

The validity of findings or data is traditionally understood to refer to the 'correctness' or 'precision' of a research reading. It is often explained as a concept with two distinct dimensions, the first, known as internal validity, concerned with whether you are 'investigating what you claim to be investigating' (Arksey and Knight, 1999); and the second, termed external validity, concerned with the extent to which 'the abstract constructs or postulates generated, refined or tested' are applicable to other groups within the population (LeCompte and Goetz, 1982) or to other contexts or settings (Lincoln and Guba, 1985). The direct overlap here between external validity and the ability to generalise are just part of why discussions about generalisation can easily become entangled. But, more crucially, such questions raise important issues about the content of a research 'reading', the accuracy or subtlety of its calibration and the extent to which it has wider applicability.

As with reliability, there has been some attempt in the qualitative literature to move away from the concept of validity and to use instead other terms which are more appropriately related to the 'correctness' of qualitative evidence. For example, Lincoln and Guba (1985) suggest that 'credibility' and 'transferability'[2] translate more appropriately for naturalistic enquiry than 'internal' or 'external' validity; Glaser and Strauss (1967), among others, talk of the 'credibility' and 'plausibility' of research claims.

Although the validity of 'measurement' is seen as a primary concern of quantitative research, and of positivist research more broadly, it is widely recognised that it is an equally significant issue for qualitative research. But the questions posed are different ones and relate more to the validity of representation, understanding and interpretation. Hammersley for example says that 'an account is valid or true if it represents accurately those features of the phenomena that it is intended to describe, explain or theorise' (1992: 69). Kirk and Miller (1986) relate validity to the interpretation of observations and whether the researcher is calling what is identified by the 'right name'.

In addition to the broad distinction between internal and external validity, a number of different forms of validity have been identified, some originally in the context of quantitative measurement, others with specific reference to qualitative research. The former include content, face, construct, predictive, concurrent and instrument validity. Altheide and Johnson's (1994) cataloguing

---

2 Transferability is also equated by Lincoln and Guba to generalisability, with which it is more commonly associated by other authors.

of interpretivist conceptions of validity include a wide and sometimes obscure set of terms (successor, catalytic, interrogated, transgressive, imperial, simulacra/ionic, situated and voluptuous validity) although all in some way concern the viability of the interpretation that has been placed on the research evidence.

Within the different forms of validity identified there is some interchange, indeed even confusion, between the concepts of the validity of a measurement or reading and its validation. This is largely because there is an underlying doubt in the minds of many qualitative researchers that there is any effective means of 'verifying' accuracy or truth in social enquiry, even if there is a 'truth' there to be confirmed. As a consequence, numerous suggestions are made about how to cross-check the validity of a finding or conclusion (validation) or to allow sufficient access to the research process for others to do so themselves (documentation). Both of these are discussed more fully below.

The primary 'validity' question which qualitative researchers have to address, at least as far as internal validity is concerned, is similar to the one posed by Hammersley (1992). Our restatement of this would be: Are we accurately reflecting the phenomena under study as perceived by the study population? This gives rise to a host of subsidiary questions all of which concern the strength of the research methods used and the quality of analysis and interpretation that takes place. In these respects it would be repetitive to rehearse all the features that matter, since these have been discussed in earlier chapters. But continual interrogation of methods is needed throughout a research study with checks of the following kinds:

- *Sample coverage*: did the sample frame contain any known bias; were the criteria used for selection inclusive of the constituencies known, or thought, to be of importance?
- *Capture of the phenomena*: was the environment, quality of questioning sufficiently effective for participants to fully express/explore their views?
- *Identification or labelling*: have the phenomena been identified, categorised and 'named' in ways that reflect the meanings assigned by study participants?
- *Interpretation*: is there sufficient internal evidence for the explanatory accounts that have been developed?
- *Display*: have the findings been portrayed in a way that remains 'true' to the original data and allows others to see the analytic constructions that have occurred?

As will perhaps be evident, there is a strong link between the validity of qualitative data and the extent to which generalisation can occur. Unless there is some degree of confidence in the internal validity or credibility of a research finding, then there would be little purpose in attempting any of the three types of generalisation previously described. External validity, on the other hand, is an inherent part of generalising since it asks whether a finding can be 'transferred' or 'applied' to other groups within the wider population or to other settings. It is thus formative in determining whether representational generalisation (to the wider population), inferential generalisation (to other contexts), or theoretical generalisation (to the development or enhancement of theory) can occur.

Validation

A number of different ways have been suggested to validate or verify qualitative data. Broadly these fall into two main sets, the first concerned with internal validation and the second concerned with verifying findings externally. Examples of the two kinds are shown below.

INTERNAL VALIDATION

- *Constant comparative method* (Silverman, 2000b) or *checking accuracy of fit* (Glaser and Strauss, 1967) which involve deriving hypotheses from one part of the data and testing them on another by constant checking and comparison across different sites, times, cases, individuals, etc.
- *Deviant case analysis* to ensure that deviant cases or 'outliers' are not forced into classes or ignored but instead used as an important resource in aiding understanding or theory development. Clayman and Maynard (1994) outline three ways that deviant cases can be used:

  - they may show an orientation to the same regularities as other cases but then deviate. This would help to support the claim that the 'regularities' are normative
  - they may contain specific individual differences which explain why the more normative behaviour is not always found
  - they may mean that a hypothesis needs to be refined or reconceptualised.

Both these methods form an inherent and essential part of developing descriptive and explanatory accounts, as was described in Chapter 9.

EXTERNAL VALIDATION

- *Triangulation* assumes that the use of different sources of information will help both to confirm and to improve the clarity, or precision, of a research finding. As was discussed in Chapter 2, there is some debate among qualitative researchers about the extent to which triangulation is useful in checking the validity of data or whether it is more a means of widening or deepening understanding of a subject through the combination of multiple readings. Nevertheless a number of authors argue that triangulation also has some role in the validation of findings. Patton, for example, states that 'It is in data analysis that the strategy of triangulation really pays off, not only in providing diverse ways of looking at the same phenomenon but in adding to credibility by strengthening confidence in whatever conclusions are drawn' (2002: 556). He, like other authors, suggests that there should be different forms of triangulation, based on a conceptualisation first introduced by Denzin (1978). These comprise:

- *Methods triangulation*: comparing data generated by different methods (e.g. qualitative and quantitative)
- *Triangulation of sources*: comparing data from different qualitative methods (e.g. observations, interviews, documented accounts)
- *Triangulation through multiple analysis*: using different observers, interviewers, analysts to compare and check data collection and interpretation
- *Theory triangulation*: looking at data from different theoretical perspectives

• *Member or respondent validation*: which involves taking research evidence back to the research participants (or to a group with the same experience or characteristics) to see if the meaning or interpretation assigned is confirmed by those who contributed to it in the first place.

All these methods of external validation can be useful although all have limitations in what they can contribute to full 'confirmation' of a finding from a qualitative study. There is much discussion in the literature about both the approaches that can be used and the limits they hold for 'testing' validity (see for example Silverman, 2000b). Indeed Hammersley (1992) argues that we can never know with certainty that an account is true because we have no independent and completely reliable access to 'reality'. We must therefore judge validity on the basis of the adequacy of the evidence offered in support of the phenomena being described. He then suggests grounds for assessing 'adequacy' including credibility, centrality and relevance, all of which would seem vital in judging the integrity of research evidence.

Documentation

As described above, there is a fairly clear consensus among contemporary commentators that qualitative research needs very clear description, both of the research methods used and of the findings, to aid checks on validity by others. This is needed not only to display the research process but also to show the conceptual processes by which meaning or interpretation has been attributed or theory developed. Such 'transparency' or 'thick description', as Lincoln and Guba (1985) advocate, will allow the reader/enquirer to verify for themselves that conclusions reached by the researcher hold 'validity' and to allow others to consider their 'transferability' to other settings.

Generalising from qualitative data

As was noted earlier, we hold the premise that generalisations can be drawn from qualitative data in relation to the parent population from which the sample is drawn (representational generalisation); about other settings in which similar conditions to those studied may exist (inferential generalisation); and as a contribution to generating or enhancing ideas and theories (theoretical generalisation). There are, however, strict limits on what can be generalised. There are also variations in the level of certainty that can be attributed to the inference, depending on the level of meaning or interpretation being assigned. In this section we discuss the kinds of questions that researchers need to have in mind when assigning wider inference.

Some key principles

There are a number of important principles to be borne in mind when generalising from qualitative data. These are illustrated below but can be broadly summarised under four broad headings: full and appropriate use of the evidential base; display of analytic routes and interpretation; research design and conduct; validation.

FULL AND APPROPRIATE USE OF THE EVIDENTIAL BASE

Use of the original data   Generalisation will be strengthened by making full use of the original data that support the phenomena under study. As was described in Chapter 8, a well-collected data set offers the qualitative researcher a rich resource in terms of evidence that can be called upon during the classificatory and interpretative stages of a study. Thus the language and content of participants' accounts, the features they display by way of segmentation, the inherent linkage and explanation they convey are all essential elements in the conduct of analysis and interpretation.

Encompassing diversity   One of the key roles of qualitative research is to identify and display range and diversity, as discussed in earlier chapters. This is particularly important for generalisation where key contributions can be made to understanding the different behaviours, perspectives, needs, groups and so on, that exist within a population. There is virtually no social or psychological phenomena that exists about which there will be only a single perspective to account.

Nature not number   The inference that can be drawn from qualitative data concerns the nature of the phenomenon being studied but not its prevalence or statistical distribution.

DISPLAY OF ANALYTIC ROUTES AND INTERPRETATION

Level of classification   The level of classification assigned to a phenomena will affect the extent to which generalisation can occur. As a very general rule, higher levels of aggregation of categories are more likely to be transferable in representational terms than more specific or individualised items since they will be less idiosyncratic in presentation (see Example 1 below). But the analytic routes to these need to be made explicit so that the unifying concepts and the rationale underlying their named meaning can be seen.

Assigning meaning and interpretation   The nature of generalisation varies as the researcher moves through the 'analytic hierarchy' although it is important to recognise that meaning is being assigned at every level (see Chapters 8 and 9). But the more a researcher places his/her own meaning or interpretation on a finding as a basis for generalisation, the more open it will be to questioning and review by others. Thus, again, display of the meanings and interpretations assigned is important.

RESEARCH DESIGN AND CONDUCT

Checks on research design and conduct   As generalisation is taking place it is important to be vigilant about any features of the research design or conduct that might limit the nature or power of the inference drawn. These checks would be along the lines of those noted above (see Reliability and validity).

Display of research methods   A full description of the design and conduct of the research will allow others to assess the research methods used and any limitations they hold.

Noted limitations   When undertaking checks on the design and conduct of the research or when considering wider applications of the evidence, it is important for researchers to note any limitations that they themselves encounter or consider. These may become evident as the research is in progress (for example, difficulties of gaining access to particular study groups) or may emerge as the analysis and interpretation is being completed (missing experiences or perspectives among the study population). Documentation of these will help the user of the research to understand the boundaries of the evidence in terms of any wider inferences that can be drawn.

VALIDATION

Validation of the inference   Once a finding appears open to generalisation, then checks against other evidence and corroboration from other sources are highly desirable.

All of these principles apply to the three forms of generalisation described earlier. But, as Lincoln and Guba (1985) argue, the central condition for inferential generalisation is similarity between the 'sending' and 'receiving' contexts. To allow others to assess this, it is necessary to provide in-depth description of the research context; of the views, processes, experiences or other phenomena that are the subject of study; of the factors and circumstances that shape those phenomena; and of how they appear or are experienced differently in different contexts or parts of the sample.

Contributing to theoretical understanding also requires robust research methods and particularly quality in data interpretation. It will be important to move beyond accounts of individual particularised cases to more collective descriptive and explanatory analyses (see Chapter 9). There should be a clear account of the logical and conceptual links made in the researcher's interpretation, and of the evidence on which they are based. A thorough understanding of existing theoretical discussion in the relevant area at the outset of the study can inform the study design and the conduct of fieldwork, but data can also be explored from a theoretical perspective after the event. A clear account of theoretical positions that have informed the study will help others to assess its contribution and credibility.

Examples of generalising from qualitative data

Two examples are given below of the kinds of thinking that has to surround generalisation and the different kinds of inference that might be drawn. In each, a small selection of data and the questions that need to be asked of the evidence are described. We have also highlighted in italics the ways in which evidence and the inferences drawn from them were subject to verification using the four sets of principles described above.

EXAMPLE 1: YOUNG PEOPLE AND POLITICS
This first example comes from a study that examined young people's political interests and behaviour (White et al., 2000). It was carried out among young people aged between 14 and 24 using a combination of individual interviews, paired interviews and focus groups.

The data
One of the aims of the study was to explore the contemporary issues that were of concern to young people. They were asked about this in very open form without any indication of the kinds of areas or subjects to be covered. The list of subjects generated was very extensive (several hundred items), of which a brief selection is summarised in the first part of Box 10.1.

The subjects generated across the interviews and discussions were classified in two ways, the first categorising the broad subject area of concern (40 categories) and the second the level at which the issue held significance (four classes). These are shown in the lower part of Box 10.1.

BOX 10.1   EXAMPLE 1: YOUNG PEOPLE AND POLITICS

Issues of concern to young people (extract)

Being bullied
Too much homework
Pressure to pass exams/get qualifications
Grants for further/higher education

Difficulties getting work/too few suitable jobs
Low wages/wages offered to young people
Nowhere to learn occupational skills/limited training opportunities
Employers' attitudes to young people

Side effects of drugs
Ease of access to drugs
Need for better information about drugs
Making cannabis legalised

Being hassled for standing around on the streets
Nowhere for young people to 'hang out' in the evenings
'Old fashioned' youth clubs
Lack of good sports/exercise facilities

Third World debt
War in Bosnia
Troubles in Northern Ireland

Categories: Broad subject area of concern included

Conditions in other countries
Preservation of wildlife
Education
Drug laws and education
Legal age limits
Policing strategies
Lack of social facilities
Job availability
Relationships
Personal safety
Self image/identity

Classes: Levels of significance

Global
National
Local
Personal

Representational generalisation

The key question for representational generalisation is whether these same categories and classes are believed to exist among the general population of young people from which the sample was drawn. There are a number of interim questions that need to be addressed on route to answering this, a selection of which follow:

Validity
Have the items been appropriately captured, as generated by the young people themselves?
The issues were originally identified and described as they were spoken by young people, so the initial answer to this is yes. But as the research team begin to classify, they move away from the formulation by the young people towards more conceptual categories. The question then becomes are these relevant and valid conceptualisations? The answer to this requires a judgement but there would certainly have been other ways in which the young people's concerns could have been categorised and classified. It is for this reason that researchers need to display their analytic routes and, in particular, the nature of the original data, so that readers and commentators can assess the evidence (display of analytic routes).

Are the issues, categories and classes comprehensive?
The list of issues is unlikely to be exhaustive because they are at a very detailed individual level. Categories, similarly, may not be fully comprehensive although they are likely to contain most major areas of concern because of the level of summation. Classes are comprehensive because of the very general level at which the items are now aggregated up to global (although not planetary) level.

Reliability
Would the issues, categories and classes be the same if another sample of young people were interviewed?
The list of concerns would probably not be exactly the same although very similar. The same range of subjects was raised at each group although the specific elements changed slightly across groups and shifted in emphasis as age increased (use of evidential base).

Categories would definitely exist – they occurred recurrently with a clear explanation as to why they were important to young people (use of evidential base). However, it is possible others might be added as noted above. Classes would almost certainly exist exactly as shown since they are conceptualised at a very general level and are comprehensive.

So the broad answer to the representational generalisation question is 'yes' although with increased certainty as specificity reduces. For the purposes of the study, however, this was sufficient to address some of the central concerns of the research. For example, in interpreting this evidence, it was observed that issues of concern to young people cover a wide range of social and political areas but are conceived and expressed in terms that are relevant to young people and thus do not necessarily have the same focus as older adults.

Although both these statements are, in theory, open to challenge or refinement, any alternative interpretation would have to accommodate the original evidence from young people.

Inferential generalisation

There is no obvious inferential generalisation to draw from this evidence and none occurred in the study concerned.

Theoretical generalisation

Evidence from the study was used to suggest that the issues that concerned young people covered a broad political agenda even if they were framed and spoken about using different terms. This challenged existing theory that young people are uninterested in 'political' issues or only interested in 'single' focus issues like animal rights. The lack of interest displayed by young people is with a narrowly conceived notion of politics in its more formalised form.

Theoretical generalisation of this kind is dependent on the robustness of the research evidence (*research design and conduct*) to draw conclusions about young people, the way the evidence is interpreted and the researcher's perspective on the meaning to attach to the data generated (*display of analytic routes and interpretation*). Provided that there is clear exposition of the theoretical construction and full description of the research methods and analysis process, such generalisation is a legitimate hypothesis but equally open to challenge by other researchers and commentators.

EXAMPLE 2: EVALUATING THE 'RESEARCHER IN RESIDENCE' SCHEME

This second example is drawn from an evaluation of the Researchers in Residence (Biosciences) scheme (Woodfield, 1999). The scheme, which was sponsored by three research councils and the Wellcome Trust, organised short placements for life science doctoral students in secondary school science departments. The scheme was intended to benefit both researchers and schools through an exchange of knowledge, ideas, experience and practice.

The data

One of the tasks of the evaluation was to examine the nature of activities in which the 'Researchers in Residence' (RinRs) were involved on their placements and how these were viewed by those involved in the scheme (RinRs, teachers and pupils). These were documented in detail but a broad classification was also produced showing the main roles that RinRs were playing. This had four categories, as shown in Box 10.2.

Both researchers and teachers identify these roles although not necessarily congruently in the same placement. It was also shown that the RinRs may play more than one role although usually one is dominant. Technically, therefore, this is not a typology as this would only allow the assignment of roles to one of the four categories (see Chapter 9).

One of the main uses of the classification was to see if other factors relate to these roles (such as what the RinRs do during their placements, how many different groups of pupils they see) and whether assessments of the value of the placement vary according to the role played. It was found that activities and placement structure/organisation did vary with the primary role but that assessments of the placement did not necessarily do so. But the assessments were very affected by a mismatch between the expected role and the role assigned or performed in practice.

BOX 10.2   EXAMPLE 2: RESEARCHERS IN RESIDENCE

Roles of Researchers in Residence

- 'Expert' scientist: to share expert scientific knowledge and research techniques with staff and pupils.
- 'Trainee' or 'potential' teacher: to observe science classes and gain a broad understanding of science education.
- 'Role model': to promote science and research, to demystify science and help to overcome stereotypes of scientists.
- 'Classroom resource': to provide assistance in the classroom and during extra curricular activities.

Representational generalisation

Validity

ROLES

Have the roles been appropriately identified in relation to the different tasks the researcher performed?

They are not detailed here, but the report contained analyses of the different activities in which RinRs were involved and the ways in which all the study groups (i.e. RinRs, teachers and pupils) perceived the functions of the researcher. This information was then used to form the above classification. The evidence was therefore drawn from multiple sources and there was commonality between them in the conception, if not the expression, of the RinRs' roles (*use of evidential base*). In addition, the analytic 'building blocks' were displayed for others to see what led to the formulation of the different roles (*display of analytic routes and interpretation*).

Is the list comprehensive?

There is no way of verifying this although the roles identified do encompass the different purposes that were envisaged in the design of the Researchers in Residence scheme (*validation*).

ASSESSMENTS OF PLACEMENTS

Were the assessments collected in a way that allowed participants to give a fair and full assessment of the value of the Scheme?

This requires revisiting methods of data collection (*research design and conduct*) to ensure that there was no potential bias that would have differentially affected the assessments in schools offering different types of placements.

Were appropriate opportunities given to determine expected and assigned/performed roles separately?

The design of the study was such that there was no contact prior to placement. 'Expected' roles were collected retrospectively and are therefore not 'pure' accounts of expectations and may well be affected by the placement experience. This was noted in the report (*research design and conduct*).

However, greater certainty about the conclusion comes from use of the evidential base where there were highly recurrent statements about what had been expected and what actually happened. Analysis of these showed the impact of dissonance between the two.

Reliability
Would the same roles be found in other schools not taking part in the evaluation?
It is very likely because all of them fit within the conceptual design of the project (*validation*). Also considerable effort was made at the sampling stage to ensure that schools sampled for the evaluation represented the full range of types of schools participating in the Scheme (*design and conduct of the research*).

Would the same assessments of placements have been made in other schools not taking part in the evaluation?
It is difficult to check the reliability of this since other features of schools or placements might have had a bearing on the assessments made. However, again, the diversity of the selection of schools is likely to enhance the potential for repetition.

Inferential and theoretical generalisation
No inferential or theoretical generalisations were made directly from the research, largely because this was a newly developed scheme and the primary concern was to evaluate its impact and operation. However, in the context of the above analyses, it would not be difficult to infer some general principles about similar postgraduate placement schemes, particularly in terms of ensuring that there is clarity, on the part of both the placed person and the host institution, about the expected roles and activities to be carried out.

Both the examples above illustrate the ways in which wider inference can be drawn from qualitative research while allowing others to check the 'credibility' of the conclusions drawn. However, it must be emphasised that there is no set prescription or water tight method for checking the generalisability of qualitative evidence. It requires careful reflection on, and questioning of, the evidence, in terms of both its quality and its potential for drawing wider inference; corroboration from other sources where these are available; and clear documentation of the research methods and analytic processes so that others can judge the inferential assessments made.

KEY POINTS

- There is much diversity among qualitative researchers in the meaning attached to 'generalisation' and whether qualitative research findings are capable of supporting wider inference. This is largely because perspectives on generalisation are strongly influenced by epistemological and ontological orientations. As a consequence there is not a clear and agreed set of ground rules for the conditions under which qualitative research findings can be generalised or what this process involves.

- Generalisation can be seen as involving three linked but separate concepts: representational generalisation, whether what is found in a research sample can be generalised to, or held to be equally true of, the parent population from which the sample is drawn; inferential generalisation, whether the findings from a particular study can be generalised, or inferred, to other settings or contexts beyond the sampled one; and theoretical generalisation, whether theoretical propositions, principles or statements can be drawn from the findings of a study for wider application.

- The validity and reliability of data have an important bearing on whether any wider inference can be drawn from a single study since, in different ways, they are concerned with the robustness and 'credibility' of the original research evidence. Because of the nature of qualitative data and the ways it is collected and analysed, the issues that surround assessments of validity and reliability have to be specifically formulated for qualitative research. This has led some authors to redefine the concepts that underpin reliability and validity so that they have greater resonance with the goals and values of qualitative research.

- There are some important principles to follow when generalisation from qualitative data takes place. These include full and appropriate use of the evidential base, the display of analytic routes and levels of interpretation assigned, checks on the research design and conduct and, where possible, validation of the inferences drawn.

KEY TERMS

Generalisation in social research concerns the potential for drawing inferences from a single study to wider populations, contexts or social theory. In qualitative research it is sometimes referred to as the **transferability** or **external validity** of research findings.

Reliability is generally understood to concern the replicability of research findings and whether or not they would be repeated if another study, using the same or similar methods, was undertaken. Because of the nature of qualitative research, the terms **confirmability**, **consistency**, or **dependability** are often preferred. All of them refer to the security and durability of a research finding.

Validity is traditionally understood to refer to the correctness or precision of a research reading. In qualitative research it concerns the extent to which the phenomena under study is being accurately reflected, as perceived by the study population. Again, alternative terms, such as **credibility** and **plausibility** are sometimes used.

Validation refers to the process of checking the validity of a finding or conclusion through analysis or cross-checking with other sources. **Member validation** involves taking research evidence back to the research participants or study population to see if the meanings or interpretations assigned are recognised and confirmed.

Further reading

Hammersley, M. (1992) *What's Wrong with Ethnography?*, London: Routledge

Kirk, J. and Miller, M.L. (1986) *Reliability and Validity in Qualitative Research*, London: Sage

Lincoln, Y.S. and Guba, G.E. (1985) *Naturalistic Inquiry*, Beverly Hills, CA: Sage

Seale, C. (1999) *The Quality of Qualitative Research*, Oxford: Blackwell

Silverman, D. (2000b) *Doing Qualitative Research: A Practical Handbook*, London: Sage

Strauss, A.L. and Corbin, J. (1998) *Basics of Qualitative Research: Grounded Theory Procedures and Techniques*, 2nd edition, Thousand Oaks, CA: Sage

11

Reporting and Presenting Qualitative Data

Clarissa White, Kandy Woodfield and Jane Ritchie

We come now to the final stage of the qualitative research process, that of reporting and presenting the findings. To do so we go full circle to a reminder that one of the key objectives of qualitative social research is to explore, unravel and explain the complexity of different social worlds. The reporting stage is critical to the success of this process. It also poses substantial challenges to the reporter because there is a need not only to represent the social world that has been researched, but also to re-present it in a way which both remains grounded in the accounts of research participants and explains its subtleties and its complexities. The reporting task, therefore, is not simply an act of recording the outcomes of the analysis but also an active construction and representation of the form and nature of the phenomena being explored.

In these respects, the reporting stage is the culmination of the analysis process. It provides an opportunity for further thought as the data are assembled into a coherent structure to convey the research evidence to the target audience(s). Data will be reanalysed, reassessed and assembled into a final package which will display the findings with ordered and reflective commentary. Reporting is then a continuation of the journey of interpretation and classification of data requiring continued data exploration, further interrogation of patterns and associations and more detailed interpretation and explanation:

> We have to approach it as an analytical task, in which the form of our reports and representations is as powerful and significant as their content. We also argue that writing and representing is a vital way of thinking about one's data. Writing makes us think about data in new and different ways. Thinking about how to represent our data forces us to think about the meanings and understandings, voices and experiences present in the data. As such, writing actually deepens our level of analytic endeavour. Analytical ideas are developed and tried out in the process of writing and representing. (Coffey and Atkinson, 1996: 109)

Many of the texts on qualitative research methods contain sections on the reporting process (for example Hammersley and Atkinson, 1995; Holloway and Wheeler, 1996; Patton, 2002; Rubin and Rubin, 1995; Seale, 1999; Strauss and Corbin, 1998). There are also a few devoted to the subject of writing up social research, both generally and specifically devoted to qualitative enquiry (Wolcott, 2001). Between them, these accounts contain much sound advice about how to organise the writing process, how to structure the written material and about how to achieve the appropriate balance between description and interpretation or between commentary and illustration. However, relatively few texts show how to display qualitative data in a way that is both faithful to the original material and provides clarity about the interpretative process that has taken place. The rare ones that have done so tend to be concerned with ethnographic accounts rather than the reporting of generated data from interviews and group discussions.

This chapter describes the process of reporting and the various tasks it involves. It begins with a discussion of the main challenges that a qualitative researcher has to face in writing up research findings and the different forms of research outputs that might be considered. It then moves on to a description of the main issues to consider when preparing a written report and the main tasks involved. This includes a discussion of how different forms of analytic output can be used in reporting and the levels of elucidation and illustration they require. We end the chapter with a short section devoted to oral presentations.

Challenges facing the qualitative reporter

As with any research reporting, the key aim in writing up qualitative evidence is to present findings in an accessible form that will satisfy the research objectives and enable the audience to understand them. Qualitative researchers will therefore share many common concerns with statistical researchers during the reporting process. But as was discussed in Chapter 8, the analytic output from qualitative research involves evidence of a very different kind from statistical reports. This poses certain challenges to qualitative researchers when portraying the different forms of descriptive and explanatory analyses that have been undertaken and the findings that have resulted. A brief review of these is given below and ways of meeting them are discussed later in this chapter.

Explaining the boundaries of qualitative research

Readers of qualitative reports may not be familiar with qualitative research, the methods it uses and the kind of evidence it produces. It will therefore be important to ensure that the audience understands what qualitative research can and cannot do. This will preferably include a discussion of the kinds of inference that can be drawn from qualitative data and its transferability to other settings.

Documentation of methods

A number of writers have stressed the importance of giving a clear account of research methods as part of displaying the 'credibility' of the evidence (Hammersley and Atkinson 1995; Holloway and Wheeler, 1996; Kvale, 1996; Lincoln and Guba, 1985; Rubin and Rubin, 1995). Indeed Kvale (1996) notes that qualitative methods are often a 'black box' which needs to be opened up to the reader or user of the findings. Written accounts therefore need to explain not only how the research was conducted but also why particular approaches and methods were chosen to meet the aims of the research.

Displaying the integrity of the findings

Integrity in reporting requires a demonstration that the explanations and conclusions presented are generated from, and grounded in, the data. Just as a survey researcher will use the tools of basic descriptive and interpretative statistics to present and explore their findings so a qualitative researcher should strike a balance between descriptive, explanatory and interpretative evidence. It is also important to be transparent about the process of analysis and interpretation so that audiences can follow through the processes of thinking that have led to the conclusions.

Being coherent

The depth and richness of qualitative data presents a considerable challenge in reporting. Findings cannot be captured in a neat series of statistics or graphs and, as a result, the reader is reliant on the author to make the story intelligible. The process requires the researcher to take the rich and detailed data that has been collected and present it in a way which effectively guides the reader through the key findings. This involves ordering what is likely to be disorderly data, unravelling complexity, and providing sufficient directions for the audience to follow the 'story' that is being unveiled. Rubin and Rubin (1995) offer a great deal of practical advice about how to keep the story cogent and clear for the reader and how to convey complexity without losing readability.

Displaying diversity

As explained in previous chapters, part of the power of qualitative research comes from its ability to explain the range and diversity of phenomena that occur. Therefore, a report or presentation which focuses only on the dominant message may well be misleading because it will provide only a partial map of the evidence. Inclusivity requires reporting and explaining the untypical as much as it does reporting the more recurrent themes.

Judicious use of verbatim passages

The temptation to pack qualitative research reports full of verbatim quotations is widely recognised by qualitative research practitioners. But there is strong advice to resist this temptation and use original passages both sparingly and for well-judged purposes (Holloway and Wheeler, 1996; Kvale, 1996; Rubin and Rubin, 1995). The overuse of cited passages can make a research account tedious to read, voluminous in length and can easily distract from the clarity of the main commentary.

Forms of research outputs

Most researchers want to make their research findings available to others and it is often an exciting moment in the research process when the outputs of many weeks, months or even years of intensive research labour are unveiled. In addition, it is usually a requirement of grant or contract funded research that the results should be available in the public domain. However, this may not always be done in the form of a final report. Researchers may choose, or be required to, present emergent or headline findings through an oral presentation or the preparation of an interim report or paper. Similarly, on completion of a project key findings and methodological issues may be disseminated through a range of different outputs such as conference papers, journal articles and books. Other possibilities include making contributions to policy forums or meetings to suggest ways of developing or changing existing programmes or interventions; involvement in media debates or programmes; or hosting conferences or workshops designed to explore theories or strategies arising from the evidence.

In addition, qualitative data take many different forms. In addition to verbal data the project may have gathered photographic or video evidence, observational notes or other materials generated through the use of projective techniques. The chosen output from the research should be appropriate to the data and provide a mechanism for displaying not only the interpretative commentary around the data but also examples of the original data collected. Photographic or documentary evidence may also be used to provide illustration of the context or environment in which the research was conducted or changes that occurred as the research took place.

Table 11.1   **The range of potential outputs from qualitative research**

Nature of output	Use when?	Objectives
Comprehensive • Substantive written report • Book	On completion	To provide a comprehensive review of research findings, research methods and wider implications
Summary • Executive summary • Book chapter • Journal article	Usually on completion of a project	To provide condensed information about key findings
Developmental • Oral presentation of emergent findings • Interim written report • Journal article • Conference or seminar paper	During ongoing project	To provide early indications of emergent findings or to offer theories or ideas for debate
Selective • Oral presentation with specific focus • Conference or seminar paper to selected audiences • Journal article • Media article or report	During or on completion of project	To focus on selected areas of research findings for specific audiences

Table 11.1 shows the range of outputs that might result from a qualitative study, or indeed any social research enquiry. These have been classified within four broad categories: comprehensive, summary, developmental and selective.

Comprehensive outputs provide a detailed and extensive portrayal of the findings from the research and are most commonly presented as written reports. The findings will be explored in detail with the necessary evidence and interpretative commentary provided for the reader. Similarly, both the implications of findings and the methodological approach will be discussed in some detail.

Summary outputs provide condensed accounts of the findings and can be delivered through a variety of oral or written mediums. They will convey key information and findings arising from the research in a distilled form. The findings will be explained in a less comprehensive fashion, the purpose being to provide the reader or listener either with an overview of important issues. In written form, these are often presented in what are termed 'Executive summaries' which allow people access to the main findings of a research study without reading the full report.

Developmental outputs, which again can be presented orally or in written form, are somewhat different from the former two. They are designed to generate discussion and debate about emergent issues arising from the research. They are often produced during the analysis stage of a project as issues and concepts begin to provide insights into the research question. Presenting interim findings or issues can allow funders or commissioners an opportunity to express particular interest in specific areas, request more analysis of areas of interest, and, in the case of evaluative projects, provide early feedback on the implementation and delivery of services or programmes. Similarly, papers given on interim findings at conferences or seminars can allow academic or other colleagues to contribute to the interpretation of the findings or to the formulation of further analyses.

Selective outputs, which may take a variety of forms, to provide accounts of specific parts of the evidence. This may be to address audiences with special interests, such as professionals or service users, or at conferences or seminars with particular substantive themes. Alternatively, it may be to offer a focused discussion on a key element of the research, as often occurs in journal articles or media reports.

There are certain factors that will determine the forms of research outputs resulting from a research study. The following are among the more significant.

REVISITING THE ORIGINS OF THE RESEARCH

The origins of the research and the purposes for which it was undertaken are important in informing the basis of the reporting strategy. For example, a piece of research conducted to inform a change in social policy can greatly differ from research designed to inform theoretical debates. The former may require a speedy presentation of headline findings to a key audience of policy-makers, followed by a comprehensive written report; the latter might lead to a journal article articulating the various theoretical implications or to material for a book.

MEETING CONTRACTUAL OBLIGATIONS

In commissioned research, the range and type of written outputs that are to be produced will have been agreed at the contractual stage with the commissioning body. For example, it is usual to find in the applied social policy arena that there are contractual obligations to deliver an oral and written report for qualitative research. Similarly in grant funded research, outputs may be determined by the funding body – for example in the form of 'good practice guides' for practitioners; or by priorities of the research institution in which the research has been conducted such as peer reviewed journal articles. Alternatively, researchers may have been asked to describe their plans for dissemination in their research proposal and these will need to be revisited when considering forms and media for reporting.

IDENTIFYING TARGET AUDIENCE(S)

The importance of keeping 'the audience in mind' throughout reporting is stressed by a number of authors (Hammersley and Atkinson, 1995;

Holloway and Wheeler, 1996; Patton, 2002; Rubin and Rubin, 1995). Audiences for the research findings will differ and it is important to bear in mind that what suits one audience may be inappropriate for another. For example, the needs of an audience of policy-makers will be different from those of an audience of academics interested in broader theoretical debates. Similarly, reporting to a group of service users may require a different focus or different levels of detail to those required by professionals. There may also be interest in feeding back to the study sample or the parent population from which they were drawn and, again, a particular form of output might be required.

THE RESOURCES AVAILABLE

Finally, there is no doubt that the resources available to a project may limit the nature of research outputs possible. Whether written, oral or other media are used to convey the research findings, there will be financial and time constraints that will require consideration. It is also worth remembering that there may be opportunities for dissemination that were not originally antici-pated. These might include journal articles or conference or seminar papers which will allow the research to be presented to different audiences.

Writing a qualitative research report

The process of reporting qualitative research is one of the most challenging stages of the research operation. It is common for researchers to encounter problems as they move from data analysis to presenting findings compre-hensively, articulately and with conceptual clarity. Yet once adept in this process, it can also become one of the most rewarding and satisfying tasks a researcher undertakes.

Although there are stages that can be followed to help with reporting there is no set formula for producing written accounts and there is no single model for a qualitative research report. There are many different approaches and con-ventions and the style and structure will vary according to the research objec-tives, the researcher, the funding or commissioning body and the target audience(s) being addressed, as discussed above. Nevertheless there are some general features of report writing that arise and some particular guiding prin-ciples for writing up qualitative evidence. We consider each of these in turn.

Some early features of reporting

GETTING ORGANISED

There comes a point in every qualitative research project where the moment of starting to write is drawing near. It is at this point that some preparation is needed in terms of both mental and physical organisation. First, it is highly likely that the researcher will be emerging from a deep involvement in analysis and ideas, hypotheses, and features of the research story will be furiously buzzing away. There is therefore a need to take the mental equivalent of a deep breath so that this buzz turns to productive output rather than becomes noisy interference. Ways of doing this may include spending a few hours writing down ideas or even half formulated thoughts, looking again at the original proposal or specification for the research or having discussions with research colleagues. It might even involve taking a few days away from the study to let the various ideas, puzzles or excitements settle down.

There will also be some more practical thing to get organised. First, it will be important to assemble all the materials that are needed for writing. These may include notes on relevant literature, fieldwork documents, notes taken during the course of the project and most certainly the outputs of analysis in whatever form they have been prepared. It may be that the researcher has decided to write up parts of the data, within an overall structure, as they move through analysis; or alternatively to wait until most of the analysis is completed before beginning to write. Either way, such assembly of 'writing materials' will be needed.

The other practical consideration is to make some space in the working programme to give consolidated time to the process of writing. It is virtually impossible to do good, reflective writing in snatched hours here and there. This is in part because of the degree of concentration needed to fulfil the delivery of analytic thinking; and in part because it becomes counterproductive to have to switch to other modes of activity. In particular, it is extremely difficult to keep alive the conceptual momentum needed for creative and penetrative writing if the researcher is simultaneously involved in other stages of another study or in totally different activities. All of this means that some space in the researcher's diary or agenda needs to be cleared for writing.

GETTING STARTED

Even if some record of the research process and preliminary findings are recorded as the research is undertaken, written reporting does not usually begin in earnest until all, or most, of the data analysis has been carried out. Beginning writing is probably the hardest part of the process.

Wolcott (2001) suggests getting started as early as possible because 'writing is thinking. Stated more contiously, writing is one form that thinking can take' (2001: 22). But much thinking also has to take place before writing begins in earnest so that the writer has a clear idea of how the journey through the research evidence is to be made. In this context, many writers emphasise the need to consider the 'story' that is to be told and how that story can best be conveyed in an organised and interesting way (Holloway and Wheeler, 1996; Patton, 2002; Rubin and Rubin, 1995: Strauss and Corbin, 1998: Wolcott, 2001). This wisdom applies both to written accounts as a whole and to individual sections or chapters.

Such preparation will also involve considerations about the structure and style of the report (see below). Wolcott (2001) suggests that this should include a sequenced outline of content but also a 'statement of purpose' as well as the basic story. Others recommend the preparation of an outline although with advice that the content and order need to remain flexible (Rubin and Rubin, 1995).

DECIDING ON SHAPE AND STYLE

Decisions about the structure, coverage and style of written accounts will all be interlinked since each of these features has an impact on the way the reader will enter and view the world that has been researched. These in turn may be affected by the research objectives, the requirements of the commissioning body and the audience(s) being targeted, as previously discussed.

Structure and content

There is much advice to be found on the components that can be included in a written report and the order in which they might appear (Wolcott, 2001; Holloway and Wheeler, 1996; Kvale, 1996). Box 11.1 outlines the key ingredients. This depicts the coverage for a comprehensive written report. The content of summary or developmental reports will vary, particularly in relation to the items shown in italics.

The main body of a written account usually contains the findings and the research evidence. Often a useful way into this is through the key themes and concepts that have been uncovered by the data analysis (Rubin and Rubin, 1995). Considerations about structure will also involve thinking about the order in which the evidence, and any conclusions reached on the basis of it, are presented. Morse et al. (2001) for example suggest two possible models, the first involving the reader in solving the 'puzzle' alongside the researcher; the second presenting a summary of the main findings and conclusions, followed by the evidence to support them. Rubin and Rubin (1995) also suggest these as possible ways of structuring reports but add two further options. These are 'analytic presentation' in which findings are organised in terms of areas of existing theory and the study evidence considered in the light of each; and through the logic of the research design, presenting through different groups of interviewee, or settings, cases or sites.

TELLING THE STORY

Whatever decision is made about the structure and organisation of the report, it is still necessary to think further about how the 'story' of the research evidence will be told. That is, how will all the different elements, themes, hypotheses, conclusions be related such that the readers attention is held and wants to know how the tale will unfold. There are certain features of research studies that can help in making these decisions.

BOX 11.1 FEATURES OF REPORT CONTENT

Title page containing the title of the study, report authors, any organisation details (where appropriate), the month and year of publication.
Acknowledgements
Abstract
Table of contents

Summary or Executive summary
Introduction explaining the objectives and scope of the research and the way in which the study was carried out.
   Literature review locating the findings within a wider policy and research context. This material can either be built into the introduction as a short contextual background section, or if a more extensive literature review has been undertaken, be the focus of a separate chapter. Alternatively, in circumstances where this material explicitly relates to the findings being reported, it may be more appropriate to integrate it into individual chapters.
Research findings and evidence
Conclusions providing a succinct review of the key themes reported and any implications arising from the research. Where appropriate it may also be useful to locate the study findings within a wider policy or theoretical context and also make recommendations for further research.
   The technical appendices provide an opportunity for a more extensive discussion of the research methods and display of any key documents used in the conduct of the research.

For example, if the research has identified and developed a strong typology (see Chapters 8 and 9), then it may be appropriate to present this right at the start of the written account. This can be done both through an exposition of the typological categories and through illustrated cases, each representing one of the different groups. This will not only bring alive the key differences within the study population but also provide a useful set of hooks on which to hang later discussion of themes and differing perspectives on them.

Another feature that may be relevant is coverage of different populations within a study. It is often the case in qualitative research that different groups will be interviewed or observed and this raises questions about how to portray the perspectives of each. A key question here is whether to deal with the evidence from each group separately or whether to integrate the different accounts and draw attention to similarities, differences and conflicts within a more thematic framework. For example, a study on parenting may have collected information from different family generations. So would it be better to report the views of children, parents, grandparents separately or should the different sets of evidence be blended in some way? The answers to these questions will depend on a number of factors, such as the likely repetition of material, the importance of constant comparison between groups and the extent to which there are very distinctive issues for the different groups concerned. But if evidence from different populations is presented separately, then there will need to be some kind of overview in which evidence from the separate groups is compared and contrasted.

Similar issues are raised by longitudinal research which aims to look at change over time. Again there are questions about whether evidence from the different time periods should be separately presented or whether the influences, or results, of time are considered in the context of each theme.

Sometimes there are very natural building blocks on which to construct a story. For example, studied programmes or processes may have an in-built progression or chronology that offers a clear narrative route. Similarly, the research may have an objective to investigate how certain phenomena relate (for example, how beliefs and attitudes influence behaviours) and there is a need to understand the individual phenomena first before considering their interrelationship. But often the path to take is not this clear and choices have to be made about which is a more captivating way to relay the data. For example, in exploratory or explanatory studies, it may be more enticing to the reader to present the meta findings or main conclusions first and then to unpack the more detailed evidence on which they are based. In other cases, it may be preferable to convey some of the mysteries or puzzles that the research presents before unveiling any new understanding that has been reached.

There are many such features of research that will affect how the 'story' generated by the research is presented and there are no prescriptions to offer about how it should be done. Each study needs to be considered in the light of its objectives, the nature of the data collected and the likely requirements of the target audiences. But reporters always need to think creatively about the best way to retain the reader's attention and to make the story 'add up', not just what would be the easiest way to relay the findings. The key objective is to find a form of presentation that has an underlying narrative and somehow compels the reader to want to find out more. This is not always simple to do but is certainly one of the safest ways to ensure that qualitative research reports get read.

Reporting style and language

The reporting voice will be determined by individual style, the requirements of the funders and the target audience(s). It will therefore vary for different types of reporting outputs. There may also be established formats and guidelines which funding bodies will require researchers to follow in the production of written reports.

Assuming there is a choice to be made, then consideration needs to be given to issues like: first or third person, active versus passive voice and present versus past tense. There are also decisions to be made about whether to adopt a 'realist' style (what you found out) or a 'confessional' style (how you did it) (Hammersley and Atkinson, 1995). There is also much debate about where the 'authorial' authority should lie and whose 'voice' – participants' or researchers' – should be dominant (Hammersley and Atkinson, 1995; Rubin and Rubin, 1995; Seale, 1999). The content of this debate will not be revisited here but it raises the important issue of how, and by whom, meaning or interpretation is being assigned and the extent to which this is evident to the reader. As has already been noted, it is our belief that there should be transparency about the 'analytic building blocks', a point we return to later in this chapter.

As with all reporting, the style of language that will be appropriate will vary according to the objectives and the target audience(s). It also needs to be accessible and preferably avoid research jargon and other technical terminology, other than perhaps for solely academic audiences. There are some debates about striking the right balance between 'aesthetics' and 'evidence' (Hammersley and Atkinson, 1995; Seale, 1999) although some general agreement that, whatever the density of the evidence, the account needs to both engage and stimulate the audience.

Describing the research context

Any research report, whether qualitative or otherwise in form, needs to provide some background information about the study. This will vary depending on the nature of the study and its objectives, but commonly includes an account of

- the origins of the research
- the aims of the study
- the theoretical or policy context in which the research is set
- the design and conduct of the study and the nature of the evidence collected
- and possibly some account of the authors' personal perspectives on the subject matter or aims of the enquiry.

In providing this kind of background, it is important to gauge how much detail to provide. In the main the reader will be keen to have some background but will need only enough to place the research evidence in its appropriate setting. The researcher, meanwhile, will have a very detailed knowledge of what led to the research and what was known beforehand and there will be a strong temptation to be overinclusive.

Balanced against this, there needs to be sufficient detail about the study's conduct for the reader to judge the 'credibility' of the research findings. Unless the research is highly 'confessional' in nature, this can often be covered in outline in an introductory chapter, supported by a methodological appendix giving further detail. It is generally preferable to keep methodo-logical detail reasonably brief in early sections of a report, while allowing people to look up the level of detail in which they are interested in an appendix.

This 'audit trail' as it has been termed (Holloway and Wheeler, 1996) allows the reader to see into the research process and follow its main stages. In addition to a discussion of the research design and fieldwork methods, which researchers commonly report, it is equally important for readers to know about the sample design and method of selection, the achieved sample composition and any known limitations within it, and the tools and approaches used in analysis. The epistemological orientation of the research team may also be useful, as was discussed in Chapter 1. Information of these kinds will offer some of the 'thick description' that many authors advocate for allow-ing wider inference from the study to be drawn (see Chapter 10).

The description of research practice should be supported through append-ing examples of relevant documentation used during the research, such as a topic guide, recruitment documents and the analytical framework. The documents might also include a copy of the thematic index used to label the data or of the thematic framework used for analysis.

Another feature that is important by way of background is to know some-thing about the composition of the sample that took part in the study. This may be in terms of socio-demographic characteristics, in relation to circum-stances or features that are central to the research or even possibly in the form of a typological classification that is heavily used in account of the find-ings. Although there need to be clear warnings that any distributions shown are there to display the internal composition of the sample only and *do not* hold any statistical significance, it is essential for readers to have some knowledge about the people who gave the original evidence. This can also be usefully illustrated by cameo descriptions which characterise the differ-ent groups or constituencies that form the sample.

Length

There is always a great temptation in writing up qualitative data to include too much material and not to be sufficiently selective about what is reported. There is inevitably a choice to be made about leaving some data out, otherwise readers will simply be swamped by the evidence and drown in the detail. Decisions about length are inevitably affected by the number and density of areas that are to be included. It is therefore always useful when drawing up an outline of content to consider whether all the topics planned can realistically be covered. If they cannot, then some selectivity will have to occur.

Wolcott (2001) also gives advice about what to do when writers are 'run-ning out of space'. The final recommendation is that if there is doubt about including material then it probably should be left out.

Integrating qualitative and quantitative findings

A discussion of how to integrate qualitative and quantitative findings within a single research account could be the subject of a whole chapter. While there is not the space for such coverage here, some useful pointers can be given, particularly for overcoming some of the difficulties that might be encountered.

First it is important for researchers who are reporting a mix of qualitative and quantitative evidence – and their readers – to understand that qualitative and quantitative evidence offer very different ways of 'knowing' about the world. They cannot just be knitted together as if from the same kind of yarn. The drawing together of the research account will therefore need careful construction – and detailed consideration of how the different types of evidence will be used in combination.

A related point concerns a decision about which kind of evidence will tell the main 'story' – it is very difficult if they both try to do so simultaneously in their different ways. So it is useful at an early stage to decide whether the qualitative account should drive the shape of the report with the statistical evidence used to support it; or whether the statistical account will provide the main structure for the report, with qualitative evidence being used to extend it. A less attractive alternative is to tell the two stories separately in different parts of the report. Usually this is very difficult for the reader because they are then left to decide how the two sets of data interrelate. It can also be rather repetitive to read because the same subject matter is likely to be covered twice.

Whichever choice is made about shaping the report, it is important that the full capacity of the qualitative data be used. There is often a temptation in these kinds of circumstances to simply use the qualitative evidence to provide quotes or case studies by way of illustration. While this will be one use of the qualitative data, it will have many other roles in amplifying and explaining the statistical findings and in providing context. There may also be evidence from the qualitative study which defines key groups within the study population which can be quantified through indicators in the statistical enquiry. These and other ways of harnessing qualitative and quantitative data were discussed in detail in Chapter 2.

When qualitative and quantitative evidence are merged in research accounts, there will always be occasions where a different 'reading' is given by the two types of data. The reasons for this need to be sorted out by the researcher(s), not left to the reader to puzzle over. There are usually good reasons for such differences in calibration because of the very different ways in which the data will have been collected, captured and analysed. These need to be explored by the researcher(s) so that any divergence in the accounts is understood.

Finally, in writing combined accounts, it is useful to tell readers which source of data has generated the evidence being discussed. Sometimes this will be very obvious – for example, in the commentary on a statistical table or in a discussion of underlying factors that have led to phenomena arising. But if the qualitative and quantitative evidence have been neatly interwoven it can sometimes be difficult to see how a particular piece of commentary was derived. Again, a brief reference to this will help the reader to understand which way of 'knowing about' the subject under study is being relayed.

Summaries

It is customary in many written accounts to provide a summary or abstract of the research findings. As noted earlier, these are sometimes called 'Executive summaries' which are intended to provide a short (between 2 and 5 pages) standalone account of the key findings and main messages derived from the research. Ideally, this should also contain a brief description of the methods used so the basis of wider inference can be judged. Sometimes there may be a requirement to produce a separate document summarising the findings, which is then published separately from the report.

As summaries are likely to be one of the more commonly viewed outputs it is important to ensure it gives a balanced and accurate report of the research and this can be a particular challenge to achieve in summarising qualitative data. Unlike quantitative data, qualitative findings are much more detailed and, as a result, important context and depth may be lost when summarising the findings to a more generic level. It is therefore wise to confine summaries to the dominant features of descriptive or explanatory outputs and any wider implications these may have for policy or social theory.

Displaying qualitative evidence – some general features and principles

It has already been emphasised that one of the main challenges in qualitative reporting is to find ways of telling the 'story' of the research in a clear and cogent way. In doing this, it is important that the subtlety, richness and detail of the original material is displayed while keeping the right balance between description and interpretation:

> An interesting and readable report provides sufficient description to allow the reader to understand the basis for an interpretation, and sufficient interpretation to allow the reader to appreciate the description (Patton, 2002: 503–4)

There will also be a need to demonstrate the bases on which interpretations have been made and conclusions reached through showing the evidence available to support them (Hammersley and Atkinson, 1995; Holloway and Wheeler, 1996; Morse et al., 2001).

BOX 11.2   STUDY ILLUSTRATION: THE RESEARCH

Two studies will be used to illustrate ways of displaying qualitative evidence. They were both carried out for the, then, Department of Social Security to explore how GPs make decisions about incapacity for employment and how they help their patients manage a return to work. The first, which was carried out in the early 1990s, was concerned with people who claimed or were receiving Invalidity Benefit, a benefit then available for people who had experienced long-term incapacity (that is, six months or more) through sickness or disability (Ritchie et al., 1993). The second, carried out around 10 years later, focused on people receiving benefits at earlier stages of incapacity (under six months). Here, GPs had a role in issuing medical statements for receipt of benefits before the state system for assessment of longer-term Incapacity Benefit came into play (Hiscock and Ritchie, 2001).[1] Both studies involved the use of in-depth interviews with GPs and, in the later study, strategic groups among GPs were also conducted.

This section describes how all these features can be attained with particular reference to the main types of analytic outputs described in Chapters 8 and 9. To aid with this, a continuing example is shown to illustrate the process (Box 11.2).

Descriptive accounts

DEFINING ELEMENTS, CATEGORIES AND CLASSIFICATIONS
In the reporting of qualitative data there will be many occasions on which descriptive and classificatory accounts will be needed to display the evidence collected. These will be required to show the nature of all kinds of phenomena, covering attitudes, beliefs, behaviours, factors, features, events, procedures and processes.

To display these to the reader it is helpful to show:

- examples of the original material on which description and classification is based
- the range and diversity of the different elements, concepts or constructs that have been found
- a comprehensive 'map' of all the categories that have been detected
- the basis of any subsequent classification and how the different elements and categories have been assigned.

---

1 Incapacity Benefit replaced Invalidity Benefit in 1995 as the main long-term state contributory benefit paid to people who are assessed as being incapable of work because of disease or bodily or mental disablement. Since the introduction of IB, judgements about longer-term entitlement to incapacity benefits (i.e. 28 weeks or over) have become the responsibility of the Benefits Agency. GPs still play a role by providing factual medical evidence but are no longer required to supply medical certificates as a basis for entitlement.

BOX 11.3 STUDY ILLUSTRATION: DISPLAYING DESCRIPTIVE ACCOUNTS

In both of the GP studies, a central area of investigation surrounded the factors that were taken into account when judging incapacity for employment. This was a complex issue partly because of the range of factors that were taken into account but more crucially because of the different weight given to varying factors in different circumstances. In order to display this complexity in the first study it was decided first to show how GPs described the process themselves. Four extracts from GP interviews were shown in the report, all from relatively longstanding GPs but each working in a different type of practice and catchment area. One of these is reproduced below:

I suppose the factors are the nature of the condition itself, certainly, yes and the person's constitution as to whether or not he is capable of overcoming what he has got sufficiently. I suppose the patient's own wishes themselves must be taken into account. I think doctors, really – I don't think anybody would say they couldn't take, don't take, that into account, they must do ... I think the change in the way the social net has been cast in recent years ... must make some people think, 'Well, it doesn't really matter if I'm on one benefit or another' because you know these people are just getting put into a slot. I think [age] must come into it really. If you get a bloke who's 63, he's coming towards the end of his thing and he's obviously just hanging on, you know, before he finally gives up and he comes to me, and he says 'Look, I can't do it any more and they don't think I can do it any more either'. I certainly do take that into consideration and if there's two years to go or something, there's no point to keep sending him back ... I often ask patients why can't they go and seek some training to do something else. Unfortunately there doesn't seem much facility for doing that – even the ones that have been retrained, I don't think they find much work at the end of it. I mean the whole exercise seems to have minimal results ...' (Ritchie et al., 1993: 23)

(Account given in 1992 by male GP who had been in general practice for 32 years; currently working in a group practice in an urban area.)

Illustrative passages of this kind were followed by a chart listing *all* the factors mentioned across the sample of GPs. There were over 30 of these and they were divided into 'main factors' and 'other factors' and presented in categorised sets. The categories displayed within 'main factors' were

- Condition(s) of incapacity
- Employment potential
- Job prospects
- Employment rehabilitation/retraining
- Motivation
- Age
- Psychological state

There are a number of different modes of presentation that can be used to do this. These require decisions about how best to display the original material in relation to the categories and classes of data found; and how much explanation to give about the categorisation and classification that has been developed. So for example one model (illustrated in Box 11.3) would be to show

---

BOX 11.4   STUDY ILLUSTRATION: DISPLAYING COMPLEXITY IN DESCRIPTIVE ACCOUNTS

The descriptions given above show the factors that GPs take into account in judging incapacity for employment, but not how the factors come into play or interact. Further commentary was therefore given about this, portraying the ways in which GPs described their judgements. This included the following paragraph describing a highly recurrent pattern in GPs' responses that also had been illustrated in earlier verbatim passages:

> The patient's condition and its impact on employment are always first on the list. But these are almost immediately interlinked with a whole range of other factors among which the patient's prospects of finding work, their age and their motivation to find work commonly occur. Interwoven with these are other influences, like the psychological or financial consequences of returning patients to unemployment or a search for jobs, or the limited availability or potential of rehabilitative training. Thus the factors influencing GPs are numerous and complex and they have to be 'weighed up' in the case of each patient (Ritchie et al., 1993: 23)

In the later GP study, a schematic representation was used to show the process that GPs used *in practice* to judge incapacity. This is reproduced in Figure 11.1. In the report, this followed another schematic representation of the 'official requirements on GPs in judging incapacity'.

---

extracts from the original material first followed by a description of the elements that have been found and the categories and classes derived; another would be to display a full map of the elements, categories and classes developed, illustrated by a selection of the original material; yet another would be to show a selection of the different elements within displayed categories and classes followed by examples in each category or class. There is no right or wrong way of doing it and the method of presentation will rest heavily on the complexity of the original data and the levels of abstraction used in categorisation and classification. But whatever choice is made, there should be some exposition of how and why classificatory systems have been reached.

In presenting lists, charts or text-based descriptions of the elements, categories or classes within phenomena, the appropriate order of the presentation has to be considered. This might be chronological, an ordering that has some logic or meaning in relation to the content of the phenomena or could be related to the weight or importance attached to the different categories by respondents. It is also important that the ordering used is explained to the reader – otherwise assumptions may be made about the sequence of display (such that it shows order of frequency of mention) which is not, in fact, significant.

There will be many cases where the complexity of the phenomena requires more unravelling than can be shown in a single list or piece of text-based commentary. In particular there may be circumstances or conditions where the elements of phenomena, or the importance attached to them, may change or there may be further refinements to add to the classification

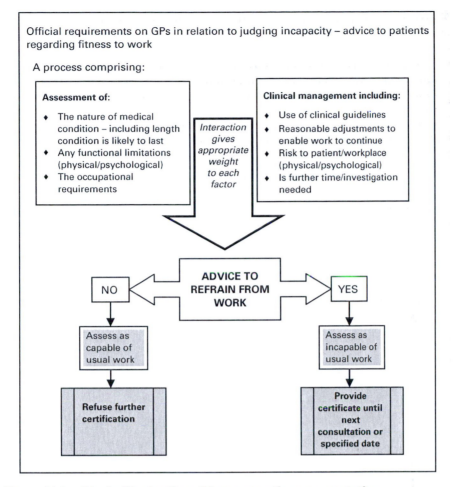

Figure 11.1 **Study illustration: Diagrammatic representation of descriptive accounts**

related to context or setting. These additional complexities might be drawn out in text-based commentary and illustration (Box 11.4), through providing case profiles of different scenarios or by presenting some form of schematic or diagrammatic representation (Figure 11.1).

TYPOLOGIES

Typologies, which provide descriptions of the different sectors or segments in the study population or of different manifestations of phenomena, may relate to particular parts of the research subject under study or have a generic use throughout a report. Well-constructed typologies provide important evidence in their own right but also act as vehicles for describing and explaining other data.

In presenting a typology, it is important to define and display the features that have led to the construction of the typology. This not only helps the reader judge its value in interpreting and presenting later evidence but

---

BOX 11.5 STUDY ILLUSTRATION: DESCRIBING TYPOLOGIES

In the second GP study, a typology was established to show different approaches to managing a return to employment after a long spell of incapacity. Three different approaches were identified which were termed the 'firm negotiator', the 'soft negotiator' and the 'non-interventionist'. Before describing the three approaches in detail, the route to establishing the typology was described. This concerned noticeable differences between GPs in:

- their perspective on the value of work in maintaining and promoting health
- the extent to which a distinction was drawn between patients on sickness absence from work and those on sickness absence from job seeking
- perspectives on the GPs' roles in sickness absence 'management'.

These three features were used in establishing the typology.

Each of the approaches was described in detail in the main text of the report in the form of general characterising features. Part of the description of the 'soft negotiator' is given below

> The 'soft negotiator' takes a more flexible, accommodating approach, which they themselves often describe as 'softy, softly'. Although they are keen to encourage the patient to return to work where possible, they are eager to do this in a gentle, coaxing manner that will not adversely affect the GP–patient relationship ...
>
> A soft negotiator will normally raise the issue of the return to work only after a period of time has elapsed, either awaiting tests or recovery ... They are likely to see their role as one of giving support and encouragement.
>
> The discussion of the return to work may involve carefully phrased suggestions such as the possibility of retraining or seeking other advice. The soft negotiator may set goals jointly with their patients in order to avoid a drift into the sick role. (Hiscock and Ritchie, 2001: 43–4)

---

should also bring some important insights into the nature of the study population and the different positions contained within it. To do this it is often helpful to describe what analytic routes led to establishing the typology accompanied by some discussion of the dimensions on which the typological groups vary (Box 11.5).

In presenting typologies it is often useful to provide a case illustration of each of the typological groups (as was done in the second GP study). This helps to bring the groups 'alive' by showing the way in which the dimensions of the typology are characterised in the sector concerned. This will often bring to readers a recognition of people or groups they have already observed – but never quite defined – themselves. More generally, case studies can be a very effective way of presenting profiles of different groups within the study population. It can also be another way of displaying verbatim text within a well-defined context.

If a typology relates to sectors within the population, then there can also be value in describing how the typology distributes across the study sample in terms of other basic characteristics. However, in doing so it is vital that the reader is warned that such distributions will hold no significance statistically because of the base and scale of sample selection. The purpose in showing the distribution is simply to give the reader some idea of the composition of typological groups for later uses in presenting the evidence.

Explanatory accounts

ASSOCIATIONS AND LINKAGES

It was noted in Chapter 9 that patterns that occur within the data, detected through associations and linkages between phenomena, often bring important insights during analysis. At the reporting stage, certain evidence needs to be conveyed to allow the reader some understanding of why two or more sets of phenomena may be linked or why certain phenomena are attached to particular subgroups.

The first and perhaps most important of these is the evidence available to support the linkage. This explanation may be explicitly or implicitly conveyed in the original text, may have been inferred through further analysis, or may simply be an explanatory hypothesis. Whatever its base, there needs to be some discussion about how the explanation has been derived (see below).

A second way of portraying linkage is to describe the circumstances in which the connection may change or become modified. To take a very simple example, let us suppose that the research evidence shows that views about systems for managing household finances differ between men and women but that this difference in perspective gets stronger with age. Then the explanation offered needs to encompass the reasons for the original linkage with gender and the factors that cause it to strengthen with age.

Finally there may well be exceptions to the association found and these can often be as helpful in explaining the original linkage as those that are in pattern. This is because the evidence from those holding an 'outlier' position often helps to identify, through absence, the conditions or factors that lead to the association in the first place. Any differences found may therefore contribute to the original explanation or may leave a puzzle, but either way it is helpful for this to form part of the evidence presented.

DISPLAYING THE EXPLANATORY BASE OF EVIDENCE

Displaying the explanatory base of evidence is one of the hardest parts of writing up qualitative research. This is in part because the source of the explanation can be hard to pin down, depending as it does on fitting several pieces of data together through iterative analysis (see Chapter 9). But it is also where the 'authorial' voice can easily become blurred between that of the study participants and the reporting researcher. Therefore to simplify the task a little, we will return to the different ways in which explanations might be formed as described in Chapter 9.

**BOX 11.6   STUDY ILLUSTRATION: EXPLICIT REASONS
AND ACCOUNTS**

In the first GP study, it was of interest for the DSS to know why doctors sometimes wrote a generic or non-specific diagnosis on a prescription. This was of concern because the recorded diagnosis was used in the review of benefit awards and it was therefore more problematic when the specific condition was unknown. The GPs identified seven main reasons why a generic diagnosis might be given, each of which was amplified in accompanying text, as illustrated below.

The main reasons for writing a non-specific diagnosis were:

- *a specific diagnosis is not possible or not known*. Commonly mentioned in this context were musculo-skeletal conditions, particularly bad backs, and nervous or psychiatric disorders. It may also happen in the case of other disorders where medical investigations are ongoing
- *multiple conditions*. In cases where there is more than one condition affecting capacity to work, it can be difficult to specify the diagnosis causing the absence from work
- *it allows for a margin of error in uncertain cases*, particularly if the cause of the condition cannot be determined
- *it avoids disclosure to the patient*, where the full diagnosis may not have been declared or where written evidence of the diagnosis could be distressing ... and so on. (Ritchie et al., 1993:19)

Explicit reasons and accounts   Almost certainly, these are the easiest to convey in describing how explanations have been reached. It can be done through presenting all the reasons that have been given by participants for a particular phenomena, either in list or textual form, accompanied by illustrative accounts if this is helpful. In such presentations, it is often useful to show why some explanations have been given more often than others and how and why explanations differ with the characteristics or circumstances of the holder (Box 11.6).

Presenting underlying logic or 'common sense'   The researcher is likely to be the originator of any underlying logic although it can often happen that one of the study participants plants the seeds of this in an analyst's mind. More commonly, it will be because there have been implicit connections within the data which suggest some explanatory link which the researcher is then left to construct either by following some logical route or because 'common sense' offers a solution. It is perfectly acceptable for this construction to be relayed although it is useful to make clear that it was the researcher, not the participants, who was the architect. It is also helpful to the reader to know the clues and linkages that led the researcher to their explanatory conclusions. This can be done quite briefly but will allow the reader to make other judgements about cause, reason or effect if their logic takes them in a different direction (Box 11.7).

BOX 11.7 STUDY ILLUSTRATION: DISPLAYING UNDERLYING LOGIC

Case illustration

On the basis of the discussions about judging incapacity it was shown that GPs were going beyond the guidelines given to them for judging incapacity. In the first study it was 'inferred' that this was happening in the following ways:

1. the judgement that the patient is '**unable to work**' because of their disorder may be extended to include **getting and retaining work**
2. the judgement that it would be 'prejudicial to their health to undertake work' may get broadened to encompass **unemployment and job search**

Thus, any patient who, because of their condition is unlikely to get a job or keep a job could be certificated on count 1. Similarly, any patient whose condition might deteriorate because of having to look for work, or through the stresses of being unemployed, might be issued a statement on count 2. (Ritchie et al., 1993: 25)

Neither of these two 'counts' were explicitly articulated by GPs. But by piecing together the evidence on assessing incapacity in a logical way, it was possible to reach the conclusion that the guidelines were being extended to include unintended circumstances of the kind described. But because this was an inference drawn from the evidence, these conclusions were written in a way that made it clear that this was based on the researchers' interpretation of the data.

BOX 11.8 STUDY ILLUSTRATION: EXPLANATORY CONCEPTS

There were no analytic concepts that evolved in the course of the two GP studies. This is largely because the concepts that were most helpful in understanding and interpreting the GPs' accounts had already been recognised and developed in other research (for example, management of 'the sick role', the doctor–patient relationship'; see below). In some studies this happens, particularly in well-researched fields, and there should be no presure to find new analytic concepts unless there is a newly emerging construct or evidence.

Relaying explanatory concepts   Very often in qualitative analysis an important concept develops that proves helpful in explaining the origins of different phenomena or sets of phenomena. This might be an underlying factor that helps to explain both convergent and divergent evidence or a newly defined concept that has emerged because of the orientation or coverage of the study. As with typologies, readers will need to be given some background about the definition of the concept, what led to recognition of its salience and some illustration of how it manifests itself in different forms. And again they will need to be given some evidence that the concept has power in explaining the existing evidence (Box 11.8).

> **BOX 11.9   STUDY ILLUSTRATION: RELATING EVIDENCE TO OTHER THEORY**
>
> The importance to GPs of maintaining a good relationship with their patients had been explored in much medical sociological research (see for example Toon, 1992). The preservation of a good doctor–patient relationship was found to be of central importance in decisions about incapacity and the issue of medical statements. This was evident both from the explicit accounts of the GPs and in the ways that GPs described their general wish not to have to 'confront' their patients. The reports therefore explored the role of the doctor–patient relationship in the ways that GPs responded to patients on incapacity benefits and its impact on decisions about medical certification.

> **BOX 11.10   STUDY ILLUSTRATION: DRAWING WIDER IMPLICATIONS**
>
> Both of the GP reports contained chapters in which the implications of the research for policy and practice are considered. All of the solutions and strategies for change that are suggested derive directly from one or more pieces of the evidence. In presenting these therefore, a brief summary of the origin of the solution or strategy and why it is needed was given. This is illustrated in the brief extract below.
>
> > There was a widespread call from both the strategic groups and the interviews with GPs for greater help with assessing incapacity and helping patients to optimise their employment or rehabilitation potential. Although these are, in practice, two quite distinct activities, or certainly can be seen as such, they were very locked together in the GPs' minds. …
> >
> > … The need for such a 'service' derives from the problems that GPs describe in judging incapacity (Chapter 3) [of study report], helping patients to identify an appropriate occupational activity and effectively manage a return to work (Chapter 4) [of study report]. The doctors were almost unanimous that some intervention is needed earlier than occurs at present. (Hiscock and Ritchie, 2001: 67–8)

Drawing on other theoretical or empirical evidence   Researchers commonly draw on ideas or concepts from other research to help explain the findings of their study. In doing so, writers will need to give some background to how the concept or theory they are using was developed. They will also need to provide evidence, in ways already described, that there is some fit between their evidence and the 'borrowed' theory or idea (Box 11.9).

Wider applications   The inferences that can be drawn from a research study, in terms of wider applications to theory or policy, evolve and develop through the course of a study. In the main, these will be inferences drawn by the researcher although again participants may well have contributed directly through thoughts, ideas or suggestions that they have offered. There are many different forms that wider applications can take and these were described in detail in Chapter 10. In written accounts of research, these are often conveyed in separate chapters in which the development of theory, hypotheses, solutions or recommendations is addressed (Box 11.10).

Displaying and explaining recurrence

The extent to which the frequency or dominance of phenomena should be displayed in reporting qualitative findings is an irksome one for researchers. This is because if the sample design is of the scale and design recommended for qualitative research, it will not support any statements about prevalence or distribution other than within the study sample itself (see Chapter 4). Any statistical inference drawn to the wider population is likely to be at best misleading and at worst erroneous because of the purposive basis of selection. As has been stated before, qualitative research should be explaining patterns of recurrence, not simply stating that they exist.

A common difficulty with qualitative reports is that they contain statements about how many people have said something – that is things like '… three people said … or nine people thought…'. Not only are such statements very tedious to read but the reader will have no idea how these numbers are meant to be interpreted. Is 'three' or 'nine' meant to be significantly high or low? And even if the reader tried to work this out in relation to the sample size, their conclusions will not be meaningful because of the small and purposive basis of the sample design.

There are ways in which these sorts of statements can be avoided so that their presentation remains more in line with the purposes of qualitative research. First it is always possible to turn the sentence around and to talk about issues rather than people. For example, instead of writing 'Seven people said that the length of benefit application forms was a problem …', this could be stated as 'Benefit application forms were criticised for their length' or 'The length of benefit application forms was seen as a problem …'.

Another way of focusing on issues rather than people is to present views or perceptions in sets such that an array of responses can be seen. So again, using the example above, this might be written as 'The problems that people noted about benefit application forms included their length …' or 'Among the problems that …' . Even more usefully, the 'array' can be presented in some more classified form. So for example, the features that people see as important in deciding on the right school for their child's education could be presented 'There were five main types of feature that parents …' or ' The features that parents saw as important fell into five broad groups …'.

If the issues that are being reported tend to differ between groups of participants, then another way of describing their occurrence is to state them in this way. So for example, 'Parents fell into four broad groups when describing the features that they thought were important in deciding on the right school for their child's education. The first mentioned ... as priorities. The second were more concerned with ...', and so on. If there is some identifiable link between the characteristics of the group and the set of issues that can be described, then this will provide even more illumination of the descriptions given.

These are just some of the few ways that the use of numbers or prevalence can be avoided in reporting. But there are occasions where it is appropriate to give some indication of the strength or weight of the findings within the study population. This can happen where a response or perspective keeps occurring, either among the population as a whole or among a particular subgroup. In such circumstances, these can be appropriately described as 'dominant', 'recurrent', 'consistent', 'widespread' or 'commonly held' provided that explanations are given to support why this is so. Conversely, perspectives that are expressed with notable infrequency can be described as 'more exceptional', 'less common', 'rare' in a similar way.

When numerical distributions within a sample are shown, for example, when describing the composition of the sample or the distribution of typological groups, then there needs to be a clear statement that these apply only to the sample studied. Indeed, it can be quite useful when describing a study sample to show how it does or does not mirror the parent population if evidence of this is available. This will show the reader the variables on which the sample is disproportionately represented and also remind them of the very different basis of qualitative sample design. If relevant evidence about the parent population is not available then it is useful for the researcher to note ways in which the distributions are unlikely to be statistically representative of the population from which the sample was drawn as well as any that might be more in pattern.

The use of illustrative material

There is a common view that verbatim passages drawn from interviews or discussions somehow constitute evidence of findings in qualitative research. Although cited passages serve vital purposes in qualitative research, their use is more often illustrative or amplificatory, rather than demonstrative. While quotations can verify features like language or some of the subtle nuances embedded in descriptive content, they can only provide partial evidence of range or diversity, linkage, segmentation or explanation (unless it is very simply explicit). Thus while quotations are essential in bringing alive the content and exposition of people's accounts, their role in providing testimony is more limited.

Despite this general warning, verbatim passages and case histories have a crucial role in qualitative reporting because of the generative and enhancing power of people's own accounts. It is therefore useful to consider some general principles that surround their use in amplifying and extending understanding of the research evidence. In summary, quotations or other types of primary data can be used effectively:

- to demonstrate the type of *language, terms or concepts* that people use to discuss a particular subject
- to illustrate the *meanings* that people attach to social phenomena
- to illustrate *people's expressions* of their views or thoughts about a particular subject and the different factors that may be influential
- to illustrate different *positions* in relation to a model, process or typology
- to *demonstrate features of presentation* about phenomena such as strength ambivalence, hesitancy, confusion or even contradictory views
- to *amplify* the way in which complex phenomena are described and understood
- to *portray* the general *richness* of individual or group accounts.

In arriving at decisions about whether it is appropriate to use primary data it is useful to reflect on whether they will contribute to and amplify the text rather than repeating commentary that has already been made. There is no point using a quotation which simply reiterates a point that has been succinctly reported in the research main text.

Quotations should also not be used without interpretative commentary. Presenting a final report which contains reams of quotes without any interpretation is akin to providing the audience with a series of statistical tabulations with no commentary. In doing so, the reader is being asked to perform the task of analyst on only a very selective data set.

There is also a need to ensure that some diversity is displayed. It is easy to end up using only the 'colourful' accounts or the views and explanations of particularly cogent or articulate respondents. This will result in giving a partial view of the evidence and may result in inaccurate and inappropriate conclusions being drawn from the research.

Finally, verbatim passages should not compromise the confidentiality and anonymity promised to the participants. This can be particularly problematic when carrying out case studies where it may be easy to identify an organisation or individual involved. For example, it may be necessary to alter the description of the location in which a person or organisation is located, broaden their age to a wider category or change insignificant points of detail.

Qualitative researchers have different views about the requirements for displaying verbatim passages authentically. Some believe that quotations should be reported exactly as they occurred, without any hesitation, repetition or incoherence removed. Others believe that some editing is desirable to provide a more fluent account for the reader. Our own view lies somewhere between these two positions in that a small amount of editing may be needed to aid comprehension but otherwise quotations should appear in their raw unedited form. Moreover, where it is felt to be appropriate to edit

The factors which influence gambling behaviour

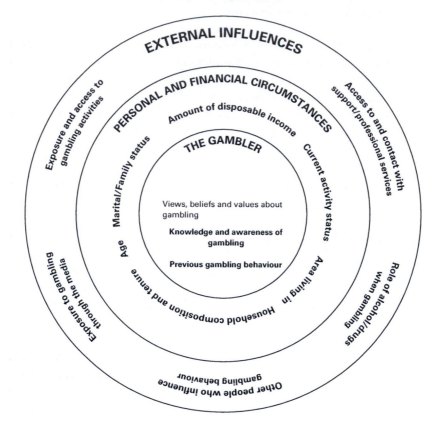

Figure 11.2 **The use of diagrams to display relationships between different factors**

quotations then this needs to be made clear to the audience. Two conventions are useful here; any omissions in a quotation are indicated by … (ellipses); and any words that need to be inserted to aid comprehension are inserted within square brackets.

The use of diagrammatic and visual representations

While text-based accounts will form the bedrock of a research report, it may also be appropriate to consider the use of diagrammatic and other visual representations of the findings in order to help make complex processes or relationships more accessible to the reader. These can range from simply placing some of the evidence in a summary box or chart to quite elaborate diagrams or pictures.

Diagrammatic and visual representations of qualitative findings can assist in a number of ways. They can help to:

- display the range and diversity of phenomena, or a typology. Sometimes these can be very effectively communicated through, for example, concept maps or a continuum of different views, behaviours or models.
- display relationships and associations between different factors. These may need several pages to describe in text form but can often be succinctly summarised in one diagram. Figure 11.2 provides an example of this kind. It was used to portray the wide variety of factors that can affect gambling behaviour (White et al., 2001).
- explain complex processes as they can display the different levels and dimensions involved and how these interact with each other. (The example shown in Figure 11.1 provides an illustration of such use.)
- provide effective means for summarising data when a number of different elements, phenomena, groups or positions have been described.
- generally help to break up the text-based format of a particular output and to bring the findings alive in a different way. As a consequence they help to refocus attention and are helpful in summarising or reinforcing points being made.

Judgements about the use of diagrammatic and visual representations will clearly depend on individual preferences as well as their appropriateness for the findings being presented. That said, it is easy to be tempted to over use them or to use them when they do not really add or contribute to the text-based description. They are most effective when they are used sparingly and when they are relatively simple and easy to follow. They should also be appropriately explained in the text.

Oral presentations

The processes of preparing and giving an oral presentation share a number of features in common with writing but there are some differences arising from the nature of the medium.

Content of an oral presentation

A key difference between written and oral accounts is the depth of coverage that can be achieved. At its best, an oral presentation can only hope to cover the key or 'topline' findings arising from the research. Judgements about content, therefore, need to be carefully considered in terms of the nature of the evidence that can be presented. The aim is to achieve a balance between overwhelming the audience with the full set of findings and presenting them at a superficial level. Perhaps even more so than with written accounts, it will be easier for an audience to take away a partial message, for example if too much emphasis is placed on the experiences of one subgroup within the sample or by not relaying the full complexity of an issue.

Decisions will also be needed about the extent to which methodological issues can be raised during an oral presentation. While it makes sense to weight the time available during an oral presentation to the research findings, the boundaries of the research undertaken as well as the type of inferences that can be drawn from the findings do need to be made clear to the audience. It is therefore helpful to provide a brief overview of the research design, the rationale for the approach taken and a profile of the sample composition. Furthermore, if the findings are emergent findings and based on a preliminary analysis of the evidence it is also important that this is emphasised during the presentation. Commissioning bodies are often operating within tight policy time scales and they may be under pressure to implement the findings of a research study before a more refined and completed analysis has been undertaken and the written report produced. Similarly, academic colleagues may be keen to learn about new theory or hypotheses in a field of enquiry and they need to be aware of the stage of analytic process these have reached.

The length of a presentation or oral paper will be determined by a number of factors. A key issue is the limit to the amount of information that an audience will be able to digest in verbal form. An hour is probably a maximum time to aim for but shorter presentations of around 30 to 45 minutes are probably ideal. Even taking account of the skills of the presenter and the techniques they can adopt to sustain interest and attention for longer periods, there nevertheless will come a point when the audience will have become saturated with information. It is far more effective to deliver the essence of the findings rather than overwhelming the audience with detail. Indeed there will usually be an opportunity for further discussion and questions following the presentation or paper.

While written reports can be targeted to more than one audience, oral presentations are at their most effective when they are specifically tailored to focus on issues that are of most salience and interest to a particular audience. Strauss and Corbin (1998) suggest that academic audiences will be more interested in abstract, conceptual material while other audiences may want more descriptive narrative or case materials to 'spice up' the conceptual evidence. Rubin and Rubin (1995) advocate a 'purposeful' and 'efficient' mode of delivery when reporting back to policy-makers. If the needs and requirements of the audience are very diverse then it may be appropriate to consider giving more than one presentation.

Structuring an oral presentation

As with written reports, the foundation of a good presentation is a coherent structure and this will be evolving in tandem with decisions about the

BOX 11.11   ORAL PRESENTATIONS

Assembling a presentation

- Begin by mapping the key themes that are to be addressed during the presentation. These will be shaped by the research objectives, the target audience, the analytical outputs as well as practical considerations like the time available
- Then take each theme in turn and identify the key findings that need to be communicated. Try to limit them to a maximum of 5 or 6 key points for each theme
- Once the key findings have been identified, consider the order and structure of the presentation. It is helpful to start with the generic points and then to move to the more subordinate or underpinning points
- It is then time to review and assess the entire coverage of the presentation. This will enable you to streamline the content and structure, seeing where points overlap, condensing or collapsing different subject areas, or by lifting the findings to a more generic level. At this stage, it is also helpful to consider how illustrative material should be used to amplify and extend understanding
- Judgements about the content and structure will need to made alongside considerations about how much material can be delivered within the time available
  Make a very rough assumption that for each overhead or slide you present, it is likely to take about 2 or 3 minutes to deliver
- Consideration will also be needed of how the presentation will start and finish. It is customary to introduce a presentation with a series of slides which outline the: agenda for the presentation, the background to the study, description of the research methods and the profile of the sample. Finally, think about ways in which you will want to conclude the presentation; are there any concluding messages or any findings that you would want to revisit or reiterate at the end. As is repeated by many advisers on oral presentations 'Tell them, what you're going to tell them, tell them and then tell them what you have told them.'

coverage of the presentation. Arriving at a structure for an oral report will involve a balance between being sensitive to the needs of the audience (which is likely to be keen to hear the findings) and ensuring that the research is conveyed in a rigorous manner, by, for example setting the findings within the context of the research method and the types of inferences that can be drawn.

Assembling a presentation

The actual mechanics of assembling a presentation will vary for different researchers and research projects. However, in order to make this process more transparent the steps that might be followed are outlined in Box 11.11.

Presentation style and delivery

Once the presentation has been assembled, there are a number of other considerations that need to be made in order to finalise preparations for delivery. These involve the following:

- *Use of handouts.* In general it is good practice to provide some form of supplementary written material to accompany presentations. These can vary from copies of the overheads/slides shown to a more detailed report which amplifies and extends some of the points being made during the presentation. While it is important to give some written account of the presentation for the audience to take away it is also important to consider how such a document may be interpreted after the presentation when there is no way to seek clarification.
- *The use of visual materials.* Irrespective of the presentation format, it is important to ensure that anything the audience will be viewing is clear, easy to read and will improve rather than hinder understanding. Simplicity, brevity and clarity are the three guiding principles when considering the design of the visual materials; principally font style, size and colour.
- *Language.* As with written presentations there are the same considerations to be made about the style of language used. There is an advantage, however, with oral presentations that it is possible to gauge how the audience is responding and adapt the style of delivery accordingly.
- *The presenting stance or voice* for an oral presentation is likely to be more personal in tone than for a written report. Otherwise the issues are the same as for written reports.

Delivering an oral presentation

Anxiety about giving oral presentations or papers is common to most researchers. Even the more practised and accomplished performers will view this task with some 'stage nerves'. While there are numerous talks and courses that focus on presentation techniques and give helpful advice and guidance about how to present, the best way to hone presentation skills is through practice and experience. There are, however, a number of useful strategies and techniques that can be easily learnt that will help effective communication. A summary of these is presented in Box 11.12.

   Oral presentations require different ways of relaying data to written presentation and some new thinking about how best to condense ideas so that they can be easily, but correctly, absorbed. But like qualitative report writing, they also require the researcher to be imaginative in methods of re-presentation and display and rigorous in conveying the inherent complexity and diversity of qualitative data. When these qualities are achieved, the interest – and even excitement – that can be generated by a well delivered presentation will leave researchers well rewarded for their endeavours.

BOX 11.12   EFFECTIVE PRESENTING

Preparation

- Know the content of the presentation
- Rehearse and time the presentation
- Identify the slides or overheads that are central to the presentation in case time is cut
- Check the ordering of the overheads, slides or a computer presentation

Delivering the presentation

- Prepare and test out any audio visual equipment before starting
- At the start, indicate the length of the presentation and the times/stages allocated for questions or clarification
- Check everyone in the audience can see any visual information being presented. Also check everyone can hear
- When showing visual information continue to face the audience and avoid blocking their view of the transparencies
- Be engaging and try to involve the audience by holding eye contact with different people
- Speak slowly and clearly
- Try to avoid reading a prepared script and either work from annotated or highlighted overheads notes on a computer screen, or cue cards
- At all times, be sensitive to the way the audience are reacting to you
- Pace yourself so as to ensure you keep to time and do not over run
- Reiterate key or important points during your summary and conclusion

KEY POINTS

- The reporting stage provides an opportunity for further thought as the data are reanalysed, reassessed and assembled into a coherent structure to convey to the target audience(s). It is a continuation of the journey of interpretation and classification of data requiring continued data exploration, further interrogation of patterns and associations and more detailed interpretation and explanation. The nature of qualitative data also poses certain challenges to the reporter.
- Reporting qualitative research requires finding a way to tell the 'story' of the research in a clear and cogent way. In doing this it is important that the subtlety, richness and detail of the original material is displayed while keeping the right balance between description and interpretation. There is also a need to demonstrate the bases on which interpretations have been made, or conclusions reached, through showing the 'building blocks' of the evidence; and to provide sufficient detail of the methods and conduct of the study for decisions about wider inference to be judged.

- There are certain temptations that need to be resisted in reporting qualitative data, all of which arise because of the intrinsic nature of qualitative evidence. These include abundantly elaborate accounts, with too little selectivity of the issues or phenomena that need to be relayed; the desire to display frequency; and overuse of illustrative verbatim text or 'quotations'. It is far more important that readers are offered a clear account of the conceptual base to the analysis and how descriptive and explanatory accounts have been derived.
- Oral presentations of qualitative data, which are commonly given, require many of the same disciplines as written accounts. But there are also features of oral presentation that present additional challenges. These include the limited level of depth and coverage that can be achieved in an oral account; and the additional difficulties of conveying subtlety and complexity. Nevertheless, oral presentations allow an immediacy of display and exposition about qualitative accounts that is often missing from written reports.

KEY TERMS

Authorial authority refers to how the research is reported and whether the voice of the participants or the researcher is dominant in presenting the descriptive and explanatory accounts.

Audit trail relates to the level of description given of the conduct of the research. In particular, it concerns the extent to which others can follow the research process that took place and any concerns or observed limitations about its conduct.

Further reading

Hammersley, M. and Atkinson, P. (1995) *Ethnography: Principles in Practice*, 2nd edition, London: Routledge

Holloway, I. and Wheeler, S. (1996) *Qualitative Research for Nurses*, Oxford: Blackwell Science

Kvale, S. (1996) *InterViews: An Introduction to Qualitative Research Interviewing*, Thousand Oaks, CA: Sage

Rubin, H.J. and Rubin, I.S. (1995) *Qualitative Interviewing: The Art of Hearing Data*, Thousand Oaks, CA: Sage

Wolcott, H.F. (2001) *Writing Up Qualitative Research*, Newbury Park, CA: Sage

References

Altheide, D.L. and Johnson, J.M. (1994) 'Criteria for assessing interpretative validity in qualitative research' in N.K. Denzin and Y.S. Lincoln (eds) *Handbook of Qualitative Research*, Thousand Oaks, CA: Sage

Arber, S. (2001) 'Designing samples' in N. Gilbert (ed.) *Researching Social Life*, 2nd edition, London: Sage

Arksey, H. and Knight, P.T. (1999) *Interviewing for Social Scientists*, London: Sage

Arthur, S. and Finch, H. (1999) *Physical Activity 'In Our Lives': Qualitative Research Among Disabled People*, London: Health Education Authority

Arthur, S. and Lewis, J. (2000) *Pensions and Divorce: Exploring Financial Settlements*, DSS Research Report No. 118, Leeds: Corporate Document Service

Arthur, S., Lewis, S., Maclean, M., Finch, S. and Fitzgerald, R. (2002) *Setting Up: Making Financial Arrangements After Divorce or Separation*, London: National Centre for Social Research

Atkinson, J.M. and Heritage, J. (1984) *Structures of Social Action: Studies in Conversation Analysis*, Cambridge, Cambridge University Press

Bannister, D. and Mair, J.M.M. (1968) *The Evaluation of Personal Constructs*, London: Academic Press

Bannister, D., Burman, E., Parker, I., Taylor, M. and Tindall, C. (1994) *Qualitative Methods in Psychology: A Research Guide*, London: British Psychological Society

Barbour, R. and Kitzinger, J. (eds) (1999) *Developing Focus Group Research: Politics, Theory and Practice*, London: Sage

Barry, C.A. (1998) 'Choosing Qualitative Data Analysis Software: Atlas/ti and Nudist Compared', *Sociological Research Online*, 3 (3), http://www.socresonline.org.uk/socresonline/3/3/4.html

Bechhofer, F. and Paterson, L. (2000) *Principles of Research Design in the Social Sciences*, London: Routledge

Becker, H.S. (1970) *Sociological Work: Method and Substance*, Chicago: Aldine

Berelson, B. (1952) *Content Analysis in Communication Research*, Glencoe, IL: Free Press

Berg, B.L. (2000) *Qualitative Research Methods for the Social Sciences*, Boston: Allyn and Bacon

Bhasker, R. (1978) *A Realist Theory of Science*, Sussex: Harvester Press

Bloor, M., Frankland, J., Robson, K. and Thomas, M. (2001) *Focus Groups in Social Research*, London: Sage

Blumer, H. (1954) 'What is wrong with social theory', *American Sociological Review*, 19: 3–10

Blumer, H. (1969) *Symbolic Interactionism*, Englewood Cliffs, NJ: Prentice Hall

Bogdan, R. and Taylor, S.J. (1975) *Introduction to Qualitative Research Methods: A Phenomenological Approach to the Social Sciences*, New York: John Wiley

Bowles, G. and Klein, R.D. (1983) *Theories of Women's Studies*, London: Routledge and Kegan Paul

Brannen, J. (1992a) 'Combining qualitative and quantitative approaches: an overview' in J. Brannen (ed.) *Mixing Methods: Qualitative and Quantitative Research*, Aldershot: Avebury

Brannen, J. (ed.) (1992b) *Mixing Methods: Qualitative and Quantitative Research*, Aldershot: Gower

Brown, C. and Ritchie, J. (1984) *Focused Enumeration: The Development of Sampling Ethnic Minority Groups*, London: SCPR

Bryman, A. (1988) *Quantity and Quality in Social Research*, London: Unwin Hyman

Bryman, A. (1992) 'Quantitative and qualitative research: further reflections on their integration' in J. Brannen (ed.) *Mixing Methods: Qualitative and Quantitative Research*, Aldershot: Avebury

Bryman, A. (2001) *Social Research Methods*, Oxford: Oxford University Press

Bryman, A. and Burgess, R. (eds) (1994) *Analyzing Qualitative Data*, London: Routledge

Bryson, C., Budd, T., Elam, G. and Lewis, J. (1999) *The New Dialogue: Women's Attitudes to Combining Work and Family Life*, London: Cabinet Office

Bulmer, M. (1982) *The Uses of Social Research: Social Investigation in Public Policy Making*, London: George Allen and Unwin

Burgess, R.G. (1982a) 'Elements of sampling in field research' in R.G. Burgess (ed.) *Field Research: A Source Book and Field Manual*, London: Allen & Unwin

Burgess, R.G. (1982b) 'The unstructured interview as a conversation' in R.G. Burgess (ed.) *Field Research: A Source Book and Field Manual*, London: Allen & Unwin

Burgess, R.G. (1982c) 'Keeping fieldnotes' in R.G. Burgess (ed.) *Field Research: A Source Book and Field Manual*, London: Allen & Unwin

Burgess, R.G. (1984) *In the Field: An Introduction to Field Research*, London: Allen & Unwin

Burgess, R.G. (ed.) (1995) *Computing and Qualitative Research,* London: JAI Press

Campanelli, C. and Channell, J. with McAulay, L., Renouf, A. and Thomas, R. (1994) *Training: An Exploration of the Word and the Concept, with an Analysis of the Implications for Survey Design*, Sheffield: Employment Department

Campbell, D.T. (1977) *Descriptive Epistemology: Psychological, Sociological, and Evolutionary.* Preliminary draft of the William James Lecture, Harvard University

Campbell, D.T. and Fiske, D.W. (1959) 'Convergent and discriminant validation by the multitrait–multimethod matrix', *Psychological Bulletin*, 56 (2): 81–105

Casey, M.A. and Kreuger, R.A. (2000) *Focus Groups: A Practical Guide for Applied Research*, 3rd edition, Thousand Oaks, CA: Sage

Chalmers, D. (1982) *What is This Thing Called Science*, Buckingham: Open University Press

Chamberlayne, P., Bormat, J. and Wengraf, T. (2000) *The Turn to Biographical Methods in Social Science: Comparative Issues and Examples*, London: Routledge

Cicourel, A.V. (1964) *Method and Measurement in Sociology*, New York: Free Press

Clayman, S.E. and Maynard, D.W. (1994) 'Ethnomethodology and conversation analysis' in P. ten Have and G. Psathas (eds) *Situated Order: Studies in the Social Organisation of Talk and Embodied Activities*, Washington, DC: University Press of America

Coffey, A. and Atkinson, P. (1996) *Making Sense of Qualitative Data*, Thousand Oaks, CA: Sage

Coffey, A., Holbrook, B. and Atkinson, P. (1996) 'Qualitative data analysis: technologies and representations', *Sociological Research Online*, 1 (1), http://www.socresonline.org.uk/1/1/4.html#top

Coote, A. and Lanaghan, J. (1997) *Citizens' Juries: Theory into Practice*, London: IPPR

Crabtree, B.F. and Miller, W.L. (eds) (1999) *Doing Qualitative Research*, 2nd edition, Thousand Oaks, CA and London: Sage

Cresswell, J. (1998) *Qualitative Inquiry and Research Design: Choosing Among Five Traditions,* Thousand Oaks, CA: Sage

Cronbach, L. (1975) 'Beyond the two disciplines of scientific psychology', *American Psychologist*, 30: 116–27

Curtis, J., Graham, J., O'Connor, W. and Park, A. (forthcoming) *Guiding Priniciples: Public Attitude Towards Conduct in Public Life*, London: Committee on Standards in Public life

Davies, H., Nutley, S. and Smith, P. (eds) (2000) *What Works? Evidence Based Policy and Practice in Public Services*, Bristol: Policy Press

Davies, S., Elizabeth, S., Hamley, B., New, B. and Jang, B. (1998) *Ordinary Wisdom: Reflections on an Experiment in Citizenship and Health*, London: King's Fund

Denzin, N.K. (1970) *The Research Act*, Chicago: Aldine

Denzin, N.K. (1978) *The Research Act: A Theoretical Introduction to Sociological Methods,* 2nd edition, New York: McGraw-Hill

Denzin, N.K. (1989) *The Research Act: A Theoretical Introduction to Sociological Methods,* 3rd edition, Englewood Cliffs, NJ: Prentice Hall

Denzin, N.K. (1994) 'Postmodernism and deconstructionism' in D.R. Dickens and A. Fontana (eds) *Postmodernism and Social Inquiry*, London: UCL Press

Denzin, N.K. (1997) *Interpretive Ethnography: Ethnographic Practice for the 21st Century*, Thousand Oaks, CA: Sage

Denzin, N.K. and Lincoln, Y.S. (eds) (1994) *Handbook of Qualitative Research*, Thousand Oaks, CA: Sage

Denzin, N.K. and Lincoln, Y.S. (1998) *Collecting and Interpreting Qualitative Materials*, Thousand Oaks, CA: Sage

Denzin, N.K. and Lincoln, Y.S. (eds) (2000) *Handbook of Qualitative Research*, 2nd edition, Thousand Oaks, CA: Sage

DePoy, E. and Gitlin, L. (1998) *Introduction to Research: Understanding and Applying Multiple Strategies*, 2nd edition, London: Mosby

Dex, S. (1995) 'The reliability of recall data: a literature review', *Bulletin de methodologie Sociologique* (49) (Dec) 58: 89

Douglas, J. (1985) *Creative Interviewing*, Beverley Hills, CA: Sage

Douglass, B. and Moustakas, C. (1985) 'Heuristic inquiry: the internal search to know', *Journal of Humanistic Psychology*, 25 (3 Summer): 39–55

Elam G. and Ritchie, J. (1997) *Exploring Customer Satisfaction*, DSS Research Report 68, London: The Stationery Office

Elam, G., Fenton, K., Johnson, A., Nazroo, J. and Ritchie, J. (1999) *Exploring Ethnicity and Sexual Health: A Qualitative Study of the Sexual Attitudes and Lifestyles of Five Ethnic Minority Communities in Camden and Islington*, London: SCPR

Farrell, C. and Lewis, J. (2000) *The Cancer Experience*, London: National Centre for Social Research

Fielding, N.G. (1995) 'Qualitative interviewing' in N. Gilbert (ed.) *Researching Social Life*, London: Sage

Fielding, N.G. and Fielding, J.L. (1986) *Linking Data*, London: Sage

Fielding, N.G. and Fielding, J. (2000) 'Resistance and adaptation to criminal identity: using secondary analysis to evaluate classic studies of crime and deviance', *Sociology*, 34 (4): 1–19

Fielding, N.G. and Lee, R.M. (eds) (1991) *Using Computers in Qualitative Research*, London: Sage

Fielding, N.G. and Lee, R.M. (1998) *Computer Analysis and Qualitative Research*, London, Sage

Filstead, W.J. (1970) *Qualitative Methodology*, Chicago: Markham

Filstead, W.J. (1979) 'Qualitative methods: a needed perspective in evaluation research' in T.D. Cook and C.S. Reichardt (eds) *Qualitative and Quantitative Methods in Evaluation Research*, Beverly Hills, CA: Sage

Finch, H. with Keegan, J. and Ward, K. (1988) *Barriers to the Receipt of Dental Care*, London: SCPR

Finch, J. (1984), 'It's great to have someone to talk to: the ethics of interviewing women' in C. Bell and H. Roberts (eds) *Social Researching: Politics, Problems, Practice*, London: Routledge & Kegan Paul

Finch, J. (1987) 'The vignette technique in survey research', *Sociology*, 21 (1): 105–14

Finch, J. and Mason, J. (1990) 'Decision taking in the fieldwork process: theoretical sampling and collaborative working' in R.G. Burgess (ed.) *Studies in Qualitative Methodology*, 2: 25–50

Fishkin, J. (1995) *The Voice of the People*, Yale: Yale University Press

Fishkin, J., Luskin, R. and Jowell, R. (2000) 'Deliberative polling and public consultation', *Parliamentary Affairs*, 53 (4): 657–66

Flick, U. (1992) 'Triangulation revisited: strategy of validation or alternative?', *Journal for the Theory of Social Behaviour*, 22 (2): 175–97

Fontana, A. and Frey, J.H. (1993) 'The group interview in social research' in D.L. Morgan (ed.) *Successful Focus Groups: Advancing the State of the Art*, Newbury Park, CA: Sage

Fontana, A. and Frey, J.H. (2000) 'The interview: from structured questions to negotiated text' in N.K. Denzin and Y.S. Lincoln (eds) *Handbook of Qualitative Research*, 2nd edition, Thousand Oaks, CA: Sage

Garfinkel, H. (1967) *Studies in Ethnomethodology*, Englewood Cliffs, NJ: Prentice Hall

Geertz, C. (1993) *The Interpretation of Cultures: Selected Essays*, New York: Basic Books

Giddens, A. (1984) *The Constitution of Society*, Cambridge: Polity Press

Gilhooly, K. and Green, C. (1996) 'Protocol analysis: theoretical background' in J. Richardson (ed.) *Handbook of Qualitative Research Methods for Psychology and the Social Sciences*, Leicester: BPS Books

Glaser, B.G. and Strauss, A.L. (1967) *The Discovery of Grounded Theory: Strategies for Qualitative Research*, Chicago: Aldine de Gruyter

Gleick, J. (1987) *Chaos: Making a New Science*, London: Heinemann

Gordon, W. and Langmaid, R. (1988) *Qualitative Market Research: A Practitioner's and Buyer's Guide*, Aldershot: Gower

Graham, H. (1984) 'Surveying through stories' in C. Bell and H. Roberts (eds) *Social Researching*, London: Routledge & Kegan Paul

Graham, J., O'Connor, W., Curtice, J. and Park, A. (2002) *Guiding Principles: Public Attitudes Towards Conduct in Public Life*. London: National Centre for Social Research

Greenfield, T. (ed.) (1996) *Research Methods: Guidance for Postgraduates*, London: Arnold

Hakim, C. (2000) *Research Design: Successful Research Designs For Social And Economic Research*, 2nd edition, London: Routledge

Hammersley, M. (1992) *What's Wrong with Ethnography?*, London: Routledge

Hammersley, M. (1996) 'The relationship between qualitative and quantitative research – paradigm loyalty versus methodological selectivism' in J. Richardson (ed.) *Handbook of Qualitative Research Methods for Psychology and the Social Sciences*, Leicester: BPS Books

Hammersley, M. (1997) 'Qualitative data archiving: some reflections on its prospects and problems', *Sociology*, 31 (1): 131–42

Hammersley, M. and Atkinson, P. (1995) *Ethnography: Principles in Practice*, 2nd edition, London: Routledge

Harré, R. and Secorde, P.F. (1972) *The Explanation of Social Behaviour*, Oxford: Blackwell

Heaton, J. (1998) 'Secondary analysis of qualitative data', *Social Research Update*, Autumn issue, Guildford: University of Surrey Institute of Social Research

Henwood, K. and Nicholson, P. (1995) 'Qualitative research (editorial)', *Psychologist*, 8 (3): 109–10

Herman, J.L., Morris, L.L. and FitzGibbon, C.T. (1987) *Evaluation Handbook*, Newbury Park, CA: Sage

Hesse–Biber, S. (1995) 'Unleashing Frankenstein's Monster? The Use of Computers in Qualitative Research', *Studies, in Qualitative Methodology*, 5: 25–41

Hinds, P., Vogel, R. and Clarke-Steffen, L. (1997) 'The possibilities and pitfalls of doing a secondary analysis of a qualitative data set', *Qualitative Health Research*, 7 (3): 403–24

Hiscock, J. and Ritchie, J. (2001) *The Role of GPs in Sickness Certification*, DWP Research Report No. 148, Leeds: Corporate Document Services

Holloway, I. and Wheeler, S. (1996) *Qualitative Research for Nurses*, Oxford: Blackwell Science

Holstein, J.A. and Gubrium, J.F. (1997) 'Active interviewing' in D. Silverman (ed.) *Qualitative Research: Theory, Method and Practice*, London: Sage

Honigmann, J.J. (1982) 'Sampling in ethnographic fieldwork' in R.G. Burgess (ed.) *Field Research: A Source Book and Field Manual*, London: Allen & Unwin

Hughes, J. and Sharrock, W. (1997) *The Philosophy of Social Research*, London: Longman

Janesick, V. (2000) 'The choreography of qualitative research design: minuets, improvisations and crystallization' in N. Denzin and Y. Lincoln (eds) *Handbook of Qualitative Research*, 2nd edition, Thousand Oaks, CA: Sage

Janowitz, M. (1971) *Sociological Methods and Social Policy*, New York: General Learning Press

Jorgenson, D.L. (1989) *Partcipant Observation*, Newbury Park, CA: Sage

Kaplan, A. (1964) *The Conduct of Enquiry: Methodology for Behavioural Science*, San Francisco: Chandler

Kelle, U. (1997a) 'Theory building in qualitative research and computer programs for the management of textual data', *Sociological Research On Line*, 2 (2)

Kelle, U. (1997b) *Computer-assisted Analyses of Qualitative Data* (Papers in Social Research Methods, Qualitative Series No. 4), London: London School of Economics Methodology Institute

Kelly, G.A. (1955) *The Psychology of Personal Constructs*, New York: Norton

Kennedy, M. (1979) 'Generalizing from single case studies', *Evaluation Quarterly*, 3 (4): 661–78

Kirk, J. and Miller, M.L. (1986) *Reliability and Validity in Qualitative Research*, London: Sage

Kitzinger, J. and Barbour, R. (1999) 'Introduction: the challenge and promise of focus groups' in R. Barbour and J. Kitzinger (eds) *Developing Focus Group Research: Politics, Theory and Practice*, London: Sage

Kreuger, R.A. and Casey, M.A. (2000) *Focus Groups: A Practical Guide for Applied Research*, 3rd edition, Thousand Oaks, CA: Sage

Kvale, S. (1996) *InterViews: An Introduction to Qualitative Research Interviewing*, Thousand Oaks, CA: Sage

Layder, D. (1993) *New Strategies in Social Research*, Cambridge: Polity Press

Lazarsfield, P.P. and Barton, A. (1951) 'Qualitative measurement in the social sciences: classification, typologies and indices' in D.P. Lerner and H.D. Lasswell (eds) *The Policy Sciences*, California: Stanford University Press

LeCompte, M.D. and Goetz, J. (1982) 'Problems of reliability and validity in ethnographic research', *Review of Educational Research*, 52 (1): 31–60

LeCompte, M.D. and Preissle, J. with Tesch, R. (1993) *Ethnography and Qualitative Design in Educational Research*, 2nd edition, Chicago: Academic Press

Lee, R.M. and Fielding, N. (1996) 'Qualitative data analysis: representations of a technology: A comment on Coffey, Holbrook and Atkinson', *Sociological Research Online* 1 (4), http://www.socresonline.org.uk/socresonline/1/4/lf.html

Legard, R. and Ritchie, J. (1999) *NDYP: The Gateway*, ES Report No. 16, Sheffield: Employment Service

Lewin, R. (1993) *Complexity*, London: Phoenix

Lewis, J. (1999) *The Role of Mediation in Family Disputes in Scotland*, Edinburgh: Scottish Office

Lewis, J., Clayden, M., O'Connor, W., Mitchell, L. and Sanderson, T. (2000) *Lone Parents and Personal Advisers: Roles and Relationships*, London: Corporate Document Services

Lincoln, Y.S. and Guba, G.E. (1985) *Naturalistic Inquiry*, Beverley Hills, CA: Sage

Lofland, J. (1971) *Analyzing Social Settings*, Belmont, CA: Sage

Lofland, J. and Lofland, L.H. (1995) *Analyzing Social Settings*, 3rd edition, Belmont, CA: Wadsworth

Loumidis, J., Arthur, S., Corden, A., Green, A., Legard, R., Lessof, C., Lewis, J., Sainsbury, R., Stafford, B., Thornton, P., Walker, R. and Youngs, R. (2001) *Evaluation of the New Deal for Disabled People Personal Adviser Service Pilot: Final Report*, DSS Research Report No. 144, Leeds: Corporate Document Services

Lynn, P. (forthcoming) 'Sampling' in R. Thomas and P. Lynn (eds) *Survey Research Practice: An Introduction for Social Researchers*, 2nd edition, London: Sage

Madjar, I. and Walton, J.A. (2001) 'What is problematic about evidence?' in J.M. Morse, J.M. Swanson and A.J. Kuzel (eds) *The Nature of Qualitative Evidence*, Thousand Oaks, CA: Sage

Marsh, P., Rosser, E. and Harré, R. (1978) *The Rules of Disorder,* London: Routledge

Marshall, C. and Rossman, G.B. (1999) *Designing Qualitative Research*, 3rd edition, Thousand Oaks, CA: Sage

Mason, J. (2002) *Qualitative Researching*, 2nd edition, London: Sage

Mauthner, N., Parry, O. and Backett-Milburn, K. (1998) 'The data are out there, or are they? Implications for archiving and revisiting qualitative data', *Sociology*, 32 (4): 733–45

Maxwell, J. (1996) *Qualitative Research Design: An Interactive Approach*, Thousand Oaks, CA: Sage

May, T. (2001) *Social Research Issues, Methods and Process*, 3rd edition, Buckingham: Open University Press

McCall, G. and Simmons, J.L. (1969) *Issues in Participation Observation*, Reading, MA: Addison-Wesley

Mead, G.H. (1934) *Self and Society: From the Standpoint of a Social Behaviorist*, Chicago, University of Chicago Press

Merton, R.K., Fiske, M. and Kendall, P.L. (1956) *The Focused Interview,* Glencoe, IL: Free Press

Miles, M.B. (1979) 'Qualitative data as an attractive nuisance', *Administrative Science Quarterly*, 24: 590–601

Miles, M.B. and Huberman, A.M. (1994) *Qualitative Data Analysis: An Expanded Sourcebook*, London: Sage

Miller, J. and Glassner, B. (1997) 'The inside and outside: finding realities in interviews' in D. Silverman (ed.) *Qualitative Research: Theory, Method and Practice*, London: Sage

Miller, R.L. (2000) *Researching Life Stories and Family Histories,* London: Sage

Mills, C. Wright (1959) *The Sociological Imagination*, New York: Oxford University Press

Mitroff, I. (1974) *The Subjective Side of Science: Philosophical Inquiry into the Psychology of the Apollo Moon Scientist*, Elsevier: Amsterdam

Molloy, D., Kumar, M. with Snape, D. (1999) *Relying on the State Relying on Each Other*, DSS Research Report No. 103, Leeds: Corporate Document Services

Morgan, D.L. (1997) *Focus Groups as Qualitative Research*, 2nd edition, Thousand Oaks, CA: Sage

Morgan, D.L. (1998) 'Practical strategies for combining qualitative and quantitative methods: applications to health research', *Qualitative Health Research*, 8: 362–76

Morse, J.M. (1994) 'Emerging from the data: the cognitive processes of analysis in qualitative inquiry' in J.M. Morse (ed.) *Critical Issues in Qualitative Research Methods*, Thousand Oaks: Sage

Morse, J.M. (1998) *Keynote address to the Qualitative Health Research Conference*, Vancouver, February, 1998

Morse, J.M., Kuzel, A.J. and Swanson, J.M. (eds) (2001) *The Nature of Qualitative Evidence,* Thousand Oaks, CA: Sage

Moser, C. and Kalton, G. (1979) *Survey Methods in Social Investigation*, 2nd edition, London: Heinemann

Nicholson, P. (1991) *Qualitative Psychology: Report Prepared for the Scientific Affairs Board of The British Psychological Society*, London: British Psychological Society

Nielsen, J.M (ed.) (1990) *Feminist Research Methods: Exemplary Readings in the Social Sciences*, Boulder, CO: Westview

Oakley, A. (1981) 'Interviewing women – a contradiction in terms' in H. Roberts (ed.) *Doing Feminist Research*, London: Routledge & Kegan Paul

O'Connor, W. and Kelly, J. (1998) *Public Attitudes to Child Support Issues,* DSS Research Report No. 46, Leeds: Corporate Document Services

O'Connor, W. and Lewis, J. (1999) *Experience of Social Exclusion In Scotland*, Central Research Unit report No. 73, Edinburgh: Scottish Executive

O'Connor, W. and Molloy, D. (2001) *Hidden in Plain Sight: Homelessness Among Lesbians and Gay Youth*, London: National Centre for Social Research

Olesen, V.L. (2000) 'Feminisms and qualitative research at and into the millennium' in N.K. Denzin and Y.S. Lincoln (eds) *Handbook of Qualitative Research*, 2nd edition, Thousand Oaks, CA: Sage

Pahl, J. (1989) *Money and Marriage,* London: Macmillan.

Patton, M.Q. (1988) 'Paradigms and pragmatism' in D.M. Fetterman (ed.) *Qualitative Approaches to Evaluation in Education: The Silent Scientific Revolution*, New York: Praeger

Patton, M.Q. (1997) *Utilisation – Focused Evaluation*, 3rd edition, Newbury Park, CA: Sage

Patton, M.Q. (2002) *Qualitative Research and Evaluation Methods*, 3rd edition, Thousand Oaks, CA: Sage

Payne, G., Dingwall, R., Payne, J. and Carter, M. (1981) *Sociology and Social Research*, London: Routledge & Kegan Paul

Perakyla, A. (1997) 'Reliability and validity in research based on tapes and transcripts' in D. Silverman (ed.) *Qualitative Research: Theory, Method and Practice*, London: Sage

Platt, J. (1988) 'What can case studies do?' in R.G. Burgess (ed.) *Conducting Qualitative Research*, Greenwich, CT: JAI Press

Plummer, K. (2001) *Documents of Life 2: An Invitation to Critical Humanism,* 2nd edition, London: Sage

Pole, C. and Lampard, R. (2002) *Practical Social Investigation: Qualitative And Quantitative Methods in Social Research,* Harlow: Pearson Education

Potter, J. (1997) 'Discourse analysis as a way of analysing naturally occurring talk' in D. Silverman (ed.) *Qualitative Research: Theory, Method and Practice*, London: Sage

Qureshi, H. (1992) 'Integrating methods in applied research in social policy: a case study of carers' in J. Brannen (ed.) *Mixing Methods: Qualitative and Quantitative Research*, Aldershot: Avebury

Reason, P. (1994) *Participation in Human Inquiry,* London: Sage

Reason, P. and Rowan, J. (1981) *Human Inquiry: A Sourcebook Of New Paradigm Research*, Chichester: Wiley

Reinharz, S. (1992) *Feminist Methods in Social Research*, Oxford: Oxford University Press

Rich, R.F. (1977) 'Uses of social science information by federal bureaucrats: knowledge for action versus knowledge for understanding' in C.H. Weiss (ed.) *Uses of Social Research in Public Policy*, Lexington, MA: DC Heath

Richards, L. and Richards, T. (1994) 'From filing cabinet to computer' in A. Bryman and R.G. Burgess (eds) *Analyzing Qualitative Data*, London: Routledge

Richardson, A. and Ritchie, J. (1989) *Letting Go: Dilemmas for Parents Whose Son or Daughter has a Mental Handicap*, Milton Keynes: Open University Press

Richardson, J. (ed.) (1996) *Handbook of Qualitative Research Methods for Psychology and the Social Sciences*, Leicester: BPS Books

Riessman, C. (1993) *Narrative Analysis*, Newbury Park, CA: Sage

Rist, R.C. (2000) 'Influencing the policy process with qualitative research' in N.K. Denzin and Y.S. Lincoln (eds) *Handbook of Qualitative Research*, 2nd edition, Thousand Oaks, CA: Sage

Ritchie, J. and Spencer, L. (1994) 'Qualitative data analysis for applied policy research' in A. Bryman and R.G. Burgess (eds) *Analyzing Qualitative Data*, London: Routledge

Ritchie, J., Duldig, W. with Ward, K. (1993) *GPs and IVB: A Qualitative Study of the Role of GPs in the Award of Invalidity Benefit*, DSS Research Report No. 18, London: the Stationery Office

Roberts, B. (2002) *Biographical Research*, Buckingham: Open University Press

Roberts, H. (1981) *Doing Feminist Research*, London: Routledge

Robinson, W.S. (1951) 'The logical structure of analytic induction', *American Sociological Review*, 16: 812–18

Robson, C. (2002) *Real World Research*, 2nd edition, Oxford: Blackwell

Rorty, R. (1980) *Philosophy and the Mirror of Nature*, Oxford: Blackwell

Rossi, P.H. and Freeman, H.E. (1993) *Evaluation: A Systematic Approach*, 5th edition, Newbury Park, CA: Sage

Rossi, P.H. and Lyall, K.C. (1978) 'An overview of the NIT experiment' in T.D. Cook, M.L. DelRosario, K.M. Hernigan, M.M. Mark and W.M.K. Trochim (eds) *Evaluation Studies Review Annual* (Vol. 3: 412–28), Beverley Hills, CA: Sage

Rubin, H.J. and Rubin, I.S. (1995) *Qualitative Interviewing: The Art of Hearing Data*, Thousand Oaks, CA: Sage

Sackett, D.L., Rosenberg, W.M., Gray, J.A.M. and Haynes, R.B. (1996) 'Evidence based medicine: what it is and what it isn't', *British Medical Journal*, 312: 71–2

Scott, R.A. and Shore, A.R. (1979) *Why Sociology Does Not Apply: A Study Of The Use Of Sociology In Public Policy*, New York: Elsevier

Scriven, M. (1967) 'The methodology of evaluation' in R.W. Tyler, R.M. Gagne and M. Scriven (eds) *Perspectives on Curriculum Evaluation,* Chicago: Rand McNally

Seale, C. (1999) *The Quality of Qualitative Research,* Oxford: Blackwell

Seale, C. (ed.) (2000) *Researching Society and Culture,* London: Sage

Silverman, D. (1972) 'Methodology and meaning' in P. Filmer, M. Phillipson and D. Silverman (eds) *New Directions in Sociological Theory,* London: Collier-Macmillan

Silverman, D. (1993) *Interpreting Qualitative Data: Methods for Analysing Talk, Text and Interaction,* London: Sage

Silverman, D. (2000a) 'Analysing conversation' in C. Seale (ed.) *Researching Society and Culture,* London: Sage

Silverman, D (2000b) *Doing Qualitative Research: A Practical Handbook,* London: Sage

Silverman, D (2001) *Interpreting Qualitative Data: Methods for Analysing Talk, Text and Interaction,* 2nd edition, London: Sage

Sloman, A. (1976) 'What are the aims of science', *Radical Philosophy,* Spring: 7–17

Smith, J.A., Harré, R. and Van Langehore (eds) (1995) *Rethinking Methods in Psychology,* London: Sage

Snape, D. and Kelly, J. (1999) *Public Attitudes to Lone Parents,* London: DSS

Social Research Association (2001) *A Code of Practice for the Safety of Interviewers,* London: SRA, http://www.thesra.org.uk/index2.htm

Spradley, J. (1979) *The Ethnographic Interview,* New York: Holt, Rinehart & Winston

Stake, R. (1978) 'The case study method in social enquiry', *Education Researcher,* 7: 5–8

Stake, R. (2000) 'Case studies' in N.K. Denzin and Y.S. Lincoln (eds) *Handbook of Qualitative Research,* 2nd edition, Thousand Oaks, CA: Sage

Stewart, D.W. and Shamdasi, P.M. (1990) *Focus Groups: Theory and Practice,* Newbury Park, CA: Sage

Stewart, J., Kendall, E. and Coote, A. (1994) *Citizens' Juries,* London: IPPR

Strauss, A.L. (1987) *Qualitative Analysis for Social Scientists,* Cambridge: Cambridge University Press

Strauss, A.L. and Corbin, J. (1998) *Basics of Qualitative Research: Grounded Theory Procedures and Techniques,* 2nd edition, Thousand Oaks, CA: Sage

Tesch, R. (1990) *Qualitative Research: Analysis Types and Software Tools,* Lewes: Falmer Press

Thomas, A. (1992) *Working with a Disability: Barriers and Facilitators,* London: SCPR

Thomas, W.I. (1931) *The Unadjusted Girl,* Boston, MA: Little, Brown

Thompson, P. (2000) *The Voice of the Past: Oral History,* 2nd edition, Oxford: Oxford University Press

Tonkiss, F. (2000) 'Analysing discourse' in C. Seale (ed.) *Researching Society and Culture,* London: Sage

Toon, P.D. (1992) 'Ethical aspects of medical certification by general practitioners', *British Journal of General Practice,* 42: 486–8

Tuckman, B. (1965) 'Developmental sequence in small groups', *Psychological Bulletin,* 63 (6): 384–99

Tuckman, B. and Jenson, M. (1977) 'Stages of small-group development revisited', *Group and Organisational Studies,* 2 (4): 419–27

Turner, V. (1982) 'The analysis of social drama' in R.G. Burgess (ed.) *Field Research: A Sourcebook and Field Manual,* London: Allen & Unwin

Walker, R. (ed.) (1985) *Applied Qualitative Research,* Aldershot: Gower

Webb, B. and Webb, S. (1932) *Methods of Social Study*, London: Longmans Green

Weiss, C.H. (ed.) (1977) *Uses of Social Research in Public Policy*, Lexington, MA: DC Heath

Weiss, C.H. (1988) 'Evaluation for decisions. Is anybody there. Does anybody care?', *Evaluation Practice*, 9 (1): 5–19

Weitzman, E.A. (2000) 'Software and qualitative research' in N.K. Denzin and Y.S. Lincoln (eds) *Handbook of Qualitative Research*, 2nd edition, Thousand Oaks, CA: Sage

Weitzman, E.A. and Miles, M.B. (1995) *Computer Programs for Qualitative Data Analysis: A Software Sourcebook*, Thousand Oaks, CA : Sage

White, C., Bruce, S. and Ritchie, J. (2000) *Young People's Politics: Political Interest and Engagement Amongst 14–24 year olds*, York: York Publishing Services

White, C., Elam, G. and Lewis, J. (1999) *Citizens' Juries: An Appraisal of Their Role*, London: Cabinet Office

White, C., Mitchell, L. and Orford, J. (2001) *Exploring Gambling Behaviour In-depth: A Qualitative Study*, London: National Centre for Social Research

Whittemore, R., Langness, L. and Koegel, P. (1986) 'The life history approach to mental retardation' in L. Langness and H. Levine (eds) *Culture and Retardation*, Dordrecht: D. Reidel

Whyte, W.F. (ed.) (1991) *Participatory Action Research*, Newbury Park, CA: Sage

Wiener, C.L. (1975) 'The burden of rheumatoid arthritis: tolerating the uncertainty', *Social Science and Medicine*, 9: 97–104

Williams, M. (1976) 'Symbolic interactionism: fusion of theory and research' in D.C. Thorns (ed.) *New Directions in Sociology*, London: David & Charles

Williams, M. (2000) *Science and Social Science: An Introduction*, London: Routledge

Wolcott, H.F. (2001) *Writing Up Qualitative Research*, 2nd edition, Newbury Park, CA: Sage

Woodfield, K. (1999) *They All Wear White Coats Don't They? Challenging Stereotypes and Promoting Science in Schools: An Evaluation of the Researchers in Residence (Bio-Science) Scheme*, London: National Centre for Social Research

Woodfield, K., O'Connor, W., Ritchie, J. and Lewis, J. (1999) *Local Labour Market Adjudication – An Evaluative Study*, London: SCPR

Woodfield, K., Swales, K., Joy, S., Lewis, J. and Grewal, I. with Bailey, M. (2002) *Disabled for Life? Attitudes Towards and Experiences of Disability in Britain*, DWP Research Report No. 173, Leeds: Corporate Document Services

Yin, R.K. (1993) *Applications of Case Study Research*, Newbury Park, CA: Sage

Yin, R.K. (1994) *Case Study Research: Design and Methods*, 2nd edition, Beverly Hills, CA: Sage

Index